First Nations
Race, Class, and Gender Relations

First Nations
Race, Class, and Gender Relations

Vic Satzewich
Department of Sociology
McMaster University

Terry Wotherspoon
Department of Sociology
University of Saskatchewan

CANADIAN PLAINS RESEARCH CENTER   2000

Canadian Plains Research Center
University of Regina
Regina, Saskatchewan S4S 0A2
Canada
Tel: (306) 585-4758
Fax: (306) 585-4699
e-mail: canadian.plains@uregina.ca
http://www.cprc.uregina.ca

Canadian Cataloguing in Publication Data

Satzewich, Vic, 1961–

    First nations : race, class and gender relations

    (Canadian plains reprint series, ISSN 1208–9680 ; 7)

Reprint, with new introduction and bibliography, of the edition published: Scarborough, Ont. : Nelson Canada, 1993.
Includes bibliographical references and index.
ISBN 0-88977-144-8

1. Native Peoples--Canada.* 2. Native peoples--Canada--Social conditions.* I. Wotherspoon, Terry. II. University of Regina. Canadian Plains Research Center. III. Title. IV. Series.

E78.C2 S335 2000   305.897'071   C00-920227-7

Cover Art: *Hand-Drum* by Sheila Orr. Collection of the artist.
        Photograph by Don Hall, University of Regina.
Cover Design: Donna Achtzehner, Canadian Plains Research Center

Printed and bound in Canada by Houghton Boston, Saskatoon, Saskatchewan

Printed on acid-free paper

This book is dedicated:

to "the guys," Linda, Lucy & Jack
—Vic Satzewich

to Barb and to my parents, Ken and Shirley
—Terry Wotherspoon

CONTENTS

ACKNOWLEDGMENTS

This book grew out of our experiences teaching courses concerning the sociology of aboriginal peoples, conducting research on major dimensions of structured inequality, and through many conversations with colleagues, aboriginal and non-aboriginal students, and other members of the aboriginal community. It became clear that while we did not have the depth of expertise and experience that would normally qualify us to undertake a project of this nature, we could make a contribution that might usefully help to broaden the analysis of the issues covered in this book. We are indebted to many people for their inspiration and assistance that made this book possible. The Department of Sociology at the University of Saskatchewan has provided us with a supportive working atmosphere. Particular mention must be made of our colleagues Gurcharn Basran, Singh Bolaria, Harley Dickinson, Peter Li, Linda Mahood, and Les Samuelson, who continually can be counted upon to deliver friendly but astute criticism and jovial encouragement. In addition, we thank Kiran Bolaria, Karen Duke, Glenda Fifield, Della Kirkham, Doug Kopko, Pat Lapierre, Rick Mirasty, and Byrad Yyelland for their countless hours of research assistance throughout various stages of manuscript preparation and completion. We are also grateful for manuscript preparation support provided by the University of Saskatchewan's Publications Fund.

We would like to reaffirm our gratitude to Dave Ward and Nelson Canada for their initial publication of this book. We also thank David Miller of the Saskatchewan Indian Federated College for his continued interest in this book, and his support in seeing that it continues to be available to students, teachers, and researchers in the area. At the Canadian Plains Research Center we thank Brian Mlazgar for helping steer this project through various phases of the publication process, and Donna Achtzehner, whose editorial skills greatly improved our Introduction to the 2000 Reprint. We continue to appreciate the comments and suggestions of the original referees for this book: Edward J. Hedican, University of Guelph, David Miller, Saskatchewan Indian Federated College, J.B. Minore, Lakehead University, Fred Shore, University of Manitoba, and John Milloy, Trent University. In addition, we received many useful and supportive comments from instructors, students, researchers, policy-makers, and community members, and we want to thank them for their feedback.

We also want to convey our appreciation to those who are closest to us, for their ongoing encouragement and support—Barb, Kurt, and Darcy, and Linda, Wally, Gail, Lucy, and Jack.

INTRODUCTION TO THE 1993 EDITION

Social scientists do not have a particularly good reputation amongst aboriginal peoples. There is a fairly widespread feeling in many communities that "Native people have been studied to death." Indeed, this was the essence of Ovide Mercredi's response to the federal government's announcement in the spring of 1991 that it planned to establish a Royal Commission on Aboriginal Affairs. The feeling is that despite the collection of massive amounts of data and the existence of numerous academic studies on aboriginal peoples, the information that has been collected over the years has not resulted in any significant improvement in aboriginal living conditions. If Ovide Mercredi is right, then how can we justify yet another study of aboriginal/non-aboriginal relations in Canada?

On one level, we agree with Ovide Mercredi: it is true that numerous studies have been undertaken to understand and explain the position of aboriginal peoples in Canada. Of all ethnic categories in Canada, it is unlikely that any other has stimulated as much academic research. Over the years, the motivations for this research have been varied, and have encompassed the rather paternalistic oriented, where the aim is to identify the "Indian problem;" an assimilationist orientation, where the aim is to facilitate the entry of aboriginal peoples into "mainstream" society; those whose aim is to facilitate the retention of traditional cultural patterns; and those whose aim is to expose past and present injustices and oppression.

At present, there are numerous studies of aboriginal peoples and issues that have been undertaken by historians, political scientists, legal scholars, and journalists. There are, for example, a number of excellent studies of particular historical experiences of aboriginal peoples. Among many others, Sarah Carter's *Lost Harvests* provides an excellent account of the demise of Indian agriculture in the prairie provinces, Jim Miller's *Skyscrapers Hide the Heavens* is a solid historical overview of Indian/non-Indian relations in Canada, and James Waldram's *As Long as the Rivers Run* is a thorough and well-documented analysis of the experiences of hydro development of three native communities in Manitoba and Saskatchewan.

With respect to political scientists and legal scholars, a tremendous amount of work has been done to examine the issues of treaty and aboriginal rights, and the struggles over self-government. Cassidy and Bish (1989) provide a solid overview of the meaning and practice of self government and Weaver (1981) provides an excellent documentary account of events surrounding the federal government's White Paper on Indian Policy.

Journalists have also made important contributions. Comeau and Santin (1990), Krotz (1990), and York (1989) provide sensitive accounts of Indian people's living conditions, concerns, and attempts to maintain dignity and strength within a context of oppression and inequality. As the reader will notice, we are rather catholic in our use of all of these sources.

However, while there are indeed numerous and excellent studies of aboriginal peoples in Canada, in many cases these studies have tended to be descriptive and have lacked an anchor within wider theoretical issues and debates. Much of the existing research, therefore, is either atheoretical, or guided by problematic theoretical assumptions. From the perspective of sociologists interested in aboriginal/non-aboriginal relations, what appears to be lacking is an integrated theoretical framework which can be used to tie together this wealth of information.

Somewhat ironically, Canadian sociologists have not kept pace with these other disciplines in the study of aboriginal peoples. While there was a flurry of sociological and anthropological studies of aboriginal peoples in the early 1970s, particularly in the context of Indian urbanization (see Dosman, 1972; Nagler, 1971; Brody, 1971; Ryan, 1978; Stymeist, 1975; Braroe, 1975), the issue of aboriginal/non-aboriginal relations has been placed on the so-called "backburner" by sociologists.

Nor have Canadian sociologists kept pace with theoretical developments in other countries, particularly in the United States and Britain. In those contexts, the political economy of groups of Afro-Caribbean origin, groups that have also been subject to varying forms and degrees of "colonization," has been advanced much further than has been the case with the analysis of aboriginal peoples in this country. In those contexts, the analysis of Afro-Caribbean populations has moved well beyond simplistic conceptions which have traditionally defined them as "underclasses" that exist outside of capitalist relations of production. The focus now is on the disentanglement of the intersections of capitalism in Afro-Caribbean people's lives.

There are now established debates within the United States, for example, concerning the articulation of "race," class, and gender in the shaping of black people's lives. Wilson (1980) argues that the position of blacks in the United States is better explained by class, than "race," while Omi and Winant (1986) argue that "race" is the central organizing principle shaping black people's lives. Boston (1988), on the other hand, argues that class and "race" intersect in complex ways to produce "racial" stratification within class categories, while Hooks (1982) argues that racism and sexism are intertwined in ways that subordinate black women in the United States.

In Britain, there is now an extensive literature which seeks to understand the position of black people in social relations in that country. Work by Phizacklea and Miles (1980) and Miles (1982), suggests that the position of black people in Britain is best explained by the concept of racialized class fractions, a position adopted with varying degrees of consistency by others in the field (see Centre for Contemporary Cultural Studies, 1982). Anthias (1990), while critical of Miles' specific formulation, suggests that "race," gender, and class intersect in complex ways to produce a multiplicity of experiences for different categories of British people.

This is not to suggest, though, that Canadian sociologists have completely ignored aboriginal issues. As we note in Chapter 1, much of the existing research has been guided by the Chicago School tradition and the internal colonial model. What is particularly interesting is that even though the tradition of political economy has been quite vibrant in the study of many areas of Canadian social, economic, and political life, it has yet to systematically address the issue of aboriginal/non-aboriginal relations. While there is an emergent, and somewhat disparate, literature rooted within the tradition of political economy which we draw upon for this book, it is also the case, as Abele and Stasiulis (1989:245) note, that "there exist few synthetic works that offer a general analysis of 'Native political economy' for any historical period."

One of our aims in this book, then, is to draw upon existing British, American, and Canadian literature to help create a "political economy" of aboriginal/non-aboriginal relations in Canada. Obviously, our aim is not to provide all of the answers to the "problems" of aboriginal/non-aboriginal relations. Rather, we hope to provide an alternative perspective on those relations, and to spark further research and debate within the area. While we are not so naive to believe that this book will result in any changes in those relationships, we do believe that efforts at social action and social change do need to be based on wider theoretical understandings of the nature of inequality and oppression within capitalist societies.

OUTLINE OF THE BOOK

In Chapter 1, we suggest that existing sociological research on aboriginal/non-aboriginal relations tends to be guided by two theoretical traditions: the Chicago School and the internal colonial model. Chapter 1 critically examines these two perspectives, and provides an outline of an alternative conceptualization, a conceptualization based on the tradition of political economy. In subsequent chapters, we focus on the social, economic, and political dimensions of the transformations and contradictions which characterize aboriginal life and relations in Canada. Chapter 2 traces the development of state policy as a tool which has been altered in accordance with distinct phases in the development of Canadian capitalism. State policy, conceptualized as a dialectic of representation and social control, has tended to emphasize the priorities of social control over aboriginal lands and peoples in order to minimize the potential impact of aboriginal interests as barriers to capitalist development.

In Chapter 3 we argue that although in general terms aboriginal peoples tend to occupy some of the most disadvantaged positions within the Canadian social structure, the argument that aboriginal peoples constitute an "underclass" within Canadian society is too simplistic. We suggest that the position of aboriginal peoples in economic relations is characterized by a complex intersection of racialization, class, and gender relations. Aboriginal peoples occupy all of the main sites within the capitalist division of labour, and their position within that division of labour reflects, in part, processes of racialization and gender stratification. Chapter 4 carries this analysis beyond the economic realm into consideration of the social conditions experienced by aboriginal peoples. We examine the impact of economic transformations and state policy upon native peoples' everyday lives, focusing upon the interaction between processes that fragment and destroy traditional social relations and the ways in which these changes are resisted and accommodated by aboriginal peoples.

Chapter 5 is concerned with the processes of social and economic transformation through formal education. We present education as a contradictory enterprise which to aboriginal peoples holds forth the promise to extend opportunities and to assert control over their lives at the same time as it contributes to their subordination and to the devaluation of their experiences. Our analysis of the multi-layered nature of disempowerment and disadvantage is continued in Chapters 6 and 7 in relation to the areas of health and crime and justice. We argue that despite official acknowledgment of a state of crisis in social justice conditions and services for aboriginal peoples, recent attempts to redress the major problems fail to address the possibility that contemporary economic and social restructuring processes entail the continuing existence of a large unemployed population, which is likely to include large proportions of the aboriginal population.

Chapter 8 discusses the historical emergence of an aboriginal leadership and political organizations to represent aboriginal peoples and their concerns in regional and national forums. We argue that these organizations have tended to be bounded by contradictory struggles over citizenship rights and the meaning of "special status." While aboriginal organizations have been engaged in struggles to eliminate the unique restrictions imposed on their rights, they have struggled simultaneously to retain particular rights stemming from their status as First Nations. Limited by the structural bases of capitalist economic and state mechanisms, aboriginal organizations run the risk of sacrificing the accomplishment of substantive social rights at the expense of struggles for formal civil and political rights. Our analysis in Chapter 9 concentrates on the prospects for meaningful social change for aboriginal peoples through processes of economic development. While successful economic development holds out the potential for aboriginal peoples to overcome long-standing positions as a generally disadvantaged and subordinate group, we conclude with a question which echoes a note of caution, a recurrent theme throughout the book: insofar as the continued growth and development of capitalist societies generates both significant levels of wealth and poverty, who are likely to be the main beneficiaries, and who are likely to suffer the main burden, of strategies for the devolution of Indian services and the emergence of an aboriginal business sector?

In the conclusion, we offer a summary of our arguments as well as discuss some of the implications our arguments have for future research.

Note on Terminology

The term aboriginal peoples refers collectively to status Indian, non-status Indian, Métis, and Inuit people in Canada. The concept of aboriginal peoples differs from the notion of First Nations insofar as the latter tends to refer to groups of status Indian origin: groups who are the first occupants of the lands that now make up Canada. Status, or registered, Indian people are those who are defined as Indians by virtue of the Indian Act. More recently, the federal government has introduced a further distinction within the status Indian category: "regular" and "Bill-C31's." The former refers to those people who were defined as Indian under the Indian Act before the passage of Bill C-31 in 1985, while the latter refers to those who have regained their status by virtue of Bill C-31. Non-status Indians are those Indians who have lost their status through enfranchisement, and who are unable, or do not wish, to regain their status as registered Indians.

There are no singular definitions of the Inuit and Métis. The 1975 James Bay agreement defined the Inuit as individuals who possessed a disc number (a disc number was assigned to each Inuk as part of the federal government's census in 1951), or who possess at least one-quarter Inuit blood, or who are considered an Inuk by the local community. Sealey and Lussier (1975) adopt a racialized definition in which the Métis are "mixed-bloods," or those of Indian and non-Indian origins. The Métis Society of Saskatchewan, on the other hand, defines a Métis as a person of aboriginal ancestry who:

1) can provide proof of his/her ancestry;
2) declares him/herself to be a Métis; and
3) meets one of the following tests:
    a) is accepted as a Métis by the Métis community,
    b) has traditionally held himself/herself out to be a Métis,
    c) has been recognized by the community-at-large as a Métis.

While our book touches on some of the issues relating to Métis and Inuit people, much of our analysis is confined to status and non-status Indian people. Political economies of the Inuit and Métis have yet to be written.

INTRODUCTION TO THE 2000 REPRINT

MIXED PROSPECTS FOR CANADA'S ABORIGINAL PEOPLE

Many significant changes have occurred within Canada's First Nations, and in the broader relations between Aboriginal people and other Canadians, since *First Nations: Race, Class, and Gender Relations* first appeared in 1993. Several important self-government agreements have been concluded, most notably in the form of the landmark establishment of Nunavut as an Inuit-governed territory. The Nisga'a agreement, one of the more prominent land claims settlements, offers the first modern-day treaty in British Columbia. First Nations have established authority to administer and deliver programs in justice, social services, education, and related areas throughout Manitoba, while other forms of devolution of authority from the Department of Indian and Northern Affairs to First Nations are being implemented or negotiated in other jurisdictions. Aboriginal people, individually or as members of co-operatives and corporate entities, have developed a diverse array of business enterprises both in and beyond their own communities, such as the establishment of a First Nations Bank based in Saskatoon. Events like the National Aboriginal Achievement Awards have helped to raise the national profile of Aboriginal people by celebrating their many artistic, literary, and cultural accomplishments. Young Aboriginal people are often expressing high aspirations and hope for the future to an extent not visible among earlier generations. Aboriginal voices are increasingly present or prominently displayed in the media, political discussions, artistic representations, and academic analyses. The Royal Commission on Aboriginal Peoples (1996a-e), which after extensive dialogue and research culminated in the five-volume report released in 1996, offers a critical examination of both contemporary and historical conditions and signals the need for a new set of relationships among Aboriginal people, non-Aboriginal people, and the federal government.

Despite these advances, there are many disturbing realities that reflect both emergent problems and those that have continued for several generations. High incidences of suicide, substance abuse, HIV infection, and serious injury or death resulting from accidents plague Aboriginal people, most disturbingly among youth in many communities. For Aboriginal people overall, and First Nations in particular, education levels and employment rates continue to lag well behind those in their age cohorts in the general population. Rates of imprisonment among Aboriginal people—especially among young males in the Prairie region—continue to soar, while relations between police and Aboriginal people in many communities are characterized by mistrust or hostility. The federal government's failure to address serious First Nation concerns on several fronts, including problems outlined in the report of the Royal Commission on Aboriginal People and the slow pace at which land claims issues are resolved, has led to court challenges and threats of other forms of protest. Efforts to improve race relations and foster the inclusion of Aboriginal people in important institutional areas are undermined by ongoing tensions and practices that exclude or victimize the indigenous population. Public concern about social problems associated with Aboriginal people is intermingled with overt questions about lack of accountability in First Nations and Métis organizations. Periodic confrontations between Aboriginal and non-Aboriginal people have emerged, leading to allegations of racism and other forms of hostility (Ponting and Kiely, 1997).

All of these factors point to the highly complex, and often contradictory, realities that characterize the social circumstances of Canada's Aboriginal people. In 2000, the national population of Aboriginal people is estimated by the federal government to be about 1.4 million, about half of whom are distributed among 610 First Nations (representing persons with formal status registered under the terms of the Indian Act, living on- or off-reserve); other major groups include the Métis (16 percent), Inuit (5 percent), and non-status Indians (persons of Aboriginal ancestry not registered under the Indian Act, constituting 31 percent of the Aboriginal population) (Indian and Northern Affairs Canada and Canadian Polar Commission, 2000:4). Living in diverse situations across Canada, split relatively evenly across cities, rural reserves, and other rural areas, Aboriginal people are most highly concentrated in the western—especially Prairie—provinces and northern territories (Statistics Canada, 1998a:4). These circumstances give rise to variations in the issues and concerns that affect diverse segments of the Aboriginal population.

The advent of the twenty-first century has been accompanied by considerable optimism among Aboriginal people regarding their potential to control their individual, if not collective, destinies. The expansion of Aboriginal economic, political, and social sectors, combined with opportunities for training, employment, and participation in mainstream organizations, has provided Aboriginal people with unprecedented chances to fulfill many aspirations and to occupy meaningful positions within Canadian society (Globerman, 1998; Santiago, 1997). However, these options remain restricted and are not equally available to all Aboriginal people. Persistent inequalities with respect to life chances, conditions, and resources exist both between the general and Aboriginal populations and within Aboriginal populations themselves (Bernier, 1997; Department of Indian Affairs and Northern Development, 1997; Federation of

Saskatchewan Indian Nations, 1997; Four Directions Consulting Group, 1997; Frideres, 1998). Consequently, in addition to negotiating relatively common everyday concerns about job, education, and family, many Aboriginal people are forced to come to grips with concerns like the impact of residential school abuse on either their lives or those of family members, lack of credentials for employment prospects, an absence of faith in conventional institutional practices, and social environments characterized by uncertainty and often hostility and violence.

Our book tries to make sense of the varied life circumstances among Canada's Aboriginal people, and the developments that have contributed to these conditions and experiences. We emphasize how a complex array of factors, discussed especially in terms of class, gender relations, and race relations, operate as powerful forces that contribute to the social and economic options and life circumstances that Aboriginal people experience in their interactions with one another and with other social groups. In this new introductory chapter, we explore some of the major changes in these conditions and relations that have occurred within the past decade. We begin with an assessment of changing dynamics in the relationship between the federal government and Aboriginal groups, followed by a brief overview of recent theoretical perspectives that have been advanced to explain these phenomena. The chapter concludes with a summary of major contemporary issues facing Aboriginal people.

CHANGING RELATIONS BETWEEN THE FEDERAL GOVERNMENT AND ABORIGINAL PEOPLE

Given the pivotal role that government regulation and control have played in defining First Nations and shaping the lives and destinies of Aboriginal people, it is instructive to start our examination of recent developments in Aboriginal affairs with an overview of changing government policies and practices. Sally Weaver (1990:9) has argued that the last decade of the twentieth century heralded the emergence of a "new paradigm" in relations between the federal government and Aboriginal people, reflecting a shift in dominant ideas within the Aboriginal affairs policy field. As we observe below, and in more detailed discussions in chapters 4 and 9, there are several reasons to agree with this general assessment. However, it is important to note, with some caution, that this change has not been absolute. We stress, further, that new policy ideas do not emerge independently but rather develop and gain acceptance as transformations occur within specific social, political, and economic environments.

Numerous recent initiatives reinforce the notion that a policy shift has occurred insofar as previous state efforts to regulate and assimilate Aboriginal people have given way to increasing emphasis on representation, negotiation, and prospects for self-determination among First

Nations and other Aboriginal groups. Self-government agreements, along with devolution of control over a broad range of social programs and government services from the federal government to Aboriginal people, have added new layers of complexity to Canada's jurisdictional landscape. The Royal Commission on Aboriginal Peoples, appointed in 1991 in the wake of frustration and fears of escalating violence in Aboriginal communities across Canada, engaged in a series of consultations that promised a new framework for the government's relationship with Aboriginal people. The final report is contained in a series of five volumes published in 1996, accompanied by an extensive series of working papers and in-depth studies on issues such as suicide and criminal justice. Widespread hope that a new relationship would be forged was reinforced in the commissioners' blunt statement that "[t]he main policy direction, pursued for more than 150 years, first by colonial then by Canadian governments, has been wrong" (Royal Commission on Aboriginal Peoples, 1996f:x). In place of this failed pathway, the commissioners propose a "renewed relationship" based on the principles of mutual recognition, respect, sharing, and responsibility (Royal Commission on Aboriginal Peoples, 1996a:677-691).

Hopeful expectations for future developments were further reinforced in the official federal government response to the commission report, presented in 1998 in the form of a document entitled *Gathering Strength – Canada's Aboriginal Action Plan*. That statement emphasizes a vision for "strong, healthy communities and new relationships founded on mutual respect, with responsible, transparent, accountable, sustainable governance structures and institutions." In order to implement this vision, the government highlights the following four strategic initiatives: (i) Renewing the Partnerships; (ii) Strengthening Aboriginal Governance; (iii) Developing a New Fiscal Relationship; and (iv) Supporting Strong Communities, People and Economies (Indian and Northern Affairs Canada, 1997). Subsequent government documents emphasize a similar vision (for example, Indian and Northern Affairs Canada and Canadian Polar Commission, 2000:2).

Despite this optimistic assessment of possibilities, questions remain as to how much really has changed. To what extent are any observed changes a consequence of incremental advancement as opposed to a full-scale shift in policy direction?

Amidst the accelerated promise for state support to address their aspirations and improve their communities, Aboriginal organizations remain highly concerned about several major issues. Among the most serious concerns are the absence of a clearly formulated definition of self-government, little or no progress towards resolution of major land claims settlements, and the perpetuation of government regulations that limit First Nations autonomy on issues like taxation, investment strategies, gaming, and other areas. Even the process of devolution, signifying the transfer of control from the federal government to First Nations in social services and other areas, has been accompanied by a new maze of fiscal and administrative regulations that limit long-range planning, make inadequate concessions to diverse social needs and band membership growth, and maintain funding constraints (Angus, 1991; Burns, 1998). Increasingly, these frustrations have been converted into litigation (and even occasional physical confrontations) initiated by Aboriginal people or their representatives against the government over land claims, taxation, regulation of First Nations resources and enterprises, residential schooling, and other matters. While often focused on specific issues, these legal challenges also point to broader questions about Aboriginal rights and the meaning and nature of "nationhood" within a First Nations context.

In many of these cases, even where there is the will or support in principle to greater First Nations autonomy, competing political and jurisdictional concerns have reduced the capacity of federal government politicians and other officials to act more decisively than they have (Brock, 1997; Graham, Dittburner and Abele, 1996; Hogg and Turpel, 1995). At least four major constitutional, political, and definitional factors compound these issues. First, while the federal government has responsibility for Indians and their lands (and the authority to transfer that responsibility to First Nations), many of the most pressing concerns for Aboriginal people, including social welfare, education, health care, and the need for services in urban areas, encompass areas of provincial responsibility. Second, Aboriginal people have a contradictory relationship with the state insofar as their claims for autonomy are bound up with fears that complete federal withdrawal from Indian affairs could signify failure to recognize Aboriginal rights and historical treaty-based obligations. Third, differential claims, rights, and entitlements are associated with different groups of Aboriginal people (including First Nations, or status and non-status Indians, the Métis, and Inuit), as designated under the 1982 Constitution Act, the Indian Act, and the treaties, resulting in periodic contestation over membership, representation, and organizational forms. Fourth, federal and provincial governments are susceptible to modifications in their policies either in response to public sentiment over Aboriginal issues or in order to conform with priorities shaped by other domestic and global concerns. In this last regard, it is noteworthy that, since the early 1990s, the federal Liberal administration has differentiated itself by taking a more proactive stance towards resolution of Aboriginal concerns than that advocated by other political parties and some provincial governments (Brock, 1997:205-207). This is not to absolve the federal government of its failure to act more decisively in a number of major areas, but it does point to the complex sets of factors that surround the state's role in Aboriginal affairs. Previous state policies and regulations have contributed to this complexity, yet contemporary state policy is not equipped to address these multiple realities.

RECENT PERSPECTIVES IN ACADEMIC RESEARCH

Just as there is no single image that can capture adequately the tremendous diversity associated with the lives and circumstances of Aboriginal people, there is no simple explanation to account for variations in these conditions, how they got to be that way, and what role the state has played in all of this. Various historical, sociological, anthropological, and legal perspectives, which will be discussed in subsequent chapters, have been advanced as means to understand First Nations people and their relations with others within various social, economic, and political dimensions. Many participants and commentators have attempted to reduce issues to the fault of a single group—from various quarters, blame is attributed to governments for genocidal actions and policies, to Aboriginal people for failing to demonstrate initiative and take responsibility for their own futures, or to an overall absence of tolerance and understanding. Numerous writers, though, have advanced a diverse range of alternative analytical positions to explain contemporary developments in Aboriginal affairs, reflecting differing political, as well as theoretical, stances.

Several writers have advocated a neo-liberal orientation, arguing that Aboriginal people can become full participants in Canadian society only when they are subject to the free operation of market forces. From this viewpoint, state regulation of Aboriginal people is regarded as undesirable, and must be extinguished through the dismantling of the Indian Affairs bureaucracy and the abandonment of "special rights" for Aboriginal people (Drost, Crowley and Schwindt, 1995; Smith, 1995; Flanagan, 2000). While there is some affinity between this argument and the desire by many Aboriginal organizations for greater autonomy from state control, the neo-liberal position is premised on the assumption that Aboriginal people are no different from any other Canadians and, therefore, that any special rights or status derived from their heritage as the first people are meaningless or even discriminatory. Consequently, this position ignores or denies many of the socially destructive forces and substantial impediments to rebuilding success that do affect Aboriginal communities through a combination of state control, racism, discrimination, and other ongoing social practices.

A more prevalent theme in recent academic analysis of Aboriginal affairs has appeared in the form of what can broadly be characterized as a conflict orientation. In chapter 1, we offer a critique of the most widely-employed conflict approach known as the internal colonial model. Internal colonial theory argues that Aboriginal people have been, and continue to be, subordinated by specific policies and institutional practices adopted first by European colonizers and subsequently by the federal government and other dominant Canadian forces. These unequal relations are maintained in the form of a process of "cultural discontinuity" in which Euro-Canadian values and institutional practices are privileged relative to

Aboriginal standards and experiences (Brady, 1996). Recent variants of the internal colonial model have moved beyond a strict focus on domination in order to acknowledge that First Nations and other indigenous people are active in the process of resisting colonization and adopting strategies to de-colonize their lands and social systems (Boldt, 1993; Gagné, 1994; Lepage, 1995; Haddad and Spivey, 1992; Pertusati, 1997). The life chances and social relations experienced by Aboriginal people are thus viewed in terms of ongoing processes of subordination, opportunity, and empowerment (Ponting, 1997:12-13).

Despite the fact that internal colonial theories attempt to take into account changing relations of power and domination, they remain limited in their ability to explain, variously, how and why particular social practices and structures reproduce already existing social relations or contribute to social transformation. Acknowledging these limitations, Frideres (1998:422-423) argues that in order to explain how Aboriginal people have been excluded from critical areas of influence and participation in social life, it is crucial "to fully understand the historical and situational contexts in which [they, like other] groups of people find themselves as they participate in the political economy of any society." The political economy approach, which underlies the analysis employed in this book, is explored more fully throughout our discussion. First, it is important to acknowledge the ways in which Aboriginal writers themselves have begun to broaden our ability to understand these social and historical realities.

THE EMERGENCE OF ABORIGINAL PERSPECTIVES

The social science literature on Aboriginal people has been augmented in recent years by the increased presence of Aboriginal voices and perspectives. In many cases, Aboriginal writers have worked within mainstream academic frameworks, often supplementing eclectic theoretical approaches (see, for example, the contributions to Long and Dickason, 1996; Ponting, 1997; and Hylton, 1999). However, several authors have made the case for a distinctly Aboriginal perspective on understanding social relations, challenging conventional analysis for its frequent misrepresentation of, or failure to take into account, Aboriginal world views and experiences. Monture-Angus (1995:14) describes, for instance, how notions like "disadvantage" employed by non-Aboriginal authors can be discriminatory insofar as there is no recognition of the social contexts to which those terms refer, and how such circumstances are produced and lived. Social science has often been accused of extending the process by which First Nations are colonized by presenting distorted images of Aboriginal people, representing them with terms such as underdevelopment, powerlessness, or disorganization (Barsh, 1994; Carter, 1995). More seriously, the depiction of indigenous peoples as preliterate has devalued the rich and varied forms of literacy that have long been central to many First Nations cultures (Battiste, 1986). There is an emerging body of scholarship to demonstrate that Aboriginal epistemologies, or distinct ways of knowing, are fundamental to the approaches that Aboriginal people take in their relations with nature and with other people (Battiste, 1998; Ermine, 1995). Our understanding of the lives and circumstances of Aboriginal people has been substantially enriched by first-person accounts and oral histories of community relationships and of the impact of government policies like residential schooling and relocation of communities on people and their families (Ahenakew and Wolfart, 1998; Assembly of First Nations, 1994; Bussidor and Bilgen-Reinart, 1997; Fournier and Crey, 1997; Treaty 7 Elders and Tribal Council, 1996). Moreover, for an increasing number of scholars, expressing their voices as Aboriginal people is vital not only for making sense of a colonial past but also, and more importantly, as a critical precondition for developing effective strategies for a post-colonial world (Alfred, 1999; Battiste, 2000).

One of the more interesting debates concerning the relationship between emergent academic and Aboriginal modes of analysis has concerned feminism. Writers from a variety of perspectives have emphasized the conspicuous absence of female representation and women's lives in accounts of both historical and contemporary First Nations societies (Carter, 1996; Emberley, 1996; Krosenbrink-Gelissen, 1996; Jackson, 1994; Peers, 1996; Smandych and Lee, 1995; Voyageur, 1996). However, several Aboriginal scholars argue that conventional feminist scholarship has not served them well in reflecting their experiences and offering political strategies to realize their aims (Monture-Angus, 1995:229–235; Turpel, 1993:187–189).

The search for effective ways to integrate Aboriginal epistemologies with other social scientific approaches has often resulted in an affinity with postmodernism. The latter, characterized by a rejection of views that see human history and the domination of nature by science as progressive forces, and an insistence that our social lives and personal identities have multiple vantage points, has provided many Aboriginal writers with a platform simultaneously to make sense of their marginalization by dominant society and to recapture their own experiences (Denis, 1997; Graveline, 1998). However, such approaches have offered little toward understanding the changing social practices and public policies that characterize relations both within Aboriginal societies and between Aboriginal and non-Aboriginal groups.

In fact, while we must not lose sight of the actions and motivations of any participants, we must also be aware of the complex social relationships and framework in which these activities occur. Our book highlights this diversity by focusing on the primary factors that shape and are shaped by people's lives, especially in the form of the intersections among class, race, and gender relations. We adopt a materialist stance, arguing that First Nations, the Europeans that they had contact with, and the subsequent relationships that have characterized Aboriginal people's lives and interactions with other groups are in the first instance determined by the social practices that different groups of people engage in to meet their basic needs. Among the most important social relations that shape people's lives, identities, and interactions with other people and groups are social class, race, and gender.

CRITICAL ISSUES IN THE ANALYSIS OF ABORIGINAL PEOPLE IN CANADA

We have identified the varied prospects that confront Canada's Aboriginal people in the twenty-first century. We conclude this new introductory chapter with a brief overview of some of the major challenges that are emerging, or indeed that remain, in understanding Aboriginal people and their relations with other groups.

Indian Nationhood, Citizenship, and Sovereignty

The meaning and nature of the terms "special status" or "special relationship" pertaining to Aboriginal people and their relationship with the Canadian state remain highly controversial and uncertain. As we discuss in chapters 2 and 8, under the *Constitution Act* of 1982, constitutional recognition is given to pre-existing Aboriginal and treaty rights of three groups of Aboriginal people—First Nations, Inuit, and the Métis. There is general agreement—except among a few who take the extreme positions either that Aboriginal people have no separate jurisdiction or that Aboriginal rights transcend nation-states—that First Nations and other Aboriginal groups have the right to regulate particular lands or jurisdictional areas within the broader framework of the Canadian federation (Allain and O'Toole, 1995; Dupuis, 1997; Dust, 1995; Grand Council of the Crees (Eeyou Astchee), 1998; Hogg and Turpel, 1995; Recherches Amérindiennes au Québec; 1995). Cairns (2000), in one of the most provocative but well-considered pieces of recent analysis, challenges all Canadians to accept First Nations as unique constituents within an integrated multi*national* (not merely multicultural) society.

With respect to working out what this means in more specific detail, though, actual events tend to outpace more abstract debates and definitions. Self-government agreements, land claims, and other arrangements completed on a case-by-case basis have the potential to produce substantive outcomes that differ widely from one context to the next. In the meantime, debate continues over fundamental issues related to jurisdiction and authority over areas such as law, taxation, and regulation of economic activity (Bartlett, 1992; KPMG, 1997; Kunin, 1998; Mallea, 1994; Tunnicliffe, 1993; Wherrett and Allain, 1995).

These issues are further complicated by questions over representation and leadership in Aboriginal communities and organizations (Atimoyoo, 1998; Duerden, Black and Kuhn, 1996; McFarlane, 1996; Sawchuk, 1995, 1998). Contending visions about which priorities should guide the direction of Aboriginal organizations, who should be centrally involved in organizational decision-making processes, and what processes should be followed in making these decisions are becoming increasingly visible at several levels, ranging from community or band councils to nation-wide bodies such as the Assembly of First Nations. Some critics are quick to dismiss these concerns as evidence of corruption or lack of responsibility among Aboriginal groups, but more serious consideration needs to be given to the impact of government policies, other external regulations, and differentiation of interests within Aboriginal populations on the procedures and alternatives that emerge within decision-making processes in Aboriginal communities.

Healthy Development of Aboriginal Communities

A variety of agencies, ranging from federal, provincial, and Aboriginal governments to non-governmental organizations and community volunteers, have expressed their commitment to restoring health and vitality of Aboriginal people and their communities. Several problems, including serious risks to individual and community health, high rates of incarceration, and inequitable participation rates in a variety of institutional, employment, and political settings, stand as immediate concerns that demand unified responses from all of these agents. Underlying many of these issues are the depth and impact of long-term legacies left by practices such as residential schooling, the removal of children by welfare agencies from Aboriginal homes and communities, and the strict regimes of regulation by Indian Affairs over many reserve communities. The effects of these policies are only now beginning to become apparent as people share their experiences and work towards healing. An Aboriginal Healing Fund, implemented by the federal government, and statements of apology from religious denominations stand as examples of the many initiatives that have been implemented in recent years as means to acknowledge some of the damages and abuses encountered by First Nations in residential schools, to foster reconciliation, and to begin rebuilding relationships within Aboriginal communities. However, the rebuilding process is complicated by tensions and contradictions reflecting competing interests and needs. The emphasis among many Aboriginal leaders and communities on massive capital investments, economic development, or casino operations, for instance, stands in stark contrast to the expressed needs of other community members for increased programming and investment in areas like child and family services or substance abuse treatment and rehabilitation programs.

Social Inequality and Opportunity

Not all Aboriginal people share the same problems or seek common strategies to overcome them. While we demonstrate throughout this book that Aboriginal people are in many respects unique relative to other Canadians, through particular historical, legal, and social circumstances, we also contend that the distinctive ways in which the "racialization" of First Nations has contributed to their specific experiences and social identities cannot be understood in isolation from other sites that they occupy within the framework of Canadian and global society. As they enter into different positions within both Aboriginal and non-Aboriginal communities and organizations, indigenous people, like anyone else, are differentiated by their gender, class relations, geographical place or locale of residence, and other factors (Laliberte and Satzewich, 1999). Consequently, people may hold in common experiences that arise from being male or female, or from being poor or being an entrepreneur, regardless of their legal status or racial origins, just as these latter factors are likely to contribute some unique dimensions to those experiences. Three of the most pressing dimensions of inequality within Aboriginal populations are gender, urbanization, and the dynamics of social classes.

Gender relations within First Nations communities are important dividing lines, as they are in other segments of plural societies (Miller and Chuchryk, 1996). There are a number of ways in which gender has become an axis of division. For instance, for many years First Nations women have raised important concerns about political processes within their communities and organizations and about their relationship with the federal government. More recent concerns about the priorities of First Nations organizations came to a head in the debate about the Charlottetown Accord in 1992. The Assembly of First Nations was prepared to support the Accord because it recognized the constitutional right to Aboriginal self-government. In the Accord, self-government was left undefined and the "notwithstanding" clause could be invoked by First Nations at the point when concrete forms of self-government were being developed. This meant that First Nations could override certain charter rights if they felt that such rights were inconsistent with their historic political philosophies, practices, and traditions. First Nations women were concerned that male-dominated community organizations could potentially develop systems of self-government that did not take into account their existing right to sexual equality. Many First Nations women, along with the Native Women's Association of Canada, were opposed to the

Accord on these grounds and worked with non-Aboriginal organizations to undermine the legitimacy of the agreement.

Urbanization constitutes another point of division. In 1991, approximately 38 percent of First Nations people were living off-reserve. This figure is expected to rise to 45 percent by 2015. Thus, in less than fifteen years, nearly 400,000 of the 900,000 registered Indians in Canada are expected to be living in cities and towns outside their reserve communities (Ponting, 1997:70).

There are a number of important implications for social inequality as off-reserve residence increases. It is not clear, for instance, how the political system will respond to the growing presence of First Nations in Canadian cities. There are several plausible scenarios. Some First Nations may become further disengaged from the political system and not participate in wider municipal, provincial, or federal politics (Calliou, 1997). This has happened to many urban Blacks in the United States, in part because they lack the economic clout to make their concerns felt within mainstream political parties. On the other hand, mainstream political parties may try to capture the urban First Nations vote by recruiting high profile First Nations candidates. The question then becomes whether those political parties are seeking genuine representation by, and participation from, First Nations or whether they are simply interested in co-opting dynamic community leaders. Yet another scenario is that Aboriginal political parties may gain increasing political significance and legitimacy. Whatever happens, these dynamics will be overlaid with First Nations' own initiatives regarding the development of modes of representation for members of their community who live off-reserve.

Another concern is whether increasing off-reserve residence will lead to further socio-economic differentiation within reserve communities. If reserves are not able to offer enough economic opportunities to keep their residents close to home, many young and better-educated members of communities may choose urban centres to pursue their careers and livelihoods. These trends may create further social distance between urban and reserve residents, and may also have implications for the size of the pool of effective leaders that communities will be able to draw from in the future.

Finally, as a number of authors have acknowledged, both First Nations and wider Aboriginal communities are themselves socially differentiated (Boldt, 1993; Mitchell, 1996). The problem of social differentiation is a fundamental concern of sociologists, and the debates are extraordinarily complex. In this book, we offer a Marxist-inspired version of class analysis that focuses on ownership and control over the means of production as a fundamental division within communities and societies. This is certainly not the only way that social differentiation within Aboriginal communities can be understood, and more conceptual work needs to be done on this issue. However, there may be equally compelling reasons for analyzing inequality from a multi-dimensional Weberian perspective. Arguably, ownership and control over the means of production may not be the main fault lines within First Nations communities. As noted above, gender is important. Moreover, status, prestige, and control over political resources may all play a role in structuring social inequality. For example, the source of respect and influence of individuals like Tom Jackson, Susan Aglukark, and Graeme Greene does not necessarily lie in their control over productive forces, but rather in the social honour they have acquired through their artistic accomplishments. Furthermore, the power of band chiefs and councillors may not be based on their ownership and control over the means of production, but rather derived from the consistency between their values and those of the wider community they represent (Crowfoot, 1997:310).

Obviously, our book does not have all the answers to these dilemmas and issues. What it does offer is a perspective on how to begin to understand the complex realities faced by First Nations in the twenty-first century.

REFERENCES TO THE 2000 INTRODUCTION AND OTHER SUGGESTED READING (1993 TO DATE)

Abele, F.
1989   *Gathering Strength*. Calgary: Arctic Institute of North America at the University of Calgary.

Ahenakew, F. and H.C. Wolfart
1998   *kôhkominawak otâcimowiniwâwa. Our Grandmothers' Lives As Told in Their Own Words*. Regina: Canadian Plains Research Center.

Allain, J. and E.G. O'Toole
1995   *Aboriginal Rights*. Current Issue Review 89-11E. Ottawa: Library of Parliament Research Branch. Minister of Supply and Services Canada.

Alfred, G.R.
1995   *Heeding the Voices of our Ancestors: Kahnawake Mohawk Politics and the Rise of Native Nationalism*. Toronto: Oxford University Press.

Alfred, T.
1999   *Peace, Power, Righteousness: An Indigenous Manifesto*. Don Mills, ON: Oxford University Press.

Angus, M.
1991   *"And the Last Shall Be First": Native Policy in an Era of Cutbacks*. Toronto: NC Press Limited.

Anderson, R.B.
1995   "The Business Economy of the First Nations in Saskatchewan: A Contingency Perspective," *The Canadian Journal of Native Studies* 15, 2:309–346.

Assembly of First Nations
1994   *Breaking the Chains: First Nations Literacy and Self-Determination*. Ottawa: Assembly of First Nations.

1995   *National Overview of First Nations Child Care in Canada*. Ottawa: Assembly of First Nations.

1998   *First Nations Issues Survey - Full Report*. Ottawa: Assembly of First Nations.

Atimoyoo, E.
1998   Representation and Political Decision-Making in a Cree Perspective, unpublished M.A. non-thesis project. Department of Sociology, University of Saskatchewan.

Awasis Agency of Northern Manitoba
1997 *First Nations Family Justice: Mee-noo-stah-tan Mi-ni-si-win*. Thompson, MB: Awasis Agency of Northern Manitoba.

Barsh, R.L.
1994 "Canada's Aboriginal Peoples: Social Integration or Disintegration?" *The Canadian Journal of Native Studies* 14, 1:1–46.

Bartlett, R.H.
1992 *Indians and Taxation in Canada*, revised third edition. Saskatoon: University of Saskatchewan Native Law Centre.

Battiste, M.
1986 "Micmac Literacy and Cognitive Assimilation." In J. Barman, Y. Hébert and D. McCaskill, eds., *Indian Education in Canada: Volume 1: The Legacy*. Vancouver: UBC Press, pp. 23–44.

1998 "Enabling the Autumn Seed: Toward a Decolonized Approach to Aboriginal Knowledge, Language and Education," *Canadian Journal of Native Education* 22, 1:16–27.

Battiste, M. (ed.)
2000 *Reclaiming Indigenous Voice and Vision*. Vancouver: UBC Press.

Bedford, D.
1994 "Marxism and the Aboriginal Question: The Tragedy of Progress," *The Canadian Journal of Native Studies* 14, 1:101–117.

Bernier, R.
1997 *The Dimensions of Wage Inequality among Aboriginal Peoples*. Ottawa: Statistics Canada, Analytical Studies Branch Research Paper Series No. 109, December.

Boldt, M.
1993 *Surviving as Indians: The Challenge of Self-Government*. Toronto: University of Toronto Press.

Brady, P.
1996 "Native dropouts and non-Native dropouts in Canada: Two solitudes or a solitude shared?" *Journal of American Indian Education* 35, 2 (Winter): 10–20.

Brock, K.
1997 "Aboriginal People: First Nations." In A.F. Johnson and A. Stritch, eds., *Canadian Public Policy: Globalization and Political Parties*. Toronto: Copp Clark, pp. 189–211.

Brown, J.S.H and E. Vibert
1996 *Reading Beyond Words: Contexts for Native History*. Peterborough: Broadview Press.

Burns, G.
   1998   "Factors and Themes in Native Education and School Boards/First Nations Tuition Negotiations and Tuition Agreement Schooling," *Canadian Journal of Native Education* 22, 1:53–66.

Bussidor, I. and Ü. Bilgen-Reinart
   1997   *Night Spirits: The Story of the Relocation of the Sayisi Dene*. Winnipeg: The University of Manitoba Press.

Calliou, G.D.
   1997   "Urban Indians: Reflections on Participation of First Nation Individuals in the Institutions of the Larger Society." In *First Nations in Canada: Perspectives on Opportunity, Empowerment, and Self-Determination*. Toronto: McGraw-Hill Ryerson, pp. 222–243.

Cairns, A.C.
   2000   *Citizens Plus: Aboriginal Peoples and the Canadian State*. Vancouver: UBC Press.

Carter, S.
   1996   "Categories and Terrains of Exclusion: Constructing the 'Indian Woman' in the Early Settlement Era in Western Canada." In K.S. Coates and R. Fisher, eds., *Out of the Background: Readings on Canadian Native History*. Toronto: Copp Clark, pp. 177–195

Chiste, K.B.
   1996   "The Aboriginal Small Business Community." In K.B. Chiste, ed., *Aboriginal Small Business and Entrepreneurship in Canada*. North York, ON: Captus Press, pp. 4–31.

Crowfoot, S.
   1997   "Leadership in First Nation Communities: A Chief's Perspectives on the Colonial Milestone." In *First Nations in Canada: Perspectives on Opportunity, Empowerment, and Self-Determination*. Toronto: McGraw-Hill Ryerson, pp. 299–325.

Daniels, D.
   1986   "The Coming Crisis in the Aboriginal Rights Movement: From Colonialism to Neo-colonialism to Renaissance," *Native Studies Review* 2, 2:97–115.

Denis, C.
   1997   *We are Not You: First Nations and Canadian Modernity*. Peterborough, ON: Broadview Press.

Department of Indian Affairs and Northern Development
   1997   *Socio-Economic Indicators in Indian Reserves and Comparable Communities 1971–1991*. Ottawa: Minister of Public Works and Government Services Canada.

Dickason, O.P.
1992   *Canada's First Nations: A History of Founding Peoples from Earliest Times*. Toronto: McClelland and Stewart.

Drost, H., B.L. Crowley and R. Schwindt
1995   *Market Solutions for Native Poverty*. Toronto: C.D. Howe Institute.

Duerden, F., S. Black and R.G. Kuhn
1996   "An Evaluation of the Effectiveness of First Nations Participation in the Development of Land-Use Plans in the Yukon," *The Canadian Journal of Native Studies* 16, 1:105–124.

Dupuis, R.
1997   *Tribus, Peuples et Nations: Les nouveaux enjeux des revendications autochtones au Canada*. Québec: Les Editions du Boréal.

Dust, T.M.
1995   *The Impact of Aboriginal Land Claims and Self-Government on Canadian Municipalities: The Local Government Perspective*. Toronto: ICURR Press.

Emberley, J.
1996   "Aboriginal Women's Writing and the Cultural Politics of Representation." In C. Miller and P. Chuchryk, eds., *Women of the First Nations: Power, Wisdom, and Strength*. Winnipeg: The University of Manitoba Press, pp. 97–112.

Ermine, W.
1995   "Aboriginal Epistemology." In M. Battiste and J. Barman, eds., *First Nations Education in Canada: The Circle Unfolds*. Vancouver: UBC Press, pp. 101–112.

Federation of Saskatchewan Indian Nations
1997   *Saskatchewan and Aboriginal Peoples in the 21st Century: Social, Economic and Political Changes and Challenges*. Regina: PrintWest Publishing Services.

Fiske, J.
1990   "Native Women in Reserve Politics: Strategies and Struggles," *Journal of Legal Pluralism* 30:121–137.

Flanagan, T.
2000   *First Nations, Second Thoughts*. Montréal: McGill-Queen's University Press.

Fleras, A.
1996   "The Politics of Jurisdiction: Indigenizing Aboriginal-State Relations." In David Alan Long and Olive Patricia Dickason, eds., *Visions of the Heart: Canadian Aboriginal Issues*. Toronto: Harcourt Brace, pp. 147–177.

Fleras, A. and J.L. Elliott
1992   *The Nations Within: Aboriginal-State Relations in Canada, the United States, and New Zealand.* Toronto: Oxford University Press.

Four Directions Consulting Group
1997   *Implications of First Nations Demography: Final Report.* Winnipeg: Indian and Northern Affairs Canada.

Fournier, S. and E. Crey
1997   *Stolen From Our Embrace: The Abduction of First Nations Children and the Restoration of Aboriginal Communities.* Vancouver: Douglas & McIntyre.

Frideres, J.S.
1998   *Aboriginal Peoples in Canada: Contemporary Conflicts*, fifth edition. Scarborough, ON: Prentice Hall Allyn and Bacon Canada.

Furniss, E.
1992   *Victims of Benevolence: Discipline and Death at the Williams Lake Indian Residential School, 1891–1920.* Williams Lake, B.C.: Cariboo Tribal Council.

Gagné, M.-A.
1994   *A Nation within a Nation: Dependency and the Cree.* Montreal: Black Rose Books.

Gilbert, S., L. Barr, W. Clark, M. Blue, and D. Sunter
1993   *Leaving School: Results from a National Survey.* Ottawa: Minister of Supply and Services Canada.

Globerman, S.
1998   "Investment and Capital Productivity." In R. Kunin, ed., *Prospering Together: The Economic Impact of the Aboriginal Title Settlements in B.C.* Vancouver: The Laurier Institution, pp. 139–168.

Goddard, J.T.
1997   "Reversing the Spirit of Delegitimation," *Canadian Journal of Native Studies* 17, 2:215–225.

Goulet, J.-G. A.
1998   *Ways of Knowing: Experience, Knowledge, and Power among the Dene Tha.* Vancouver: UBC Press.

Graham, K., C. Dittburner and F. Abele
1996   *Public Policy and Aboriginal Peoples 1965–1992. Volume 1. Soliloquy and Dialogue: Overview of Major Trends in Public Policy Relating to Aboriginal Peoples.* Ottawa: Minister of Public Works and Government Services Canada.

Grand Council of the Crees (Eeyou Astchee)
1998   *Never Without Consent: James Bay Crees' Stand Against Forcible Inclusion into an Independent Quebec.* Toronto: ECW Press.

Graveline, F.J.
1998   *Circle Works: Transforming Eurocentric Consciousness*. Halifax: Fernwood Publishing.

Haddad, T. and M. Spivey
1992   "All or Nothing: Modernization, Dependency and Wage Labour on a Reserve in Canada," *The Canadian Journal of Native Studies* 12, 2: 203–228.

Helin, C.
1991   *Doing Business With Native People Makes Sense*. Victoria, BC: Praxis Publishing and Native Investment and Trade Association.

Hogg, P.W. and M.E. Turpel
1995   "Implementing Aboriginal Self-Government: Constitutional and Jurisdictional Issues," *The Canadian Bar Review* 74, 2, (June): 187–224.

Hylton, J.H.
1999   "The Case for Aboriginal Self-Government: A Social Policy Perspective," in J.H. Hylton, ed., *Aboriginal Self-Government in Canada: Current Trends and Issues*, second edition. Saskatoon: Purich Publishing, pp. 78–91.

Indian and Northern Affairs Canada
1997   *Gathering Strength: Canada's Aboriginal Action Plan*. Ottawa: Indian and Northern Affairs Canada.

1998   Basic Departmental Data 1998. Ottawa: Minister of Public Works and Government Services Canada.

Indian and Northern Affairs Canada and Canadian Polar Commission
2000   *2000–2001 Estimates. Part III: Report on Plans and Priorities*. Ottawa: Minister of Public Works and Government Services Canada.

Jaccoud, M.
1995a   "L'exclusion sociale et les Autochtones," *Lien social et politiques - RIAC* 34:93–100.

1995b   *Justice blanche au Nunavik*. Montréal: Méridien.

Jackson, M.A.
1994   "Aboriginal Women and Self-Government." In J.H. Hylton, ed., *Aboriginal Self-Government in Canada: Current Trends and Issues*. Saskatoon: Purich Publishing, pp. 180–198.

Jhappan, C.R.
1992   "Global Community?: Supranational Strategies of Canada's Aboriginal Peoples," *Journal of Indigenous Studies 3*, 1:59–91.

KPMG
1997   *First Nations and Canadian Taxation*, second edition. Toronto: KPMG.

Krosenbrink-Gelissen, L.E.
1996 "Sexual Equality as an Aboriginal Right: Canada's Aboriginal Women in the Constitutional Process on Aboriginal Matters, 1982–1987." In R. Kuppe and R. Potz eds., *Law and Philosophy*, Volume 8. Dordrecht: Kluwer Law International, pp. 147–160.

Kunin, R. ed.
1998 *Prospering Together: The Economic Impact of the Aboriginal Title Settlements in B.C.* Vancouver: The Laurier Institution.

Laliberte, R. and V. Satzewich
1999 "Native Migrant Labour and the Alberta Sugar Beet Industry." *Canadian Review of Sociology and Anthropology* vol. 36, no.1, pp. 65–86.

Langford, T. and R.J. Ponting
1992 "Canadians' responses to Aboriginal issues: The role or prejudice, perceived group conflict, and economic conservatism." *Canadian Review of Sociology and Anthropology* vol 29, no. 2, pp. 140–166.

LaPrairie, C.
1996 *Seen But Not Heard: Native People in the Inner City.* Ottawa: Minister of Public Works and Government Services Canada.

Lepage, P.
1995 "Un regard au-delà des chartes. Le racisme et la discrimination envers les peuples autochtones," *Recherches amérindiennes au Québec* 25, 3: 29–45.

Long, D.A. and O.P. Dickason, eds.
1996 *Visions of the Heart: Canadian Aboriginal Issues.* Toronto: Harcourt Brace Canada.

Mallea, P.
1994 *Aboriginal Law: Apartheid in Canada.* Brandon, MB: Bearpaw Publishing.

McBride, S. and P. Smith
1998 "The Impact of Aboriginal Title Settlements on Education and Human Capital." In R. Kunin, ed. *Prospering Together: The Economic Impact of the Aboriginal Title Settlements in B.C.* Vancouver: The Laurier Institution, pp. 169–206.

McFarlane, P.
1996 "Aboriginal Leadership." In D.A. Long and O.P. Dickason, eds., *Visions of the Heart: Canadian Aboriginal Issues.* Toronto: Harcourt Brace, pp. 117–145.

Miller, C. and P. Chuchryk
1996 *Women of the First Nations.* Winnipeg: University of Manitoba Press.

Miller, J.R.
1996   *Shingwauk's Vision: A History of Native Residential Schools.* Toronto: University of Toronto Press.

Mitchell, M.
1996   *From Talking Chiefs to Native Corporate Elite. The birth of class and Nationalism among Canadian Inuit.* Montreal: McGill-Queen's University Press.

Monture-Angus, P.A.
1995   *Thunder in my Soul: A Mohawk Woman Speaks.* Halifax: Fernwood Publishing.

1996   "Lessons in Decolonization: Aboriginal Overrepresentation in Canadian Criminal Justice." In D.A. Long and O.P. Dickason, eds., *Visions of the Heart: Canadian Aboriginal Issues.* Toronto: Harcourt Brace and Company, pp. 335–354.

Newhouse, David R.
1993   "Modern Aboriginal Economies: Capitalism with an Aboriginal Face." In *Sharing the Harvest: The Road to Self-Reliance,* Royal Commission on Aboriginal Peoples, 90-100. Ottawa: Minister of Supply and Services Canada.

Norris, M.J.
1996   "Contemporary Demography of Aboriginal Peoples in Canada." In D.A. Long and O.P. Dickason, eds., *Visions of the Heart: Canadian Aboriginal Issues.* Toronto: Harcourt Brace and Company, pp. 179–237.

1998   "Canada's Aboriginal Languages," *Canadian Social Trends* 51 (Winter):8–16.

_____ **and D. Beavon**
1999   "Registered Indian Mobility and Migration: An Analysis of 1996 Census Data," paper presented at the Canadian Population Society meetings, Lennoxville, Québec, June.

Peers, L.
1996   "Subsistence, Secondary Literature, and Gender Bias: The Saulteaux." In C. Miller and P. Chuchryk, eds., *Women of the First Nations: Power, Wisdom, and Strength.* Winnipeg: The University of Manitoba Press, pp. 39–50.

Perley, D.G.
1993   "Aboriginal Education in Canada as Internal Colonialism," *Canadian Journal of Native Education* 20, 1:118–128.

Pertusati, L.
1997   *In Defense of Mohawk Land: Ethnopolitical Conflict in Native North America.* Albany, NY: State University of New York Press.

Peters, E.J.
1996   "Aboriginal People in Urban Areas." In D.A. Long and O.P. Dickason, eds., *Visions of the Heart: Canadian Aboriginal Issues*. Toronto: Harcourt Brace and Company, pp. 305–333.

Petipas, K.
1995   *Serving the Ties that Bind*. Winnipeg: University of Manitoba Press.

Ponting, J.R.
1997   "Editor's Introduction." In J.R. Ponting, ed., *First Nations in Canada: Perspectives on Opportunity, Empowerment, and Self-Determination*. Toronto: McGraw-Hill Ryerson, pp. 3–18.

1997   "The Socio-Demographic Picture." In J.R. Ponting, ed., *First Nations in Canada: Perspectives on Opportunity, Empowerment, and Self-Determination*. Toronto: McGraw-Hill Ryerson, pp. 68–114.

Ponting, J.R. and J. Kiely
1997   "Disempowerment: 'Justice,' Racism, and Public Opinion." In J.R. Ponting, ed., *First Nations in Canada: Perspectives on Opportunity, Empowerment, and Self-Determination*. Toronto: McGraw-Hill Ryerson, pp. 152–192.

Recherches Amérindiennes au Québec.
1995   *Autochtones et Québécois: La recontre des nationalismes*. Montréal: Recherches amérindiennes au Québec.

Rogers, E.S. and D.B. Smith
1994   *Aboriginal Ontario: Historical Perspectives of the First Nations*. Toronto: Ontario Historical Series for the Government of Ontario.

Royal Commission on Aboriginal Peoples.
1993   *Aboriginal Peoples in Urban Centres: Report of the National Round Table on Aboriginal Urban Issues*. Ottawa: Minister of Supply and Services Canada.

1995   *Choosing Life: Special Report on Suicide Among Aboriginal People*. Ottawa: Minister of Supply and Services Canada.

1996a   *Report of the Royal Commission on Aboriginal Peoples, Volume 1: Looking Forward, Looking Back*. Ottawa: Minister of Supply and Services Canada.

1996b   *Report of the Royal Commission on Aboriginal Peoples, Volume 2: Restructuring the Relationship*. Ottawa: Minister of Supply and Services Canada.

1996c   *Report of the Royal Commission on Aboriginal Peoples, Volume 3: Gathering Strength*. Ottawa: Minister of Supply and Services Canada.

1996d   *Report of the Royal Commission on Aboriginal Peoples, Volume 4: Perspectives and Realities*. Ottawa: Minister of Supply and Services Canada.

1996e   *Report of the Royal Commission on Aboriginal Peoples, Volume 5: Renewal: A Twenty Year Commitment.* Ottawa: Minister of Supply and Services Canada.

1996f   "A Word from Commissioners." In *Royal Commission on Aboriginal Peoples, People to People, Nation to Nation: Highlights from the Report of the Royal Commission on Aboriginal Peoples.* Ottawa: Minister of Supply and Services Canada, pp. ix–xi.

Santiago, M.
1997   *Post-Secondary Education and Labour Market Outcomes for Registered Indians.* Ottawa: Indian Affairs and Northern Development Canada.

Saskatoon Star-Phoenix
1999   "HIV infecting more Natives," Saskatoon *Star-Phoenix*, January 18:A1-2.

Satzewich, V.
1997   "Indian Agents and the 'Indian Problem' in Canada in 1946: Reconsidering the Theory of Coercive Tutelage," *Canadian Journal of Native Studies* 17, 2:227–257.

Sawchuk, J.
1995   "Fragmentation and Realignment: The Continuing Cycle of Métis and Non-Status Indian Political Organizations in Canada," *Native Studies Review* 10, 2: 77–95.

1998   *The Dynamics of Native Politics: The Alberta Métis Experience.* Saskatoon: Purich Publishing.

Schissel, B. and T. Wotherspoon
1998   *An Investigation into Indian and Métis Student Life Experience in Saskatchewan Schools.* Saskatoon: Research Report Prepared for the Saskatchewan Indian and Métis Education Research Project.

Silverman, R.A. and M.O. Nielsen, eds.
1992   *Aboriginal Peoples and Canadian Criminal Justice.* Toronto: Harcourt Brace & Company.

Smandych, R. and G. Lee
1995   "Women, Colonization and Resistance: Elements of an Amerindian Autohistorical approach to the Study of Law and Colonialism," *Native Studies Review* 10, 1:21–46.

Smith, M.H.
1995   *Our Home or Native Land? What Government's Aboriginal Policy is Doing to Canada.* Victoria: Crown Western.

Statistics Canada
1998a   "1996 Census: Aboriginal data," *The Daily*, January 13.

1998b "1996 Census: Ethnic Origin, Visible Minorities," *The Daily*, February 17.

1998c "1996 Census: Education, mobility and migration," *The Daily*, April 14.

1998d "1996 Census: Sources of income, earnings and total income, and family income," *The Daily*, May 12.

Sub-Committee on Aboriginal Education
1996 *Sharing the Knowledge: The Path to Success and Equal Opportunities in Education*. Report of the Standing Committee on Aboriginal Affairs and Northern Development. Ottawa: Canada Communications Group.

Treaty 7 Elders and Tribal Council
1996 *The True Spirit and Original Intent of Treaty 7*. Montreal and Kingston: McGill-Queen's University Press.

Tunnicliffe, R.D.
1993 "Barriers to Business Financing: The Legal Context." In *Financing First Nations: Investing in Aboriginal Business and Governments*. Vancouver: Conference manual, June.

Turpel, M.E./Aki Kwe
1993 "Patriarchy and Paternalism: The Legacy of the Canadian State for First Nations Women," *Canadian Journal of Women and the Law* 6:174–192.

Voyageur, C.J.
1996 "Contemporary Indian Women." In D.A. Long and O.P. Dickason, eds., *Visions of the Heart: Canadian Aboriginal Issues*. Toronto: Harcourt Brace and Company, pp. 93–115.

Weaver, S.
1990 "A New Paradigm in Canadian Indian Policy for the 1990s," *Canadian Ethnic Studies* 22, 3:8–18.

Wherrett, J. and J. Allain
1995 *Aboriginal Self-Government*. Current Issue Review 89-5E. Ottawa: Library of Parliament Research Branch. Minister of Supply and Services Canada.

Williams, A.M.
1997 "Canadian Urban Aboriginals: A Focus on Aboriginal Women in Canada," *Canadian Journal of Native Studies* 12, 1:75–101.

CHAPTER 1

POLITICAL ECONOMY VERSUS THE CHICAGO SCHOOL AND INTERNAL COLONIALISM:
Class, "Race," Gender, and Aboriginal Peoples

Even though it is readily acknowledged that as a collectivity aboriginal peoples occupy disadvantaged positions within social, economic, and political relations in Canada, there is little agreement as to why there are such inequities and social differences between aboriginal and non-aboriginal peoples. While there is an emergent literature rooted in the tradition of political economy (Abele and Stasiulis, 1989), existing sociological analyses of aboriginal peoples in Canada have been dominated by two apparently distinct schools of thought: the Chicago School tradition and the internal colonial model.

This chapter critically evaluates the Chicago School and the internal colonial models' interpretation of aboriginal peoples experiences in Canada. Despite the appearance that the internal colonial model is a radical alternative to the Chicago School (Frideres, 1988), we suggest that both approaches share some conceptual terrain and, therefore, have similar conceptual problems and reproduce similar silences (see also Wolpe, 1975). We argue that both approaches are limited in their ability to analyze and understand aboriginal issues and experiences in Canada. In the final section, we offer an alternative conceptualization based on political economy.

THE CHICAGO SCHOOL AND ABORIGINAL PEOPLES

One of the central terms within the Chicago School is the concept of assimilation. For many academics and non-academics, there is confusion surrounding the concept of assimilation (Li, 1988). Much of this confusion stems from the failure to differentiate between assimilation as a political strategy and assimilation as a sociological term used to describe and explain particular social processes. As a social science perspective, the Chicago School does not necessarily approve or disapprove of attempts by states to assimilate groups of people, although there are at times clear political implications associated with the school (Shore, 1987). As a social science perspective, it examines the issues of how and why groups of people become more culturally alike, how and why groups of people resist becoming more culturally alike, and the social and economic consequences of cultural differences and conflicts. Our concern, then, is primarily with the utility of the concept of assimilation and the adequacy of the Chicago School as a social science perspective.

There are several specific approaches stemming from the Chicago School which over the years have been popular in explaining different patterns of minority-majority group relations in North America (Ballis Lal, 1990). However, within all versions of Chicago School-based theories, analytical emphasis is placed on the concepts of culture, cultural difference, and cultural change. The central assumption is that cultural differences exist and that these differences structure, regulate, and have consequences for social interaction between groups. In this light, Chicago School theories have generally examined two sets of issues: 1) the dynamics of the process of assimilation; 2) the social and economic consequences of assimilation or the lack of assimilation.

In terms of the first issue, some, like Robert Park (1950; see also Nagler, 1975), view assimilation as the end result of a race relations cycle. For Park, the cycle begins with contact between two different groups of people. This contact leads to competition, usually over scarce economic resources. Competition leads to the development of racism, the formation of group boundaries, and some form of accommodative relationship between groups in which inequality is institutionalized. Eventually this accommodative order breaks down and gives way to the incorporation of the minority group into the dominant group.

Others, like Milton Gordon (1964), emphasize the multivariate nature of assimilation. Gordon argues that there are seven types, or stages, of assimilation. Behavioral assimilation refers to learning the culture of the host society; structural assimilation is the large-scale participation in primary groups within the dominant society; marital assimilation is the large-scale intermarriage between majority and minority group members; identificational assimilation is the development of a sense of community based on the definitions of the dominant society; attitude-receptional assimilation refers to the absence of prejudice; behavioral-receptional assimilation is the absence of discrimination; and civic assimilation refers to the absence of ethnic conflict (see Geschwender, 1978, for a summary and critique).

Types of assimilation do not follow each other sequentially. However, Gordon does argue that cultural assimilation is a necessary, but not a sufficient, condition for the latter types of assimilation. Learning the culture, values, and norms of the dominant society is necessary in order for other types of assimilation to occur, but this does not guarantee that they will follow. The major barrier to total assimilation is structural assimilation: when minority group members come to participate in the various cliques, clubs, and institutions of the dominant society, other forms of assimilation usually follow.

The second set of issues Chicago School theorists examine are the social and economic consequences of assimilation and the lack of assimilation. In North America, some have suggested that European and aboriginal cultures are completely dissimilar, and the unwillingness and/or inability to assimilate on the part of the latter is the cause of various problems such as poverty, job segregation, and low levels of upward occupational mobility and educational achievement.

Mark Nagler, in *Natives Without a Home*, has provided one of the most systematic applications of Chicago School-type analysis to the condition of aboriginal peoples in Canada. Even though his work is somewhat dated, as well as eclectic, his arguments remain popular within some academic and non-academic circles, and are part of the larger "common sense" of aboriginal relations in Canada. Nagler (1975) argues that aboriginal peoples in Canada possess a specific cultural complex that is quite different from that of non-aboriginals. Aboriginal peoples, he suggests, have a present rather than future time orientation (1975:20); they value free mutual aid without the expectation of return (1975:18-19); they do not place a high value on the possession of wealth or material goods (1975:20); they do not save for the future; they have a different conception of time and do not live according to "clock time" (1975:21); they do not have an appreciation of the monetary value of time; they do not have a work ethic (1975:22); and they do not place the same value on education as do non-aboriginal people.

Nagler (1975:22) argues that taken together, "these normative patterns or values are universal among native groups." He also argues that these elements of aboriginal culture create a culture of poverty. Alternatively, Henry Zentner (1973), in a way which sounds like he is describing dinosaurs, refers to this complex of culture as the "preneolithic ethic." The culture of poverty refers to a cultural system in which people are unable to succeed and achieve economic mobility because of the absence of a culturally-sanctioned work ethic. The absence of this work ethic means that "a large segment of the Indian population refuse or find themselves unable to partake in full time economic pursuits" (Nagler, 1972:131).

In sum, the work of theorists working within the Chicago School tends to regard the subordinate status of aboriginal peoples in Canada primarily as a problem of "race" and ethnic relations. Aboriginal and non-aboriginal peoples are two relatively homogeneous groups whose cultures are incompatible. The incompatibility of cultures is the cause of various social problems for aboriginal peoples.

Explanations of aboriginal peoples' positions in Canada stemming from the Chicago School have been challenged by social scientists, although they remain popular on the level of common sense. There are several conceptual problems with this school of thought when applied to aboriginal peoples.

First, Chicago School approaches do not specify which behaviors are indicative of assimilation at an empirical level. Gordon's model of multi-variate assimilation avoids this problem to some extent, but even it is plagued by imprecision. With respect to behavioral assimilation, there is a wide variety of behaviors in which people within the majority group engage. Some people attend movies and the ballet during their leisure time and others like to consume alcohol in a bar; some eat and drink things that others find unpalatable. The models of assimilation do not indicate which actual behaviors minority group members need to engage in before they are judged to be behaviorally assimilated. Nor do these models tell us which institutional structures are the most important to be assimilated into. It is unclear, for example, whether membership in the Lions Club, the Canadian Legion, or the Canadian Manufacturers Association all have the same social significance. These are not inconsiderable problems given the analytical importance of the concepts of behavioral and structural assimilation. If the model is to prove useful either in policy or practical terms, then it must be able to justify theoretically, and specify empirically, the standards of assimilation. Otherwise, there is considerable potential for shifting the goal posts of assimilation to make it impossible to achieve.

Second, the use of the concept of culture is ambiguous. In the work of Nagler, for example, it is unclear to which aspects of aboriginal peoples' lives "culture" refers. One of Nagler's associated arguments is that aboriginal peoples are different from ethnic groups of European origin because the former lack a common sense of group identity. The absence of a group identity stems from their varying religious, geographical, social, and linguistic backgrounds. Thus, Nagler suggests that because aboriginal peoples in Canada are so diverse, they do not have a common cultural tradition to draw upon in order to forge an ethnic identity and hence an effective political strategy.

However, as already noted, Nagler also provides a catalogue of beliefs, attitudes, and values that all aboriginal peoples are deemed to possess: they do not value wealth and consumer goods; they are collective rather than individually oriented; and they do live according to European conceptions of time, etc. He attributes these values to all aboriginal peoples in Canada. Aside from the fact that this description of aboriginal peoples' values uncritically reproduces many common-sense negative stereo-types, this argument is contradictory. If we are to believe his description of aboriginal values and beliefs, then it seems that aboriginal peoples do in fact possess many common "cultural" traits that could, in theory, provide the basis for a common ethnic identity. Thus, at some points in Nagler's analysis, aboriginal peoples seem to possess common cultural traits and at other points, they are said not to possess a common culture. This demon-strates the confusion surrounding the concept of culture.

Third, we question whether culture is a cause of material circum-stances. As noted above, the application of Chicago School arguments to the case of aboriginal peoples suggests that cultural differences cause inequality, poverty, unemployment, job turnover, and low rates of upward occupational mobility. There are, however, empirical and theoretical grounds to suggest that culture is not something primordial which exists abstractly and transhistorically (Mason, 1986). Rather, it is rooted in a range of material circumstances and is situationally determined (Yancey, Erikson, and Juliani, 1976). Thus, the values and beliefs that appear to be the cause of unemployment, low incomes, and high rates of job turnover may actually be consequences of a rational assessment by aboriginal peo-ples of their chances within the context of limited opportunities (Wien, 1986).

This cause-and-effect problem is evident in Nagler's interpretation of interview material. In an interview he conducted with an aboriginal person who worked for a time in a southern community, but whose home was in an isolated reserve in northern Canada, the interviewee stated that

> I wanted to buy a car there but it is even hard to walk on the road some-times at home. I really do not know why people want lots of money. At home, we have what we want but we work and if I have a radio or T.V., it is no good because you can't hear it up there (Nagler, 1975:19).

Nagler interprets this response as indicating that aboriginal culture teaches people not to value wealth and consumer goods, which in turn leads to a lack of motivation to work hard. However, a very different, and more plausible, interpretation can be offered. As the respondent indicated, the lack of value placed on the possession of an automobile has largely to do with the practicalities of driving in a community that does not have good roads. Furthermore, not wanting a radio or television also seems to be logical when reception is poor. The problem, then, is not that aborigi-nal peoples do not value cars, televisions, and radios because of their cul-ture. Rather, some may not value these commodities because, in the context of their own material circumstances, it makes little practical or economic sense to do so. Thus, what Nagler interprets as a primordial cultural trait of aboriginal peoples may instead be a rational reaction to their own circumstances. One can only wonder what a social scientist would say about "the problem" with aboriginal culture if a person worked eight hours a day so that her family could sit in front of a television screen that contained nothing but static electricity.

Fourth, we question whether all minorities undergo the same process of assimilation. Reflecting his usage of Park's race relations cycle, Nagler suggests that in the process of urbanization, "like all newcomers, Native Peoples must go through a period of adjustment when they first come to an urban environment . . . . The Native Peoples are more in the position of the first group of immigrants of any particular ethnic origin, who usually encounter considerable difficulty when they arrive" (Nagler, 1975:52). This argument assumes that all "newcomers" face the same material circumstances, labour market conditions, and economic opportunites as previous generations of newcomers to a country or city.

Steinberg (1981) has argued, however, that in the United States different rates of upward social mobility of ethnic groups have been affected primarily by the state of the job market they faced upon arrival. Given that the nature of the job market and occupational structure of a country is constantly shifting, it is unrealistic to assume that all groups who migrate to a new country, or to an urban area within a country, will face the same job opportunities and life chances as previous generations and experience the same patterns of upward mobility (see also Wilson, 1980). As we suggest in Chapter 2, aboriginal migration to urban areas in the early 1970s coincided with a sharp decline in the fortunes of Canadian capitalism, which has resulted in a reduction of opportunities for upward structural social mobility.

Our reservations about the work of Nagler, who is one of the main proponents of the Chicago School tradition in Canada, are shared by others interested in the sociological understanding of aboriginal peoples (Lithman, 1984:10). In fact, problems with the arguments led in the 1970s to the development of an alternative conceptualization: the internal colonial model.

THE INTERNAL COLONIAL MODEL: A "RADICAL" ALTERNATIVE?

The application of the internal colonial model to aboriginal peoples in Canada draws on literature developed originally in the context of the debates about the position of black people in America (Blauner, 1969; Geschewnder, 1978). Blauner (1969) argues that traditionally the concept of colonialism referred to unequal and exploitative relations among Europe and Asia, Latin America, and Africa. Colonialism in those contexts involved the domination by a "mother country" of an external "subject country" or colony. The mother country was interested in either the exploitation of labour power or the extraction of resources from the environment. Colonialism usually referred to an unequal political and economic relationship between two or more spacially distinct regions of the world.

Blauner argues that colonial relationships not only exist between different geographical units but also can be found within a singular spatial and political unit. Thus, he introduces the term *internal colonialism* to refer to those situations where Europeans have settled in "new lands," have established European institutions, and have subjugated both indigenous and non-indigenous groups.

Since the 1970s the internal colonial model has become increasingly popular in the explanation of the position of aboriginal peoples in Canada. There are several proponents of the model in Canada, each with a somewhat different emphasis. Kellough (1980) and Bienvienue (1985) provide general historical overviews of the colonization process. The model has been applied to aboriginal peoples and development in the North by Mel Watkins in his edited collection, *The Dene Nation: A Colony Within*, and by Coates and Powell in *The Modern North: People, Politics, and the Rejection of Colonialism*. In more specific studies, Brady (1984) uses the model to explain the poor health status of aboriginal peoples and Boldt (1981a, 1981b, 1981c, 1982) presupposes the existence of an internal colonial relationship in his study of Indian leadership.

Given that there is not a singular internal colonial model on which all theorists would agree, our focus will be on the version offered by James Frideres in the final chapter of the third edition of *Native Peoples in Canada*. Frideres' work is chosen here because it has been the version that has been most accessible to students over the years, it is the most comprehensive and theoretically refined, and because he presents the internal colonial model as an explicit alternative to "micro" models, or Chicago School analyses of aboriginal/non-aboriginal relations.

Following Blauner, Frideres conceptualizes the colonization process into seven parts. The first involves the incursion of the colonizing group into a geographical area. In Canada, it was a combination of French and British interests that initially entered the territory in their search first for fish, and later for fur and other staples. Second, colonization involved the destruction of the social and cultural structures of the indigenous group. In Frideres' (1988:367) terms, the "white colonizers destroyed the Native's political, economic, kinship and in most cases, religious systems. The values and norms of Native people were either ignored or violated."

The third and fourth aspects of colonization involve the establishment of systems of external political control and aboriginal economic dependence. Indian and Northern Affairs Canada (INAC) along with the Indian Act have been the main vehicles by which external political control has been advanced. Both are external political structures that have been imposed on aboriginal peoples. Through the Indian Act and the activities of INAC, Indian people were denied many basic civil and political rights that other Canadians have taken for granted. Among other things, Indians were denied the right to vote in federal elections until 1960, faced restrictions on their movement off reserve until the 1930s, and were not allowed to consume alcohol. In addition, traditional cultural, religious, and political practices were systematically attacked. Frideres notes, however, that since the 1960s a process of decolonization has occurred: aboriginal peoples are becoming more politically active in their struggles for citizenship rights and control over their own lives and institutions.

In relation to economic dependence, the reserve system is regarded as a geographical hinterland for white exploitation. Indian reserves are internal colonies that are exploited by white Canadians. White colonizers exploit the non-renewable resources of Indian lands and the labour power of Indian workers, who work at unskilled jobs in seasonal industries controlled by whites. In addition to draining resources from aboriginal communities, economic dependence is further fostered by provisions of the Indian Act and the Income Tax Act, which limit Indian people's access to credit: they prohibit the placement of reserve property as collateral for bank loans and hence deter the development of free enterprise amongst native peoples.

The fifth aspect of the colonization process is the provision of low quality social services for the colonized people. The inadequate provision of health and social services is indicated by the low health status, the low educational status, and the extensive welfare dependency of native peoples.

The sixth and seventh aspects of this process relate to the nature of social interactions. An ideology of racism and a colour line emerge to regulate social interaction between groups. Social significance is attached to skin colour, and ideologies of biological superiority and inferiority emerge to justify the exploitation of aboriginal peoples and their resources, to break down their resistance to exploitation, and to deter them from becoming full members of Canadian society.

In sum, Frideres (1988:372) argues that while the motives for colonization may have been religious, economic, and political, the rewards of colonization are primarily economic: "White Canada has gained far more than it has lost in colonizing its Natives." In many ways the internal colonial model is compelling. When compared with the Chicago School, it has several advantages. Since it is a macro model, it is better able to link aboriginal peoples' experiences to larger structural processes occurring within Canadian society. It also recognizes the existence of power differentials between aboriginal and non-aboriginal peoples. Despite these merits, doubts remain about the ability of the model to explain aboriginal peoples' experiences in a satisfactory fashion (see Hartwig, 1978; Wolpe, 1975 for critiques of the model in other contexts).

First, the internal colonial model is imprecise on the question of timing. The model is ambiguous as to when the colonization process began.

Furthermore, while there is a recognition that a phase of de-colonization has recently been entered, it tends to assume that aboriginal-white relations, and the process of colonization, have been rather static for the previous 300 years of contact. It is unclear whether there have been shifts in the motives, techniques, and practices of colonization over time.

When the issue of timing is specifically addressed, there is a tendency to suggest that the colonization process began with European arrival in North America in the 16th and 17th centuries. As we suggest in Chapter 2, European interest in systematically transforming aboriginal culture and exploiting their lands occurred after the decline of the fur trade and the rise of industrial capitalism. While there certainly were concerted efforts on the part of Europeans to induce Indians into the fur trade and to form both military and economic alliances, in relation to later periods, this was a period of comparative laissez-faire with respect to the aboriginal way of life. While relations of dependence and subordination emerged during the course of the fur trade, in part because of Indian people's reliance on European commodities, some anthropologists and historians nevertheless suggest that this was a period of "non-directed cultural change" (Miller, 1989). Aboriginal lifestyles were central to the economic reproduction of the fur trade, and Europeans generally did not want to tamper with a successful system of commodity production (Trigger, 1985; Wolf, 1982).

It was at the point when ruling classes deemed that future economic expansion should occur on the basis of agriculture and industrial capitalism that aboriginal peoples and their culture became systematically defined as a "problem." Thus, in marking the beginning of the colonization process with contact, the model is unable to grasp the changes in the social and economic forces that have affected the position of aboriginal peoples in Canada.

Second, the model may have some relevance to Indian people who live on reserves, but its applicability to other categories of aboriginal peoples is questionable. The economic benefits of appropriation of Indian land have been enormous, and Indians on reserves historically have played key roles in the seasonal labour force, particularly in agriculture and logging (Knight, 1978). In some ways, Indian reserves can be considered as sites where a portion of the reserve army of labour for capitalist economic activity has been reproduced. However, the model offers little help in understanding the position and experiences of non-status Indians, Métis, and those aboriginal peoples (status, non-status, and Métis) who live in urban areas. It is unclear how the model applies to aboriginal peoples who, while they may be subject to various forms of racist hostility and exclusion, are not subject to the social, economic, and political controls of INAC and the Indian Act. These groups have different relationships to the Canadian state than do reserve-based Indians.

Third, like the work of the Chicago School, the internal colonial model tends to assume that aboriginal and white are homogeneous groups. Frideres (1988:366) conceptualizes the problematic nature of the relations between the two groups as "White Canadians are . . . the colonizing people while Natives are . . . the colonized people." In conceptualizing the colonization process as rooted in the process of contact between whites and aboriginals, there is a tendency to reify the two categories. That is, it sees the categories of "white" and "native" as actual groups that have real social interaction. It further assumes that all whites have similar interests in relation to the maintenance of an internal colonial relationship with aboriginal peoples, and that all aboriginal peoples have a singular set of economic, social, and political interests that revolve around resistance to internal colonial domination.

As we suggest in Chapter 3, despite attempts on the part of some aboriginal leaders and organizations to forge a common national identity through the development of pan-Indianism, there are economic, political, ideological, and gender divisions within the aboriginal population. Aboriginal peoples are distributed across the range of class sites within Canadian society, and their distribution reflects complex intersections of class, "race," and gender. In Wolpe's (1975:321) terms, the "consequence of the failure to relate classes within racial or ethnic groups to the class structure of the society as a whole, is that racial or ethnic entities are treated abstractly and as if their internal class structures are irrelevant to their existence as groups and to their political and ideological practices."

In terms of the conceptualization of European or "white" society, the model tends to imply that all Europeans have had, and continue to have, an equal interest and voice in the oppression and exploitation of native peoples. While there is no doubt that many white people have benefitted both directly and indirectly from the exploitation of aboriginal peoples, we question the extent to which all whites have derived an equal benefit, have had an equal interest in, and have had an equal voice in such exploitation. We suggest that the "exploitation" of aboriginal peoples occurs in the context of an extant class system in which benefits have been unequally distributed.

Thus, like the Chicago School, the internal colonial model is silent on the form of social and economic organization which characterizes white society, and whether this social and economic organization has had a formative impact on aboriginal peoples' lives. Within the model, there is no mention of the fact that it was a European society characterized by the presence of a particular mode of production, and that within this mode of production, there are certain social classes and genders that have differential relationships and access to the means of production. Differences in economic power have a determinate impact on the political power that they possess.

Fifth, even though the state is accorded a central role in shaping aboriginal peoples' lives, little attempt has been made by proponents of the internal colonial model to theorize the nature of this role. At best the model tends to adopt a voluntaristic view of the state where policies are formulated in isolation from other social, political, and economic relations. This leads to analytical formulations which emphasize either the mean-spirited, malicious, ethnocentric, and/or racist politicians and bureaucrats who did not have aboriginal peoples' best interests at heart when they formulated policy (see for example, Ryan, 1978), or the "bad planning" that went into the design and implementation of policy (Driben and Trudeau, 1983). The implication of these arguments is that had better people implemented better plans for aboriginal peoples, then things would have been much improved.

We question the notion that failed policies are simply the result of bad planning or bad individuals. As we suggest in subsequent chapters, the failure of state policies relating to aboriginal peoples may actually reflect rather "good planning" by state officials who are structurally interested in maintaining the subordination of aboriginal peoples (Ponting and Gibbins, 1980:103-104). Furthermore, some state policies also appear to be formulated in the context of pressure from particular sets of non-aboriginal interests to curtail the ability of aboriginal peoples to compete for scarce resources.

Finally, the internal colonial model tends to portray aboriginal peoples as the passive victims in a process that they did not understand and were incapable of changing. While there have been, and are, power differentials between aboriginal peoples and representatives of the state, it is also the case that in some circumstances aboriginal peoples have resisted state policies and practices, and have struggled to maintain their special rights stemming from treaties. Thus, aboriginal resistance is not a new phenomenon, but rather extends throughout the history of aboriginal/non-aboriginal relations.

In light of these comments, it is important to be clear about our concerns regarding the Chicago School and the internal colonial model. We do not question the existence of culture or cultures, or the potential of culture to impact on social and economic conditions. Nor do we question whether cultural change and assimilation occur. In relation to the internal colonial model, we do not question whether internal colonization actually occurred. Clearly, a colonial relationship has characterized aboriginal and non-aboriginal relations in Canada.

However, we do question the ability of these models to understand these processes and grasp the wider social and economic sources of oppression of aboriginal peoples. Even though the two models differ in their emphases, they share certain conceptual problems and silences. Both models assume that the aboriginal and non-aboriginal populations are homogeneous. Both suggest that aboriginal peoples are a relatively homogeneous "racial" minority whose position and experiences in Canada have been shaped outside of the larger system of class relations in the country. In Wolpe's (1975:230) terms, domination and exploitation are conceived by the internal colonial model "as occuring between 'racial,' 'ethnic' and 'national' categories. To this extent, the 'internal colonial' thesis converges with conventional race relations [Chicago School] theory."

TOWARDS A POLITICAL ECONOMY OF ABORIGINAL PEOPLES

A political economy approach, in contrast to the Chicago School and internal colonial explanations of aboriginal experiences and issues in Canada, begins with an emphasis on the changing material circumstances which shape and are shaped by aboriginal life experience. Asch (1985:152) observes that the analysis of native peoples in Canadian political economy traditions constitutes "the study of the effect on the indigenous population of the development of its territory into a majority European-settler state under liberal-democratic government and capitalism." Unfortunately, a central preoccupation with the transformation of labour/capital relations has left aboriginal issues at the margins of, and often entirely absent from, the political economy literature in Canada, presumably under the assumption that native peoples either are subsumed under general patterns of development or are marginalized from the whole process of class and nation formation. Nonetheless, there has emerged an extensive body of literature which has incorporated an analysis of aboriginal peoples and their societies into explanations of the processes of national development in the context of First Nations as well as Canadian state and global formations (see Abele and Stasiulis, 1989, for a useful critical review of this literature). In the following pages, we outline a framework for the political economic analysis of aboriginal peoples.

As with other approaches to the analysis of social relations, political economy both in general and as it applies more particularly to native peoples includes divergent and sometimes conflicting variants. Underlying the major Canadian political economy traditions is a recognition of Canada's historical domination by Britain (and France to a lesser extent) and the United States, and the limitations to national development through reliance upon a resource-based staples economy. Around these central concerns have emerged debates about Canada's developing role in the global capitalist economy; the nature and significance of class relations; the role played by state activity in cultural, economic, and political relations; the significance of regional, linguistic, and cultural struggles for questions of nation formation and national unity; and the interaction between material structures and social, cultural, and political agents (Clement and Williams, 1989:10-11; Dickinson and Bolaria, 1992:27; Drache and Clement, 1985; Marchak, 1985:673ff.).

These issues constitute in various ways the focus of analysis of aboriginal peoples as addressed by liberal and Marxist accounts, the two prevailing strands of political economy. The liberal tradition, especially as influenced by the landmark analysis of the fur trade by Innis (1956), has tended to emphasize the progressive deterioration of native society through resource development strategies employed by white European and North American interests. Marxist analysis, carrying on a line of analysis started notably by Ryerson (1960), shares with liberal political economy the view that native peoples and their institutions have been highly marginalized or destroyed through wider processes of dependency and development, but places emphasis on the internal dynamics of capitalism and class formation. Where these dynamics are interpreted in a stringent or mechanistic fashion, orthodox Marxist analysis of aboriginal societies and their relations with non-native societies can sometimes be simplistic and inaccurate, ignoring the richness of historical variations and struggles that have characterized these relations. At its best, however, Marxist analysis has stimulated the emergence of a "new" political economy that provides the basis for understanding the interpenetration of class, gender, and racism within changing material contexts (Clement and Williams, 1989). As Marchak (1985:673) indicates, political economy has come to challenge Marxism "in growing recognition of . . . property rights [other than the relations of production] in capitalist systems; as well, of the importance of the sources of inequality, subordination, and resistance either unrelated to or not adequately explained within a standard class analysis."

At the heart of a political economy analysis is a concern for the ways in which people socially produce and reproduce the conditions for their existence. Production and reproduction are accomplished by people who act not strictly as individuals but as interacting social subjects who are situated in particular social locations and who bear distinct social and cultural characteristics including class, gender, ethnicity, age, and so on. Class relations flow from the ownership of property and resources that are utilized in the production of basic goods and services. The understanding of class relations is central to political economy insofar as such relations shape people's opportunities through the parameters within which a society's fundamental survival needs are met. However, people, regardless of their class interests, also act on the basis of opportunities and limitations which are defined by these other social characteristics. As active subjects, individuals make choices that are both unique to their particular circumstances and indicative of their positions as boys and girls, men and women, and members of particular racial and ethnic formations. Within this complex array of characteristics, people's social actions further shape and are shaped by settings in various institutional areas of public and private life such as work, school, family, and political relations.

Presented in these terms, a political economy analysis of Canada's aboriginal peoples must be grounded in the consideration of native peoples' struggles for subsistence and survival under changing material circumstances. Whether arranged around an autonomous quest for existence or strongly immersed in relations with other social formations, aboriginal economic and cultural organizations encompass a diverse range of patterns. Additionally, there are variations in the types of individual subjects and activities that prevail within each form of social arrangement. What is of primary analytical concern is how these social relations are regulated by dominant class and other institutional interests, including the state, and what kinds of organized responses, with what impact, subordinate groups have provided to these arrangements.

This book is organized around the theme of domination over and resistance by aboriginal peoples within processes of social and economic production and reproduction. Although we represent aboriginal peoples as being involved, both historically and even in contemporary times to a certain extent, in several different modes of production, our emphasis is upon the transformation of native life through the introduction and extension of capitalism throughout Canada and beyond. While this transformative process refers largely to patterns of economic development, our analysis emphasizes the closely interconnected nature of social, economic, political, and ideological relations. Changes, and resistance to those changes, in one sphere of life are highly interdependent upon practices and relations that are characteristic of other spheres. This is nowhere so evident as in the prominent role played by the Canadian state in regulating aboriginal life. We are concerned, in particular, with the ways in which state policies and actions have served over time to manage aboriginal peoples and native/white relations. The state's central concern, we argue, has been with pressures to reconcile the contradictory position of aboriginal peoples as subjects and citizens who have general as well as special rights, and who as a collectivity have occupied highly marginalized and disadvantaged positions within the dominant institutional framework of Canadian life.

CHAPTER 2

THE STATE AND THE CONTRADICTIONS OF
INDIAN ADMINISTRATION

*[In North America] ... Western Europeans entered more or less a com-
plete societal vacua and settled in those areas establishing themselves as
their permanent residents.... They came to the new lands with 'capitalism
in their bones' and meeting no resistance worth the name — the exploits
of Davey Crockett notwithstanding — they succeeded in a short time in
establishing on virtually virgin (and exceptionally fertile) soil an
indigenous society of their own. From the outset capitalist in its structure, unencumbered by the fetters and barriers of feudalism, that society
could single-mindedly devote itself to the development of its productive
resources* (Paul Baran, 1973:273).

In Canada, aboriginal peoples have a historically unique position in political-legal relations and a unique relationship to the state. Today, many
agree that this relationship has had long-term negative consequences for
aboriginal peoples. In a recent public-opinion poll, over 50 percent of
Canadians believed that the problems facing aboriginal peoples are due to
the damaging system established by the government (Saskatchewan *Star-
Phoenix*, 1990). It is frequently argued that the reason this relationship
has been so negative for aboriginal peoples is that it has been premised on
the existence of personal and institutional racism within the state.

Upton (1973), for example, argues that economy and racism were
the main factors leading to the Canadian government's policy of assimilation in the 19th century. He states "the policy of assimilation was the
result of a concurrence of sentiment and interest: the sentiment that a

15

superior race (the British) had definite responsibilities towards an inferior (the Indians) coincided with the self interest of the British government in cutting the costs of colonial administration" (Upton, 1973:51).

Others, perhaps more charitably, argue that ignorance and misunderstanding have been the defining characteristics of state officials in their dealings with aboriginal peoples. In *The Unjust Society*, Harold Cardinal has put this case most eloquently:

> throughout the hundreds of years of the Indian-government relationship political leaders responsible for matters relating to Indians have been outstanding in their ignorance of the native people and remarkable in their insensitivity to the needs and aspirations of the Indians in Canada. More often than not, government people simply do not know what they are doing.... (Cardinal, 1969:6; see also Cardinal, 1977:15).

It is not difficult to find, either in the historical or contemporary record, evidence of institutional racism, or of personal racism and ignorance amongst personnel within the state apparatus. The titles and contents of much 19th- and 20th-century legislation pertaining to aboriginal peoples are laced with racist assumptions. For example, the 1857 Act for the Gradual Civilization of the Indian Tribes and the 1859 Civilization and Enfranchisement Act clearly suggested, in a racist fashion, that Indian people were uncivilized human beings who required considerable coaching to be elevated to a social position in which they would be comparable to Europeans. The contemporary Indian Act is regarded by many aboriginal peoples as the embodiment of two centuries of racist thinking which must be carefully dismantled.

Over the years, statements made by those who administered Indian people, be they state officials or missionaries, are also replete with racism and ignorance. During the late 19th century, some missionaries described Indian people as "in many ways like children. At any time they will act just so foolishly; thankless beyond measure, strangers to the truth and right, depraved and filthy in the extreme; they typify man having reached the lowest level of the human ladder ..." (quoted in Kellough, 1980:359).

The argument that racism and ignorance are the key explanations of the Canadian government's policies and practices directed towards Indian people is rooted in an elite theory of the state. Such explanations assume that it is the "racial," ethnic, and personal makeup of political parties, judiciary, police, and bureaucracy which are the key determinants of state policy and actions. They further imply that had a less racist and more knowledgeable group of people occupied positions of state power, government policies and practices would have been more sensitive to the needs of aboriginal peoples. Other "racial" origins might have been less malevolent and more knowledgeable in their dealings with aboriginal peoples. In such a context, the 500-year period following the arrival of the first Europeans in North America would have been much less negative for aboriginal peoples.

The 500th anniversary of Christopher Columbus' arrival in North America has sparked considerable debate about the outcome of history had the circumstances of contact been different. Historically, it is the case that the state elite in Canada has been made up of men primarily of British, but also of French, origins (Porter, 1965; Olsen, 1980). There is also evidence to suggest that European powers had different objectives and used different means in their efforts to colonize aboriginal peoples in the "New World" (Cumming and Mickenberg, 1972:13-22).

However, there is also reason to believe that other factors, in addition to racism and ignorance, affected the administration of aboriginal peoples in Canada. First, in addition to being of English or French origins, those who occupied positions of political power in Canada also held significant degrees of economic power, that is, they were men who occupied particular class positions. In describing the class makeup of the 1878 Canadian parliament, Gustavus Myers noted that

> Politics was, in fact, a business; the Canadian parliament was crowded with men who were there to initiate, extend or conserve class interests; of the 206 members of the Dominion House of Commons ... there were 56 merchants, 55 lawyers, 12 gentlemen of leisure, and an assortment of manufacturers, insurance company presidents, shipbuilding and lumber capitalists, contractors, and a few journalists, physicians and farmers (1972:265-266; see also Leadbetter, 1984:17)

Second, evidence also suggests that reserve systems were established in contexts where individuals of English origin had little influence over the determination of state policy. For example, reserves for the segregation and control of First Nations were established in a wide variety of ethnic contact situations. According to Guillemin (1978:319), "the incarceration of relict native tribes in reservations in South American and African states barely influenced by British colonialism implies functions independent of Anglo solutions to the problems of race relations." These observations suggest that factors rooted in the particular nature of the capitalist mode of production also impacted on the development of aboriginal policies and administration. State policies and practices were formulated not only on the basis of "race" and ethnicity, but also on the basis of class and gender.

Our aim in this chapter is to redefine the contexts of the history of Indian administration and policy in this country. Racist ideas, and the practices based on those ideas, are not autonomous, but rather have been formed within the context of the emergence and reproduction of a particular mode of production. Thus, the history of Indian administration is tied to the development of a capitalist mode of production characterized by racism and class and gender relations.

THE PROBLEM OF PRIMITIVE ACCUMULATION

Contrary to the views of Paul Baran cited at the beginning of this chapter, the capitalist mode of production was not part of the original baggage Europeans brought to Canada. Capitalism, a system of commodity production which is premised on the existence of private property and the purchase and sale of free wage labour in the market, has complex social and historical origins. Given that the lands that now make up Canada have not always been characterized by the existence of a capitalist mode of production, there has been a social process whereby these relations of production have come into existence. Marx (1967:713), in his book *Capital*, refers to the transformation of non capitalist into capitalist relations of production as the process of primitive accumulation.

The form that primitive accumulation takes is historically specific and is based on the nature of pre-existing cultural, economic, and political relations. In Britain, primitive accumulation involved, in part, a process of proletarianization: a process where agricultural producers were denied access to land and who were therefore forced by the condition of being without property to sell their labour power for wages (Miles, 1987:36). Primitive accumulation also involved the concentration of wealth (in the form of money and precious metals) in the hands of a particular class of people. This wealth was then transformed into expanding the means of production. In Britain, the state played a central role in primitive accumulation through a variety of legislative and political interventions: holding down wages, organizing the national debt, and legalizing the privatization of common lands (Miles, 1987:36-37).

There are a number of studies of various dimensions of the process of primitive accumulation in Canada. The Canadian state played a central role in the process. Clement examines the formation of a class of owners of the means of production (Clement, 1975; Naylor, 1975), while Pentland (1981) and Palmer (1983; see also Katz, 1975) have examined the social origins of the working class in Canada. Yet others have examined the formation of a transportation and communications infrastructure which provided preconditions for the expansion of commodity production (Pentland, 1981). A fourth dimension of primitive accumulation, and one which has ironically received somewhat less attention from political economists, was the separation of Indian people from the land and the transformation of that land into private property. We suggest that the treaty-making process was a moment in the primitive accumulation of capital in Canada.

Before examining this process, it is first necessary to make a distinction between merchant and industrial capital. Merchant capital involves the accumulation of wealth through the process of the exchange of money and commodities. Profit is derived from the purchase or exchange of commodities below their value which are then sold above their value elsewhere

(Miles, 1987:38). Industrial capitalism, on the other hand, refers to a particular set of social relations of production. Industrial capital involves the direct organization of production of use values where accumulation occurs on the basis of the exploitation of labour power. The defining feature of industrial capitalism is the production of commodities via the purchase and sale of "free" wage labour (Dobb, 1963).

Initial European interest in the territory that makes up Canada was merchant capitalist in nature. The discovery of rich stocks of cod off the coast of Newfoundland in the late 15th century meant that by the early years of the 16th century, a number of European countries had established a presence in the region (Easterbrook and Aitken, 1961:25). Europeans who came to Canada were initially in search of fish, which was destined for consumption by the emergent working class and peasantry in Europe. The nature of the European presence depended, in part, on techniques used to preserve fish. The French, Spanish, and Portuguese fleets had access to large quantities of salt which was used as a shipboard preservative (termed the "green cure" method). They tended to go ashore only occasionally to replenish supplies of water, food, and fuel. Fishermen from more northerly climates such as Britain did not have access to large stocks of salt and therefore had to dry fish on the land (the "dry cure" method) before it could be sent to Europe (Innis, 1970; Miller, 1989).

In the course of catching and preserving fish, occasional contacts were established with aboriginal peoples. European fishermen soon discovered that the lands and inland waterways also contained valuable pelts which aboriginal peoples were willing to barter. Coupled with a demand in Europe for pelts, this discovery gave rise to Canada's second great "staple" industry, the fur trade (Innis, 1970).

During the 17th and 18th centuries, North America became the site of a series of economic and military conflicts between the Netherlands, Spain, England, and France. In order to achieve military and economic objectives, European merchant capitalists elicited aboriginal peoples as allies. The nature of alliances between Europeans and aboriginal peoples shifted over time and were based, in part, on complex economic and political jockeying by both sides (Miller, 1989). Thus, in order to consolidate control over the fur trade and establish military supremacy in the territory, Europeans required the cooperation of Indian people. This involved, in part, the formation of various treaties of peace and friendship between European merchant capitalists and Indian people between the 16th and 18th centuries (Purich, 1986).

Europeans' need for military and economic alliances in North America contrasts sharply with the case of Australia, which was settled by Europeans much later. Unlike Canada, Australia

> seemed to grow no bush or flower or grain which Europe wanted. It
> seemed to yield no animal or fish for which European merchants were

willing to risk their ships in long voyages. Its Aboriginals were not ocean seafarers, nor were they traders or collectors of precious stones, and they could show visiting seamen no commodity of value (Blainey, 1983:3-4, quoted in Miles, 1989:95).

Australia was deemed to have little value for either military or economic reasons. Since it was defined initially as a penal colony and not as a source of mercantile wealth, there was not the same need to elicit the cooperation of aboriginal peoples as there had been in Canada. Since no treaties were signed between the representatives of the British crown and aboriginal peoples, this placed Australian aboriginal peoples in a more disadvantaged position than their North American counterparts (Buckley and Wheelwright, 1988:21-22).

In Canada the critical moment for late 19th- and early 20th-century treaties oriented towards the surrender of aboriginal lands was the Royal Proclamation of 1763. The proclamation followed Britain's victory over France in the Seven Years War and was, in part, a statement of Britain's mercantile interests in its newly acquired territories. The proclamation involved the establishment of three new governments in the newly acquired territories of Quebec, East Florida, and West Florida, and provided guidelines for dealing with aboriginal peoples (Purich, 1986:45). In relation to land and land rights within the territorial confines of the three new governments, the proclamation stated that because "it was just and reasonable, and essential to our Interests, and the security of our colonies," land that had not been formally ceded by the Indians "are reserved to them or any of them, as their Hunting Grounds." In lands outside of the territories of the new governments, the proclamation attempted to block further settlement. It reserved "for the use of the said Indians, all the Lands and Territories not included within the Limits of Our Said Three New Governments, or within the Limits of the Territory granted to the Hudson's Bay Company." It stated that those who had willfully or inadvertently settled on unceded Indian land should remove themselves from that land. The proclamation also required that Indian lands be purchased, "and prohibited their sale to anyone other than an authorized crown agent" (cited in Cumming and Mickenberg, 1972:291; see also Slattery, 1987). By this measure, the British colonial state inserted itself directly into the process of land acquisition and conveyance.

There are three important implications of the Royal Proclamation for the issue of treaties and aboriginal rights. First, it is defined by aboriginal peoples as the "Indian Charter of Rights" (Purich, 1986:45; Cardinal, 1969). For Indian people, the proclamation retains a profound contemporary importance. Since it has never been specifically repealed, it provides aboriginal peoples with formal-legal support for their argument that they are a nation which possesses *aboriginal rights*: "those property rights which inure to native peoples by virtue of their occupation upon certain lands from time immemorial" (Cumming and Mickenberg, 1972:13; Slattery, 1987). Second, in protecting the land rights of aboriginal peoples in the Royal Proclamation, British authorities were interested in securing peace with Indians and maintaining the economic viability of the fur trade. The proclamation provided a political-legal basis for the continued existence of a non-capitalist mode of production involved in the extraction of fur from the environment. In a clear statement of the significance of the proclamation for British mercantile interests in the fur trade, the Lords Commissioners (the equivalent of the Canadian Senate) stated: "Let the savages enjoy their desserts in quiet .... Were they driven from the forests the peltry trade would decrease" (quoted in Ryerson, 1960:238).

The third implication is that the proclamation's recognition of aboriginal title to land created a contradiction when there was a shift in the nature of the European definition of what was valuable in the territory. This contradiction was resolved, in part, through formal land surrender treaties.

Primitive Accumulation and Land Surrender Treaties

The 19th century witnessed a shift in the nature of the global development of capitalism. Described as a shift from mercantile to industrial capitalism, this change had profound implications for Canada and the position of aboriginal peoples. Generally, this move involved a transformation of the Canadian economy away from single-minded extraction of raw materials from the environment and their export to Britain, towards the development of commercial agriculture and secondary manufacturing via industrial capitalism (Pentland, 1981). While the fur trade did continue into the 20th century, its importance within the wider economy became diminished (Ray, 1990). In Canada, then, the timing of the move from mercantile to industrial capitalism varied according to region. In the Atlantic provinces and eastern Canada, it occurred around the middle of the 19th century (Pentland, 1981), while in western Canada, it occurred in the 1870s and 1880s (Leadbetter, 1984:4; Friesen, 1984).

With the emergence of industrial capitalism during the course of the 19th century, the affirmation within the Royal Proclamation of Indian people's right to occupy and use land created a contradiction for Canadian authorities. A policy that recognized aboriginal title to land which was consistent with the aims of merchant capital came to constitute a political-legal obstacle to the development of an industrial capitalist mode of production. As noted above, industrial capitalism is premised on the existence of private property, in both land and the means of production. Thus, as in the case in Britain, a transformation of collectively-owned land into private property was required. In order to effect this transformation, Canadian authorities were forced to enter into land surrender treaties with First Nations. With the exception of lands in Quebec, the Maritimes, and British Columbia, where no treaties were agreed to, most of the land that now makes up Canada was formally surrendered by First Nations to the Canadian state. Between the Royal Proclamation of 1763 and 1818, land transfers were effected by one-time payments to Indian people. For example, in 1792, the Mississauga Indians surrendered approximately 300 000 acres of land to British authorities for £1180, and in 1805 they surrendered over 250 000 acres of land in York county for ten shillings (Ryerson, 1963:241). In these cases, land was transferred from Indian people to the state, which was then sold or given away to European settlers, speculators, or corporate entities.

After 1818, authorities tended to pay for the land via annuities. Between 1871 and 1921 in western Canada and northern Ontario, there were eleven numbered treaties agreed to between the federal government and Indian bands (see Map 2.1 and Map 2.2). With the exception of British Columbia, these treaties involved the formal alienation of most of the land in western Canada. The numbered treaties tended to be different from previous ones in that they tended to involve the surrender of much larger tracts of land. They were also different in that land transfers were paid for via annuities to aboriginal peoples. Map 2.1 and Map 2.2 provide information about the timing of treaties in eastern and western Canada.

Currently there are debates about what the treaties meant from the First Nations' perspective. Indian oral tradition points to a discrepancy between verbal agreements and those contained in the written record. In some treaty negotiations, particularly Treaty 8, Indian people felt that the government agreed to provide them with medical care and education for their children, but no such provisions were included in the written text of the treaty.

In addition, there is also the likelihood of fundamental conflicts over interpretations of what was being agreed to. According to Harold Cardinal:

> We did not, by treaty surrender our sovereignty; we did not, by treaty surrender our water, our timber, our mineral resources; we did not surrender our way of life. The only thing that we agreed to was to live in peace with the white man, and to share with him the available land so that he could come into this country, and bring his livestock, and support his families (Cardinal, 1977:147-48).

Hugh Dempsey (1978) argues that there could not have been a "meeting of the minds," one of the essential features of a legally binding contract, between groups of people with such radically different world views. Purich (1986:109) argues that "words like 'surrender', 'convey', 'cede', 'yield up' and 'release', which had a precise legal meaning, probably meant nothing to Indian leaders." Even more strongly, the Manitoba Indian Brotherhood in 1968 argued that "... forever and a day it will be obvious to all who read the said Treaties and the history of their making,

Map 2.1

The Eastern Canadian Treaties

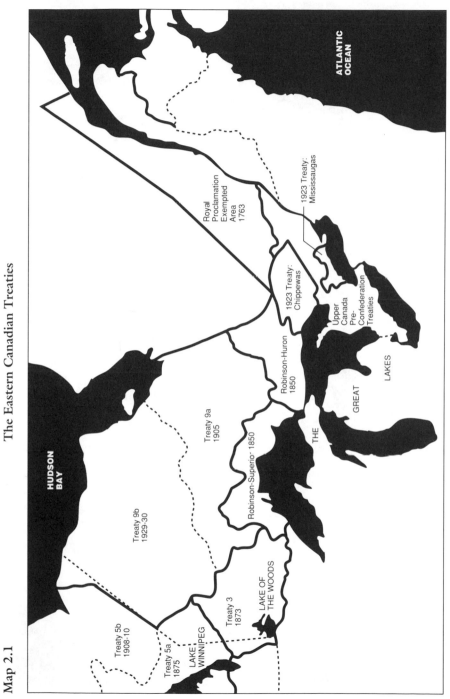

Source: J. Waldram, *As Long as the Rivers Run*. Winnipeg: University of Manitoba Press, 1988: p. 26.

Map 2.2

The Numbered Treaties in Western Canada

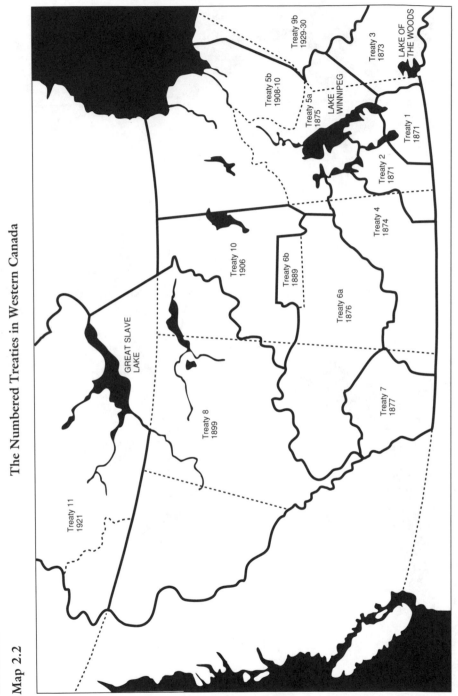

Treaty 11
1921

Treaty 8
1899

GREAT SLAVE
LAKE

Treaty 10
1906

Treaty 6b
1889

Treaty 6a
1876

Treaty 7
1877

Treaty 5b
1908-10

Treaty 5a
1875

LAKE
WINNIPEG

Treaty 9b
1929-30

Treaty 3
1873

LAKE OF
THE WOODS

Treaty 1
1871

Treaty 2
1871

Treaty 4
1874

Source: J. Waldram, *As Long as the Rivers Run*. Winnipeg: University of Manitoba Press, 1988, p. 30.

that the officials of Her Majesty the Queen committed a legal fraud in a very sophisticated manner upon unsophisticated, unsuspecting, illiterate, uninformed natives" (Cardinal, 1969:36).

Others, however, argue that Indian people were eager to enter into treaties and were cognizant of their implications (Stevenson, 1991). Some suggest that Indian people welcomed the prospect of entering into treaties which would formalize the land surrender process because they clearly saw the negative consequences of the absence of land cession treaties in the United States. They realized the inevitability of European incursion into their territory and actively sought to forestall their total disinheritance from the land. Indian people feared the encroachment of white settlers on their lands, and therefore wanted some form of state intervention to ensure future generations a land base (Carter, 1990:54-57).

Moreover, Carter (1990) and Stevenson (1991) argue that Indian people actively negotiated terms of treaties, the implication being that they were at least partially cognizant of the implications of the treaties. Carter (1990) argues that in terms of the numbered treaties in western Canada, the government's initial position was that the treaties would only contain provisions for the establishment of reserves and the payment of annuities. Indian leaders, wishing to enter into treaties, sought wider protection and support from the government negotiators. In the negotiation of Treaty 6, Indian leaders also sought aid to agriculture by the provision of hoes, seed, twine, harnesses, and livestock. Thus, Carter (see also Miller, 1989, and Stevenson, 1991) suggests that Indian people were amenable to treaties, and were rather skillful bargainers in the process in that they were able to win certain concessions from the negotiators.

For Canadian authorities, though, the chief significance of treaties was that they focused on one major commodity—land. Indian people surrendered their land and in return received annual payments, assistance for agriculture, schools, and reserves. Treaty 3, the North-West Angle Treaty, was agreed to in 1873 and was fairly typical of the other treaties effected between Indian people and state representatives. The treaty covered southeastern Manitoba and western Ontario around Thunder Bay and Lake of the Woods. In return for the cession, release, surrender, and yield all of the rights, articles, and privileges of the land in question, Indian people received the following:

> 1) reserve lands of one square mile for every family of five, or a proportionate amount depending on the size of the family;
> 2) a one-time payment of $12 to every man, woman, and child in existinguishment of all claims to the land;
> 3) a $5 yearly payment in perpetuity to each man, woman, and child in the band;
> 4) the establishment of a school;

5) a commitment that no intoxicating liquor would be allowed to be brought onto the reserve;
6) that Indian people had the right to pursue hunting and fishing activities on unsettled lands;
7) $1500 per year for ammunition and twine for nets;
8) for every family cultivating the soil, two hoes, one spade, scythe, axe, cross cut saw, hand saw, and pot saw; for every ten families, one plough; for every twenty families, five harrows; and for every band, one file, grindstone, auger, chest of ordinary carpenters' tools, one yoke of oxen, a bull, and four cows, and enough wheat, barley, potatoes, and oats to plant the land broken for cultivation;
9) each year the Chief was to receive $25, and each subordinate officer $15; once every three years, the chief and subordinate officers received a suitable suit of clothing; and at the close of the treaty negotiations, the chief would receive a medal and a flag.

In addition to provisions similar to the above, chiefs negotiating Treaty 6, which covered much of central Saskatchewan and Alberta, were able to insert a clause which provided for the government to supply a medicine chest, to be kept at the residence of the Indian agent (Cumming and Mickenberg, 1972).

The compulsion of state authorities to enter into treaties was not experienced evenly across the country. As noted, there were no land surrender treaties signed between government authorities and Indian people in Quebec, the Atlantic provinces, British Columbia, and the Yukon. Quebec was exempted from the Royal Proclamation's requirement that Indian lands had to be formally extinguished because it was believed that aboriginal title was extinguished by prior French occupation of New France (Frideres, 1988:60). Pressures to settle quickly United Empire Loyalists on the land and the relative political weakness of Indian people in the Maritimes in the late 18th century appear to have been the key factors in explaining why land surrender procedures outlined in the Royal Proclamation were not adhered to in the Maritimes (Cumming and Mickenberg, 1972:104-105).

The importance of clearing away political-legal obstacles to capitalist development has been brought into focus in the case of land struggles in contemporary British Columbia. With the exception of agreements pertaining to portions of Vancouver Island, there were no treaties between the state and aboriginal peoples. During the colonial period, the governor of the colony of Vancouver Island recognized the existence of Indian title to land and that that title had to be formally extinguished via a treaty before settlement could occur on a clear legal basis. However, with the incorporation of British Columbia into Canada in 1871, the provincial government refused to recognize Indian title to land, and refused to enter into treaty negotiations with Indian people. While the provincial government continued to grant reserve lands to Indian bands, this was not done on the basis of formal land surrender treaties, but rather as a means to facilitate settlement (Cumming and Mickenberg, 1972:185-91).

This means that most Indian people in B.C. do not possess treaty rights. However, they claim that they have aboriginal rights to land which they have yet to cede to the government. They argue that given the Royal Proclamation's affirmation of aboriginal rights, they remain the legal owners of most of the land that now makes up the province. They have used the courts, and increasingly civil disobedience, to block economic development projects and to pursue their claims for recognition of their aboriginal rights. Clearly, the decision made over one hundred years ago to not enter into land surrender treaties will continue to place the further development of capitalism in the province on a contested legal basis.

In addition to being a method of land conveyance and a moment in the primitive accumulation of capital in Canada, treaties also took on class-specific meaning for particular sections of Canadian business. Of particular interest is the state's offer of what are now rather insignificant annuities to Indian people in return for the surrender of land. While the annuities were initiated in 1818 as a cost-cutting measure during colonial rule (Miller, 1989:92-93), they assumed a heightened significance for the Hudson's Bay Company when they were included in the provisions of the numbered treaties in western Canada.

According to Ray (1989), in order to maintain loyalty to particular posts and to ensure a regular supply of furs, the Hudson's Bay Company provided income support, in the form of credit and gratuities, for Indian people with whom they had been involved in the fur trade. By the 1860s the fur trade in western Canada was in an economic crisis as both the demand for, and supply of, furs decreased. The costs of support for the Indian work force became burdensome for the company and it was eager for the government to assume these reproduction costs. In addition to encouraging Indian people to enter into treaties with the government to reduce the costs of maintaining their aboriginal work force, Hudson's Bay Company officials also encouraged government to provide an annual payment in exchange for the surrender of land. Given the company's prominent position in the western Canadian commercial system, it appears that company officials saw an annual payment as a potential source of stable future revenue.

In his account of the aftermath of the negotiations for Treaty 3, Alexander Morris provided a revealing account of the significance of treaty money for the company. He commented:

> As soon as the [treaty] money was distributed the shops of the HBC and other resident traders were visited, as well as the tents of numerous private traders, who had been attracted thither by the prospect of doing a good business. And while these shops all did a great trade — the HBC alone taking in $4,000 in thirty hours — it was a noticeable fact that many took home with them nearly all their money (Morris, 1880).

Thus, while annuities now constitute meager monetary compensation to Indian people for the surrender of their land, annual treaty payments appear to have been an indirect subsidy given by the state to the Hudson's Bay Company and smaller traders and shopkeepers. In addition, it appears that the HBC was the main supplier to the government of many of the commodities agreed to in the treaties.

Stanley Ryerson (1960:241) has put the meaning of the treaties most bluntly when he wrote "the fact of the matter is that the Indians were dispossessed of their lands by a colossal operation of fraud, misrepresentation and legalized theft," a process which was not unlike primitive accumulation in other colonial contexts.

INDIAN POLICY AND THE CREATION OF SUBJECTIVITY

Treaties in themselves did not resolve the issue of how Indian people were to be incorporated into the post-fur trade society. Once the Indians were dispossessed of their land via treaties, the "problem" state authorities faced was what should be done about them. As noted earlier, the setting aside of reserve lands was a central component of treaty agreements, and while no treaties were signed with Indian people in Quebec, the Maritimes, and British Columbia, reserve lands were nevertheless set aside there.

For Indian people, reserves were defined as "homelands" upon which they could continue to engage in traditional hunting and gathering practices. For government authorities, however, reserves were intended to be sites for the creation of certain forms of subjectivity, that is, reserves were to be locations at which Indian people would be resocialized (Tobias, 1988). The project of resocialization has been more particularly framed in terms of the Christianization and assimilation of Indian people. The Indian people were increasingly seen as a problem population after the decline of the fur trade and Christianization came to be defined by government authorities as one of the prerequisites for future citizenship within Canada. The Christianization of "savage tribes," in addition to imparting in Indian people proper forms of Christian relations, was also seen as the means by which aboriginal peoples would become civilized.

The policy of assimilation did not mean the physical annihilation of Indian people; rather it referred to the cultural and behavioural change of Indians such that they would be culturally indistinguishable from other Canadians. The charge of "cultural genocide," while serious in its implications, is not inappropriate. Sir John A. Macdonald, the Minister of Indian Affairs in 1880, stated that the aim of government policy was "to wean them by slow degrees, from their nomadic habits, which have become almost an instinct, and by slow degrees absorb them on the land." Seventy years later, this view was shared by Walter Harris, the Minister of Indian Affairs, who stated that "The ultimate goal of our Indian policy is the integration of the Indians into the general life and economy of the country" (quoted in Ponting, 1986:26).

While clearly racist in both content and intent, these expressions were not formed in isolation from other social forces. They emerged within the context of capitalist relations of production. As demonstrated in Chapters 4 and 5, the aim was not simply to transform Indian people into Christian "Europeans," but into Christian Europeans who also occupied particular positions in the relations of production, namely as people who would work for someone else for wages, or for themselves as farmers.

The formalization of this policy was left to the Indian Act and the implementation rested with the Indian Affairs Branch of the federal government.

The Indian Act

Section 91, subsection 24 of the 1867 British North America Act defined the nature of Indian people's relationship to the Canadian state. The act provided that Indians and lands reserved for Indians would be the responsibility of the federal government. Whereas non-Indian people would face a plurality of government departments and agencies in their dealings with the state, Indian people would face a singular government apparatus — the Indian Affairs Branch, which later became the Department of Indian Affairs and Northern Development. Unlike non-Indians, where legislative control over such things as education, health care, and social services was accorded to provincial government authorities, for Indian people each of these areas was the responsibility of the federal government.

In part, the initial rationale for according the federal government legislative authority over Indian people stemmed from the nation-building role of the state. As potential obstacles to that nation-building strategy, the clearest expression of which was Macdonald's "National Policy," control over Indian people was rationalized into a single state agency. Furthermore, British colonial officials felt it unwise to vest control over Indians and lands reserved for Indians in the hands of provincial governments. Based on a recognition of the role of class interests in the determination of state policy, they felt provincial levels of government would be too closely tied to local merchant, industrial, and agrarian elites, who had interests which were opposed to those of Indian people. British colonial officials assumed that the federal government was more insulated from the direct power of capitalist forces and therefore better placed to protect the interests of Indian people (Manuel and Polsuns, 1974:162). In retrospect, the federal government appears to have been unable to fulfill the rather lofty expectations of those who helped draft the BNA Act. The federal government has been far from immune to class pressures that would have negative effects on Indian people.

The Indian Act of 1876 was a consolidation and revision of previous legislation pertaining to Indian people. The aim of the act was to systematize the disparate legislation covering Indian people. There were three central elements to the Indian Act of 1876: 1) it defined who was an Indian; 2) it provided for the protection of Indian lands; 3) and it provided for the concentration of authority over Indian people (for more details of the development of the Indian Act, see Jamieson, 1978, and Leslie and Maguire, 1979).

The Indian Act defined who was and who was not an Indian person in order to delineate precisely who came under its jurisdiction. In the Act of 1876, an Indian "was defined as any male person of Indian blood reputed to belong to a particular band, any child of such person and any woman who is or was lawfully married to such a person" (Ponting, 1986:21). In 1924, the Inuit were defined as "Indians" for the purpose of the Indian Act.

Various groups of people have lost their status as Indian persons under the Indian Act by means of enfranchisement. Over the years, Indian people could lose their status as Indians if they received a university education, if they lived outside of the country for five years or more, and, for a time in the early 1920s, involuntarily if they were deemed to be "assimilated" by an Indian Affairs official.

It was, however, Section 12(1)(b) of the Indian Act which was to have the most long-lasting, conflictive, and divisive consequences for Indian communities. Basically, this section of the Indian Act provided for the loss of Indian status if an Indian woman married a non-Indian man. Jamieson summarized the meaning of this provision in the following terms:

> The woman, on marriage, must leave her parent's home and her reserve. She may not own property on the reserve and must dispose of any property she does hold. She may be prevented from inheriting property left to her by her parents. She cannot take any further part in band business. Her children are not recognized as Indian and are therefore denied access to cultural and social amenities of the Indian community. And, most punitive of all, she may be prevented from returning to live with her family on the reserve, even if she is in dire need, very ill, a widow, divorced or separated. Finally, her body may not be buried on the reserve with those of her forebears (Jamieson, 1978:1).

Section 12(1)(b) of the Indian Act concerning the process of enfranchisement of Indian women who married non-Indian men, and the loss of status of her children, has been the subject of heated academic and political debates. Since an Indian man who married a non-Indian woman did not lose his status as an Indian (in fact his non-Indian wife and their children also became Indians under the Indian Act), these debates have been primarily about sexism and the double standard used to define who was an Indian. The academic debate has focused on the reasons for this provision and the political debate has focused on what should be done to redress the situation.

In relation to the former, an unpublished paper by Weaver (n.d.) argues that the differential treatment accorded Indian men and women in the Indian Act was rooted in Indian Affairs officials' concern over the protection of Indian land. She suggests that the logic of government officials in their introduction of this measure was that if white males were granted Indian status through intermarriage with Indian women, they might come to dominate band councils and gain access to the use of Indian lands. Thus, while sexist in its contemporary implications, the policy was aimed not at the penalization of Indian women but rather the protection of collective property rights of Indians (cited in Jamieson, 1978).

Others, like Jamieson (1978:38), argue that the federal officials held three convictions that determined the content of the legislation: 1) Indians and their land were to be assimilated. The number of Indians was to be gradually reduced ...; 2) Indians were not capable of making rational decisions for their own welfare and this had to be done by the department on their behalf ...; 3) Indian women should be subject to their husbands as were other women. Their children were his children alone in law. It was inconceivable that an Indian woman should be able to own and transmit property and rights to her children. Thus, Jamieson argues that this provision was structured by prevailing conceptions of patriarchy.

The political debate has focused on what should be done to redress this double standard. In the 1970s, several Indian women and Indian women's organizations became actively involved in struggles to regain their Indian status. In 1970, Jeanette Lavell contested her loss of status in the courts on the grounds that this provision was contrary to the 1960 Canadian Bill of Rights. While Lavell won her case at the Federal Court of Appeal in 1971, the Supreme Court ruled against her in 1973 (Jamieson, 1978:82). Other struggles involved the lodging of a formal complaint against the Canadian government to the United Nations Human Rights Committee in Geneva, marches to Ottawa, and occupation of band administration offices (Silman, 1987).

In addition to resistance from the federal government, many mainstream (and male-dominated) Indian organizations allied themselves against women who had lost their status. Politically, the National Indian Brotherhood (NIB) and several chiefs were supportive of the discriminatory status quo. Some have argued that their resistance to the reinstatement of Indian women and children who lost their status was, in part, a result of sexism within the Indian community (Jamieson, 1978).

However, the NIB's argument was that if the Federal Court of Appeal decided in favor of Lavell on the grounds that it was contrary to the Bill of Rights, this would have provided the federal government with a legal basis upon which to "knock out" the special status of Indian people more generally (Cardinal, 1977:110). Furthermore, the NIB did not want the government to "open up" the Indian Act to address only one issue. Male Indian leaders wanted a more general reconsideration of the Indian Act, and they defined an amendment to the act on this issue as a precedent which would undermine their claims to the maintenance of special status within Canadian confederation (Cardinal, 1977). In the 1980s, the Assembly of First Nations, while not opposed to reinstatement in principle, was concerned about the financial implications of reinstatement and was thus opposed in practice, on the grounds that this would result in a situation where already poor bands would have fewer resources to spread among even more people. Thus, Indian leaders have argued that their opposition was not based on sexism but rather on important political considerations which affected the entire status Indian population.

In 1985, the federal government passed Bill C-31, which was An Act to Amend the Indian Act. The stated purpose of the legislation was to redress the issue of gender discrimination in the Indian Act. The most important features of the legislation provided for the abolition of the concept of enfranchisement and the reinstatement of Indian status to certain categories of people who had previously lost their status. Thus, under the new legislation, Indian women who marry non-Indian men do not lose their status as Indians, and Indian women and their children who had previously lost their status can now regain that status. However, while they may regain their status as Indians under the Indian Act, they must apply to become a band member. Thus, Indian status no longer automatically entails band membership. Table 2.1 gives an indication of the growth in the status Indian population of Canada in the 1980s, along with a projection of the size of the population in 2001. It shows that by 1989, 66 904 individuals had their status as Indians reinstated under the legislation, while 399 433 individuals were non-Bill C-31 Indian people. It also shows that by 2001, it is expected that the total Indian population will grow to just over 620 000.

The particular legal definitions of an Indian person and the regulations surrounding the processes of enfranchisement gave rise to the category of non-status Indians. Non-status Indians are those persons who have lost their Indian status either voluntarily or involuntarily. The term Métis initially applied to children of "mixed" Indian and French marriages, but is now used to apply to the children of Indian and European marriages more generally. Before the patriation of the constitution in 1982, non-status Indians and Métis people had the same legal status as non-aboriginal peoples. They were in the same legal position as other non-Indian Canadian citizens: they could not claim special rights or privileges, nor were they subject to regulations of the Indian Act. However, with the Constitution Act of 1982, the existing aboriginal and treaty rights of Indians, non-status Indians and Métis people were affirmed, and their relationship with the various levels of the Canadian state are currently being renegotiated.

Table 2.1

**Registered Indians and Indians Registered Under Bill C-31,
Average Annual Growth Rates,
Canada, 1981-2001**

	Registered Indians			Average Annual Growth	
Year	Excluding Bill C-31	Bill C-31 Population	Total	Excluding Bill C-31	Including Bill C-31
1981	323 782	0	323 782	2.59	0.00
1982	332 178	0	332 178	2.95	0.00
1983	341 968	0	341 968	2.00	0.00
1984	348 809	0	348 809	2.82	3.28
1985	358 636	1605	360 241	3.16	7.66
1986	369 972	17 857	387 829	2.40	7.24
1987	378 842	37 056	415 898	2.71	6.73
1988	389 110	54 774	443 884	2.65	5.06
1989	399 433	66 904	466 337	3.66	5.75
1991	429 178	92 282	521 461	1.99	1.91
1996	473 559	99 710	573 269	1.78	1.67
2001	517 226	105 675	622 901		

Source: Department of Indian and Northern Affairs, *Basic Departmental Data*. Ottawa: Minister of Supply and Services, 1989, pg. 7.

Collectively, status (or registered) Indians, non-status Indians and Métis, and the Inuit make up Canada's aboriginal population. In addition to the approximately 470 000 status Indians, there are an estimated 35 000 Inuit people, and anywhere from 368 000 to 750 000 non-status Indians and Métis in Canada (see Purich, 1986:34 and Statistics Canada, 1989:2 for the dramatically different estimates).

The second dimension of the Indian Act was its protection of Indian lands. This dimension of the act was, however, contradictory when considered in the light of other government practices. Indian people's property and land were protected through clauses that "excluded Indian people from taxes, liens, mortgages, or other charges on their lands and from loss of possessions through debt or through pawns for intoxicants" (Ponting, 1986:22).

This protection, however, was relative, not absolute. In practice it appears that the protection of Indian lands was not a priority of those who were charged with the administration of Indian policy. In the face of an influx of immigrants to the Prairies in the first decade of this century, the emphasis of government Indian policy was to facilitate the transfer of land from Indian to state, and then farmer or land speculator, control. The Department of Indian Affair's view was that

> So long as no particular harm nor inconvenience accrued from the Indians' holding vacant lands out of proportion to their requirements, and no profitable disposition thereof was possible, the department firmly opposed any attempt to induce them to divest themselves of any part of their reserves. Conditions, however, have changed and it is now recognized that where Indians are holding tracts of farming or timber lands beyond their possible requirements and by so doing seriously impeding the growth of settlement, and there is such demands as to ensure profitable sale, the product of which can be invested for the benefit of the Indians and relieve *pro tanto* the country of the burden of their maintenance, it is the best interests of all concerned to encourage such sales (Leslie and Maguire, 1979:106-107).

Clearly, then, the aim of state policy was to protect Indian people in the land conveyance process. The aim did not appear to be to maintain Indian lands in perpetuity (Ponting, 1986: 30). It is for this reason that Jamieson's interpretation of the origins of section 12(1)(b) of the Indian Act which discriminated against Indian women is likely to be correct.

The third feature of the Indian Act of 1876 was the concentration of authority. The act defined the legitimate forms of band government by providing for the establishment of band councils. Many of the powers of band councils were, however, largely symbolic as the Minister of Indian Affairs had the power to overturn band council decisions, a power which the minister, incidentally, still retains. Essentially, the act vested control of many of the day-to-day affairs of Indian people in the hands of an Indian agent.

There have been a number of amendments to the Indian Act over the years and a new Indian Act was introduced in 1951 in which many of the formal restrictions on Indian people were eased. These changes will be discussed in more detail in subsequent chapters.

STATE THEORIES AND THE DEPARTMENT OF INDIAN AFFAIRS AND NORTHERN DEVELOPMENT

If it is true that the unique position of Indian people within Canada stems largely from the nature of their relationship to the state, then in order to understand fully Indian experiences in Canada, it is necessary to clarify the nature of the Canadian state.

According to the internal colonial model of Indian/non-Indian relations, Indian peoples' relationship with the Canadian state is unlike other groups' relationship with the state (Ponting, 1986). This relationship is seen as exceptional in that no other group has a similar relationship of total domination and subordination. The Indian Act and the apparatus established to administer the act, the Department of Indian Affairs and Northern Development, have been described as a total institution (Frideres, 1988; Ponting and Gibbins, 1980:9): a set of practices and arrangements that control all aspects of Indian people's lives. Their lives are not unlike individuals who have been imprisoned or who have been confined to psychiatric institutions.

There are both empirical and theoretical grounds to challenge the view that Indian people's relationship to the state is entirely exceptional and characteristic of a total institution. First, the concept of a total institution tends to imply that aboriginal peoples have been passive victims in the colonization process. Although the scope for autonomous social-action was severely curtailed by various state policies and practices, aboriginal peoples have not simply been objects of forces outside of their control. As Miller (1989), Van Kirk (1980), Barron (1988), and others have demonstrated, aboriginal peoples have resisted this "total institution" and have attempted to carve out and define their own experiences on their own terms. Second, there are strong similarities in relations with the state and Indians and other state service recipients. In order to test the hypothesis that aboriginal peoples' relationship to the Canadian state is unlike that of other Canadians, Ponting (1986) examines the nature of client-state relationships between Indian people and the federal government and injured workers and the Newfoundland Workmen's Compensation Board. While the client groups (Indians and injured workers) differ in obvious ways, Ponting argues that they have structurally similar relationships to the respective levels of the state with which they must deal. For example, both government departments: 1) face fiscal restraints and must be accountable for their expenditures to higher authorities; 2) are beseiged by the activities of a number of contradictory interest groups; and 3) are bound by existing rules, procedures, and acts which limit possible courses of action.

The two client groups also share many similarities: 1) both need to be adept at the process of grantsmanship — the ability to convince the respective agency that their considerations, needs, and concerns are worthy of state funding; 2) both distrust bureaucrats and the bureaucratic process with which they deal; 3) both are subjects of paternalistic thinking on the part of the official representatives of the institutions, where those officials know what is good for their clients; 4) there are different "languages" that are used by the client groups and the officials with whom they deal — client groups have difficulty communicating with officials; 5) both experience inconsistencies and contradictions in what are supposed to be impersonal and universalistic criteria for decisions.

Ponting suggests, then, that the experiences of Indian people at the hands of state officials are not qualitatively different from those of other subordinate client groups within Canada. Even though the specific issues addressed in the two relationships vary, the form of client-state relationships are similar. But if it is true that Indians and non-Indians share certain experiences in their dealings with various levels of the state, the next task is to make sense of these relationships theoretically.

According to Stasiulis (1988:227), despite different emphases, there are four "connecting threads" to the theory of the state within the tradition of political economy. First, there is a primacy of material conditions in shaping social structures, social relations, and human consciousness. This means that state institutions and policies are shaped and constrained by the nature of the distribution of economic power within a society. Second, the state does not represent equally the interests of all groups in society. Since economic power is closely linked to political power, and since state policies are formulated in the context of unequal power relations, policies work to the benefit of some people over others. Third, the existence of democratic freedoms such as the rights to vote, to stand in elections, and to free speech are not incompatible with the existence and maintenance of fundamental economic inequalities. And fourth, the "state" consists of more than simply the particular government of the day. It consists of a more complex array of institutions which include "the government, the public service, military and police, judiciary, subcentral governments and various national, provincial and local assemblies" (Stasiulis, 1988:227-228).

Mahon (1977) applies these general considerations to the specific analysis of the structure of the public policy process and the nature of the contemporary Department of Indian Affairs and Northern Development. She argues that each branch of the public service has one or more client groups, or target constituencies, which are its concern. For example, the main client group of the federal Department of Labour is the organized working class; the main target group of the Canada Employment and Immigration Commission is immigrant workers and their families; the main target groups of the Department of Industry, Trade and Commerce are small and medium-sized businesses.

Mahon argues that each government department has two main roles in relation to their respective client groups: one is to represent their interests at the cabinet table and the other is to act as an agent of social control over them. Thus, the relationship between federal government departments and their client groups is one of representation and social control.

All groups are not equally well represented at the cabinet table and within the ranks of the state more generally. Similarly, all groups do not experience the same dialectic of representation and social control. Given that political power in capitalist societies is closely related to economic power, it is clear that economically powerful groups are better represented at the cabinet table than are others. There is an unequal structure of representation within the Canadian state. Mahon argues that the Department of Finance occupies the "seat of power" within the federal government to the extent that it provides the final approval, and in some cases, determines the budgets, priorities, and activities, of all other government departments. The activities of other government departments must be cleared by the Department of Finance before they are implemented (Mahon, 1977:175-177). The department's primary relationship is with Canadian merchant and finance capitalists; that is, the department represents the interests of a particularly powerful class within Canadian society. Thus, economically powerful classes have their interests better represented within state policy than do less powerful subordinate groups.

Within this view, the state is a complex set of social relations and a site of class- and non-class based struggles over the distribution of resources, and state policies are the outcomes of complex relations of political and economic power within the society as a whole.

How then, does the Department of Indian Affairs fit into this conceptualization?

During the first half of the 19th century, the locus of administration of Indian affairs shifted a number of times between military and civilian authority. Responsibility over Indian affairs was transferred from imperial control to the Province of Canada in 1860, and to the federal government in 1867. Four years after passage of the Indian Act in 1876, the Department of Indian Affairs was established. While it was a separate government department between 1880 and 1936, the Minister of the Interior remained the Superintendent-General of Indian Affairs. In 1936, the department was subsumed under the Department of Mines and Resources, and in 1949 it was transferred to the Department of Citizenship and Immigration. In 1965, the Indian Affairs Branch was merged with the Department of Northern Affairs and Natural Resources, and in 1966 the present Department of Indian Affairs and Northern Development was created. According to Mahon, there are two distinct target groups stemming from the present structure of DIAND: Indian people and large corporations interested in the exploitation of northern resources. Since the mid-1960s the department has forged relations of representation and social control with Indian people and large resource development multinationals. The dual nature of the representation and social control activities of DIAND is evident in the division of departmental programs into four areas: the Indian and Inuit Affairs Program (IIAP); the Northern Affairs Program; the Canada Oil and Gas Lands Administration; and the Administration Program.

The first three programs reflect the split between controlling and representing the interests of Indian people and resource multinationals. The Indian and Inuit Affairs Program's mandate is to fulfill the government's obligations to Indians arising out of treaties, the Indian Act, and other relevant legislation; deliver basic services to status Indians and Inuit communities; assist in employment and business development of Indian and Inuit people; negotiate the transfer of decision making to the community level;

and support constitutional discussions (Department of Indian and Northern Affairs, 1990).

The Canadian Oil and Gas Lands Administration and the Northern Affairs Program have as their primary client group northern resource companies, although the latter is also mandated to deal with all people in the two northern territories. In addition to the provision of support for the development of political, social, and cultural institutions and processes in the North and the management and protection of the northern environment, the mandate of the Northern Affairs program is the "direct funding and coordination of economic initiatives by industry and other federal governments." The Canadian Oil and Gas Lands Administration reports jointly to the Department of Indian Affairs and Northern Development and Energy, Mines and Resources Canada. It administers the Canadian Petroleum Resources Act and the Oil and Gas Production and Conservation Act, and its mandate is the "regulation of oil and natural gas exploration and development of Canada's frontier lands" (Department of Indian and Northern Affairs, 1988a:8).

The administration program provides financial, administrative, and management services to the department's programs, human resource services to its employees, and coordinates the communication of the department's activities to aboriginal peoples and the general public.

Historically, the Indian and Inuit Affairs Program, or what was once the Indian Affairs Branch, has been more interested in the control of Indian people rather than representation. Given that Indian people had no access to the federal or provincial franchise until after World War II, there was little need to be politically concerned about representing their interests. Since the acquisition of the franchise and the subsequent politicization of Indian people both nationally and locally in the 1960s, IIAP has become more concerned with the representation of Indian interests at the cabinet table. The dialectic of representation and social control is now more complicated than ever.

Since the Diefenbaker government's recognition of the potential wealth of the Canadian North (Rea, 1968:357), which was further spurred by the discovery of vast amounts of oil in Alaska in 1968, the interests of resource multinationals have come increasingly to impinge on the formulation of aboriginal policies. Thus, the contradiction between the interests of Indian people and those of resource development corporations has become increasingly acute. This contradiction was brought to a head in the Mackenzie Valley Pipeline inquiry in the mid-1970s. While the weight of the DIAND's support was thrown behind the development of the pipeline and the exploitation of northern resources, some sectors of the department, particularly within the IIAP, were sympathetic to the interests of aboriginal peoples to the extent that they sought to slow the pace of exploration and to assess the social and cultural impact of the pipeline (Mahon, 1977:190-191). With the help of Thomas Berger, aboriginal peoples in the North and certain factions within the Indian and Inuit Affairs Program were able to win a temporary victory with the ten-year moratorium placed on further development in the North.

However, the commitment of the Mulroney government in the mid-1980s to settling outstanding land claims in the Yukon and Northwest Territories may reflect once again a shift in the balance of power within the DIAND towards resource extraction interests. In the Northwest Territories, the Dene-Métis agreement-in-principle involved the transfer of land to aboriginal control and cash compensation. The monetary value of the settlement was $500 million, plus a $20-million capital fund, and $75 million for the Norman Wells project. In addition, the Dene-Métis were given a share of resource royalties, special harvesting rights, title to 70 000 square miles of land, of which 3900 square miles included subsurface rights, and representation management boards (Coates and Powell, 1989:124-125).

While the agreement may appear to have been a victory for the aboriginal peoples of the Northwest Territories, the monetary value of this compensation package is not particularly large in light of the amount of potential wealth that is at stake in the North. Between 1987 and 1989 for example, the total value of mineral production alone in the Yukon and Northwest Territories was nearly $4.2 billion (Department of Indian and Northern Affairs, 1988a, 1990), considerably more than the one-time payouts associated with the settlement.

While political pressure has been placed on the government by the Dene-Métis of the Northwest Territories to settle their outstanding land claims, the agreement-in-principle between the government and the Dene Métis also appears to reflect a desire on the part of the state to clear away the political-legal obstacles to resource exploitation in the North stemming from unfilled land entitlements. The Auditor General of Canada, in its 1990 Annual Report to the House of Commons, outlined the "problems" faced by resource extraction companies in the North in the following terms:

> In the North, creating business certainty is a challenge, especially for mining. Unfortunately, the regulatory and approval processes are slow, often confusing, and sometimes unpredictable because they involve many government agencies and pieces of legislation administered from two territorial governments. Furthermore, land claims negotiations and subsequent implementation and environmental initiatives have an effect over time on mineral exploration and development. Along with world-wide market trends, these uncertainties affect the climate for investing in the mining sector in the North (Auditor General of Canada, 1990:473).

Thus, the political will to settle outstanding land claims in northern Canada, and the agreement-in-principle may reflect an increase in the political and economic pressure placed on the federal government by resource extraction companies interested in beginning a new phase of "economic development" in the North. Clearly, the settlement of land claims is a small price to pay for unobstructed multinational access to northern resources.

Ironically, this assessment was supported by the federal government's own 1985 Task Force to Review Comprehensive Claims Policy. In the context of land claims issues more generally, the members of the Task Force observed that, "settlements [of land claims] have been achieved only when the federal government was eager to facilitate an economic development project" (Task Force to Review Comprehensive Claims Policy, 1985:13).

The contradiction between the representation of business and aboriginal interests within the federal government in general, and within DIAND in particular, is evident more generally in what Weaver calls the "Indian policy field." She argues that in the mid-1980s there were two distinct paradigms (systems of values, and premises that shape the definition of problems and the proposal of solutions) within the federal government for dealing with Indian issues. One paradigm, represented by the Report of the Task Force on Program Review, chaired by Erik Nielsen, entailed "the premise that aboriginality did not exist and should not be given validity as the basis for new Indian-government relationships." It stressed that Indian people should conform to existing federalist and economic arrangments, and did not recognize the constitutional affirmation of aboriginal rights.

The second paradigm, represented by David Crombie, then Minister of Indian Affairs, was oriented more toward the needs and interests of aboriginal peoples. It was premised on the formal recognition of aboriginality and that it could form the basis for the formation of new political relationships within Canada. This paradigm also stressed that the federal government should be flexible in its negotiations over self-government for aboriginal peoples and allow Indian people the freedom to negotiate new political relationships.

Weaver (1986:31) argues that the former paradigm tended to be supported by those sections of the government that represented the interests of the provinces and of Canadian business. She suggests that the locus of support for this policy was "at the apex of the cabinet among more powerful, right wing, ministers whose portfolios had government-wide application." In contrast, the latter "Indian oriented" paradigm was supported by "the less senior level of a line department and represented the less powerful left wing of the cabinet and party" (Weaver, 1986:17-18). She argues that the native policy field is fluid. While the Nielsen paradigm was ascendant in the mid-1980s, she suggests that more recent developments may reflect a shift towards the Crombie-type paradigm (Weaver, 1990).

Conclusion

Several arguments have been developed in this chapter. First, we have suggested that treaties were a method of land conveyance: they were designed to transfer land from Indian to governmental and then to settler control. The treaty-signing process was part of a state strategy to clear away political-legal obstacles to the development of capitalism in Canada that were created, in part, by the Royal Proclamation of 1763. To the extent that treaties between government officials involved the transfer of land from Indian to state and subsequent private settler control, the treaties clearly were a moment in the primitive accumulation of capital in Canada. As such, the treaty-making process was structured not only by racism, but by the structure of emergent class relations in Canada.

Second, the factors leading to the particular configuration of Indian administration in Canada were structured by a complex set of factors rooted in class, gender, and "race." Indian policy and the Indian Act, while clearly racist in content and intent, were also formulated in the context of ideas about the appropriate position of women in a society and by prevailing definitions of what constituted legitimate economic activity. Thus, policies and practices were also shaped by the desire to transform aboriginal men into either commercial farmers or wage labourers, and aboriginal women into their subordinate spouses.

Third, what is unique about Indian people's relationship to the state is not that it has been one of domination and subordination, or that the state has sought to control Indian people. In a sense, all groups of people who have an organized interest in relation to the Canadian state are subject to the similar dialectic of representation and social control. What is unique about the position of aboriginal peoples is the balance of representation and social control. This balance was clearly in the direction of the latter. Historically, federal authorities were more concerned over the social control of aboriginal peoples than the representation of their interests at the cabinet table.

Fourth, there are two orders of contradictions within the contemporary structure of the Department of Indian and Northern Affairs Canada. First, there is a contradiction between the representation and control of each of its client groups, and there is a contradiction between servicing the concerns of each of these groups. Policies that directly or indirectly impinge on Indian people reflect, then, the outcomes of complex struggles and contradictions within DIAND and the civil service more generally. Neil Sterritt, hereditary chief of the Gitskan Nation and candidate for the position of national chief of the Assembly of First Nations in 1991, recognized the complex power relations within the federal cabinet that have an impact on state policy. Commenting on the present Minister of Indian and Northern Affairs Canada, Sterritt stated that despite being pleased with Tom Siddon's performance, he did not expect any great strides to be made in Indian Affairs since "you'd have to change the whole cabinet to do that" (Santoro, 1991; see also Erasmus, 1986:53).

CHAPTER 3

ABORIGINAL PEOPLES AND ECONOMIC RELATIONS:
Underclass or Class Fractions?

During the past two decades, sociologists in the United States and Britain have been keenly interested in the determination of the key variables that influence the life experiences, social chances, and position in production relations of various minority groups (See Boston, 1988; Wilson, 1980; Centre for Contemporary Cultural Studies, 1982; Miles, 1982). Within the political economy literature, debates have focused on the impact of racism, sexism, and class relations in shaping the positions and experiences of groups of people. While specific formulations vary, in part, on the basis of which variable or variables are accorded analytical priority, there is a recognition that these variables intersect in complex ways to structure the social position of groups.

In Canada, however, it is more common to assume that the social position and experiences of aboriginal peoples have been determined by a singular set of factors, namely factors stemming from their aboriginality. Studies undertaken by academics, government officials, and aboriginal peoples and their organizations have demonstrated that as a collectivity, aboriginal peoples occupy disadvantaged positions within social and economic structures of Canada. In relation to non-aboriginals, aboriginal peoples have lower average incomes, lower rates of labour force participation, higher rates of unemployment, and tend to be overrepresented in unskilled manual-labour positions. On the basis of this information, the impression is created that all aboriginal peoples, because they are aboriginal, share a structurally similar position within economic relations in Canadian society. Like some versions of the internal colonial model, there is presumed to be a convergence of "race" with class position.

In this chapter, we suggest that such aggregate statistics obscure more than they reveal about the nature of the position of aboriginal peoples within wider class relations in Canada. We also question the extent to which "race" overlaps with class in the determination of the location of aboriginal peoples in economic relations. As such, there are three specific objectives of this chapter. First, we examine debates about the position of aboriginal peoples in post-fur trade economic relations. Second, we critically evaluate the underclass thesis of the contemporary position of aboriginal peoples in socioeconomic relations. Third, we examine the distribution of aboriginal peoples in economic positions. We suggest that the differences in economic position between aboriginal and non-aboriginal peoples are relative and not absolute, that aboriginal peoples are distributed across the range of class sites, and that aboriginal peoples' position in economic relations reflects a complex intersection of class, gender relations, and racialization.

WHAT HAPPENED AFTER THE FUR TRADE?

Our concern in this chapter begins with the post-fur trade era in Canada. The onset of this period varies on the basis of region. The fur trade was of limited importance by around 1700 in the Maritimes (Wein, 1986), while in western Canada it remained the key industry until the 1870s and 1880s. In the North, the fur trade continued to be a significant force until the middle of this century (Rea, 1968:439).

The position of aboriginal peoples in the fur trade has been the subject of extensive historical and anthropological research. In addition to documenting the central role of aboriginal peoples as military allies of European powers (Miller, 1989), several scholars have documented the key roles Indian and Métis men and women played as primary producers and traders in this staple industry. For more detailed analysis of aboriginal peoples' involvement in the fur trade, readers are directed to Chapter 4, and to the work of Innis (1970), Bourgeault (1983), Van Kirk (1980), Trigger (1985), and Brown (1980b).

Ironically, it seems that more is known about the position of aboriginal peoples in economic relations during the fur trade than after its decline. However, within the sociological, anthropological, and historical literature, there are two divergent interpretations of what happened to the economic position of aboriginal peoples following the fur trade.

The first view suggests that aboriginal peoples were unable to make the transition to either waged work or farming following the fur trade and therefore were never incorporated into commercial agriculture and the emergent industrial capitalist economy. With the decline of the fur trade, aboriginal peoples became superfluous to economic activity and were economically marginalized. It is suggested that the end of the fur trade saw the placement of Indian people on reserves and the emergence of a range of "social problems," not least of which was a state of permanent unemployment and welfare dependency. In short, this view assumes that there were no Indian workers in the Canadian economy after the decline of the fur trade (Abele and Stasiulis, 1989:252).

Reflecting this traditional view, Krauter and Davis' (1978) textbook on minorities in Canada suggests that

> Before the white man came, Indians were self sufficient. Sedentary or roving, they were able to care for their own needs. Later, as trappers and hunters, they traded with whites. When Indians withdrew to the reserves, their employment problems began to multiply (Krauter and Davis, 1978:17-18).

From a different perspective, Wardhaugh (1983:225) suggests that the decline of the Indian began with the Indian Act, while Elias argues that "there appears to have been almost a direct shift from a trapping subsistence economy associated with the colonial situation to an economic position based upon permanent unemployment and social assistance associated with a class situation" (Elias, 1975:7). Similarly Palmer (1983:24), in his study of working class formation in Canada, argues that "reduced to a state of dependency by 1850, [aboriginal people] ... were, for the most part, marginalized, and over the course of the nineteenth century were shunted into increasingly restricted areas within the reserve system."

Several explanations of the lack of transition to waged work and farming are advanced. First, as noted in Chapter 1, the Chicago School-type of explanation focuses on cultural differences, and suggests that aboriginal peoples were either unwilling or unable to alter their traditional cultural and religious behaviours, which in turn inhibited their incorporation into post-fur trade economic relations. Traditional aboriginal cultural patterns were inconsistent with modern industrial society: aboriginal peoples lacked the cultural capital to succeed in a competitive, individualistic economic environment. In Zentner's (1973:4-9) terms, aboriginal peoples possessed a "pre-neolithic" work ethic that was, and remains, inconsistent with the work ethic required in an industrialized society. Yet others have suggested more specifically that aboriginal culture and religion were inimical to the development of modern European farming (see Carter, 1990, for a review of this literature). The problems with such explanations have been noted in Chapter 1 and shall not be reviewed here.

A second view attributes the economic marginalization of aboriginal peoples to the racist hiring practices, both consciously motivated and not, on the part of capitalist employers and within other institutions in society (Hull, 1982:24). Thus, according to Elias (1975:8), when European sources of labour were available to employers, aboriginal peoples were displaced and put in positions of permanent unemployment or semi-employment.

While racist hiring practices explain part of the process of economic marginalization, racism in itself is an incomplete explanation. Under some circumstances, to be discussed in more detail later, aboriginal peoples did participate in the post-fur trade economy. Furthermore, racism rarely has an autonomous existence. The meaning and significance of racist ideas are remarkably fluid and are subject to shifting conditions in the labour market. Depending on historical and economic conditions, racist ideas have been used as justifications for both exclusion from, and inclusion into, certain economic positions (Satzewich, 1991).

A third explanation, and one which requires further research and substantiation, involves the notion of resistance: conscious and unconscious resistance on the part of aboriginal peoples to waged work may have been partially responsible for their relative non-incorporation into industrial capitalism. Based on the analysis of colonialism in Africa, it can be suggested that this resistance was not rooted in an inherent inability or unwillingness of aboriginal peoples to alter their culture, but rather was a consequence of their continued access to land through the reserve system.

One of the contradictions inherent in the reserve systems established in colonial East Africa in the late 19th and early 20th centuries was that they provided a basis for African resistance to incorporation as wage labour. In Kenya, tracts of land were initially set aside by Europeans for the reproduction of the African population. Africans were engaged in both subsistence and market-oriented agriculture on reserve land (Brett, 1973:165-212). Continued access to that land provided the material basis for social reproduction outside of a wage economy.

The ability to resist incorporation as wage workers was, however, undermined by a shortage of labour and the political power of European settlers. The reserve system was contradictory to the extent that Europeans faced shortages of labour to work on their plantations. One of the ways in which this contradiction was resolved was through the implementation of various ordinances, as well as hut and poll taxes, which forced Africans to make cash payments to the state. In order to earn the cash to pay taxes, Africans were forced out of subsistence activities on reserves and into waged work on plantations. Such taxes were simply devices used by farmers to acquire a labour force (Miles, 1989). What is instructive about the case of colonial East Africa is that the reserve system initially provided a basis for resistance to incorporation as wage labour.

The relative non-incorporation of aboriginal peoples into the post-fur trade Canadian economy may be attributed, in part, to similar forms of resistance. Arguably, aboriginal resistance was more successful in Canada than in Kenya because alternative sources of labour power were in better supply here, and therefore there was not the same need to force them off reserves through legislation. Thus, even though from the point of view of Canadian state officials reserves were to be sites where Indian people would learn how to become commercial farmers and wage labourers —

and hence be incorporated into the emergent capitalist economy (Tobias, 1987) — one of the consequences of the reserve system and the treaties is that they provided a material basis for Indian people to retain at least partial access to land as a means of production. To some degree Indian people could economically and socially reproduce themselves outside of a cash economy.

Furthermore, this allows some Indian people to move into and out of the wage economy and use reserve lands and hunting and trapping rights to facilitate the temporary entry and withdrawal from the labour market. Contemporary studies of the articulation of modes of production in northern Canada provide some evidence to support this view. Michael Asch (1989), an anthropologist, argues that there are two modes of production in the Canadian North. One mode of production is capitalist, while the other is the "bush subsistence mode of production." While there are debates about whether these modes of production are contradictory or complementary (Asch, 1989; Berger, 1977; Daniels, 1986), what is clear is that a portion of aboriginal peoples engage in both subsistence production and wage labour in resource industries during the course of the year (Loxley, 1981:162; Watkins, 1972; Asch, 1989). An indication of the importance of the former is gained through an analysis of country food in the diet of northern aboriginal peoples. Research prepared for the Mackenzie Valley Pipeline Inquiry during the mid-1970s suggested that approximately 50 percent of adult males participated in "traditional" activities which involved subsistence food production through hunting and fishing, as well as commercial trapping (Rushforth, 1977). Bone's (1989) study of the use of country food during the construction phase of the Norman Wells pipeline in the Northwest Territories in the mid-1980s confirms these earlier findings. Fifty percent of aboriginal peoples he surveyed said that 40 percent of their diet consisted of country food (see also Usher, 1976; Stabler, 1989a, 1989b).

While this explanation is more compelling than the first two, it too underestimates the degree to which aboriginal peoples were incorporated into the post-fur trade economy. Furthermore, while it may have some applicability to northern reserves where continued access to traditional hunting, fishing, and trapping lands could provide enough resources for subsistence either outside of or in conjuction with a wage economy, it does not appear to be applicable to those aboriginal peoples who live on reserves closer to more densely-populated areas in southern Canada, where the resource base has been depleted.

A second view of the timing of the economic marginalization of aboriginal peoples points to a more complicated picture in which their experiences were closely tied to the vagaries of industrial capitalism. Rolf Knight (1978), in *Indians at Work* (see also Lithman, 1984; Dyck, 1983), questions the conventional wisdom which suggests that after the decline of the fur trade aboriginal peoples were economically marginalized from the "mainstream" economy. While not disagreeing that racism, discriminatory hiring practices, and the Indian Act have had negative impacts on their incorporation into waged work, he demonstrates that in the case of British Columbia, Indian people were incorporated extensively into the post-fur trade economic structure of the province via their participation in a range of wage labour activities. Aboriginal men worked for wages in commercial fishing, canning, road construction, logging, milling, mining, railroad construction, longshoring, and coastal shipping. Many of the jobs were unskilled and manual in nature, but others were skilled supervisory non-manual jobs. According to Mitchell and Franklin (1984), aboriginal women in British Columbia worked as domestic servants, cannery workers, seasonal agricultural labourers, and in some circumstances as prostitutes. The canning industry was particularly reliant on aboriginal labour such that by the late 19th century, most of the northern canneries were staffed by aboriginal women and children.

This view is also shared by Gonzalez (1981) and Wien (1986) in their studies of the Micmac in Nova Scotia. Both suggest that during the period from 1868 to 1940, aboriginal peoples were quite familiar with waged work. Micmac men and women sold their labour power on either a full- or part-time basis in a variety of sectors. In Nova Scotia, Micmac men worked in dowel factories, sawmills, brickworks, lobster factories, and construction, and in New England worked in shoe and textile factories (Wien, 1986:24-25). Micmac women appear to have been less involved in wage labour but were nevertheless employed in fruit and vegetable harvesting and processing and a number of other manufacturing concerns. In short, both Gonzalez and Wien argue that during the post-fur trade era, the Micmac in Nova Scotia were showing signs of a successful transition into waged work: they were able to "gain a foothold in the prevailing economy" (Wien, 1986:27).

Further to this view, Elias (1988:221) argues that during the turn of the century, the Dakota people on the Prairies pursued a variety of economic strategies. Depending on local conditions, some Dakota bands continued to engage in traditional hunting and gathering activities while others specialized in commercial grain production, ranching, and wage labour, or a combination of forms of economic activity. Thus, in Elias' terms,

> A continuum of strategies can be seen to range from H'damani's people, who lived closest to a customary lifestyle with only modest concessions to local labour and commodity markets, to the bands at Portage la Prairie and Prince Albert, whose members sold their labour power with enthusiasm and took what little they could from nature. Between are the farmer bands that developed strategies based upon the soil and an increasing experience in commercial agriculture and individual skills useful in the local labour markets (Elias, 1988:222).

In relation to agriculture, Carter (1990; see also Hull, 1982) argues that during the late 19th and early 20th centuries, Indian people showed signs of becoming successful farmers. She demonstrates that in the Treaty Six and Seven areas in Saskatchewan, Indian people were actively interested in becoming farmers, that Indian farmers steadily increased the number of acres under cultivation, and that they were able to grow enough food for both subsistence and occasional sale in the market. As Figure 3.1 demonstrates, agriculture was the single most important source of Indian people's income between 1899 and 1929.

Both Knight (1978) and Lithman (1984) argue that before the 1950s, aboriginal peoples' employment patterns generally followed larger economic cycles. The period from 1884 to 1930 was the zenith of aboriginal employment due, in part, to a general shortage of labour. The depression marked the collapse of the large-scale use of Indian wage labour, but with the emergence of labour shortages during World War II and their persistence in the immediate aftermath of the war, Indian wage labour activity increased again.

Evidence provided in the annual reports of the Department of Indian Affairs during the first half of this century tends to support this view. Figure 3.1 shows that wages were the second most important source of income for Indian people between 1899 and 1929. While Indian people

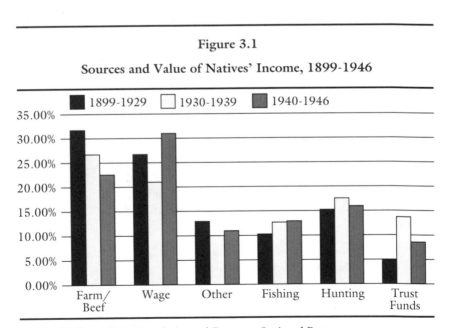

Figure 3.1

Sources and Value of Natives' Income, 1899-1946

Source: Indian Affairs Branch Annual Reports, *Sessional Papers.*
Ottawa: Kings Printer, 1899-1946.

gained 31.5 percent of their total income from farming and ranching activities, they also gained 26.2 percent of their total income from wages. The remaining sources of income were derived from fishing, hunting, trust funds, and handicraft production. As might be expected given our knowledge of employment patterns for non-aboriginal peoples during the 1930s, wages as a source of Indian people's income declined to 20.8 percent of their total income during the depression. However, wages became the most important source of income for Indian people during World War II when general labour shortages were acute. While farming and ranching operations constituted 22.1 percent of their total income between 1940 and 1946, wages made up 30.8 percent of their total income.

Collectively, then, these sources suggest that the economic marginalization of Indian people began not with the end of the fur trade, but rather sometime in this century. If it is true that aboriginal peoples were making a successful transition to waged work and agriculture, then the question of why they were pushed out of these spheres is much more difficult to answer.

In relation to the expulsion of Indian people from wage labour, Wien (1986; see also Elias, 1975, 1988:223) suggests that the depression was the crucial turning point in the history of Indian participation in wage labour in the Maritimes. He suggests that while the high levels of unemployment during the depression created hardships for many Canadians, the depression had more devastating and long-term effects on Indian people. The concentration and centralization of capital during the depression resulted in the elimination of many of the jobs that aboriginal peoples previously held, particularly as farm labourers and workers in resource-based industries.

Both Knight and Lithman suggest that it was only during the post-1945 period that there developed a "welfare economy" on reserves (Knight, 1978:202; Lithman, 1984:40). Like women who were mobilized into wage labour during the war effort, aboriginal peoples appear to have been displaced from their jobs by returning war veterans and immigrant workers who were recruited for unskilled manual-labour employment beginning in the late 1940s (Lithman, 1984:39-40; Satzewich, 1991). In addition, they suggest that the large-scale, but never complete, economic marginalization of aboriginal peoples in the economies of various provinces began with the renewed capitalization, mechanization, and "decasualization" of labour that was associated with the resource boom in the 1950s and 1960s (Knight, 1974:201; Clement, 1988).

Carter (1990), in her explanation of the demise of Indian agriculture, argues that the initial success of Indian farmers created conflict with non-aboriginal farmers. Given the limited nature of local markets for the sale of produce in western Canada in the late 19th and early 20th centuries, Indian farmers were competing for the same urban markets as non-Indian farmers. The latter saw government assistance to Indians for farming as

unfair competition. Local farmers in western Canada appear to have successfully lobbied federal and provincial levels of government to engage in
practices and implement legislation to undermine Indian farmers' ability
to compete. This involved the forced sale of more productive Indian
lands, restrictions on the sale of produce, and restrictions on Indian farmers' use of technologies to increase productivity.

Additionally, it appears that the depression had a more negative
impact on Indian than non-Indian farmers. Tyler summarizes the changes
in Canadian agriculture following the depression in these terms:

> Farms abandoned during depression became productive units during the
> war years. Men were replaced with machines, while productive units
> became steadily larger in size and fewer in number as the period pro-
> gessed.... [T]he development of large farms was difficult prior to 1939,
> due largely to the limitations of the horse as the major power source for
> production. This limitation disappeared after the war when the techno-
> logical developments of several years became available (Tyler, 1966:287)

In addition to reducing opportunities for aboriginal wage labour on
Canadian farms, the depression and its aftermath put Indian farmers in an
even more disadvantaged position than they had experienced before 1929.
In the context of the mechanization of agriculture and the growth in farm
size, Indian farmers were less able to compete than they had been. Given
that Indian farmers could not mortgage reserve-based property, they had
restricted access to credit to finance expansion and mechanization
(Dempsey, 1978:28). This process is also reflected in Figure 3.1, which
shows that while Indian wage labour was able to rebound somewhat after
the depression, farm income for Indians decreased.

Thus, while somewhat disparate, this alternative view suggests that
the fortunes of aboriginal peoples as wage labourers and farmers were
directly and indirectly tied to the larger fortunes of Canadian capitalism.
Their fate was determined not solely by their status as Indians but rather
as Indians who were living in particular locations within a capitalist
society.

ABORIGINAL PEOPLES AND THE CONTEMPORARY CLASS STRUCTURE

With certain exceptions (Adams, 1990; Dosman, 1972; Daniels, 1986),
social scientists who attempt to locate aboriginal peoples within the class
structure suggest that they form an *underclass* within contemporary
Canada (see Rex, 1970 for a British example). There is a certain consensus
between otherwise distinct theoretical traditions in that the underclass
thesis is put forward in general textbooks on social stratification and ethnicity in Canada, as well as in studies concerned specifically with aboriginal peoples (Stymeist, 1975). Dennis Forcese, in *The Canadian Class*

Structure, argues that "always at the bottom of the class order [are] the 'non-people', the Indians and Metis" (Forcese, 1975:46); "the Indians, Eskimos and the Metis, who even lack treaty rights, have been relegated to the lowest rung on the Canadian stratification hierarchy, one somewhat analogous to that of the outcastes or untouchables of [East] Indian society" (Forcese, 1975:55). Wardhaugh (1983:225), using similar imagery, describes aboriginal peoples as "a population living largely apart from other Canadians in a kind of a caste system, with high unemployment, and poor education, housing and health.... To be an Indian in Canada is to be at the very bottom of the Canadian social hierarchy; it is to be last in everything."

From the internal colonial model, Kellough (1980:349), somewhat confusingly, argues that Indians form the underclass within the larger metropolis/hinterland structure: "in most cases, Indian reserves have been at the bottom of the Canadian hinterland ladder. When communities other than reserves form this lower level hinterland, native Indians form the underclass within that community, an underclass of unemployed who are incorporated into the structures and processes of local capitalism" (Kellough, 1980:349). And within a Marxist framework, Elias (1975) in his study of class relations in Churchill, Manitoba, suggests that aboriginal peoples have become permanent members of the underclass within Canada. He suggests that "'Native' and 'underclass' are almost synonymous: to be native is almost sure to be a member of the underclass and to be a member of the underclass is almost sure to be native" (Elias, 1975:17). The assumption of the underclass thesis is that the class position and experiences of aboriginal peoples are completely unlike those of other groups of people within Canada. Given their experiences of racism, their unique position in political-legal relations, and the associated material disadvantages, aboriginal peoples exist not as a part of the extant class structure, but as distinct and separate from it. Collectively, aboriginal peoples occupy a common position of subordination, marginality, and dispossession within Canada. Thus, all aboriginal peoples, by virtue of their common background, occupy the same socially and economically disadvantaged position.

The underclass thesis is inadequate on both theoretical and empirical grounds. First, the thesis tends to unwittingly perpetuate negative stereotypes about aboriginal peoples. The portrayal of all aboriginal peoples as a class of permanently unemployed and decrepit people reinforces the common sense impression that all aboriginal peoples live either off welfare on reserves or on "skid row" in cities.

Second, as we shall demonstrate in more detail, even though aboriginal peoples have lower rates of labour force participation and higher rates of unemployment than non-aboriginal peoples, they are nevertheless distributed across the range of class sites within Canada. Thus, the underclass thesis ignores the fact that many aboriginal peoples are economically active, that the majority of those in the labour force earn a wage, and that at least some aboriginal peoples own property and are employers.

Third, the underclass thesis posits a homogeneity of experience for different genders, classes, and socio-legal categories of aboriginal peoples. In other words, it is silent on the theoretical and political significance of class and gender divisions within the aboriginal population. The specific dimensions and meanings of class, gender, and socio-legal divisions within the aboriginal population will be discussed in more detail in the remainder of this chapter and in subsequent chapters.

In sum, we suggest that the underclass thesis is unable to capture the full complexity of aboriginal peoples' position in economic relations. In the remainder of this chapter, we attempt to disentangle the effects of racialization, sexism, and class in the distribution of aboriginal peoples within economic relations. We demonstrate that aboriginal peoples are distributed in all of the main class sites within Canada. Like the non-aboriginal population, aboriginal peoples have differential relationships to the means of production: they occupy economic sites as part of the lumpenproletariat, reserve army of labour, working class, petite bourgeoisie, and bourgeoisie. We also suggest, however, that their placement in these positions has been affected by racism and a pre-existing gendered division of labour.

The Lumpenproletariat

Marx defined the lumpenproletariat in typically Victorian terms as a group consisting of "thieves and criminals of all kinds, living on the crumbs of society, people without a definite trade, vagabonds, [and] people without a hearth or a home" (quoted in Giddens, 1971:38). Veltmeyer, in a no less graphic way, defines the lumpenproletariat as

> people who are not regularly employed and, not owning property or other forms of income-producing wealth, are forced into lives of crime, parasitical dependence or other forms of social deviance. In this situation are a wide assortment of people — burglars, muggers, hustlers of all kinds, small time pimps, drug addicts, beggars, street prostitutes, alcoholics, tramps, low level dope dealers, main-streeters, hippies and others who have given up trying to find regular work. They reject productive labour and live off the system (Veltmeyer, 1986:105).

While Veltmeyer overemphasizes the criminality dimension of the lumpenproletariat, the category refers more generally to a group of people who do not own any means of production, who do not work for wages, and who are incapable of, or unwilling to engage in, regular wage labour in order to maintain themselves. Along with certain criminal elements, they are the permanently unemployed who lack the educational, personal, or social skills to find and retain permanent, or even occasional, employment (Anderson, 1974:129). Characterized by high rates of alcohol use, poor health status, and high rates of welfare dependency, the latter are those who have been marginalized by, and are superfluous to, the direct process of production within capitalism.

When applied to aboriginal peoples, the lumpenproletariat is that portion of the aboriginal population who live on skid row in cities and on permanent welfare on reserves. The aboriginal lumpenproletariat is the most socially visible section of the urban aboriginal population in Canada. This is the group of aboriginal peoples we regularly "see" on the street-corners of skid row in Canada's cities. However, because of their social visibility, and because of the process of selective perception where people rarely take notice of aboriginal peoples who do not conform to skid row stereotypes (Dyck, 1986), the aboriginal lumpenproletariat appears to be larger than it really is.

As we note in the appendix to this chapter, only a small proportion of people who make up the census category of "not in the labour force" are of lumpenproletarian status. The census category of "not in the labour force," while not an entirely appropriate measure of the lumpenproletariat, can, however, provide a general indication of the relative differences between aboriginal and non-aboriginal participation in economic activities. Thus, Table 3.1 provides information on the labour force participation (LFPR) and non-participation rates (NPR) for all Canadians and for single origin Indian, Métis, and Inuit men and women. It shows that for all Canadian men over the age of 15, the LFPR was 77.5 percent and the NPR was 32.5 percent. For all Canadian women, the corresponding rates are 55.9 percent and 44.1 percent respectively. For single origin Indian people, men had a LFPR of 59.5 percent and women a rate of 39.0 percent, with corresponding NPRs being 40.5 percent and 61 percent respectively. For single origin Métis men, the LFPR was 66.4 percent and NPR 33.6 percent, and for women the figures were 44.5 percent and 55.5 percent. For single origin Inuit men, the LFPR was 59.5 percent and for women it was 43.7 percent. Non-participation rates stood at 40.5 percent and 56.3 percent for Inuit men and women.

Thus, when compared with the total Canadian population, aboriginal peoples are clearly overrepresented in the category of "not in the labour force." The two difficult empirical questions, however, are what percentage of those not in the labour force are of lumpenproletarian status, and how large is the aboriginal lumpenproletariat compared with the non-aboriginal lumpenproletariat? While this is discussed in more detail in the appendix, Brody's (1971) participant observation study of Indians on skid row in a western Canadian city suggests that about 10 percent of the urban aboriginal population can be classified as constituting the lumpenproletariat, compared with approximately 3-5 percent of the non-aboriginal population.

Table 3.1

Labour Force Participation Rates, Aboriginal and
Non-Aboriginal Men and Women, 1986

	Single Origin N.A. Indian		Single Origin Métis		Single Origin Inuit		Total Canada	
	M	F	M	F	M	F	M	F
Labour Force Participation Rate (LFPR)	59.5	39.0	66.4	44.5	59.5	43.7	77.5	55.9
Non Participation Rate (NPR)	40.5	61.0	33.6	55.5	40.5	56.3	32.5	44.1
Total	100.0	100.0	100.0	100.0	100.0	100.0	100.0	100.0

Source: Statistics Canada, *A Data Book on Canada's Aboriginal Population from the 1986 Census of Canada*. Ottawa, 1989, pp. 15-16

The aboriginal lumpenproletariat has been the object of considerable curiosity on the part of social scientists and government officials. One line of research, stemming from the work of Herbert Gans (1974), examines the aboriginal lumpenproletariat in the process of commodity circulation via their roles as consumers. While the lumpenproletariat are not direct producers of goods or services, they are important elements of capitalist societies to the extent that they are consumers of state-sponsored social, as well as police and prison, "services" (Stymeist, 1975). In other words, the existence of a lumpenproletariat helps maintain a whole range of state-financed white-collar and professional jobs such as social worker, prison guard, life-skills counsellor, and police officer. As some aboriginal leaders have noted, "Indians are a big business" in many western Canadian cities.

Some private-sector businesses also derive large parts of their sales from the expenditures of the aboriginal lumpenproletariat. It appears that most beverage rooms frequented by the aboriginal lumpenproletariat, both in urban and rural areas, are owned by non-aboriginal peoples. In fact, for some white-owned skid row hotels, the sale of alcohol to aboriginal peoples seems to be the main source of revenue. In addition, some corner grocery stores are known to stock large supplies of cleaning fluids under their counters which they sell to aboriginal peoples, knowing of course that they use it to get high. Without a reserve-based aboriginal population reliant on government transfers in close proximity, many rural communities in western Canada would be considerably worse off than they are presently. The so-called "welfare money" which some aboriginal peoples rely on is a silver lining for the pockets of skid row beverage rooms and other businesses who cater to this group of people. Thatcher

(1986:285) observes that "the management and control of Native people as deviants is a thriving industry in Canada." He stresses that aboriginal disadvantage works to the benefit of several others including slumlords, pawnbrokers, liquor vendors, public health workers, Christian reformers, and a sizeable federal bureaucracy. The cruel irony is that while many people are critical of aboriginal peoples' dependence upon social assistance and their patterns of consumption, few are critical of those private-sector interests which take advantage of, and perhaps help perpetuate, these situations.

Other studies in the urban context are more concerned with the nature of social interaction on skid row. Hugh Brody (1971), in his study *Indians On Skid Row*, argues that contrary to popular perceptions, skid row is characterized by a certain sense of community. Rather than being characterized by community disorganization, skid row life contains a logic of its own in which there are certain rewards for participation. Skid row provides a support and income distribution network for participants with expectations of reciprocity. It also constitutes a location in which aboriginal peoples can physically and socially isolate themselves from the pressures of the outside world. Morinis (1982:102) argues further that skid row lifestyles are forms of political defiance, rejection, and opposition to "modern Canada."

More importantly, however, Brody (1971) also argues that despite skid row whites' verbalization of racist hostility directed towards aboriginal peoples living on skid row, there is a certain sense in which this animosity is superficial. He suggests that aboriginal and non-aboriginal peoples on skid row have certain common experiences and concerns, and that they exist in a state of mutual dependency. Skid row whites rely on native peoples to prop up their own egos, while skid row Indians gain a certain sense of status by being able to associate with whites, even though they are whites who possess rather low social standing. Thus, their common experiences, concerns, and lifestyles mean that whites and Indians share a structurally similar position within the society, with the exception being that whites on skid row are not subject to the racist hostility of native peoples (see also Morinis, 1982; Dosman, 1972).

The Reserve Army of Labour

The reserve army of labour consists of those individuals who have been displaced from the process of capitalist production but who are available for work when demand warrants. They constitute a portion of people who are forced, by their condition of absolute or relative lack of property, into selling their labour power for wages, but who, for various reasons, are not part of the active labour army. They are those who can be brought into the production process when the cyclical demands of capital accumulation require their labour power. Several sources of the reserve army of labour were identified by Marx (1967). The two most important categories for our purposes are the latent and floating surplus populations. The reserve army of labour consists of a latent surplus population of those who have been displaced by the penetration of capitalist relations of production in agriculture, and a floating surplus population of those who have been displaced by technological innovations which reduce the demand for labour (Marx, 1967:640-648).

Aboriginal peoples are clearly overrepresented within both of these sections of the reserve army of labour. Using census terms, the reserve army of labour consists of those who are out of work but who are actively seeking work. Aboriginal peoples possess anywhere from two to nearly four times the unemployment rates of non-aboriginal peoples. According to the 1986 census, aboriginal people's unemployment rates ranged from a low of 20.9 percent for single origin Inuit women over 25 to a high of 44.5 percent for single origin Indian males between 15 and 24 years of age (see Table 3.2). This compares with a Canada-wide unemployment rate of 9.6 percent for men and 11.2 percent for women.

Official unemployment rates on reserves are highly variable. Some reserves in northern Manitoba and Saskatchewan have unemployment rates of more than 95 percent while some reserves closer to urban centres in eastern Canada have relatively low rates of unemployment (Durst, 1990:197).

Aboriginal youth are considerably overrepresented in the ranks of the reserve army of labour when compared with both older aboriginal peoples and non-aboriginal youth. According to Table 3.2, the unemployment rate for single origin Indian men between 15 and 24 is 44.5 percent, and for women it is 42.7 percent. The unemployment rates for single origin Métis and Inuit youth are somewhat lower, but nevertheless remain more than twice as high as the non-aboriginal youth unemployment rate of 17.3 percent for 15-24 year old males and 16.6 percent for 15-24 year old females.

As is evident from Table 3.2, the reserve army of labour does not consist solely of aboriginal peoples. Since it is a structural feature of the capitalist mode of production, members of all ethnic groups and both genders make up the reserve army of labour. What is unique about aboriginal peoples is that they are overrepresented within the ranks of the reserve army of labour. It is not, however, entirely their preserve.

The reasons for the disproportionate placement of aboriginal peoples into the reserve army of labour are complicated, and it is not due to a singular set of factors. As noted, in some cases the existence of the reserve system and treaties allows Indian people access to land and means of production that can be used for subsistence activities in conjunction with only occasional sale of labour power for wages. Also as noted earlier, over the years many aboriginal workers have been displaced by technological innovations which have reduced the demand for labour in resource extraction and agricultural sectors in rural Canada. Many aboriginal peoples live in relatively isolated rural areas where opportunities to sell labour power for wages are limited. As well, labour market discrimination, low quality education, and inadequate training also contribute to placing aboriginal peoples disproportionately into the reserve army of labour (Hull, 1982; Armstrong, Kennedy, and Oberle, 1990:19).

Table 3.2

Unemployment Rates for Aboriginal* and Non-Aboriginal People, 1986

	Indian		Métis		Inuit		Canada	
	M	F	M	F	M	F	M	F
Unemployment Rate								
15 yrs.+	32.7	28.7	30.3	27.0	28.9	26.0	9.6	11.2
15-24	44.5	42.7	39.0	38.8	42.7	34.9	17.3	16.6
25 yrs. +	28.5	23.1	26.8	21.7	23.0	20.9	7.7	9.6

* Statistics are for single origin Indian, Métis, and Inuit people.

Source: Adapted from Statistics Canada, *Profile of Ethnic Groups — Dimensions.* Ottawa: Minister of Supply and Services, 1989.

However, some sectors of the Canadian economy, particularly those which require large amounts of relatively unskilled seasonal labour, have relied historically on the aboriginal reserve army of labour. Until the 1970s, Indian people from reserves in northern Alberta, Saskatchewan, and Manitoba were crucial to the commercial viability of the sugar beet industry in southern Alberta and Manitoba (Satzewich, 1991; Lithman, 1984). During the mid-1960s, for example, 95 percent of the members of the Witchekan Lake Reserve, 90 percent of the Pelican Lake Reserve, 65 percent of the Big River Reserve, and 25 percent of the Montreal Lake and One Arrow Reserves (all in Saskatchewan) migrated on a seasonal basis to thin, hoe, and harvest sugar beets in the southern Alberta sugar beet industry. Similarly, Micmac Indian families in Nova Scotia have migrated on a seasonal basis to the blueberry and potato harvests in Maine since the 1920s (Wein, 1986:22). In these cases, Indian people constituted a particularly useful labour source to the extent that they were available when demand warranted, they could be mobilized via state intervention, and they "disappeared" back to the reserve when their services were no longer required. With the mechanization of these production processes in the 1970s, the demand for their labour power has decreased.

Clearly, one of the main aims of recent state policy is to reduce the size of the aboriginal reserve army of labour by placing them into the active labour army, or working class. Located on the reserve and in cities, this group has been the object of a number of state programs involving training for both temporary and permanent waged employment. It is estimated that the Canada Employment and Immigration Commission (CEIC), the Department of Indian Affairs and Northern Development, and the Department of Justice spent nearly $770 million between 1973 and 1988 on job training and mobility programs for aboriginal peoples (Bherer, Gagnon, and Roberge, 1990:22-23). In Saskatchewan in 1989, aboriginal peoples made up 21 percent of the participants in all programs of the Canadian Jobs Strategy (CJS) and 48 percent of the participants in the Job Development option of the CJS (CEIC, 1989).

In addition, private-sector and crown corporations have been forced, or have voluntarily implemented programs, to hire aboriginal workers. Most notably, Nova-an Alberta Corporation, Inco Metals Company-Manitoba Division, Saskatchewan Power Corporation, the Manitoba Telephone System, and Syncrude, have all undertaken initiatives to recruit an aboriginal work force (Grant, 1983).

There is a sense of urgency associated with various levels of the state in their attempts to reduce the size of the aboriginal reserve army of labour. This urgency is linked largely to the perception that high levels of unemployment lead to militancy on the part of aboriginal youth. Given that the aboriginal population is comparatively young in demographic terms, and given trends towards greater urbanization of aboriginal peoples in the future, considerable concern has been expressed over the future of social stability and "race relations" in urban areas. In a review of affirmative action programs in Canada in 1983, it was noted that in Saskatchewan, "there is an acute awareness that the inordinately high native unemployment and the resultant poverty combine to create an atmosphere of serious discontent and potential unrest.... [C]urrently one out of four school children are of native ancestry. These children represent 25 percent of the potential labour force in the next decade" (Cohen, 1983:28-29). Without jobs and a stake in the system, the fear is that aboriginal youth may follow in the path of protest pursued by minority youth in the United States and Britain in the 1970s and 1980s (Solomos, 1989).

The Proletariat

Like the reserve army of labour, the proletariat, or working class, consists of individuals who do not own or control the means of production and who are compelled by the condition of relative or absolute lack of property to sell their labour power for wages in the market (Veltmeyer, 1986:72). Unlike the reserve army of labour, however, they are actually in paid employment. The majority of aboriginal peoples who are in the labour force and who have jobs occupy working-class positions.

Tables 3.3 and 3.4 provide an indication of the relative distribution of aboriginal and non-aboriginal men and women within specifically working-class sites. Before proceeding with an examination of these data, a word of explanation is necessary. The data provided in these two tables are for those who were in the labour force during the 1986 census. Census data provide an imperfect measure of class, and some caution is required in the interpretation of these data. Furthermore, those who were employed and those who were out of work but seeking work are included in the same category. Since unemployed aboriginal peoples have already been defined as part of the reserve army of labour, and since aboriginal peoples have higher rates of unemployment than non-aboriginal peoples, the figures do not give an accurate indication of the absolute size of the respective classes, but rather an indication of the relative distribution of the aboriginal and non-aboriginal populations within the working class.

For analytical purposes, the working class is divided into white- and blue-collar fractions. Based on 1986 census categories, the former includes clerical, sales, and service occupations. The blue-collar fraction consists of primary, processing, fabricating, construction and other.

Table 3.3

Distribution of Single Origin Aboriginal and Non-Aboriginal Men in Working-Class Sites*, 1986

	Indian	Métis	Inuit	Canada
Working Class				
Clerical	4.3	4.2	7.8	6.8
Sales	2.9	3.3	2.9	8.8
Service	10.0	10.4	10.6	10.2
Total White Collar	17.2	17.9	21.3	25.8
Primary	17.9	16.3	7.6	7.9
Processing	7.6	7.5	3.3	8.2
Fabricating	5.2	6.1	5.7	9.9
Construction	19.7	20.4	18.4	10.1
Other blue collar and n.e.s.**	16.3	19.7	25.1	13.1
Total Blue Collar	66.7	70.0	60.1	48.9
Total Working Class	83.9	87.9	81.4	74.7

* Percentages based on totals employed in all occupations.
** Not elsewhere classified categories.

Source: Gerber, 1990, p. 75

Table 3.3 shows that in 1986, 17.2 percent of the single origin Indian male labour force, 17.9 percent of the single origin Métis male labour force, and 21.3 percent of the Inuit male labour force were in white-collar working-class positions, compared with 25.8 percent of the total male labour force of Canada. Each category of aboriginal men tended to be underrepresented in each white-collar position. The only exception was Inuit men who were overrepresented in clerical positions. Table 3.3 also shows that 66.7 percent of single origin Indian men, 70 percent of single origin Métis men, and 60.1 percent of Inuit men were in blue-collar positions, compared with 48.9 percent of the male population of Canada. In blue-collar positions, aboriginal men tended to be overrepresented in construction and primary and other occupations, and were underrepresented in product fabricating and processing jobs. The larger proportion of aboriginal men in "other and not elsewhere classified" categories may reflect the difficulty that census takers have had in measuring "traditional" economic activities. On the whole, however, aboriginal men were overrepresented in working class sites when compared with the male Canadian labour force.

Table 3.4 shows that in 1986, aboriginal and non-aboriginal women were distributed in roughly similar proportions in blue- and white-collar locations. It shows that 55.5 percent of the single origin Indian female labour force, 59.8 percent of the single origin Métis female labour force, 58.1 percent of the single origin Inuit female labour force, and 59 percent of the total female labour force in Canada were in white-collar positions. Within this category, however, aboriginal women were underrepresented in the somewhat better-paying clerical and sales positions, and overrepresented in more poorly-paying service positions. It also shows that 15.5 percent of the single origin Indian female labour force, 21.9 percent of the single origin Métis female labour force, 11.6 percent of the single origin Inuit female labour force, and 12.3 percent of the total female labour force in Canada were in blue-collar positions. Overall, with the exception of Métis women, aboriginal and non-aboriginal women were distributed in roughly similar proportions in working-class sites.

What is of particular interest here is that a comparison of data in the two tables suggests that aboriginal men and aboriginal women have somewhat different labour market experiences. Aboriginal women, like their non-aboriginal counterparts, are overly concentrated in white- and "pink-collar" occupations and are underrepresented in blue-collar occupations when compared with both aboriginal and non-aboriginal men. While occupying the most disadvantaged position overall, the position of aboriginal women tends to parallel the position of non-aboriginal women more than the position of aboriginal men.

This observation also appears to hold for differences in earnings. Indian women who worked full time all year long in 1985 earned on average $17 100 and non-aboriginal women earned $20 000. Indian men who worked full-time all year earned on average $23 300, and non-Indian men $30 500. Thus, whereas Indian women earned 85.5 percent of what other women earned, they only earned 73.4 percent of the income of Indian men. Differences in earnings between aboriginal and non-aboriginal men, and between aboriginal and non-aboriginal women, reflect, in part, segmentation within class categories. However, employment opportunities and levels of earnings of aboriginal men and women are also determined, in part, by prevailing conceptions of what constitutes "women's" work and what constitutes "men's" work. This suggests that the gendered division of labour may have an equally, if not more important, influence on the position of aboriginal women in production relations than their status as aboriginal peoples. According to Gerber (1990:76) "while more marked in some respects, gender segregation in employment among natives is similar to that experienced by Canadians as a whole."

One of the major differences, though, between the aboriginal and non-aboriginal working classes is the source of employment income for

Table 3.4

Distribution of Single Origin Aboriginal and
Non-Aboriginal Women in Working-Class Sites*, 1986

	Indian (Percent)	Métis (Percent)	Inuit (Percent)	Canada (Percent)
Working Class				
Clerical	24.4	22.0	26.5	33.5
Sales	5.7	5.7	3.5	9.4
Service	25.4	32.1	28.1	16.1
Total White Collar	55.5	59.8	58.1	59.0
Primary	3.0	2.6	0.6	2.5
Processing	3.3	2.1	2.5	2.4
Fabricating	3.4	2.9	4.1	4.2
Construction	1.2	1.1	1.7	0.3
Other blue collar and n.e.s.**	4.3	13.2	2.7	2.9
Total Blue Collar	15.5	21.9	11.6	12.3
Total Working Class	71.0	80.7	69.7	71.3

* Percentages based on totals employed in all occupations.
** Not elsewhere classified categories.

Source: Gerber, 1990, p. 75.

the two groups. As Figure 3.2 shows, in 1983, 37 percent of on-reserve status Indians made a living from private-sector employment, while 63 percent made a living from public-sector employment. For off-reserve status Indians, 42 percent and 58 percent of their employment income was from private- and public-sector sources respectively. Within the Canadian economy as a whole, 75 percent of the population made their living from private-sector employment, while 25 percent made their living from public-sector employment. Compared with the Canadian economy as a whole, then, the aboriginal working class is overly concentrated in employment which is directly or indirectly funded by the state.

Figure 3.2

Breakdown of 1983 Payroll for Status Indians

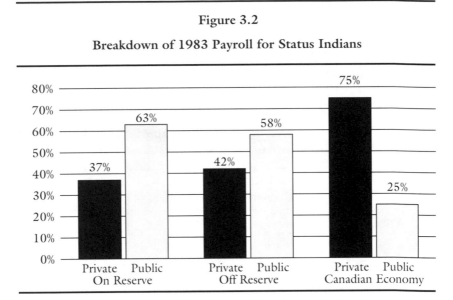

Source: Indian and Northern Affairs Canada, *Task Force on Indian Economic Development.* Ottawa: Minister of Supply and Services, 1986, p. 12.

The nature of the experiences and concerns of aboriginal working-class men and women needs to be the subject of much more research in order to fully disentangle the complex intersections of class, "race," and gender in their daily lives. Additionally, more research is needed on the extent to which the concerns and struggles of aboriginal peoples who occupy working-class sites are similar to, and different from, the concerns and struggles of the non-aboriginal working class, particularly when they are of the same gender and live in urban areas.

Feminist researchers are divided over whether the social positions, experiences, and struggles of aboriginal women are similar to those of European women. Evidence suggests that the nature of the struggles of

aboriginal women (both working class and petite bourgeois) are both similar to, and different from, the struggles of non-aboriginal women in similar class positions (Ng, 1988a; Jamieson, 1981; Lachapelle, 1982;
Stasiulis, 1987; Kline, 1989). While aboriginal and non-aboriginal women
share similar concerns over sexual harrassment in the workplace, working
conditions, unionization, wages, health care and day care, it is also the
case, that aboriginal women's

> demands are very different from those of white women who claim to
> speak on their behalf. Rather than seeking the end of the nuclear family,
> they are trying desperately to hold onto the extended and everchanging
> Native family that is under attack by unemployment, alcoholism, prison
> and child apprehension. They show little interest in breast feeding and
> home child-birth but in proper clinics and medical care in their commu-
> nities (Daniels, 1986:104).

Thus, while struggles in the workplace may be similar, the call for the
dismantling of the nuclear family rings hollow for aboriginal women who
have had their families torn apart by welfare bureaucracies and the residential school system.

Other evidence suggests that under certain conditions both the aboriginal and non-aboriginal working class have united in common struggles. In their study of unionism in the fishing industry of British
Columbia, Gladstone and Jamieson (1950) demonstrate that prior to
World War I, Indian men and women working in the salmon canning
industry, in conjunction with their "white" counterparts, were actively
engaged in strikes over wages and agitation against Japanese fishermen
and cannery workers. A more contemporary study of the fishing industry
in British Columbia suggests that there are complex ways in which aboriginal and non-aboriginal boat owners and shore workers are united by
common class positions and at the same time divided by "racial" barriers
(Clement, 1988:129-130).

One of the key issues confronting the future of the aboriginal working class is whether they will experience the same degrees of upward
mobility, in terms of class position and income, as previous generations of
working-class Canadians and Canadian immigrants. In the context of
assumptions stemming from the Chicago School that aboriginal peoples
will eventually experience these same patterns of upward mobility, Doug
Daniels has argued:

> The Canadian immigrants who made it 'under the wire' so to speak —
> the Italians, the Portuguese, and the Greeks of the late 1950s and 1960s
> — were able to take part in some of the upward mobility that has
> become the official model for Canadian minorities. Those who arrived
> later, including the off-reserve Indians who migrated to the cities in the
> late 1960s and Third World newcomers from the Caribbean, Philippines

and Latin America, came in a period of steady [economic] contraction (Daniels, 1987:57).

In other words, Daniels argues that the restructuring of Canadian capitalism since the 1970s has resulted in reduced opportunities for aboriginal peoples for structural upward mobility through job ladders and internal labour markets.

While not specifically addressing aboriginal employment, this assessment is confirmed more generally by the Economic Council of Canada (1990). It argues that since the 1950s, there has been a dramatic shift in the nature of employment in Canada away from goods-producing activities to service-based industries. This has resulted in an increasingly bifurcated occupational structure into "good jobs" and "bad jobs." Whereas previous generations of working-class Canadians could look forward to relatively long-term employment and experience upward mobility with a single employer in the goods-producing sector, present generations of the working class are increasingly faced with the prospect of short-term, low-paying employment in non-unionized small firms in retail trade, accommodation and food, and personal service sectors (Economic Council of Canada, 1990:2-6).

The implications of these changes for aboriginal peoples are far-reaching. The coincidence of increasing rural to urban migration of aboriginal peoples, along with the fundamental reorganization of the Canadian economy, may mean that aboriginal peoples will be put in an even more difficult situation than they have been. While the aboriginal working class clearly has a set of experiences that are unique from the non-native working class, in part because of racism and their distinct citizenship status in Canada, their fate, like that of other Canadians, is tied to events largely beyond their control.

The Aboriginal Bourgeoisie and Petite Bourgeoisie

In addition to occupying positions as parts of the lumpenproletariat, the reserve army of labour, and the working class, aboriginal peoples also occupy bourgeois and petite bourgeois positions. For analytical purposes the latter is divided into the "old" and "new" petite bourgeoisie.

The bourgeoisie consists of those who own and/or control the means of production and who employ others. For the non-aboriginal population, power tends to be based on the ownership of the means of production. While this is also the case with the aboriginal bourgeoisie, the primary basis of their power stems from the control which they exercise over capital and the means of production. Thus, the aboriginal bourgeoisie is made up of those people who either own large sums of capital privately, or who control large sums of "communally"- or band-based capital. As Martin O'Malley (1980) notes, recent land claims settlements, and the likelihood of future settlements (however slow the process), have resulted in large transfers of funds to aboriginal peoples' control.

Even though the funds transferred to aboriginal peoples through land claims settlements and resource royalties are in many cases nominally "owned" by all people in a band, control over the disbursement of these funds usually rests in the hands of a few individuals. Thus, relatively small groups of people exercise control over the investment decisions and how these resources are to be used. While they may face certain ideological and political constraints over how they dispose of these resources because they do not formally own the capital, in many ways they are able to act like the non-aboriginal bourgeoisie. They exercise effective control over capital and can operate, in effect, as merchant bankers (Daniels, 1986).

The aboriginal bourgeoisie is still in its embryonic stage. It is likely that this group constitutes no more than 1 percent of the total aboriginal population in Canada compared with 2.4 percent of the total Canadian population (Veltmeyer, 1986:110). Over ten years ago, Martin O'Malley provided a profile of a handful of aboriginal men who can be said to occupy bourgeoise class positions. While some of their wealth has been based on privately-owned capital, others have been able, through the control they have exercised over land claims settlements, to establish power and control over small regional airlines, snowmobile manufacturing companies, oil and gas exploration companies, land companies, and companies that provide services to resource multinationals. While the basis of their power may be different from that of the non-aboriginal bourgeoisie, their lifestyles are strikingly similar (O'Malley, 1980).

Thus, despite its small size, this class appears to be one of the most dynamic sectors of the aboriginal population, and is one that is able to wield a considerable amount of power and influence. As Calvin Helin, president of the Native Trade and Industry Investment Association has stated, "be prepared to do business with native pople, because the land claims situation is not on your side" (Saskatoon *Star-Phoenix*, 1991a).

The aboriginal petite bourgeoisie consists of two strata: the old and the new petite bourgeoisie. The old petite bourgeoisie consists of aboriginal peoples who are independent commodity producers who do not employ other people (or do so only on a limited scale), or who make use of family labour. They are involved either in commercial fishing, trapping, and farming or are owners of small restaurants, garages, grocery stores, commercial trucking operations, school buses, and taxis. Most aboriginal businesses are small in size and are individually- or family-owned and operated.

Figure 3.3 shows that in a sample of 2000 Indian-owned businesses in 1981, 86.3 percent were on-reserve operations, 13.3 percent were off-reserve operations, and 0.4 percent were on surrendered lands. Figure 3.4 shows that 87 percent of the sample of Indian-owned firms had 1-4 employees, 7 percent had 5-9 employees, and 6 percent had 10 or more employees. This compared with 75 percent of all Canadian businesses which had 1-4 employees, 10 percent which had 5-9 employees, and 15 percent which had 10 or more employees. Figure 3.5 shows that in comparison to all-Canadian businesses, aboriginal businesses are relatively "young": 56 percent were in business for 5 years or less, 31.7 percent were in business for 6-10 years, and 12.3 percent for 11 years or more. Nationally, 17 percent of businesses were under 5 years old, 38 percent were between 6-10 years old, and 55 percent were more than 10 years old (Department of Indian and Northern Affairs, 1986).

Figure 3.6 examines the sectoral distributions of Indian-owned businesses. It shows that in 1981, 33.3 percent of the businesses were in the resource sectors of fishing, wild rice production, farming, and hunting, while 16.9 percent were in transportation and construction, 15.1 percent were in services and communications, 15.2 percent were in retail or wholesale trade, 13.2 percent were in tourism and recreation, and 6.3 percent were in manufacturing.

Figure 3.3

Location of Indian Business Operations, 1981

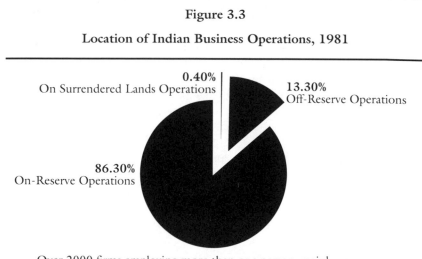

0.40%
On Surrendered Lands Operations

13.30%
Off-Reserve Operations

86.30%
On-Reserve Operations

Over 2000 firms employing more than one person, mainly on reserve.
On reserve, Indian business to population ratio is about 1:100, for Canada, 1:30.

Source: Indian and Northern Affairs Canada, *Task Force on Indian Economic Development*. Ottawa: Minister of Supply and Services, 1986.

Figure 3.4

Size of Indian Businesses (By Number of Full-time Employees)

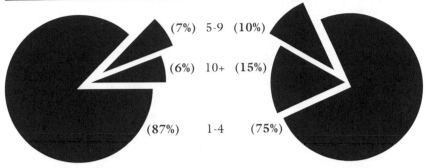

(7%)	5-9	(10%)
(6%)	10+	(15%)
(87%)	1-4	(75%)

Indian-owned firms   **All Canadian businesses**

In all, 87% of businesses have 1-4 employees, 7% of businesses have
5-9 employees, and 6% of businesses have 10 or more employees.
These percentages are relatively small by national standards (75% 1-4).

Source: Indian and Northern Affairs Canada, *Task Force on Indian Economic
Development*. Ottawa: Minister of Supply and Services, 1986.

Figure 3.5

Length of Time in Business, Indian Businesses, 1981

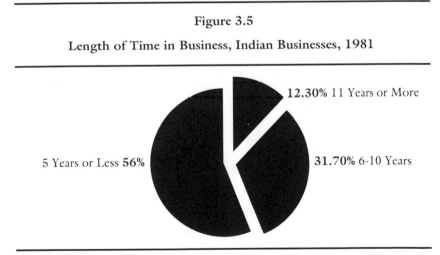

12.30% 11 Years or More

5 Years or Less **56%**

31.70% 6-10 Years

Source: Indian and Northern Affairs Canada, *Task Force on Indian Economic
Development*. Ottawa: Minister of Supply and Services, 1986.

Figure 3.6

Sectoral Distribution of Indian Businesses, 1981

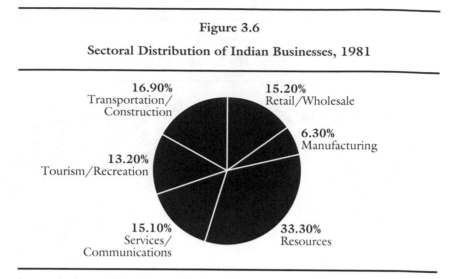

Source: Indian and Northern Affairs Canada, *Task Force on Indian Economic Development.* Ottawa: Minister of Supply and Services, 1986, p. 11.

The new petite bourgeoisie consists of aboriginal peoples who hold managerial or administrative positions, either in the private or public sector (most usually the public sector), whose authority is delegated to them from either the bourgeoisie or the political system (Veltmeyer, 1986:61). This group also consists of relatively small numbers of professionals such as lawyers, accountants, college professors, and engineers, who have control over certain skills and knowledge and who have certain degrees of autonomy over their conditions of work.

According to Table 3.5, 7.1 percent of single origin Indian men occupied managerial and administrative positions and 9.0 percent occupied professional occupations, compared with 12.6 percent and 13.1 percent, respectively, of all Canadian males. On the other hand, 5.8 percent of Indian women were in managerial and administrative occupations and 23.2 percent were in professional occupations. For all Canadian women, 7.8 percent and 20.9 percent were in managerial and professional occupations. Thus, 16.1 percent of Indian men and 31 percent of Indian women made up the new petite bourgeoisie, compared with 25.7 percent of all Canadian men and 28.7 percent of all Canadian women. While care must be used in the interpretation of these data to the extent that some of these positions may involve relatively little control over the means of production or knowledge, they nevertheless demonstrate that some aboriginal peoples are better placed occupationally than others.

As already noted in Figure 3.2, a significant proportion of this group is employed in government or government-financed positions. While not all are professionals, approximately 20 percent of the Department of

Indian Affairs and Northern Development's employees are of aboriginal ancestry (Department of Indian and Northern Affairs, 1988a:47; Gerber, 1990:76).

Historically, state policy has been contradictory with respect to its impact on the development of the aboriginal bourgeoisie and petite bourgeoisie. Some suggest that the state, in its efforts at colonization, attempted to promote an aboriginal "middle class" during the turn of the century (Dosman, 1972). This involved the creation and subsequent promotion of "leading families" on the reserve. These were the families who were most cooperative with the Indian agent; they were rewarded for their cooperation by the allocation of various political and economic resources. Like colonization strategies in other contexts, this was an attempt to create a comprador class that would drive a wedge into Indian communities to divide and rule the population and to act as agents of social control over other aboriginal peoples (Frank, 1967). As we shall discuss in more detail in Chapter 9, this remains one of the strategies of the federal government.

Other state policies, however, have directly deterred the formation of an aboriginal bourgeoisie and petite bourgeoisie. With the exception of revoking the Indian status of Indian women who married non-Indian men, state policies have nowhere had as great an impact as on these two groups. Historically, both the size and sheer existence of these classes within the aboriginal population have been severely limited by status Indians' restricted access to credit stemming from the Indian Act and the Income Tax Act. Restrictions on the mortgage of property and limited access to private-capital markets have played havoc with capital formation for the aboriginal bourgeoisie and petite bourgeoisie. As will be discussed in more detail in Chapter 9, this has forced actual and potential Indian entrepreneurs to rely on direct and indirect state financing.

However, even though the process has been painfully slow, banks now appear to view favourably money lending to Indian entrepreneurs. While obstacles to aboriginal capital formation remain, Canada's major chartered banks are coming to discover, in Martin O'Malley's (1980:37) terms:

> the potential wealth of Canada's Indians and Inuit. They see it in oil, gas, minerals, fishing, farming, residential subdivisions, native-owned and operated construction companies and scrap metal factories, and most of all in whopping land leases and land-claim settlements.

Furthermore, non-aboriginal businesses are interested in the development of joint ventures with bands. In the context of high taxes in other parts of the country, the favourable taxation regimes on reserves may make them attractive sites for future investment. In a fashion similar to Free Trade Zones in the Third World (Sassen, 1988), joint ventures established with status Indians will have access to a large and youthful

Table 3.5

Distribution of Single Origin Aboriginal and Non-Aboriginal Men and Women in "New" Petite Bourgeois Sites*, 1986

| | MALES | | | |
	Indian (Percent)	Métis (Percent)	Inuit (Percent)	Canada (Percent)
Managerial	7.1	5.3	7.8	12.6
Professional	9.0	6.8	10.9	13.1
Total Men "New" Petite Bourgeoisie	16.1	12.1	18.7	25.7
	FEMALES			
Managerial	5.8	4.7	5.8	7.8
Professional	23.2	13.6	24.5	20.9
Total Female "New" Petite Bourgeoisie	29.0	18.3	30.3	28.7

* Percentages based on totals employed in all occupations.

Source: Gerber, 1990, p. 75.

work force and natural resources, as well as a 61 percent tax write-off on investments located on Indian reserves (Saskatoon *Star-Phoenix*, 1991a).

Other bands are attempting to dovetail their interests in economic development with the Immigrant Investors Program. Bands, like many provinces, are seeking to capitalize on uncertainties surrounding mainland China's takeover of Hong Kong in 1997 by attracting resources from the immigrant entrepreneur program to help finance reserve-based industries (Saskatchewan Indian Agriculture Program, 1989).

Other programs are more specifically dovetailed to promote a petite bourgeoisie. The British Columbia Indian Fisheries Assistance Program was established in 1968 and involves loans and grants to make Indian fishermen in that province more competitive. This program provided the basis for the formation of Indian Agriculture Programs in Manitoba (MIAP) and Saskatchewan (SIAP) in 1975 and Alberta (AIAP) in 1979. These programs assist Indian people to become commercial farmers.

There appears to be some resistance on the part of other sectors of the aboriginal population to support private initiatives and to patronize privately-owned Indian businesses. For example, in order to qualify for funding under agricultural assistance programs like SIAP, AIAP, and MIAP, band members require long-term leases from the band council.

Some band councils appear reluctant to provide long-term leases to band members who wish to become farmers (Nielsen, 1985:98-99) on the grounds that reserve lands should not be used for the enhancement of individual interests. Conversely, some prospective farmers resent having to pay for land which they define as part of their treaty entitlement.

In relation to the managerial, administrative, and professional fractions of the aboriginal petite bourgeoisie who usually have a university education, state policies historically have been aimed at co-opting them through the provision of government jobs. While federal employment equity programs can be regarded as an effort to create fairness in what has been a discriminatory system of hiring and promotions, some have argued that efforts to recruit aboriginal peoples into positions within the state bureaucracy are part of a co-option strategy designed to buy off the more capable, articulate, and ambitious aboriginal leaders (Ponting and Gibbins, 1980; Boldt, 1981a).

Given the new petite bourgeoisie's participation in the bureaucratic institutions which have been the bane of many Indian people, they have been the target of some hostility and political abuse by other aboriginal peoples, and are defined as new agents of social control. In some cases, they have been characterized as "apples" — red on the outside and white on the inside — suggesting that they have sold out to "white society" because they work for the government. It appears that Phil Fontaine was unsuccessful in his 1991 bid for the national leadership of the Assembly of First Nations, in part, because of his previous employment with DIAND and his close association with the federal Liberal Party (Platiel, 1991).

Obviously, one of the key issues that will emerge if the trend towards the development of "red capitalism" continues is the extent to which economic development based on the private ownership and control of the means of production will provide the basis for new forms of conflict within aboriginal communities based on economic exploitation. Doug Daniels has perceptively highlighted a potential down side to this process:

> because labour by Indians on reserves ... are [sic] not subject to federal and provincial income taxes, Indians can be apparently paid less by multinationals and still leave a relatively high 'take home' wage. This formula could be expanded if deductions for the social programs such as Canada pension, unemployment insurance, and workman's compensation were dropped. Further savings of course could be made by ensuring non-union labour and that issues of occupational health and safety and environmental protection were skirted. In short, the 'red capitalists' have opted for the free trade zones of South East Asia and other parts of the Third World (Daniels, 1986:111).

Animosities directed to the bourgeoisie and the new and old petite bourgeoisie are reflective of antagonistic class relations; they are not solely an "Indian" phenomenon. Such conflicts within minority communities are not uncommon and reflect a complex intersection of racism, sexism, and class in the shaping of people's lives.

Conclusion

Many people assume that all aboriginal peoples share a structurally similar position in the class structure as the "underclass" of Canadian society. In this chapter, we have challenged the assumption that in the case of aboriginal peoples' "race" corresponds perfectly with class by suggesting that the position of aboriginal peoples in economic relations reflects an intersection of racism, class, and gender. While the position of aboriginal peoples stems, in part, from their aboriginality, it also stems, in part, from wider class and gender relations in Canada.

The implications of our argument are rather far-reaching. The delineation of class and gender differences within the aboriginal community is not simply an academic exercise in which aboriginal peoples are slotted into pre-existing categories simply for the sake of demonstrating the utility of a particular theory. The delineation and specification of such differences has important practical implications for the patterns of accommodation and resistance to oppression, the struggles for self-government, the nature of efforts to change the existing order, and the wider character of aboriginal politics. Thus, our discussion of class and gender within the aboriginal population is not undertaken with the aim of introducing "artificial" divisions within aboriginal communities. Such differences already exist, and it is important to begin to discuss, in an open and effective way, the consequences and potential consequences of these divisions for the future of aboriginal/non-aboriginal relations in Canada.

APPENDIX A — PROBLEMS WITH DETERMINING THE CLASS LOCATION OF ABORIGINAL PEOPLES

Measuring unemployment, labour force participation, and the class composition of capitalist societies is a difficult task, regardless of whether we are dealing with aboriginal or non-aboriginal peoples. Census data do not use typical sociological class categories, so flexibility and interpolation are necessary if such data are to be used meaningfully. When considering the position of aboriginal peoples in economic relations, the use of census material entails an additional problem. Many aboriginal peoples are distrustful of the census. Many feel that they have been "studied to death," and that information collected by the government or other agencies is not likely to be used for their benefit. It is this distrust which led, in part, to the unwillingness of 136 Indian reserves to be enumerated in the 1986 census. Members of these reserves made up about one-fifth of the reserve-based Indian population in Canada. While these are the most comprehensive and systematic data available, reservations nevertheless need to be raised about the quality of data on aboriginal peoples collected by the government.

With respect to unemployment, differing definitions and methods of data collection mean that there is no sure measure of the "real" rate of unemployment in Canada. Problems of measurement are compounded by the politically sensitive nature of high unemployment, and governments have been known to change the definitions of employment and unemployment in order to further their own political objectives (Stirling and Kouri, 1979).

Census statistics pertaining to those "not in the labour force" provide an imperfect measure of the lumpenproletariat. First, the category of not in the labour force includes those people who are unable to work for some physical reason. The largest group within this category are the aged, but it also includes those with injuries, disease, blindness, or mental illness (Veltmeyer, 1986:101). Approximately 4 percent of the aboriginal population is 65 years of age or older, and therefore should not be counted as lumpenproletarian. Also included in the category not in the labour force are those people who are attending educational institutions. These individuals should not be included in the category of lumpenproletariat.

Second, the census overestimates the size of the reserve-based aboriginal lumpenproletariat in that traditional, non-market hunting and gathering activities are not counted as "economic activity." The 1981 Canadian census, for example, did not define aboriginal peoples living on the land who consumed what they produced as participating in the labour force. If they had sold what they produced in the market, then they would have been counted as economically active. Furthermore, in rural areas where employment opportunities are more scarce than in urban areas, many aboriginal peoples have been discouraged from job search activities. While eager and able to work, some are counted as not in the labour force because they did not look for work in the week preceding the collection of information.

Third, evidence points to the existence of a hidden economy in reserve communities. This hidden economy involves small-scale, informal "businesses" involved in the exchange of goods and services. Most of these activities are legal, such as car repairs, crafts, and taxi rides, while others such as bootlegging, are illegal (Wolfe, Cunningham, and Convey, 1989). Such underground activities tend not to be recorded in census data as economic activity.

Fourth, the category of "not in the labour force" includes women who work in the household. While there are debates about the status of housework as productive labour (see Hamilton and Barrett, 1986), it is clear that homemakers should not be counted as lumpenproletarian.

Fifth, census data underestimate the size of the urban lumpenproletariat. The census has not been able to record information on urban populations that are homeless or transient, nor on those who make frequent moves to and from reserves and urban areas. The 1991 census attempted to rectify this, and estimates suggested that approximately 3 percent of urban populations are homeless and therefore not enumerated.

CHAPTER 4

SOCIAL REPRODUCTION AND THE WELFARE STATE

The title of a well-known study by anthropologist Hugh Brody (1971), *Indians on Skid Row*, expresses a stereotype of native peoples that many Canadians hold. This view is augmented by the opinion held by a plurality of Canadians, in particular by a majority of those in western Canada as well as of residents in rural areas and smaller urban centres, that native peoples receive an excessive amount of state financial assistance (see Gibbins and Ponting, 1977:66-68; Ponting, 1988a:9-10; Ponting, 1988b:16-17). Alcohol dependency, family problems, criminality, and reliance upon welfare round out this portrayal. While writers such as Brody, Gibbins, and Ponting point out that the reality, and the perceptions of this reality, are more complex than they often are assumed to be, the subtleties of native life experiences tend not to be viewed by most people as part of a coherent whole; as Ponting (1988b:17) concludes, "Native issues remain on the periphery of Canadians' consciousness." This marginalization and lack of public awareness of native concerns is gradually dissolving as the native voice assumes a significance that can no longer be excluded from the current process of national reconstitution. However, a thorough elaboration is required in order to take account of the changing and contradictory worlds occupied by First Nations peoples.

This chapter is concerned with the social relations of native life, in particular as these have been shaped through interaction with the Canadian state. This theme will be expanded upon in the analysis in the next three chapters which focus, respectively, upon education, health, and the criminal justice system. Here, we are concerned to extend our analysis of state policy from the previous two chapters in order to incorporate an understanding of the ways in which capitalist transformation and state actions affect and are affected by everyday aspects of aboriginal social life. In considering these relationships, we stress the need to avoid stereotypical images that tend to take a one-sided view of native life which either represent discriminatory positions derogatory towards native society or glorify a romanticized aboriginal lifestyle.

Consistent with positions advanced by writers as disparate as Marx (see especially Marx, 1973) and Giddens (1979; 1985), we represent culture and society, for aboriginal and non-aboriginal peoples, as integrated components within a social framework which both produces and is produced by people's everyday lived experience. Participation in society bestows upon individuals particular life chances, opportunities, and characteristics which, in turn, mold future social actions. Although individual choices and personalities influence whatever courses of action are followed, we emphasize that material conditions set the parameters within which active social forces are able to operate. With respect to Canada's native peoples, these conditions, as we have argued in the previous chapter, have involved a gradual transition from autonomous subsistence to incorporation into various types of capitalist relations. This transformative process has been accomplished to a large extent through the activities of the Canadian state and, we conclude, will not terminate in the context established by the recent focus on questions of aboriginal self-government and economic development.

NATIVE PEOPLES, SOCIAL REPRODUCTION, AND THE STATE

The relationship between Canada's aboriginal population and the state, as we have noted previously, is commonly characterized as one of wardship and paternalism. Though in many respects this is an accurate description of prevailing relations, we have argued that such a view is somewhat limited and simplistic for at least three major reasons. First, because of legal and political distinctions, governments in Canada do not treat all native peoples in the same way. Second, these terms do not take into account changing state policies and practices. Third, any analysis which focuses only upon state domination ignores the impact of aboriginal peoples upon state actions through accommodation, resistance, and conflict.

An alternative way of conceptualizing native-state relations in Canada is to examine the extent and nature of state involvement in the regulation and reproduction of social as well as economic activities. This approach enables us to emphasize how state activities are shaped by social struggles centred around the maintenance or transformation of ongoing social practices and structures. We begin by showing, briefly, how a regulation/reproduction analysis of the state stands in contrast to the major contending theories of pluralism and orthodox Marxism that have influenced, respectively, the Chicago School and internal colonial models which we discussed in Chapter 1 (see, e.g., Carnoy, 1984, for a useful extended discussion of state theories).

Pluralism, in either its liberal guise, such as the Chicago School approach, or its more conservative manifestations, views the state as an arbiter among diverse social interests. The state's role is to serve the common good, to ensure that all individuals and social groups have the right to participate democratically in decision-making on matters of public concern. While pluralists differ in terms of what they see as the most appropriate form of representation and regulation — liberals emphasize individual liberty, limited state intervention in social life, and direct participation, while conservatives stress the role of representative and corporate bodies which make decisions in the name of groups of individuals — they agree that an effective state must remain neutral from intervention by any particular social body.

This view stands more as a description of an ideal than as an explanation of real state activity. The presumption of formal political equality, for example, is contradicted by restrictions on several groups, including Canada's status Indians, who were denied the right to vote or run for public office in most provinces until after World War II and federally until 1960. Moreover, the state, by virtue of its direct and indirect linkages with the dominant economic class and other powerful social interests, is not the neutral vestige of the public interest depicted by pluralist theory. As signified by contention over such issues as aboriginal land claims and recent widespread public cynicism over Canada's elected governments, the legitimacy of state power is something that must be cultivated rather than taken for granted as part of a natural political order.

Marxist and internal colonial analyses of the state, by contrast, view state power as repressive and class interested. The modern state is not neutral, but stands as a capitalist state in the sense that it must foster the conditions which contribute to the production of commodities for profit in private hands. Orthodox Marxism portrays the state as acting directly in the interests of capital through overlapping personnel, institutional structures, and economic interests. However, in recognition of the limited ability of the orthodox analysis to account for the contradictory nature of state activity, more recent political economic analysis has attempted to address questions that concern the changing nature of state policy and practices, the role of social struggle in those changes, the potentially unique dynamics of state bureaucracies, and the relationships among the state, the economy, and other spheres of social life (Carnoy, 1984:8-9; Urry, 1981:99-100).

In order to analyze adequately the relations between the Canadian state and aboriginal peoples, it is important to recognize the central role the state has played in managing both the development of the Canadian nation and the place of aboriginal peoples within the national framework. In many respects, consistent with the Marxist orthodoxy, this has been an economic task involving policies which facilitate primitive accumulation and subsequent conditions for the emergence of industrial capital through arrangements for accessible, cost-effective land, labour power, and material resources. As we have emphasized in the previous chapters, this process has subjected native peoples to varying degrees of displacement, marginalization, and integration with respect to their economic practices.

State formation, however, also involves an administrative and inter-subjective dimension that entails the consolidation of a population as a manageable political unit. The process is one of struggle over gender and "race" identities and concerns, as well as over the production and distribution of wealth (Stasiulis, 1988). Various cleavages, whether they are constituted along the lines of gender, "race," ethnicity, language, religion, age, geography, or some other characteristic, frequently produce situations which are problematic from the point of view of those concerned with governance of the population. In Canada, repeated crises over minority language rights represent perhaps the best examples of the problems of political management (Brown, 1969). Ideally, stable and consistent administration requires an internally disciplined populace that is willing to accept the legitimacy of those who rule. However, in some instances, a successfully organized and mobilized minority group may be able to extract particular concessions from the state, while in other circumstances, political or military coercion may be employed by the state to manage its affairs. In this and subsequent chapters, we provide examples of how the Canadian state has drawn upon each of these strategies periodically — individualized discipline, political concessions, and coercion — in its efforts to manage Indian affairs.

It must be emphasized that the state, like First Nations themselves, is not a unified or monolithic organization. Divergent factions within state operations and tensions among participants at various levels of government commonly operate on the basis of particular, sometimes conflicting, agendas such as can be seen in ongoing federal-provincial conflict over the recognition of Indian land claims and the provision of social services to native peoples. Similarly, groups that seek to influence state policy and programs may strategically put pressure on or align themselves with participants in different positions or levels of government. Nonetheless, while an analysis of state activity must take into account these diverse alliances and agendas, it is important also to recognize that the state is characterized by less ephemeral structured patterns that are predominant over a long period of time. Examples of these include the gradual emergence of the welfare state in the 20th century and the subsequent neoconservative attacks on state growth since the early 1980s (Panitch, 1977; Mishra, 1986). Put in the language with which we began this section, there is ongoing struggle and indeterminacy as well as systematic regularity in the ways in which the state regulates social life for the reproduction of economic and political relations.

STATE ORGANIZATION AND THE TRANSFORMATION OF ABORIGINAL PEOPLES' SOCIAL CONDITIONS

Prior to contact with Europeans, aboriginal peoples in North America engaged in a diverse range of cultural practices that reflected their geographical and social milieu. There is an abundant literature that details the richness and variety of native peoples' interpersonal and institutional experiences over several centuries. (Our intention is not to replicate these descriptions here. See, e.g., Jenness, 1977; McMillan, 1988; Patterson, 1972; and Trigger, 1985, for details). What is significant is that, usually more directly than with the abstract aspects of modern nation-states, the social formations emerged around the specific material needs of each particular group (Cox, 1987a). First Nations political, economic, and social practices provided a resiliency that had contradictory implications. Initially, at least, these cultural practices contributed to tribal survival and offered a basis of resistance against colonization by Europeans, but they sometimes proved dangerous, such as in instances when healing rites and contact with kinship networks intensified the spread of epidemics; at the same time, they were both useful and threatening to Europeans who had alternative agendas. Rituals such as the potlatch ceremony, which to an outside observer might appear to be a primitive remnant of an unsophisticated society, and which were actively suppressed by missionaries and government officials in the late 19th and early 20th centuries, were important for maintaining social cohesion even after their immediate economic purposes were no longer apparent (LaViolette, 1973).

Intertribal contact and subsequent relations with Europeans produced a vast array of modifications in social arrangements as new alliances, hunting and trading patterns, and material resources and products were imposed or assimilated within existing patterns. Aboriginal peoples' ability, at least in a selective manner, to accommodate social and economic transformations was particularly important for the first European traders and colonizers who depended upon natives' knowledge and skills in order to survive in unfamiliar and often hostile environments (Wilson, 1986:66). With greater European self-sufficiency, however, the ongoing erosion of aboriginal self-sufficiency became both a by-product and an objective of colonial policy. Under the fur trade, for example, traditional subsistence skills were necessary for survival and success on the traplines. At the same time, though, it was in the interests of the trading companies to compel the trappers to trade their furs for trading post goods or cash rather than to be left with the opportunity for autonomous subsistence.

In short, the expansion of the mercantile system was characterized by contradictory dependencies and modes of integration. A discriminatory pricing system, especially after the merger of the Northwest and Hudson's Bay Trading companies in 1821, combined with growing reliance upon imported goods and shortages of traditional game, created poverty, dependence, and the fragmentation of clan networks among Indian people in the West (Driben and Trudeau, 1983:18). European officers employed political restrictions upon and sexual liaisons with Indian women to facilitate both alliances with and destruction of clan networks (Bourgeault, 1983). Intermarriage and relationships with the children of mixed European and Indian parentage produced further social categories within the complex class and social organization of both the fur trade and aboriginal societies (Brown, 1982:44). While tribal groups had some ability to control their own affairs, sometimes resisting and imposing conditions upon Europeans' activities, their material circumstances became fundamentally altered as they followed new trapping and trading circuits or settled in communities around trading posts. As Van Kirk (1980) demonstrates, fur trade society was multidimensional as class, "race," and gender alignments did not neatly correspond to any single power dimension or division of labour.

Indian conditions across Canada therefore varied widely during the first half of the 19th century amidst the declining importance of the fur trade and its associated military alliances, accompanied by an influx of settlers and the development of alternative forms of economic enterprise. As the previous chapter has shown, Indians in some regions, particularly in eastern Canada, came to be integrated into wage labour markets, while impoverishment and lack of a resource base was common among natives in regions most affected by the fur trade and subsequent displacement due to economic development; at the same time, Indians in northern and other remote areas were often able to maintain traditional patterns of subsistence (Cox, 1987b). It was within this setting that the nascent Canadian state consolidated its jurisdiction over Indian affairs in the context of a shift from mercantile to industrial capitalist development.

Conceptualized as forms of regulation and social reproduction, the state has had to contend with two major preoccupations in its efforts to manage Indian affairs — first, the removal of aboriginal peoples and aboriginal title as possible impediments to competing priorities of economic and political development; and second, the establishment of political and social conditions which ensure that Indian affairs are consistent with wider national development policies and practices. The first task, as we elaborated in Chapter 2, was accomplished formally through several pieces of legislation, notably the enactment of a comprehensive, consolidated Indian Act in 1876, and the signing of the treaties whereby native peoples' aboriginal title to most of Canada's land mass was ceded to the state between 1850 and 1923 in exchange for certain legal obligations (see Frideres, 1988:25ff., for details). The enforcement of both tasks was facilitated by the gradual creation of an administrative and institutional apparatus that penetrated, often in minute ways, Indians' daily lives.

In other words, state actions have been motivated in large part by a desire on the part of reformers as well as employers to regulate the kinds of people that are produced within a political unit (Corrigan and Sayer, 1985; Curtis, 1988). Part of the rationale for the state's involvement in the restructuring of natives' lives, as the previous chapters stress, was the desire to wean aboriginal peoples from either traditional subsistence (for which opportunities were diminishing in the face of non-aboriginal settlement and development of lands) or dependency and starvation, through entry into agricultural and wage labour pursuits. These economically motivated actions, in turn, were also guided by social and political considerations intended to "Christianize" natives and transform their total way of life.

Diverse Indian cultural practices designated as "traditional" were undermined both ideologically (viewed as uncivilized, backwards, and heathen) and materially (through the creation of circumstances which prohibited or restricted opportunities for their realization). The term "reserves," for instance, denotes the holding in trust by the state not only of lands, but also of human labour power. Aboriginal peoples, insofar as they constitute a minority excluded from opportunities and privileges determined by Eurocentric visions of Canadian society, share a common position with non-white immigrant groups. However, there is a significant difference in that whereas the state can control and monitor, through immigration policy, the initial entry of non-white labour into the country, the prior existence of First Nations peoples has been problematic for the state. Consequently, the twin goals of protection and assimilation as established in the federal government's 19th-century Indian policy provided the state with a potential means to monitor and regulate both the supply and the movement of Indian labour power. The basis upon which this policy emerged, one of careful regulation combined with exclusion from certain legal rights, was recognized as early as the mid-19th century by a British Commonwealth organization, the Aborigines' Protection Society, which in its 1846 annual report commented in reference to Indians in New Brunswick that

> Though the Indians recognize the authority of the British Government, and are entitled to the protection of British law, their position is anomalous, inasmuch as they do not participate in some of the most important rights of British subjects — they have no individual property in the land, and they take no part in elections or other public affairs of a local or general character, in which respect their position is far worse than that of any foreign emigrant (Aborigines' Protection Society, 1846:15-16).

Until 1985, the Indian Act required evidence of readiness for assimilation as determined by the Minister of Indian Affairs (or, in the case of women, marriage to a non-Indian man) as the prerequisite for enfranchisement, signifying the formal designation of citizenship rights. Even before confederation, as Tobias (1987:148) stresses, the reserve system "came to be regarded as a training ground in 'civilization' where the

Indian could be taught to live like a European with European values, and thus made capable of being assimilated." The assimilationist project, then, consisted not only of an economic dimension, as determined by successful farming practice or paid employment, but also, significantly, of a moral dimension which involved the attainment of personal characteristics deemed to be worthy by Indian Affairs officials.

The interlocking nature of these dual state objectives of economic discipline and sociopolitical control is illustrated by the words of Duncan Campbell Scott, who, in 1931, as Deputy Superintendent of Indian Affairs, defended the federal government's policy of banning Indian cultural activities such as the sundance and potlatch ceremonies:

> The department is confronted with serious problems in the slow process of weaning the Indian from his primitive state.... [Through participation in the sundance at fairs, stampedes and other events] the Indians are induced to leave their reserves for considerable periods, and generally at times of the year when they should be engaged with their agricultural duties....
>
> [Moreover],... Before the advent of the white man, this plan [the potlatch ceremony] undoubtedly served a useful purpose and was adequate to the needs of the people. Obviously, however, with the introduction of the new money system of economics; the engagement of Indians as wage earners in industry, the effects of the pot-latch, if the practice were unchecked, would be disastrous (Scott, 1931:25-26).

Government policy towards Indians, notably as encoded in legislation such as the Indian Act, is inherently contradictory in that it obligates the state to recognize the "special status" of those it defines as Indians, while at the same time the state is authorized to set the conditions for the extinguishment of any distinct status. A document produced late in the 19th century to quell the fears of prospective immigrants to western Canada about a potential "Indian problem" outlines clearly the many facets of those policies, including the settlement and dispersal of the aboriginal population on scattered reserves; the "civilizing and Christianizing" impact of missionaries; the policy of domestification on agricultural lands; the provision of state services through hospitals and education; and police and military roles in the maintenance of "law and order" (Richardson 1886: 26-29).

State activity, as we argued in Chapter 2, signified as a whole nothing less than a prolonged, systematic process of cultural genocide in the sense that the administration of economic, justice, welfare, education, and health care policies sought to destroy the fabric of First Nations life. Administratively, the main dilemma for state officials was what, if anything, the abandoned life practices were to be replaced with and how resistance by Indian communities could be dealt with.

Reconstructing Family and Kinship Relations

From a Eurocentric viewpoint, families stand at the centre of private life, supplying individuals and family members with a nurturing environment separate from the demands of the outside public realm. However, as critics like Christopher Lasch (1977) emphasize, this apparent public/private dichotomy which portrays families as "havens in a heartless world" ignores the complex ways in which internal family dynamics interact with forces outside the family unit. Images of "the family" that adopt uncritically a notion of what constitutes the "ideal" family serve as ideologies which oversimplify the real diversity of family forms and which, when used to guide public policy, have serious consequences for the lives of particular groups of people (Eichler, 1988). The family ideal of a husband employed outside the household whose children and domestic needs are catered to by a stay-at-home wife, for instance, has emerged as a means to stabilize labour force patterns and social relationships based on high economic productivity and mass consumption of commodified goods and services (Gaffield, 1990). However, under advanced capitalism, the conditions for maintaining stable family life are also undermined by such factors as changing labour markets, declining real wages and the need for multiple family wage earners, and new demands in the domestic sphere. Consequently, intervention increases by state officials, professional experts, and social reformers who often have a direct interest in normalization, or the active promotion and enforcement of policies and lifestyles which facilitate adherence to, and penalize deviation from, specific family forms (Miller, 1991).

The history of state intervention in aboriginal affairs has revolved in large part around such attempts to decenter and reconstruct family relations amidst distinct periods of capitalist development. In effect, state institutions and activities assumed the role of determining what kinds of persons Indians were to become and in what conditions they would exist. Civil life had to be restructured because "Indianness," however it was conceptualized, was deemed to be inadequate for people whose eventual destinies were intended to be as full Canadian citizens. The process of normalization involved the creation of regulations that simultaneously undercut long-standing kinship and tribal relations and forced their replacement with European-based standards appropriate to emergent positions in or at the margins of wage labour markets.

For several centuries, there was not a single, unitary pattern of aboriginal family and kinship relations across North America (Jenness, 1977:154-158). This diversity, particularly with respect to alternative marriage practices, came to signify for missionaries and state officials an abhorrent, culturally backward social life. Especially with the decline of the fur trade, Christian missionaries engaged in what LaViolette (1973:18) calls "an institutionalized mode of cultural dismemberment and reconstruction" through the exposure and denunciation of presumed practices of heathenism such as cannibalism, random violence, lack of respect for private property, pagan spiritualism, and sexual promiscuity. These efforts were not always successful. Because of varying forms of economic activity and institutional linkages with white communities, class and occupational factors as well as gender divisions of labour tended to be at least as important as, if not more significant than, ethnicity in the determination of marital and family patterns (Gorham, 1987:48; Jamieson, 1978:19). Some practices such as "customary marriages" of common-law relations between European traders and Indian women even gained legal sanction between 1869 and 1951 (Jamieson, 1978:17).

Nonetheless, the thrust of ongoing intervention by the state was aimed at producing both the material and cultural conditions which would further the degree of conformity with anglo-European standards. The federal government's intentions were spelled out by Lieutenant-Governor Archibald of Manitoba in an address to Indians involved in negotiations for Treaty Number One, in 1871:

> [The Queen] wishes her red children to be happy and contented. She wishes them to live in comfort. She would like them to adopt the habits of the whites, to till land and raise food, and store it up against a time of want. She thinks this would be the best thing for her red children to do, that it would make them safer from famine and distress, and make their homes more comfortable.
>
> But the Queen, though she may think it good for you to adopt civilized habits, has no idea of compelling you to do so. This she leaves to your choice, and you need not live like the white man unless you can be persuaded to do so of your own free will (Morris, 1880:28).

The task of "persuasion" was accomplished through a variety of mechanisms which restricted the practice of alternatives. The process of settlement and land cultivation involved the assumption, sometimes stated explicitly, that the nuclear family system composed of a legitimately married male and female and their direct offspring, would prevail. The treaties signed after the mid-19th century made reference to families as the basis for the allocation of land and annuity payments, with the post-confederation treaties specifying five family members as the norm (Morris, 1880). The dispersal of land to individual family units, combined with temporary prohibitions against the use of mechanized devices on the land, sought to ensure a gradual evolution from a state of tribal autonomy to one of supposedly complete integration into capitalist social and political relations (Tobias, 1987:152). The treaty-making process replaced informal social and community structures with a rigid distinction between Indians and non-Indians that, as Jamieson (1978:41) observes, signified "the imposition on the Indian families and bands of categories and racial divisions which were against the expressed desire of the Indians and contrary to their perception of band affiliation."

The Indian Act, in addition to granting broad powers to the Department of Indian Affairs to define who is an Indian and to regulate Indian band activities, empowers the government, among other things, to direct entitlement money to the dependants of an Indian who deserted or separated from a spouse or family under particular conditions (R.S. 1985, c.I-5, s. 68) and to regulate housing, sanitary, and other living conditions on reserves (R.S. 1985, c.I-5, s. 73). The presence of the Indian agent in the structure of administration of Indian affairs provided the state with a cadre of local authorities who were empowered to regulate a detailed range of social and economic life activities on the reserves. Government trusteeship of Indian lands, as Shumiatcher (1971:51) observes, was akin to "the kind of arrangement that a far-seeing and beneficent Victorian father might well create for the use and protection of his spendthrift and improvident son in order to save him from his own folly or stupidity," thereby restricting the Indians' ability to accomplish the responsible self-development that was the declared aim of Indian policy.

One of the key tools employed by the state in the intended process of Indian settlement and assimilation was formal education, which is discussed in greater detail in the next chapter. What is noteworthy here is that education, like other state practices, had contradictory implications for native peoples. Significantly, formal guidelines for state jurisdiction over Indian children were consistent with, and sometimes exceeded, the establishment of more general initiatives to regulate childhood and family life throughout Canada. Beginning in the last two decades of the 19th century, and influenced by moral reformers seeking "proper" modes of child development in the context of industrial development, provincial and federal governments introduced a variety of legislative regulations including compulsory school attendance, sanctions against juvenile delinquency, and the empowerment of state authorities such as teachers and court officials to act as surrogate parents "in the best interests of the child" through *parens patriae* and *in loco parentis* (Sutherland, 1976). The federal government's prior assertion of sweeping paternalistic powers over Indian affairs made education a central priority in its efforts to treat as children, and acculturate, all Indian people.

While schooling under the tutelage of missionaries and trading company officials had emerged on a sporadic basis throughout the 19th century, several groups acknowledged the advantages of formal educational provisions as a means to transform Indians' lives. Initial educational efforts were only partially successful in this endeavour. Patterson (1972:110) observes that, "The new education had grown out of a different cultural experience and was being grafted on imperfectly, so that it did not 'take' as had been intended." In the latter half of the 19th century, native elders, in the face of the demise of traditional means of self-sufficiency and cognizant of the advantages of literacy, pressed for the inclusion of education rights in treaty negotiations on the Prairies (Stevenson, 1991). Educators and other school promoters stressed the benefits of schooling not merely in terms of useful skills and content, but primarily for its ability to shape the moral and political development of individuals as worthy citizens. Missionaries, not always naively, also viewed schooling as a vehicle through which the Indian could be transformed from an uncivilized state to a valued Christian subject with distinctly new class and gender identities.

Under these conditions, the federal Conservative government of John A. Macdonald, linking its task of stabilizing the native population with its national policy of providing conditions for domestic economic growth, was receptive to Nicholas Flood Davin's recommendation in 1879 to establish a system of residential and industrial schools for Indians. These schools were organized in such a way as to provide maximum control by educational authorities over Indian children. Children were separated from their families and communities for most of the year. Strict daily regimens of activity and prohibitions against the practice of native customs were justified by the aim of assimilation. For several decades, widespread incidences of physical, mental, and sexual abuse, which only recently have become matters of public concern, contributed to the destabilization of native personalities and communities. Despite their serious problems, the residential schools did have contradictory consequences for native peoples. Many individuals were able to acquire useful skills and knowledge and the schools provided a basis for the emergence of a corps of native leaders who were familiar with the workings of the wider political system. In some instances, reflecting a combination of student resistance and, at times, acquiescence by school authorities, Indian traditions remained alive due to the practice of cultural activities and the development of strong school-community ties (Gresko, 1986). Nonetheless, the overall impact of the schools, in conjunction with other socioeconomic factors, was highly detrimental to native solidarity and survival.

Liquor, disease, and atrocities committed by white traders and settlers contributed to the further demise of aboriginal community structures. Describing changes that occurred to the Blackfeet Indians of the southern Prairies in a short time span between the early 1860s and 1876, for example, missionary C. Scollen wrote to Lieutenant-Governor Morris of the Northwest Territories that

> [Over a fifteen year period] their number has decreased to less than one half, and their systematic organizations have fallen into decay; in fact they have been utterly demoralized as a people. This sudden decadence has been brought on by two causes: 1. About ten years ago the Americans crossed the line and established themselves on Pelly River, where they carried on to an extraordinary extent the illicit traffic in intoxicating liquor to the Blackfeet. The fiery water flowed as freely, if I

may use the metaphor, as the streams running from the Rocky Mountains, and hundreds of the poor Indians fell victims to the white man's craving for money, some poisoned, some frozen to death whilst in a state of intoxication, and many shot down by American bullets. 2. Then in 1870 came that disease so fatal to Indians, the small-pox, which told upon the Blackfeet with terrible effect, destroying between six hundred and eight hundred of them. Surviving relatives went more and more for the use of alcohol; they endeavoured to drown their grief in the poisonous beverage. They sold their robes and their horses by the hundred for it, and now they began killing one another, so that in a short time they were divided into several small parties, afraid to meet (Morris, 1880:248).

The disasters outlined in this account illustrate the interpenetration of several factors that contributed to the demise of aboriginal solidarity and self-sufficiency. While these conditions cannot be generalized to all aboriginal peoples because of significant regional and temporal variation, they demonstrate the powerful forces that have operated to create dependency and marginalization among large segments of the native population.

The Impact of Child Welfare Practices

A further factor in the destruction of First Nations has been the impact of child welfare policies and practices. Some commentators, such as Hudson and McKenzie (1981), see a direct connection between residential schooling and child welfare patterns through the extension of colonial control over native peoples. As with residential schooling, however, the implementation of child welfare has also been marked by contradictory motivations and developments. Early missionaries and European officials, for instance, often encouraged the adoption of Indian children by whites to "save" the child from heathen influences and to demonstrate the advantages of Christian family life. Selected children of mixed marriages or common-law relationships were sent to Europe for training and education, especially by fathers who had sufficient wealth and status in colonial economic and political hierarchies. These arrangements facilitated the process of colonial rule by posing an elite class of intermediaries between the administration and local aboriginal communities (Bourgeault, 1983), but they also produced political and social linkages that were important for the development of organized native resistance groups (Brown, 1982). State efforts to "normalize" family relations posed new problems for the re-establishment of stable social relations in aboriginal communities, especially as questions about legitimacy of marriage and offspring became intertwined with legal definitions and treaty rights concerning Indians. Moreover, practices such as slavery continued into the 20th century despite official pronouncements and legislation prohibiting them. Correspondence between Indian Affairs officials, for example, notes the case in 1912 of a young Indian girl named Daisy, less than 13 years old, purchased for $500 to live with a man in northwestern British Columbia (Campbell, 1912; McLean, 1912). The dual process whereby initiatives to strengthen and stabilize family relations often coexisted with practices that had the opposite effect of destroying kin and community support has remained a continuing reality produced by the interplay among government activity, economic development, and aboriginal peoples.

The post-World War II expansion of industrial capitalism into northern Canada and the "welfare economy" that characterized native peoples' economic marginalization were accompanied by the formalization of many previous experiences with the child welfare system. Social workers, armed with a mandate to seek out and provide assistance to "problem" families, and possessed by a reformist zeal, engaged in what would become in some communities nearly a wholesale removal of children from their family environments. Norms of child care based upon standards of constant in-home parental presence did not take into account the more open extended family relationships in which aunts, uncles, cousins, and grandparents shared with parents and their offspring in informal but well-established ways the tasks of communal welfare. Upon the death of a parent, or in cases of economic need or temporary absences, relatives by custom are available to provide child care or to arrange adoptions. Until recently, these arrangements have not been regarded by social services authorities as legitimate, with important implications for aboriginal family life. The existence of informal support mechanisms has meant that native society has in many instances been more stable than commonly supposed. Failure to recognize their legitimacy makes children living in such conditions vulnerable to apprehension by state agencies, thereby contributing to social dislocation and potential family breakdown.

In addition to the welfare system's potential definition of unproblematic situations as problematic, disadvantaged social and economic conditions have produced circumstances that do make it difficult for many native peoples to raise and maintain children adequately (Ward, 1984:46-47). These problems, it must be stressed, are related to the realities of social class and poverty, not to characteristics of native peoples. Factors such as unemployment, migration from reserves to urban areas, and lack of affordable housing and food supplies frequently become intertwined with problems such as alcoholism and physical and emotional abuse of family members, contributing to family instability. As with the delivery of other social services to native communities, the programs and facilities that deal with real problems are often severely inadequate, while mechanisms which label and treat somewhat benign phenomena as problems have a powerful and enduring presence. Recent revelations about the traumas of residential schooling and inappropriate foster home placement, for example, have pointed to a cycle of victimization that is passed on to succeeding generations.

Native peoples have come to be extensively involved with the child welfare system, usually as clients. Data, though often incomplete or defined across inconsistent baselines, reveal that in virtually all Canadian provinces and territories, native children are overrepresented as a proportion of children who are in foster homes, placed for adoption, or in the care of government agencies. The relative recency and magnitude of this phenomenon is illustrated by the case of British Columbia, which is by no means atypical, where between 1955 and 1964 the proportion of native children relative to the total number of children under the care of the provincial child welfare branch increased from less than 1 percent to 34.2 percent (Johnston, 1983:23). By the end of the 1970s, the degree of native overrepresentation in the child welfare system had increased even further:

> Over 3.4% of status Indian children are in the substitute care of provincial and federal child welfare agencies — more than three times the rate for all Canadian children. Native children make up 39% of the children in care in British Columbia, 40% in Alberta, 50% in Saskatchewan and 60% in Manitoba. Yet while Indian kids are entering care at an increasing rate, their rate of discharge is well below that of white children (National Council of Welfare, 1979:7).

As the data in Table 4.1 indicate, these proportions have begun to decline from the high levels of the late 1970s, with 4.0 percent of on-reserve children under non-parental care in 1990-91. This shift, as will be discussed later in this section, can be attributed in large part to a recent emphasis upon the transfer of child welfare services to band control.

These trends reveal that what is significant is not only the magnitude, but also the nature, of native child welfare practices. Aboriginal children have tended to be placed predominantly in homes and institutions outside their own communities, largely in urban centres far from their homes, in other provinces and, in cases of adoptions, the United States. The problem was particularly acute in the prairie provinces and northern territories, especially in Manitoba, where 55 percent of all treaty Indian children and 40 percent of all Métis children placed for adoption in 1981 were placed outside the province, compared with 7 percent of all Caucasian children placed for adoption; just over 12 percent of the total placements were made in the United States, 98 percent of which were aboriginal children (Review Committee on Indian and Métis Adoptions and Placements, 1983:6). The absence of services and care facilities on or adjacent to reserves and remote communities exacerbated the problem. In the North, typically, children were airlifted from their home communities to urban centres by social workers who were unprepared for life in the region, while in southern centres, a growing number of migrant natives became a ready source of new clients for an expanding corps of social services personnel (Hudson, 1987:252).

Table 4.1

On-Reserve Children in Care, Registered Indian Population,
Canada, 1966/67 - 1990-91

Fiscal Year	Children in Care [1]	Children Aged 16 and under	Fiscal Year	Children in Care [1]	Children Aged 16 and under
		Percent			Percent
1966/67	3201	93 101	3.4	1978/79	6177	94 866	6.5
1967/68	3946	93 484	4.2	1979/80	5820	94 414	6.2
1968/69	4310	94 616	4.6	1980/81	5716	94 916	6.0
1969/70	4861	94 698	5.1	1981/82	5144	94 608	5.4
1970/71	5156	95 048	5.4	1982/83	4577	96 105	4.8
1971/72	5336	94 777	5.6	1983/84	4105	98 379	4.2
1972/73	5336	94 906	5.6	1984/85	3887	97 586	4.0
1973/74	5582	94 634	5.9	1985/86	4000	99 213	4.0
1974/75	5817	96 960	6.0	1986/87	3603	101 841	3.5
1975/76	6078	96 493	6.3	1987/88	3836	101 537	3.8
1976/77	6247	96 417	6.5	1988/89	3989	102 529	3.9
1977/78	6017	96 780	6.2	1989/90	4178	105 992	3.9
				1990/91	4352	109 165	4.0

Notes:
1. The total number of children in care calculated by Social Development Branch is obtained by dividing the total number of case-days by 365. Child care cases do not include preventive and alternate approaches to child and family services (eg. homemakers). Excludes Indians residing in the N.W.T. and Newfoundland. Children in care is defined as the number of children who had to placed away from parental care in order to protect them from neglect and/or abuse or prevent neglect and/or abuse.

Source: Indian and Northern Affairs Canada, *Basic Departmental Data 1991.* Ottawa: Minister of Supply and Services Canada, 1991, Cat. No. r-12-7/1990E; p. 47.

The massive transfer of native children from parental care into the child welfare system was a result of several interrelated developments. Specific events must be understood in the context of the changing position of aboriginal peoples under capitalist development, first as marginalized from wage labour participation during economic restructuring in the 1930s and then, especially after the late 1960s, increasingly reintegrated from low cost labour into a more sophisticated range of labour market positions under advanced capitalism. Prior to the 1960s, provincial governments were reluctant to extend their delivery of child welfare and other social services to children on reserves because of federal responsibility for registered Indians. Government jurisdictional matters were reassessed in the wake of state responsiveness to the economic crisis of the 1930s and the federal government's subsequent efforts to coordinate Canada's involvement in World War II. After the war, increasing northern development and migration from reserves to urban areas brought into focus previously hidden questions about native welfare. Under these circumstances, the federal government appointed in 1946 a Special Joint Committee of the Senate and House of Commons to investigate the Indian Act. As part of its recommendations for wholesale changes to the act in order to facilitate "the gradual transition of Indians from wardship to citizenship," the committee recommended that arrangements be made between federal and provincial governments for the delivery and financing of provincial social services to Indians (Leslie and Maguire, 1978:143-145). The latter points echoed arguments made in several submissions to the committee, notably by the Canadian Welfare Council and the Canadian Association of Social Workers (1947:158-161), which argued with respect to existing child welfare services in residential schools that "we feel that the existing program falls short of social adequacy in that it fails to provide Indian children with standards of care comparable to those developed by the more advanced child care services in the country," and by the Vancouver Branch of the Canadian Civil Liberties Association (1947:2) which sought an end to policies that made Canadian Indians "a backward and a depressed race whose morale is shattered and whose self-confidence is lost." Changes to the Indian Act in 1951 that moved in the direction of authorizing (but without federal funding) provincial governments to provide child welfare services to on-reserve Indians facilitated the emergence of a haphazard series of arrangements whereby, as Johnston (1983:3) observes, "only some provincial child welfare programs were extended to residents of some reserves in some provinces." Where provincial assistance was offered, it tended to be limited only to the most high-risk cases, and usually involved the apprehension of the child rather than the extension to family members of preventative or remedial services (Hepworth, 1980:113; Johnston, 1983:66).

Paradoxically, lack of attentiveness to the underlying causes of socially and economically inadequate conditions on many reserves placed extremely high numbers of Indian children at risk or in situations where authorities defined them as being at risk. Several "common patterns of practice" as identified by a federal Child and Family Services Task Force in 1987 have contributed to what could mildly be characterized as a crisis of Indian child welfare:

1. Indian children predominantly have been placed into care under court orders (vs consent agreements);
2. Indian children predominantly have been placed into care outside their community;
3. Indian children have remained in care longer than non-native children;
4. Indian children have more frequently moved out of care through

adoption or self-care (at age 18 or 19) than through returning to their parent's home;

5. the first action by the provincial child authority predominantly has been apprehension of Indian children; and

6. little, if any, support and assistance has been provided to Indian parents (Indian and Northern Affairs Canada, 1987:9).

The large-scale apprehension of Indian children and their subsequent placement into institutional care, foster homes, or under-adoption contributed to severe disruptions in many aboriginal families and communities. However well-intended some of the practices may have been, their consequences surfaced in what has become a familiar litany of problems: families were broken up, with siblings often placed in different homes or agencies separated by vast physical and social distances; inadequate and culturally insensitive screening, placement, and follow-up services contributed to and perpetuated emotional suffering and sometimes physical abuse of native children; frequent movement between placement settings, particularly among foster homes and institutional care, created a sense of abandonment and an unstable climate for personal development; and the symptoms generated by family breakdown for children and parents alike, including personality disorders, substance abuse, violent behaviour, and criminal activity, became, in turn, the foundation for the recurrence of these phenomena from generation to generation.

Mounting public concern over the problems of native child welfare in the 1970s and 1980s corresponded with rising native demands for self-governance, the federal government's search for alternatives to its jurisdiction over Indian affairs, and the increasing value placed upon aboriginal labour power in different class positions. Consistent with the desire by First Nations organizations that aboriginal peoples become integrally involved in the organization and delivery of services in areas such as education, health care, and economic development, the question of Indian control over Indian child welfare became a matter of central concern. The National Indian Brotherhood, for example, in 1979 stressed the need for "Indian development of Indian policy" based on the principle that "The Indian family is the integral foundation of Indian social structure." These declarations were given substance by several initiatives beginning with such notable cases as the 1975 tripartite agreement, whereby the Blackfoot Band in Alberta administered on-reserve child welfare services under the provincial Department of Social Services and Community Health, funded by the federal government; the 1980 by-law passed by the Spallumcheen band council, and subsequently consented to by the British Columbia and federal governments, which authorized the band to have exclusive jurisdiction over the welfare of its children; and the 1982 Canada-Manitoba-Indian Child Welfare Agreement which, following earlier agreements covering northern Manitoba and eight bands in the province's south, spells out the framework by which bands may administer, deliver, and fund on-reserve child and family services (see Hudson, 1987; Johnston, 1983:106-115; and MacDonald, 1987, for details).

Child welfare services have also been transferred to bands as part of more comprehensive aboriginal self-government agreements including the 1975 James Bay and Northern Quebec Agreement, the 1978 Northeastern Quebec Agreement, and federal and British Columbia legislation, which in 1988 gave the Sechelt band the powers of municipal self-government (see Hawkes, 1989, for details of these arrangements). By 1986-87, over half of the Indian bands in Canada had entered into various service agreements — 155 in total — which entitled the bands, with federal funding, either to provide their own child welfare services or to have access to provincial services (Indian and Northern Affairs Canada, 1987:1). In 1989-90, 36 of these agreements, involving 193 bands, were renewed (Indian and Northern Affairs Canada, 1990b:20). In addition, a variety of service arrangements for non-status Indians, Métis, and Indians living off reserve have been developed across the country in recent years.

In a relatively short period of time, the changes in child welfare administrative and program delivery procedures have had some positive impact on band, community, and family relations. In particular, participation by and consultation with First Nations peoples have provided avenues for raising and responding to critical issues in a manner sensitive to local needs. The federal Child and Family Services Task Force reported that the shift to band control has had several beneficial consequences, including gradual reductions in the numbers of children in care and in the period of time under substitute care, a high proportion of parental consent in placement decisions, a relatively low rate of placement in out-of-home institutional settings, a high proportion of placements in the child's home community, and emphasis on preventive, remedial, and family support services rather than on mere crisis intervention (Indian and Northern Affairs Canada, 1987:10-11).

However, some commentators, including Wharf (1989:33-34), caution that, despite the favourable impact of a general shift towards community control and away from prevention to intervention in child welfare practices, First Nations programs have not been entirely successful due to such problems as domination by local elites, community isolation from better-equipped outside programs and services, and inadequate resources. Allegations that political considerations outweighed concern about child welfare, for example, surrounded reports in 1987 of child abuse resulting from improper placement of children by the Awasis Agency into homes on reserves in northern Manitoba (York, 1987:A4).

Aboriginal control over child welfare services is highly constrained by ambivalence or conflict produced through existing jurisdictional boundaries, institutional arrangements, and federal and provincial legislation (Hudson, 1989:257-259). These problems, in many respects, reflect the contradictory positions of aboriginal peoples with regard to their changing economic and political status under advanced capitalism. A comment made in 1966 by British Columbia's then Minister of Municipal Affairs, Daniel Campbell, is instructive in this regard. Campbell argued that while in principle it would be a "good idea" to enable Indian reserves to have legislative powers equivalent to municipalities, a practical barrier was posed through government trusteeship of Indian land: "The problem is that municipal government has only one good reason for existence, and that is the looking after of private property" (Indian-Eskimo Association of Canada, 1966:9). The result, in the midst of the transformation of property relations among aboriginal peoples as observed in Chapter 3, is a disparate collection of arrangements which displays little uniformity across the country. The provision of services to some Indian bands, to Indians living off reserve, and to non-status Indians and Métis in particular, is often uncertain and inadequate (Barkwell, Longclaws, and Chartrand, 1989). Moreover, any child welfare programs that do not address the underlying social, economic, and emotional causes of family problems are limited in the degree to which they can be effective.

In many ways, the shift to First Nations control over their own child welfare services signifies a major gain for native peoples in their struggles to escape widespread marginalization and to attain self-government. The demise of the highly interventionist regimes of residential schooling and child welfare practices has provided native peoples with opportunities to re-establish stable patterns of family and community life. However, the struggle for aboriginal self-determination involves differing visions of the nature of and the means to accomplish self-government, with each often contended vigorously by particular organizational alliances (Boisvert, 1985). The consequences of this fragmentation, with ensuing outcomes reflecting both coordinated planning and active responses to exigencies, can be seen, in part, in the tremendous diversity of arrangements which exist with respect to child welfare initiatives. Ultimately, the move to establish child welfare practices "in the best interests of the child" continues to leave unanswered questions about who is defining and directing those interests, and to what end.

Social Conditions

One indicator of change in native communities is provided by a comparison over time of the social conditions which characterize aboriginal life. As with other areas of aboriginal life and history, it is important to dispel myths and stereotypes that assume a uniformity among Indian people and their living conditions. Native peoples live in tremendously diverse situations across the country, exacerbated by recent political and economic developments. Bands which have access, both geographically and through agreements signed with federal and provincial governments, to fertile land

and resources, for example, afford opportunities for their members which are not available to less well-situated bands or to non-status Indians and Métis. Similarly, social conditions are affected by the availability and nature of such factors as employment, state support, and social programs, which are experienced differentially by people in distinct class and gender locations.

The phenomenon of migration from reserves to other regions illustrates the growing disparities among native peoples as they encounter distinctive forms of labour market, political, and social opportunities and barriers (see Figure 4.1). In 1966, about 15 percent of Canada's registered Indians lived off reserve, while by the end of 1989, that proportion had increased to 40 percent, ranging from 19.2 percent in the Northwest Territories to 50.6 percent in the Yukon, with about one-quarter of registered Indians in Quebec living off reserve, along with about one-third in the Atlantic region, Manitoba, and Alberta, and just under one-half in Ontario, Saskatchewan, and British Columbia (Department of Indian Affairs and Northern Development, 1980:134; Indian and Northern Affairs Canada, 1989b:xiii). Part of this trend can be explained by legal changes in status as a consequence of Bill C-31 which, as discussed in Chapter 2, amended the Indian Act in 1985 to reinstate band membership to eligible individuals and their offspring who previously had been defined as non-status. In 1985 and 1986, over 94 percent of the Bill C-31 population, compared with less than one-third of the "regular" registered Indian population lived off reserve (Loh, 1990:43-44). These figures are, in part, an indication of how legal status interacts with social and economic trends. In addition, given that Bill C-31 Indians constituted less than 5 percent of the total registered Indian population during those years, the trend to migration off reserves is also of more general significance.

Problems in identifying the size and distribution of the aboriginal population, especially those who are not registered Indians, makes it difficult to provide a clear comparison of social conditions between Indians living on reserves and aboriginal peoples living in other locales. However, a patchwork of studies and surveys reveals some striking disparities among native peoples as well as between natives and non-natives. Indians who live off reserve are proportionately overrepresented relative to Indians living on reserves in the middle age cohorts and underrepresented in the uppermost and lowest age cohorts: in 1986, 31.5 percent of Canada's registered Indians lived off reserve, with comparable figures of 32.1 percent for those aged 15-24, 38.3 percent for the 35-44 year cohort, and 35.5 percent for the 45-54 year cohort; by contrast, the figures were 28.0 percent for those under 15 years, 27.2 percent for those aged 65 and older, and 31.1 percent for those in the 55-64 year cohort (calculated from Loh, 1990:83-85). A greater proportion of status Indian women than men live off reserves. Off-reserve and non-status Indians and Métis peoples are also more likely to be in the labour force and to be employed, and to have higher levels of education and income than status Indians living on reserves (see Table 4.2). The relative disadvantage experienced by Indians living on reserves as depicted by these indicators reflects the consequences of a continuous cycle of events in which young Indians tend to leave the reserve in search of education and employment opportunities, thereby depriving reserve communities of a valuable supply of human resources which is crucial for future band success. These patterns are to a large extent a consequence of the absence, until relatively recently, of any sustained social and economic development opportunities on reserves, giving depth to the sense in which reserves have been holding grounds for "reserve armies of labour" which are available upon demand to perform short-term, low-cost wage labour.

Figure 4.1

Registered Indian Population Growth On and Off Reserve

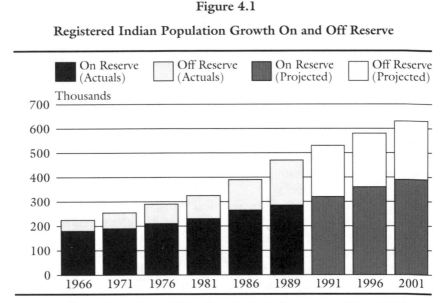

Source: Indian and Northern Affairs Canada, *Basic Departmental Data 1990.*
       Ottawa: Minister of Supply and Services Canada,
       Cat. No. R-12-7/1990E, 1990, p. 4.

Differences in living conditions on and off reserves are revealed in other ways as well. While some of these data, particularly from the 1986 census in which ninety bands refused to cooperate, must be interpreted with caution due to variations in population bases and analytical categories, the trends are sufficiently pronounced to demonstrate the existence of real disparities. Housing conditions on reserves are more likely than in other locales to be characterized by overcrowding and in need of improved facilities, utilities, and services. In 1988, the average number of persons per dwelling on reserves was 4.2, compared with a Canadian average of 2.7 (Indian and Northern Affairs Canada, 1989b:61; Statistics Canada, 1988:25). While nationally the proportion of private dwellings occupied by persons other than registered Indians and which had more than one person per room was 1.7 percent in 1986, the comparable figures for registered Indians living in dwellings which had more than one person per room were 11.3 percent for those living off reserve and 28.9 percent for those on reserve (Larocque and Gauvin, 1989:29). In that same year, 37.5 percent of dwellings occupied by Indians living on reserves, and 9.5 percent of those off reserve, compared with 5.3 percent of other private dwellings, did not have a central heating system, while figures for 1989 reveal that for dwellings on reserves, 13.9 percent lacked an adequate water supply and 20.9 percent did not have adequate sewage disposal (Larocque and Gauvin, 1989:31; Indian and Northern Affairs Canada, 1990:63). Despite the discrepancies between groups, these conditions do mark an improvement over previous years. In the early 1970s, for example, less than one-half of houses on reserves in British Columbia were considered by the Department of Health and Welfare to be in good condition, nearly two-thirds of reserve houses had inadequate heating, over one-quarter had inoperative or no toilets, over one-third had no bath or shower, one-quarter had no kitchen sink, and one-fifth had no refrigerator (British Columbia Socio-Economic Development Commission, 1977:77, 91). In 1977, only about half of dwellings on Canadian Indian reserves were considered to have adequate sewage disposal and water supply, while the average number of persons per dwelling has declined steadily since that time (Indian and Northern Affairs Canada, 1989b:61, 63). Nonetheless, the improved housing conditions belie fundamental problems related both to the unequal distribution of resources among native peoples and the continued lack of control by many natives over their lives. House (1989:50) illustrates the situation with reference to a northern Labrador coastal Inuit village, Nain, in which

> houses are provided for the people by government programmes. Contracts are awarded to white building contractors from outside the region; outside workers come in and build the houses; the unemployed Inuit wait around with little to do while their houses are being built; and the houses are built to suburban specifications with little attention to the specific housing needs of Native peoples living in the North. Native families are then assigned to the houses according to bureaucratic criteria. Often, they cannot afford to heat them properly and they are ill-equipped to look after, repair and maintain them.

While self-government provisions offer the promise of transferring benefits and employment from off-reserve sources to reserve residents,

Table 4.2

Selected Socioeconomic Indicators, National Registered Indian
and Non-Indian Populations Aged 15 And Over, Canada, 1986

Socioeconomic Indicator	Registered Indian Population			Non-Indian Population
	On Reserve	Off Reserve	Total	
Proportion with less than Grade 9 education (%)	44.7	24.4	37.2	17.1
Proportion with at least high school education (%)	21.7	37.5	27.6	55.8
Employment rate(%)	28.2	36.8	31.4	59.8
Average gross income, 1985 ($)	9300	11 000	9900	18 200

Source: Data from Larocque and Gauvin (1989, 17-25).

there is no guarantee in a class-divided society that these benefits will be shared equally among band members.

The absence or shortage of basic amenities also causes other related problems. Driben and Trudeau (1983:40), describing four native communities in northern Ontario in which running water, electricity, and sewer systems were either not available or were limited, observe that gathering fuel and water and activities such as washing and cleaning were difficult and time-consuming daily tasks, while health and safety risks were posed in the form of reliance upon combustible fuels such as kerosene, water pollution through contamination from sewage, and chill and disease from poorly-constructed, overcrowded houses.

Migration of Indians from reserves to other areas, especially to urban centres, began in the 1970s to generate a growing interest in the social conditions of native peoples living off reserves. Most studies of off-reserve natives have focused upon the disadvantages experienced by native peoples relative to other groups and the related problems of adjustment and social disorganization (see, e.g., Dosman, 1972; Nagler, 1973; Stanbury and Siegel, 1975). As with reserve life, a chronicle of unemployment or sporadic employment, poor housing conditions and overcrowded dwellings, lack of basic services, alcoholism, and ill health runs throughout portrayals of native life off the reserve. In addition, several problems such as high mobility, high crime and arrest rates, prostitution, lack of family or community support, and overt racism in employment, housing, and general social circumstances are often more pronounced for native persons who do not live on reserves. A recent survey of Indians living in

Vancouver, for example, notes that only 36.7 percent of native persons surveyed in the city had been living in the same locale for the past five years, that less than half (48 percent of the men and 42.1 percent of the women) were currently employed, despite the fact that nearly all respondents had at least some high school education, that only 9.2 percent owned their own house, and that many had experienced problems with the criminal justice system (Rowe and Associates, 1989). The report's most notable finding was the degree of migration both into and out of the Vancouver area by native peoples, especially among men in the 22-25-year age group, with an average length of stay in the area of twenty-eight weeks (Rowe and Associates, 1989:13). Similarly, Clatworthy (1981:28) observes that nearly half of native family heads who had recently migrated to Winnipeg indicated that they had lived in the city on at least one previous occasion, though he cautions that patterns of migration out of the city are not as strong as often supposed. Of status Indian household heads surveyed, only 4 percent of females aged 25 years and over, and 7 percent of males in this age group, compared with 16 percent of females under 25 and 21 percent of males under 25, planned to leave the city in the near future (Clatworthy, 1981:29).

In many ways, these trends both give rise to and reinforce common stereotypes about native peoples. Urban concentration exacerbates and makes visible problems which are otherwise hidden away on reserves out of view of the general public, sometimes leading to simplistic conclusions such as native peoples are lazy, incompetent, or culturally unable to adapt to a new environment. But the complex interpenetration of living conditions with differential labour market, political, and social circumstances contributes to a complex array of experiences within broader structures of class, "race," and gender given shape by distinct opportunities, resources, and barriers.

The phenomenon of living arrangements serves as an illustration of how these perceptions and patterns emerge. Because of apparent similarities in housing conditions for native persons living in urban centres and on rural reserves, including overcrowding and co-residence among extended family members, it is commonly concluded, as Peters (1984) points out, that natives' urban living patterns and difficulties are a result either of disorganization produced by migration to an unfamiliar setting (e.g., Dosman, 1972) or of the awkward transposition of traditional lifestyles upon a more modern urban setting (e.g., Nagler, 1973). However, Peters argues to the contrary that family and household relations among urban natives reveal a patterned system of adjustment to real limitations, notably the lack of steady employment for native males combined with the relatively greater stability provided by welfare support for women with children, rather than a "scenario of complete family disorganization and break-down" exacerbated by a constant flow of persons into and out of the household: "The method financial resources were distributed among household members suggests that there was a distinct hierarchy of responsibility: parents first supported their offspring, and aid was given to members of the extended family only when there were suffi- cient financial resources" (Peters 1984:33, 37). These patterns, it should be emphasized, tend to reinforce class inequalities among native peoples in that individuals or families with financial resources or valued skills, edu- cation, or political ties have greater opportunities for self-sufficiency. Moreover, these realities are experienced differently by men and women, who tend to have different labour market opportunities and household responsibilities.

THE MULTIFACETED EXPERIENCES OF NATIVE PEOPLES

While aggregate statistics are helpful in providing a profile of a general population, we have noted in several places that they often hide the rich diversity of the peoples being described. This is increasingly true of Canada's First Nations peoples. The urban squalor and run-down reserves that characterize life for the poorest of the nation's native peoples stand in marked contrast to the worlds occupied by the leading aboriginal profes- sionals and business and political leaders, as well by bands which have benefitted from social and economic development initiatives. Images of the "skid row" Indian are far removed from the realities of First Nations leaders negotiating complex land claims settlements and constitutional issues in elaborately furnished office complexes and hotel rooms across the country. Yet these contradictory circumstances are bound inextricably together in the unfolding scenario around which is being defined the nature and meaning of contemporary aboriginal life.

As a whole, native peoples are among the poorest and most disadvan- taged groups in Canada. The National Council on Welfare (1985:70) identifies native persons, along with the disabled, elderly widows, and per- sons with limited education, as the groups with the highest risks of poverty. Similarly, Osberg (1988:16), in a background paper prepared for the Canadian Council on Social Development, identifies native peoples, along with single parents and older workers, as groups most at risk of unemployment and dependency upon social assistance in the face of Canada's changing labour markets. Native peoples are less likely to have any income, and to have lower-than-average levels of income, than Canadians as a whole, while in terms of average incomes, all categories of native peoples rank near the bottom relative to the incomes of other eth- nic and racial groups (Gerber, 1990). Native peoples, like members of other visible minorities, are frequently the victims of social discrimination, but they are less likely to be employed and less likely to be in higher wage occupations (Commission on Equality in Employment, 1984).

Aboriginal women bear the heaviest burden of disadvantage. According to 1986 census data, women aged 15 years and over who reported aboriginal origins had a labour force participation rate of 40.2 percent, which is about two-thirds of the participation rate of 60.8 percent for aboriginal men, and just over two-thirds of the rate of 56.0 percent for non-aboriginal women; by contrast, native women had an unemployment rate of 28.2 percent, slightly lower than the comparable rate of 32.1 percent for aboriginal men and more than double the unemployment rate of 11.0 percent for non-aboriginal women (Statistics Canada, 1990:191). Of persons who reported an income in 1986, aboriginal women's median income of $6817 ranks below the median income of $8533 for aboriginal men and $9601 for non-aboriginal women, and is barely one-third the median income of $20 001 for non-aboriginal men (Statistics Canada, 1990:191). The extent of poverty among aboriginal women is severe — in 1985, one-quarter of aboriginal women had no income, compared with proportions of 13 percent among aboriginal men, 19 percent among all Canadian women, and 7 percent among all Canadian men (National Council on Welfare, 1990:112). Natives are overrepresented in female-headed lone parent families, which constitute another of the major categories of Canada's poor. In 1986, while one-tenth of all Canadian families were headed by a single-parent mother, the comparable proportion among aboriginal families was 16 percent (National Council on Welfare, 1990:113).

The problems experienced by off-reserve Indians are most intense for women. Over half (54.7 percent in 1986) of Canada's registered Indians who live off reserve are women, compared with less than half (48.0 percent) who live on reserve (Larocque and Gauvin, 1989:13). This trend is compounded by the effects of Bill C-31 since, as noted earlier, by the nature of previous discriminatory legislation which denied Indian status to Indian women who married non-status men, most of the persons who since 1986 have been eligible for reinstatement of status are women living off reserve. After the first year of the bill's implementation, about 60 percent of persons who registered under Bill C-31 were women, while over 60 percent of registrants lived in urban areas (Loh, 1990:39, 70). While the new legislation has allowed some native women access to previously denied services, community ties, and funding resources, a combination of inadequate government funding to accommodate increased band memberships, barriers to the reinstatement process, and political divisions among bands over C-31 registrations has meant that the legislation has contributed to the perpetuation of inequalities among Indian people (Holmes, 1987). High costs of housing and other living expenses, combined with inadequate or inaccessible community services, especially for women with young children, compound the dilemmas of unemployment and low-wage work. Several other factors also interact to make life difficult for off-reserve and urban native women, including the amount of time women tend to be engaged in domestic labour and child-care activities and the matriarchal traditions of many native societies, which place added burdens on women to host and care for newly-arrived family members as they search for work or stability in urban environments. At the same time, formal services are seriously inadequate in most cities, while informal community supports have been eroded or left behind for women who leave the reserve. In the words of Cherly Brooks, who in 1991 chaired hearings in British Columbia for the Aboriginal Child Care Commission, "We leave reserves to find employment ... and come to the city where we find ourselves caught up in an even worse situation. Because now we don't even have an aunt or an uncle or a grandparent that we can rely on to sometimes take our children" (cited in Bell, 1991:E2). Moreover, domestic labour tends to be intensified for households with limited income, as extra effort is required to seek low-cost groceries and services, while family members are more induced to provide labour-intensive services in areas such as food preparation, cleaning, and clothing repair which are too expensive to be purchased (Armstrong, 1984:104-105). These activities, in turn, make it difficult to devote time to job seeking and training or educational upgrading. Domestic stress and financial necessity sometimes force the individual to follow alternatives such as petty theft and prostitution, activities which are also subject to discrimination and further social problems. Prostitution, for example, is racially segmented so that persons working in the more prestigious services such as escort agencies and higher priced street locations tend to be almost exclusively non-native while, in western Canadian cities especially, natives constitute 50 percent and more of prostitutes working the less desirable street corners (McLean, 1991).

The often bleak portrayals of native social conditions and life opportunities can be tempered by the success stories of individual and organizational initiatives in communities both on and off reserve in various forms, such as self-help groups, local jurisdiction over social assistance to reserve residents, housing cooperatives, and social planning councils. In addition, coordinated district tribal, provincial, and regional efforts in the direction of self-government and economic development have advanced well beyond the days when white bureaucrats and planners, if they took any action at all, imposed from the outside remedial programs directed at specific social ills. Nonetheless, as recently as 1984, the Royal Commission on Equality in Employment (1984:38) summarized the key issues for native peoples as being

> their exclusion from relevant decision-making, the fragmented and unco-
> ordinated policy approaches, the absence of federal/provincial/munici-
> pal coordination of service delivery systems, and the constant sense that
> they are forever subject to the discretion of people who do not under-
> stand their culture. As much as any group, they complained of the prolif-
> eration of discussion and research, and of the absence of corresponding
> political action. They feel a sense of urgency that is intense — the human

cost of their political and economic positions has been enormously and inexcusably high.

One of the devastating consequences of the social conditions experienced by native peoples is that very few of them have gone untouched by widespread poverty and related social afflictions either in their own experiences or through someone close to them. At their worst, these problems have created a certain inertia and hopelessness among some segments of the indigenous population. At the same time, though, there has emerged a generation of articulate, educated, and politically experienced native leadership whose members know firsthand the tragedies of an unjust society.

SHIFTING PATTERNS OF SUPPORT FOR ABORIGINAL AFFAIRS

Indigenous peoples' intensive efforts to mobilize and press the government for effective political action has converged with an apparent growing willingness on the part of the state to address native concerns. Weaver (1990:15) argues that since the 1980s, federal policy regarding First Nations peoples has been characterized by a shift from an "old paradigm" in which antagonistic relations arose from the state's "preoccupation with law, formality and control," towards a "new paradigm" of conciliation and recognition of fundamental state obligations as part of a policy "concerned with justice, adaptation, and workable inter-cultural relations." This policy transformation is not without precedent, as will be discussed in Chapter 8, and as Weaver (1981) shows in her detailed and widely-cited book which describes the federal government's efforts to reorganize the administration and delivery of Indian Affairs services during the 1960s. Between 1963 and 1969, when the much criticized White Paper on Indian policy was produced, the federal government made a concerted effort to link the administration and funding of Indian services to wider questions about federal-provincial arrangements. In particular, the federal government sought to establish conditions whereby native bands and the provinces could become more directly involved in the delivery of services to Indian people amidst the expansion of the welfare state and growing concern about poverty as a social problem which required state attention (Weaver, 1981:24-26). The furor that followed the White Paper's release, with Indian organizations denouncing the government's unilateral declaration of intent to repeal the Indian Act and dismantle the Department of Indian Affairs, and declaring as unacceptable the proposed termination of Indians' special status with the state, prompted somewhat greater caution by the state and a move to make more explicit the state's recognition of aboriginal peoples' distinct status (Frideres, 1988:124-127; Weaver, 1981). This process was entrenched in the 1982 Constitution Act (The Charter of Rights and Freedoms) which recognized the special place and rights of aboriginal peoples with respect to other Canadians (Pratt, 1989:43-44). More recently, the federal government has outlined in its Annual Report on Indian and Inuit Affairs its commitment to aboriginal self-government, defined as the goal "to establish new relationships between the government and the aboriginal peoples of Canada that respect the distinctive characteristics and needs of Indian and Inuit communities" (Department of Indian and Northern Affairs, 1989a:5).

One of the ways in which to examine potential changes in state policies is to look at shifting patterns of state funding for Indian Affairs. As the data in Table 4.3 show, federal government spending on Indian Affairs has increased from about $200 000 in 1870 to over $3.3 billion in 1990. These figures should be read as indicators of general trends rather than as accurate accounts of federal spending on aboriginal peoples, since they refer to government departments which historically have had some jurisdictions beyond Indian Affairs (such as Northern Development), and they do not include expenditures by other federal departments or by other levels of government on programs and services for aboriginal peoples. In 1987-88, for example, federal departments other than the Department of Indian Affairs and Northern Development spent over $711 million on programs and services in the native sector (Neilsen, 1985:52-53). As a proportion of total federal spending, expenditures on Indian Affairs have been relatively low, fluctuating between a high of nearly 3 percent in 1890 and a low rate of less than half of 1 percent in the periods immediately following World Wars I and II, but rising steadily since the 1950s.

Table 4.4 illustrates with reference to major program areas the changing federal spending patterns on Indian Affairs between 1973-74 and 1989-90. The contradictory nature of federal policy is evident when we examine the areas of expenditure which have experienced the highest rates of growth over this time period — spending on welfare, infrastructure (the provision of community services and utilities such as roads, sewers, and community centres), and band management have each increased nearly nine times, while spending on economic development and land claims have also increased at high rates, as has spending on health care, which is delivered primarily through the Department of Health and Welfare. These spending trends are indicative of a dual concern by the state to manage the realities and recognition of aboriginal peoples as a "problem" population. On the one hand, especially since the late 1960s, the state has increased its expenditures on welfare and other social services directed toward provision for inadequate social conditions and the needs of a largely dependent, marginalized population. On the other hand, as evident in the more recent shift toward economic development and band management priorities, it appears that the state is focusing its expenditures upon the establishment of opportunities for aboriginal self-sufficiency. This, though, is an overly simplistic assessment of the direction of state policy that ignores many of the limitations that continue to be built into state control over and guidance of aboriginal affairs. It is also instructive to observe the correspondence between these funding priorities and the reinforcement of a distinct capitalist class structure consisting of a bourgeoisie (to direct economic development), a petite bourgeoisie (to manage both small-scale businesses and clients within the subordinate population), a proletariat (consisting of waged employees of business initiatives and of aboriginal peoples who have work off reserve), and a lumpenproletariat (constituted by those who are out of the labour force or unemployed and managed by the welfare state).

Table 4.3

Federal Government Expenditures on Indian Affairs, 1870-1990

Year	Total Federal Government Expenditures ($ millions)	Federal Expenditures on Indian Affairs ($ millions)	Indian Affairs Expenditures as a Proportion of Total Federal Expenditures
1870	19	0.2	0.9
1880	33	0.7	2.0
1890	39	1.1	2.8
1900	56	1.0	1.8
1910	122	1.3	1.1
1920	529	2.4	0.4
1930	442	5.3	1.2
1940	1250	5.7	0.5
1950	2901	12.4	0.4
1960	6551	41.1	0.6
1970	15 089	311.4	2.1
1980	53 362	1126.0	2.2
1990	142 703	3372.8	2.4

Sources: F.H. Leacy (ed.), *Historical Statistics of Canada*, second edition Ottawa: Minister of Supply and Services, 1983, H 19-34; Canada, Department of Finance, *Public Accounts*, various years; Canada, Department of Indian Affairs, *Annual Reports*, various years.

Emerging out of movements towards aboriginal self-government are questions about why these shifts are occurring now and what their implications are for the apparent end of strict government regulation over the lives of indigenous peoples. These transformations commonly tend to be analyzed as part of a gradual process of political or legal evolution (see, e.g., Bartlett, 1990; Boldt, Long, and Little Bear, 1984; Schwartz, 1985). Other commentators, such as Weaver (1990), portray the policy changes as representing a shift in ideas. Clearly, as these and many other studies

Table 4.4

Federal Government Expenditures In Indian Affairs
By Selected Categories For Selected Years, 1973-74 to 1989-90

Area or Program	Annual Expenditures ($ million)			
	1973-74	1978-79	1983-84	1989-90
Social Programs and Community Development:				
Education	131	252	479	681
Welfare	62	133	278	541
Infrastructure	31	60	195	262
Housing	24	43	133	152
Health*	2	7	10	23
Administration of Justice	n/a	6	13	13
Economic and Native Claims				
Economic Development and Regional Agreements	107	271	502	874
Native Claims	0	10	51	66
Band Management and Reserves and Trusts				
Band Management	25	53	118	213
Reserves and Trusts	11	13	22	73

* Note: Figures do not include the following health care costs for native peoples
     under the Department of Health and Welfare (in $ millons): 1973-74:
     60; 1978-79: 126; 1983-84: 273; 1989-90: 436.

Sources: Task Force on Program Review, *Indian and Native Programs.*
     Ottawa: Minister of Supply and Services Canada, 1985, pp. 52-53;
     Indian and Northern Affairs Canada, *1991-92 Estimates. Part III.*
     Expenditure Plan. Ottawa: Minister of Supply and Services Canada,
     1991.

show, the political, legal, and ideological machinations of change are complex, intricate, and often highly volatile. However, such changes cannot be fully comprehended without addressing the material conditions within which policy decisions are grounded, particularly as they relate to general strategies to promote northern development and reserve-based enterprise.

    The phenomena of northern development and economic development on and near reserve lands, and their implications for the social conditions experienced by aboriginal peoples, have been the subject of intense controversy. It is common to assume that economic development will provide sufficient security to overcome a wide range of social problems. The presence of enterprise offers possibilities for waged work, demand for skilled labour, capital for housing and other infrastructural material, and a shift away from reliance upon government assistance. Successful cases like the West-Bank Reserve, near Kelowna, B.C., the Tyendinaga Reserve near Belleville, Ontario, and the Huron Reserve, near Quebec City, have been able to reduce unemployment drastically while creating a substantial community network of services through business development, while other reserves, such as the Blood Reserve near Lethbridge, Alberta, have been able to finance similar accomplishments through oil and gas revenues (Dolan, 1980:21). Across Canada, there are many further examples of bands that have mobilized community members to create agencies, on their own or through an extensive and often frustrating process of lobbying the federal government, to counter effectively serious social and economic problems.

However, the glamour of an influx of apparent "windfall" levels, sometimes in the hundreds of millions of dollars, of compensation from land claims settlements and resource royalties, hides several harsh realities. Despite images of huge cash payouts, the funds that actually reach Indian bands are often limited and conditional, subject to extensive legal costs and administrative barriers. Even where bands do benefit financially, the rewards are limited because of lack of opportunity on reserves and off-reserve spending. The federal Task Force on Indian Economic Development (Department of Indian and Northern Affairs, 1986b:56) reports an estimate from one large band "that 92 cents of each dollar doesn't circulate within Reserve even once; for smaller bands, it may be worse."

These problems are not new ones. In the early 1930s, for instance, Indians who had been members of the Kitsilano Reserve in Vancouver received just over one-third (35.9 percent) of a total award of $44 988.58 made by arbitrators for land held in trust that was to be used to construct footings for the Burrard Bridge, while the majority of the funds were paid out as costs — $15 145.65 for lawyers for the city of Vancouver and $13 708.85 to the Indian Affairs department (Matthews, 1934). A little over a decade later, members of the Squamish tribe, which the Kitsilano Indians had joined after being moved out of the city lands in 1912, were in a state of destitution and attempted to use tribal funds held in trust by the government in order to provide for desperately needed community services, especially adequate housing. However, the Indian Affairs department refused to grant an expenditure of $25 000 which had been approved for these purposes by the Squamish Tribal Council, even though the trust fund contained in excess of $300 000. The extent to which Indians lacked control over their tribal affairs was illustrated by claims that over 50 percent of health care expenditures on the reserve were allocated to administrative costs and the salaries of white officials, and a report that one Indian agent had used relief orders for food for starving reserve residents as the basis on which to make over $10 000 in graft money (British

Columbia Indian Arts and Welfare Society, 1948:24-25).

Although recent steps towards aboriginal self-government and the devolution of control by Indian Affairs officials have removed some of the intermediaries that previously have impeded First Nations social and economic development, many political and fiscal barriers remain. The experience of the Cree-Naskapi peoples, who in 1976 signed an agreement with the federal and Quebec governments which provided the Cree and Inuit with $225 million in compensation for the dislocation and use of lands to construct the James Bay Hydro-Electric Development Project, is instructive in this regard. Despite the promised benefits that the northern natives were expected to reap from the arrangement, by 1988 Cree and Naskapi communities continued to suffer from inadequate housing, infrastructure, and capital programming as a result of unstable and insufficient financial resources (Cree-Naskapi Commission, 1988:40-41). Projects such as the completion of social housing have been jeopardized because of federal funding cutbacks at the same time as the demands of northern development have placed added strain on northern communities through population growth and the need to provide services for further development. This problem, whereby development promotes demands for new resources and changing standards of living at the same time as general service levels remain constant or are reduced, is a common one. The Lysyk Inquiry into the construction of the Alaska Highway Pipeline, for example, observes how pipeline construction in Alaska drew resources away from existing community services such as housing construction, alcoholism treatment, and courtworker programs at the same time as new services in such areas as health care, education, social welfare, and housing were required to meet the needs of changing labour force and community profiles (Lysyk, 1977:94). In a similar fashion, Thomas Berger, in his report on the Mackenzie Valley Pipeline Inquiry, cautions that industrial development in the north has had two major consequences:

> first, that native people have not participated in the industrial economy on a permanent basis; and secondly, that the native people have paid a high price in terms of social impact wherever the industrial economy has penetrated into the North (Berger, 1977:148).

Unfortunately, political and ideological factors tend to divert attention from the impact of the social changes brought about by economic development. The erroneous assumption that compensation funds immediately offer social and economic relief for northern communities provides justification for further curtailment of state services by creating an impression that native peoples are the recipients of excessive levels of undeserved wealth and programs. In its strong rebuttal to this view, the Cree-Naskapi Commission (1988:11) expresses its concern over

> a widely held misconception that the Cree and Naskapi should pay for

these needs [including housing, roads, water, sewage, administration buildings and equipment, a land registry system, court facilities and police, salaries and training for personnel] using the compensation monies they received under the two Agreements. Suggestions that the "Cree are rich" or that "the Naskapi have money" and that public funding of their activities should be curtailed are ill-founded and must be answered. The compensation monies paid to the Cree and the Naskapi nations were for granting permission to construct one massive hydro-electric project on their territory. The Cree and Naskapi did not give up their entitlement to the benefits received by all Canadians, by all Quebecers or by other Indians. This point is seldom made.

Even where benefits accrue to bands and community members, they are not evenly distributed. The development and reinforcement of a class system around newly-created jobs and administrative positions is a mounting problem among aboriginal peoples. LaRustic et al. (1979:157-158), for example, observe the emergence of class differentiation among the James Bay Cree "in the concentration of political power and administrative activities at the level of regional structures, which are essentially controlled by a group which is tending to close itself off." New administrative and political powers are possible in cases in which a community elite has access to an influx of capital from land claims, resource revenue, and economic development. In addition, the need for adequately qualifed personnel to accompany community infrastructural growth provides opportunities for persons who have particular skills and training, most likely acquired outside of the community, to become entrenched into community decision making to the disadvantage of longer-term residents.

These patterns, though, are not unilateral. As the resource and social base of a community changes, so do its internal social relations as well as its relations with other communities and organizations. Involvement by community members in previous struggles for resources and services has provided a base of expertise that is crucial for identifying new priorities and developing future strategies. Skewed priorities related to economic and political inequalities within bands often heighten the disproportionate disadvantage faced by certain groups such as aboriginal women, particularly those who are single parents or who have limited credentials for entry into labour markets. In the process, however, new struggles are emerging as challenges to both aboriginal and non-aboriginal leadership have risen from aboriginal women's organizations as well as from other groups concerned about democratic rights and responsiveness to deep-rooted community needs. As with capitalist societies in general, then, aboriginal communities are grappling with the choice between potentially conflicting priorities of social justice and economic development at any cost.

Challenges by aboriginal organizations and community members to prevailing models of economic development have also questioned the

extent to which new enterprises actually do constitute a break from traditional patterns of dependency (McArthur, 1989). The co-existence of different modes of production continues to be an important factor in the
social organization of northern communities. As we observed in Chapter
3, there is substantial evidence that, despite industrial development in the
North, a mixed economy prevails. Bone (1989), in a survey of food consumption changes in four communities in the Mackenzie River Valley
affected by the Norman Wells energy project, observes that between 1982
and 1985, while there were differences among native households in the
degree of reliance upon country foods such as berries, wild game, and
fish, most natives continued to consume consistently moderate to high
rates of such foods. Similarly, Cox (1987b), reviewing the evidence from
communities affected by several northern development projects, argues
that the "bush economy" remains a central part of northern life and a
necessary means of survival in the absence of adequate wage labour and
state support.

The perpetuation of subsistence opportunities in the North is a real
problem for aboriginal peoples and not a matter that can be solved simply
by the supposed miracles of economic development. In the wider
Canadian and international context of economic and labour market
restructuring, native peoples are highly at risk without alternative means of
support. Economic shifts have in particular reduced employment in the
resource and manufacturing sectors, areas in which natives have been predominantly employed in the labour force, while urban migration is risky
given the combined phenomena of urban labour market shifts and the
financial and social costs of moving from rural to urban communities
(Osberg, 1988:16-17)

Conclusion

This chapter has examined several dimensions of aboriginal social organization and state involvement in native life. We have argued that, while
political, organizational, and legal factors are rarely fully cohesive, rational,
and successful, the thrust of state activity in the area of indigenous affairs
has been an attempt to reproduce a group of peoples who are politically
and economically manageable within the broad framework of national and
international capitalist development.

Native life has been shaped by a dialectic of domination and resistance constituted, within the terms of reference of our analysis, through
the emergence and transformation of capitalist social relations. The
Canadian state, as signified in the actions of its agencies and officials, has
intervened actively, both directly and indirectly, in aboriginal societies in
order to produce particular kinds of individuals or subjects as required
within particular phases of capitalist development and state formation.
This chapter has examined many of the ways in which the state has
employed legislative and regulative mechanisms, including ideologies and

policies concerning marriage, family, child welfare, and other cultural practices, as tools to accomplish the "project" of reshaping aboriginal life. However, we have also stressed that this "project" is highly complex, subject both to changing and sometimes conflicting ideologies and interests, and to varying forms of resistance, modification, and accommodation from within aboriginal communities.

The process of social transformation has produced several crises as material and administrative circumstances have warranted shifts in policy orientation. It has also been part of a situation in which aboriginal peoples engage in a diverse array of social relations, usually in a disadvantaged position subject to variations along class, "race," and gender lines. Recent initiatives to promote self-government and economic development, prompted and resisted in different ways by aboriginal organizations and governments, have tended to be focused upon either very specific programs or general philosophical orientations. Questions about who will benefit, and at what cost, tend to be ignored by many aboriginal and non-aboriginal commentators alike. These questions are explored more fully through an analysis of the continuing historical development of aboriginal social relations in the areas of education, health care, crime and justice, and political organizations in the chapters that follow.

CHAPTER 5

EDUCATION AND JOB TRAINING[1]

New prospects for economic and political advancement of native peoples have been linked increasingly to the attainment of formal education and vocational training. The federal government's 1985 Task Force on Indian Economic Development, for example, cites the urgent need for expanded and enhanced job training and education programs in order to overcome Indians' disadvantaged status with respect to employment opportunities (Indian and Northern Affairs Canada, 1986:46-48). Indian organizations, articulated especially since the National Indian Brotherhood's (1972) call for "Indian control of Indian education," have made the demand for improved educational services a central part of their quest for self-government and social justice. General concern over the educational development of Canada's aboriginal peoples is motivated in part by desires for the achievement of real opportunities and equity. More importantly, growing attentiveness to the problems associated with native education is deeply rooted in the search by business and political leaders for readily available supplies of appropriately qualified workers amidst the restructuring of Canada's labour force. A recent report by Employment and Immigration Canada (1989:19) makes the case directly for the emerging significance of aboriginal peoples to national economic growth by observing that "with a relatively high birth rate, the aboriginal population is, on average, young and represents an important human resource that has largely been undeveloped and underutilized." Education and training, in other words, are proposed as tools in the transformation of native peoples into citizens who are capable of fulfilling the tasks set out for them within the framework of national economic agendas.

This chapter, following the analysis of native social conditions in the previous chapter, portrays education as a contradictory endeavour. The hope and possibilities for social and personal advancement which education offers is counteracted by real barriers to educational attainment and benefits. Education and training are conceptualized as means by which individuals are transformed in accordance with wider social standards and expectations. While people are potentially empowered through education, in the sense that they gain knowledge and skills by which they may be able to transform themselves and their communities, educational possibilities are also constrained by the development of the capitalist mode of production through its labour force requirements and the organization of its political and civil institutions.

Viewed in this way, the history of native education in Canada revolves around a conflict between opportunities for self-sufficiency and pressures towards marginalization. After European contact, natives' steady and decided loss of control over their educational practices was an integral part of the deterioration of their conditions of social existence. In the process, schooling aided in the transformation of natives into individual subjects who were formally "free" to pursue alternative patterns of work and social life. These freedoms, and the struggle to define and use them in meaningful ways, are analyzed in terms of aboriginal peoples' changing status relative to the development of the capitalist mode of production. We conclude that contained within educational conflict are possibilities for new forms of domination as well as liberation through native self-determination.

HUMAN CAPITAL AND STRUGGLES FOR EDUCATIONAL CONTROL

There is little dispute with the notion that education is a central tool in the process of economic development. This view is given its fullest expression in human capital theory, which conceptualizes education and training as investments which are expected to produce a future return for the individual and for society as a whole. While this position was articulated most strongly to justify human resource development through educational expansion in the post-World War II period (see, e.g., Schultz, 1961), it has appeared widely in many different guises throughout the advanced industrial nations. In 1990, for example, the Economic Council of Canada (1990:20) posed the question of "why Canada, as a nation, does not appear to be getting a greater economic return on its substantial investments" in education. The implication is that education systems are expected to be tailored in such a way as to ensure that people are trained to fit existing labour force requirements.

A human capital approach serves as a convenient, but, as we will argue, inadequate, explanation for aboriginal peoples' relative lack of economic success. As Armstrong, Kennedy, and Oberle (1990) argue in their analysis of Indians' education levels and economic status, native peoples' economic well-being and labour force status would improve markedly if only more Indians completed high school and post-secondary studies. Findings from the 1986 census highlight the disparities that exist between the educational attainment of natives and non-natives. Of those registered Indians aged 15 and over who were reported in the census, 37.2 percent had less than Grade 9 education and only 27.6 percent had at least a high school education, compared with corresponding figures of 17.1 percent and 55.8 percent, respectively, for the general population (Larocque and Gauvin, 1989:17-19). Under human capital theory, consistent with pluralist and Chicago School approaches to race and ethnic relations, the general social and economic success of any group depends upon the ability of its members to adapt to prevailing social norms and to compete on an equal basis with other individuals. Schooling is particularly important as a means of ensuring that all youths have the "cultural capital" required for social survival and as a mechanism for allocating credentials to determine placement in the job market. Native peoples' low socioeconomic status is viewed in this light as a product of cultural barriers to their educational success (Nagler, 1975). The education and social systems are regarded as fundamentally sound, while reasons for educational failure are sought in the home, language, cultural norms (Kirkness, 1974), or even the genetic endowment of the individual. Thus, the individual must be tailored, perhaps with the benefit of cultural enrichment or other special resources, to meet educational and labour market demands.

Despite its common sense appeal to the notion that educational and social success should be linked, a human capital approach to native education, as well as to education in general, is severely limited. The primary inadequacy of the theory is its assumption of a free labour market. The theory is premised upon the notion that, with equitable opportunities and resources to promote educational attainment, the most capable persons, regardless of social background, will be available to fill positions requiring skill and qualifications. Such an assumption, however, fails to recognize the importance of structural factors which systematically restrict opportunities for large segments of the populace. Racism and discrimination of various forms produce barriers which restrict the educational and occupational advancement of aboriginal peoples as well as members of other minority groups. Education and training require a commitment of financial and personal resources which are not available to many groups such as single parents or the poor. Even for persons from a disadvantaged background who do gain educational credentials and other qualifications, there are informal limitations to their occupational success if they lack personal contacts or other assets. Finally, human capital theory ignores the realities of labour force structures in which there are relatively few "good" or meaningful jobs being created so that, if everyone did gain improved educational qualifications, there would be an extreme surplus of qualified workers.

More recent variants of human capital theory have attempted to account for some of these problems by arguing that the state should take an active role in the coordination of labour markets so as to provide a careful match between labour demand and supply (Economic Council of Canada, 1990). In some cases the state has been called upon to become even more directly involved in ensuring that members of minority groups such as aboriginal peoples have access to education, training, and employment opportunities in proportion to their representation in the general population (see, e.g., Employment and Immigration Canada, 1990; Commission on Equality in Employment, 1984). However, like the theory in general, these concerns ignore the underlying features of social reality, including labour market structures, that give rise to social and economic inequalities. These approaches also tend to reduce education to a matter of economic concern, thereby undermining the significance of formal education to character formation and personal development.

In fact, these latter dimensions of education have been recognized as crucial by several interests, including the colonizers of native peoples as well as native organizations themselves. This is a central premise of a contending approach to the analysis of the education of native peoples in Canada, one which emphasizes the colonization process. Theories of colonization focus more directly on structural problems. Natives' depressed socioeconomic conditions in this view are seen to emerge through the subordination of natives by dominant groups. The historical subjugation of natives enabled colonizers to "liberate" aboriginal land and resources for capitalist development and to provide a surplus pool of labour (Kellough, 1980). Educational institutions were employed by colonial authorities as a tool to assert their hegemony (Gustafson, 1978). Education served to separate and widen the gulf between natives' traditional social practices and belief systems and the colonial institutions, thereby reducing the need for coercive means of control such as military occupation. In Canada, for example, the introduction of residential schools enabled authorities to subject native children to near total control, thereby contributing to the destruction of kinship ties and posing the supremacy of European language and institutional forms over aboriginal ones (Gresko, 1979).

The colonial model's depiction of the school system as an instrument of domination presents a sharp contrast to human capital theory's claim that schooling is a vehicle for social mobility. The analysis of education as a tool for colonization demonstrates that schooling does not exist solely for economic purposes, showing that formal education can be used to suppress as well as nurture the development of human resources. Despite these insights, however, a strict emphasis on education for colonization tends to present the colonization of native peoples in a static way, ignoring the changes that have occurred in educational practices and government policies (Frideres, 1988:372). The colonization process involved different phases of efforts by capital and the state to assert control over land, resources, and labour, but it has also been met by varying forms of resistance on the part of native peoples.

As recent analysis has pointed out, native education and wider social relations are interconnected in very complex ways (Barman, Hébert, and McCaskill, 1986; Frideres, 1987). The question of control over education is often centrally involved in struggles to shape the character and destiny of a group of people. Education can be employed variously as a form of domination and subordination and as a means to express cultural autonomy and growth. Its power lies in its ability to shape people's consciousness about surrounding social and natural conditions and possibilities. In the case of native-white relations in Canada, missionaries and state officials readily employed schooling as a means to destroy traditional native cultures and promote the assimilation of aboriginal peoples, but native bands have also looked to education as a vehicle for the resurrection of traditional native values and the reconstitution of native identity.

In order to understand the development of education and training for Canada's native peoples, it is important to examine within any mode of production the interplay of the two sets of factors, the economic and the social. Educational policies and practices are shaped by the labour force needs of a society, but they are also responsive to political agendas and struggles over the kinds of persons and characteristics that are valued by particular social interests. Schooling has been employed variously by the state as a device for the political containment of native peoples and as a means to prepare them for possible labour force participation. It has attempted to provide native children with discipline, habits, and skills which would make them ready for particular social positions within or at the margins of the mainstream of society. The remainder of this chapter examines the historical role played by political, social, and economic factors in transforming education and training for different segments of native populations through distinct stages of capitalist development.

THE ROLE OF EDUCATION IN THE COLONIZATION PROCESS

Characteristic of general social relations in pre-industrial societies, education was not separated institutionally from other aspects of aboriginal life prior to European contact. Social practices and spiritual beliefs were unified around the fulfillment of material needs. Childhood constituted a process of general apprenticeship to life in order to ensure social stability (Jenness, 1977:152-153). These practices, while often varied and highly sophisticated, were very much integrated into everyday life and not formalized in the way in which contemporary educational institutions are organized.

Initially, for the first Europeans who entered North America, native society was adequate as it existed. Aboriginal peoples' familiarity with the land and resources and their skills in endeavours such as trapping were essential for the survival and enterprise of Europeans in the "new world." Alliances with native tribes also had a military value for the procurement and protection of land, resources, and settlements. It was in the interests of the early British and French in North America to secure the cooperation of Indians as "Indians" in the sense that natives possessed traits which were desirable from the Europeans' perspective. Consequently, a degree of native cultural autonomy was useful.

At the same time, though, forces were in operation to undermine the natives' autonomy. The very fact of contact, which embodied definite purposes for each interacting group, had altered social and material relations. Practices like intermarriage between Indians and fur traders, for example, created new social groupings. Racism was often institutionally embedded in social and economic relations, such as the importance of colour lines which regulated divisions of labour in trade and community activities and the multi-tiered pricing system of the Hudson's Bay Company (Bourgeault, 1988a:50-51; Hull, 1982:7-8). Similar changes in the gender division of labour produced new roles and identities for men and women. Moreover, various groups were concerned to cultivate natives' loyalty for their own intentions. Education was at the core of the missionaries' agenda for religious imperialism through efforts to "Christianize" and "civilize" the "heathen" Indians. These developments had the effect of undermining traditional social cohesion and substituting European-based models or new hybrids (Sealey, 1974).

However, consistent with the contradictory nature of educational practices in general, not all such efforts had or were intended to have destructive consequences. In some instances, for example, where native youth were trained in European schools in order to prepare them for leadership positions that would advance colonial political or religious mission interests, the apprentices came to have either no effective influence or else became active agitators for the advancement of radical native organizations (Bourgeault, 1988a:60; Trigger, 1985:252). Formal education provided access to knowledge as well as literacy and analytical skills which enabled native peoples to function in the white world. For these reasons, education came to be valued and, in the case of prairie Indians, sought actively as a treaty right (Stevenson, 1991:215-216).

By the 1820s, colonial consolidation had been accomplished through the merger of the North West Company and Hudson's Bay Company in 1821, massive land transfers, and the establishment of stable territorial boundaries. As resource development and settlement emerged as new priorities, aboriginal issues were subject to redefinition. As Indians' utility as Indians was vanishing (Wilson, 1986), it became imperative either to marginalize native peoples or to seek their assimilation into the cultural mainstream. Both options were pursued, although the latter became official state policy. The 1830 transfer from the military to civil state authorities of responsibility for natives brought education to the core of Indian affairs.

Education and the Process of State Formation

The shift from mercantile to industrial capitalism occurred both unevenly and in conjunction with the alteration of the political and social landscapes in 19th-century Canada. Industrialization accompanied, and was often preceded by, Canadian state formation, which involved the consolidation of Upper and Lower Canada with the vast outlying territories to the east, west, and north, as well as the creation of a political unity out of fragmented populations. Bourgeois authorities saw education as a primary vehicle for accomplishing the latter task (Stamp, 1977). The offering of public schooling provided opportunities to develop, democratically and without coercive intervention, a common moral purpose and to attract and retain a settled population (Curtis, 1983; Corrigan, Curtis, and Lanning, 1987). In eastern Canada, and in settlements in the southern territories of the West, where regularized contact had become established, it was viewed as possible and often desirable to include natives in the general school population The inclusion of Indian children in regular classrooms, for example, was sought by school promoters who wished to inflate school registers for financial and political purposes. In other instances, however, native education was accomplished in isolation from the public school system. In any event, school officials stressed the importance of education as a tool which could contribute simultaneously to character formation and the development of useful political and economic attributes. An authority from the Brandon Industrial School expressed the task clearly, by identifying the state's educational purpose as:

> The preparation of Indian youth for the duties, privileges and responsibilities of citizenship.... This implies training in the industrial arts, the development of the moral and intellectual faculties, the formation of good habits, the formation of character.... The task we have before us is to win over the Indian children by sympathetic interest and a firm, kind, guiding hand; there is no other way.... The foundation must be the development of character — learning is a secondary consideration; but what we give him should be adapted to his immediate practical needs (Ferrier, 1906:13, 15).

To these ends, the Indian Affairs Branch and other colonial and local authorities involved in the governance of natives expressed their verbal commitment to education as a major priority.

In practice, however, a somewhat haphazard approach to native education emerged, signifying the low priority of Indian affairs amidst the exigencies of national development once title to desired aboriginal lands was attained by the state and private interests. In the vast outlying regions of the territories, Indians received little or no formal education until con-

tact was imminent. Where schooling was provided, there was no guarantee that children would be receptive to the educational services offered.
Since the basis of schooling constituted a denial of their previous social
existence, Indians tended to resist schooling when no tangible benefits
were evident (Barman, Hébert, and McCaskill, 1986). Educational officials continually lamented the dismal record of native school attendance.
Moreover, government authorities tended to leave the education of
natives to missionaries in exchange for annual grants and certain land entitlements. Bourgeois reformers were concerned about the parochial nature
of denominational education, which ran contrary to the aims of those who
sought to develop a cohesive and secular state. In addition, the missionary
schools were replete with severe problems in their programs and operations.

As state officials saw the matter, Indians needed to be educated under
some form of compulsion in order to be liberated both from their "primitive" conditions of wandering and subsistence and from the mediating
religious influence of the missionaries. They had to be guided in such a
way as to reap the benefits of new, "civilized" freedoms:

> Some of the most difficult problems in connection with the education of
> the Indians toward full citizenship arise from the transmission of traits
> developed by primitive conditions from generation to generation; com-
> pulsion in any form has terrors for the Indians. They resent it with vigor.
> Before a compulsory law can be made effective, and can be enforced
> without much friction among Indians, they must understand that such
> compulsory law is absolutely necessary for the furtherance of their inter-
> ests (Jamieson, 1922:4-5).

Federal government attempts to consolidate native education also
came increasingly to emphasize the injection of useful content into the
schooling process in order to aid in the processes of agricultural settlement and assimilation. The nation building project created the likelihood
that Indians would not for long remain marginalized and isolated from
"civilized" society.

Indian affairs officials began to look at industrial schools to serve their
varied purposes. As early as 1847, Egerton Ryerson, who was instrumental
in the establishment of a system of public schooling in central Canada,
advocated industrial schools as the most appropriate measure by which to
provide Indians with "a plain English education adapted to the working
farmer and mechanic," as well as offering in a residential setting the means
to "improve and elevate his character and condition" with "the aid of religious training" (Welfare and Training Service of the Indian Affairs
Branch, 1947:322). David Laird, the federal Minister of the Interior,
wrote in 1875 that Indian youth "require not only the elements of an
English Education, but also to be taught and trained in some useful
industrial pursuit" (Department of the Interior, 1875:6). Industrial

schools, separated geographically from native communities, would provide state authorities with the means to discipline and control Indians and enforce attendance so as, in the words of the Indian Superintendent for British Columbia, J.W. Powell, to develop the natives' "natural gifts" and "render them good and useful members of society" (Indian Affairs Branch, 1873:9-10).

Federal commitment to industrial schools was entrenched as official policy following the 1879 report of Nicholas Flood Davin, a journalist and lawyer whom the Department of the Interior had commissioned to examine the system of Indian schools in the United States. Davin was impressed with the success of many of the American boarding schools, and recommended that a carefully planned system of boarding and industrial schools be established in Canada. Like Ryerson, but contrary to the wishes of several federal authorities and school reformers, he stressed that Indian schools should continue to be operated as much as possible by missionaries, subject to federal regulation and regular inspection. Davin recommended that inducements such as rations of tea and sugar should be offered by schools to parents and children in order to encourage and reward regular attendance. Indians required the benefits of Christian values. It was also imperative that teachers be of utmost moral character. Virtuous living and moral guidance, for Davin, were essential to elevate the Indian character to a higher, self-regulating level. Only then could Indians be weaned from direct religious authority (Davin, 1879).

Despite the opposition by some officials to denominational schooling, the federal cabinet under John A. Macdonald readily embraced Davin's report. Besides providing a framework for a cohesive native education policy, the report's recommendations did not require extensive outlays of additional funds by the federal government. The new policy was oriented to offer what in effect became a three-step process towards Indians' assimilation — boarding schools for the young would remove traditional native cultural attributes from the child and provide habilitation into the dominant culture; industrial schools would provide further character formation and controlled work-training skills for older children who were to be integrated into agricultural work and labour force positions; and day schools would signify the complete assimilation of natives into Euro-Canadian cultural and employment patterns.

The trend to industrial and training schools was not as pronounced in practice as had been recommended by Davin. By the end of the 1880s, each of the provinces and territories from Ontario west had industrial schools in operation, numbering fifteen in 1896 and twenty-two, with a total enrollment of 1913 students, by 1901. The number of boarding schools increased from thirty-four in 1896 to forty-two, with 1542 students on the rolls, in 1901. By comparison, the number of day schools dropped from 239 in 1896 to 226 in 1901, but the total number of students attending these schools increased from 3131 to 6121 during that time period (Department of Indian Affairs, 1902; Welfare and Training Service of the Indian Affairs Branch, 1947:323). In 1901, 250 of the 290 Indian schools in Canada, including all but two of each of the industrial and boarding schools, were run by denominational groups, most prominently Roman Catholic and the Church of England (Department of Indian Affairs, 1902:xxx).

There was, in certain instances, a limited but real commitment to native education, and some success was attained at each of these levels. Significantly, formal education contributed to an array of distinctly different opportunities among aboriginal populations. Some children returned home from school with real skills in literacy and leadership, and training in agriculture and other trades offered selected Indians a restricted range of practical occupational alternatives (Barman, Hébert, and McCaskill, 1986:7). The schools, paradoxically, also stimulated native rights and resistance movements and, at times, facilitated native involvement in traditional spiritual and cultural practices (Gresko, 1979).

It was clear, however, that the schools constituted a basis for the low-cost production of native labour power. Accommodations, food, books, and other school supplies were less than adequate in most Indian schools, and schools were often forced to close as a result of teacher attrition. The denominational schools tended to favour deprivation as a means to instill what they considered "discipline." Schools tended to benefit more from students than vice versa, with the operation of Indian schools highly dependent upon student labour. Most industrial schools survived by virtue of an elaborate system of child labour, such as the one described at the turn of the century at Emmanuel College in Prince Albert:

> All the general work required on the premises is performed by the pupils. The boys attend the horse and cattle, milk the cows, draw water, chop wood, do all the farm work, and any ordinary work required. We have a carpenter's shop, and the elder boys are practised in the use of tools. The girls are taught housework, cooking, sewing and knitting (Department of Indian Affairs, 1901:350).

A combination of a relative absence of labour force opportunities for aboriginal youth, and the potential availability of schooling in the public school system for Indians who sought enfranchisement or assimilation, contributed to the general disregard for sufficient learning and living conditions in the Indian schools. At the turn of the century, federal authorities began to acknowledge that provisions for Indian schooling were ineffective. On the one hand, officials who had some sympathy for native peoples saw that natives were being marginalized between waylaid traditions and non-integration into industrial capitalist society (Nock, 1978). A contrary view, however, indicated that educational provisions perhaps were overly generous in that some successful native graduates were competing economically with non-native workers and enterprises. This position became especially prominent in the context of massive labour recruitment through immigration from Europe and the United States early in the 20th century (Barman, Hébert, and McCaskill, 1986:8-9).

With a few scattered exceptions, Indians were not becoming the kinds of subjects that authorities desired them to be. The problem, ironically, was compounded by the fact that the "heathen" natives were responding to their circumstances in a rational manner. That is, while many native peoples actively sought schooling as a means to provide them with social and economic opportunities, they found it detrimental to allow their children to attend schools which provided them with few tangible benefits. The deputy superintendent of Indian Affairs wrote in 1901 that:

> So long as Indians remain a distinct people and live as separate communities, their attitude towards education will in all likelihood remain much as it is today, which means that they will not be anxious for further education for their children than will serve as a convenience and protection with regard to such dealings as they have with the white population (Department of Indian Affairs, 1901:xxxiii).

In summary, education occupied a central role in Indian Affairs policies during the period of state formation and industrial expansion in the late 19th and early 20th centuries. However, educational policies and practices were not strictly oriented to the formation of an industrial work force, especially given sometimes considerable resistance by both aboriginal peoples and non-aboriginal interests to the employment of native peoples in industrial and agricultural pursuits. While, clearly, training for wage labour and the provision of useful skills constituted part of the educational agenda, education for native peoples was primarily a socio-political enterprise intended to ensure that they were politically contained if not integrated into mainstream society. In subsequent years, the management functions of education would come to predominate as authorities moved to institutionalize the increasing marginalization of natives from education and labour force participation.

Segregation and the Deterioration of Indian Education

In 1909, federal administration of Indian affairs was reorganized to emphasize functions of population management and the facilitation of economic development by non-native enterprises on Indian and northern lands. Native education policy reflected the broader strategy of confinement of Indians on reserves and isolated lands. While formally intended to "fit" Indian education with social and labour market conditions in these areas, little formal acknowledgment was made of the depressed state of existence that tended to prevail on reserves and in native communities. Indians were acknowledged to have little value to white society as workers and subjects, and were abandoned with few means of survival. The value of traditional native pursuits like hunting, fishing, and trapping had declined to about one-third of total native income by 1909 (Department of Indian Affairs, 1910), while few new sources of meaningful work were imminent and little real effort was given to promote education and other investment in native peoples' labour power. Conditions in native communities were allowed to stagnate at the same time as the isolationist policy was justified by reference to the need for Indians to learn on their own the importance of integration into the socioeconomic mainstream.

In communities characterized by malnutrition, unemployment, and high rates of illness and death, schooling became important primarily for purposes of political containment and efforts to ensure the stability of native populations in isolation for some future possible use. The superintendent of Indian education observed in 1911 that "without education and with neglect the Indians would produce an undesirable and often a dangerous element in society," while the deputy superintendent general wrote in the same year that Indians

> manifest a certain apathy as to the prolongation of a life which affords comparatively few interests and enjoyments and is lived mainly for the supply of the arising necessities of the day.
>
> It is to be hoped that dissemination of Christianity and expansion of the somewhat curtailed limits of their knowledge and interests may gradually work a change in this regard (Department of Indian Affairs, 1911:xxiii, 273).

The use of schooling to regulate the lives of native peoples was made evident in legislation concerning mandatory education. In 1919, the Indian Act was amended to make schooling compulsory for Indians between 7 and 15 years of age, while in 1930 the upper age limit was raised to 16 for girls and to 18, at the request of the superintendent of Indian Affairs, for boys. However, schooling was restricted in that the legislation specified these limits as the maximum age to which Indian children were entitled to attend school, while individual progress was retarded by provisions to hold classes only on a half-day basis (Stevenson, 1991:222). Moreover, investment in schooling was limited to those Indians who were deemed to be "physically fit," which enabled the state to exclude large numbers of native children in the context of massive health and nutritional problems. In school, learning materials were scarce, facilities were substandard and frequently destroyed by fires, and few means were available to provide any worthwhile activity for students who attended. Procurement and retention of qualified teachers posed a constant difficulty for school officials, especially in the outlying areas away from larger settlements. The federal government maintained little direct contact with the schools, preferring instead to let denominational groups operate the schools. Consequently, Indian children rarely advanced beyond the early elementary grades (Barman, Hébert, and McCaskill, 1986:11).

With the new education policy, residential schools which combined half days of instruction with chores and practical training replaced the boarding and industrial schools. Enrollment of Indian children in day schools increased slowly, from 7775 in 1920-21 to 8651 in 1940-41, while enrollment in boarding and industrial schools and the residential schools which replaced them nearly doubled, from 4783 in 1920-21 to 8774 in 1940-41 (Department of Indian Affairs, 1921:27; Department of Indian Affairs, 1941:165). Some schools did attempt to offer experimental programs and provide practical training. In selected schools in British Columbia, for example, Indian youth were given courses in such areas as wool preparation and knitting, fruit preservation, and auto mechanics, while in Alberta an experimental mink ranch was started in the late 1930s.

However, the chief advantages of the school system, particularly through the residential schools, lay in its ability to contain costs and maximize control over the Indian population. Per-pupil expenditure remained low throughout the period — in 1940-41, total federal funding for Indian education averaged $40.94 per pupil in day schools compared with an average of $58.26 for general public schooling in Canada; the cost per pupil in Indian residential schools, including food, boarding, and other services, was $166.74 (calculated from Department of Indian Affairs, 1941:165-166; and Statistics Canada, 1978). The residential schools operated cheaply according to a funding arrangement whereby a federal government grant was augmented by funds raised by the school agencies themselves, most of which were religious denominations. Moreover, while the costs of running the schools were kept low through the use of child labour, justified as vocational preparation, the schools sold agricultural products, handicrafts, and other goods to support denominational coffers. The Secretary of the British Columbia Advisory Committee on Indian Affairs observed in 1951 that

> the Dominion Government grant made to residential schools did not cover the expense of maintaining these schools, and in many cases the children were expected to work on school farms, etc., to make up the deficit. This was not considered child labour, but a useful preparation for after life for many of the students attending these schools, and in some cases it provided vocational training (Advisory Committee on Indian Affairs in B.C., 1951:2).

This "vocational preparation" was mostly restricted to domestic work for girls and manual or agricultural chores for boys, providing the schools with cheap labour. In many cases, the schools barely disguised the exent to which they relied upon student labour as work, paying only lip service to the possibility of useful training, as evident in the following description from 1928 of the domestic economics program at the United Church's Coqualeetza Residential School in Sardis, B.C.:

Coqualeetza Residential School girls have, during the past eight months enjoyed their Domestic Science classes very much, and have shown marked improvement *in their work of preparing 740 meals* each day.

Many new appliances have been installed in the kitchen *to lighten the work* for the girls, such as a canning machine, stationary can openers, knife sharpeners, etc. (Coqualeetza Residential School, 1928:19, emphasis added).

It is questionable how useful this "preparation" would be for the students' future lives, given that these appliances were not available for most reserve residents under prevailing socioeconomic conditions. Where anyone besides school authorities derived any benefit from the work programs, it tended to be white officials who had at their disposal a ready supply of cheap, unemployed, or underemployed native labour available to carry out domestic and manual chores.

In many instances, residential school students were also disciplined and beaten into submission by the rigours of ascetic living conditions and religious ritual, as well as physical, emotional, and spiritual abuse, and disease which often ran rampant in the closed environments of the residential schools. Basil Johnston (1988: 137) recalls of his residential school days that:

Food was the abiding complaint because the abiding condition was hunger, physical and emotional.... Perhaps more than anything else the boys resented the never-ending surveillance that began in the morning and ended only late at night, after they had all fallen asleep; a surveillance that went on day after day, week after week, month after month, year after year.

Only recently has the dismal legacy of violence, alcoholism, and child abuse that was often a direct consequence of the residential schools become a public issue. Aboriginal leaders such as Phil Fontaine, head of the Assembly of Manitoba chiefs, have emphasized the destructive nature of the "distorted morality" in which, "The same people who tell you to be pure are violating you. You don't know what's right or wrong. The abused become the abusers. Then we blame ourselves and those around us" (cited in Adam, 1991, A10).

Further problems arose around the fact that students who survived their schooling years had few employment opportunities outside of service to local communities. The superintendent-general of Indian Affairs observed in 1931 that, "Except in those Indian communities where successful farming is found, the school graduate presents a problem which is very difficult of solution" (Department of Indian Affairs, 1931:13).

Indian education had taken a decidedly backwards turn in the first half of the 20th century. By mid-century, a national system of education for non-natives was moving into place, with consolidated larger school districts replacing scattered, single-room schools, secondary education was becoming the norm, and average daily attendance rates of over 90 percent were achieved in elementary and secondary schools (see Phillips, 1957; Statistics Canada, 1983:W68). Aboriginal children, by contrast, particularly in western Canada, tended to be schooled in an array of small, under-equipped schools, separated from ongoing community life, and ill-prepared for or isolated from all but a handful of employment situations. Through their isolation and repressive social conditions, native peoples had been marginalized from the turbulence of wider social unrest and educational development in the period leading up to and during World War II. After the war, however, the search for social stability and capitalist expansion began to have a more direct impact on native issues.

Steps Towards the Integration of Natives into the Educational System

Initiatives to reorganize Canadian state activities and structures were prominent in the wake of the economic crisis of the 1930s and Canada's subsequent involvement in World War II. The need for broad coordination given the national and international scope of the major problems led to a reassessment of federal-provincial funding and program delivery arrangements. As part of this process, the provinces, which had primary jurisdiction over health, education, and welfare, were becoming increasingly involved in Indian affairs (Hawthorn, 1966). It was now appropriate to acknowledge as a failure the previous reserve policies and recommend, as did the Special Joint Committee of the Senate and House of Commons on the Indian Act in 1948, that Indians should be encouraged to enter the provincial school systems. A growing sense of dissatisfaction with Indian education conditions under the churches and small employers' search for new sources of low-cost labour power in the post-war economy contributed to a restructuring of priorities in the delivery of education services for natives.

The federal government gradually began to shift the burden of Indian schooling to the provinces by reducing or terminating funding for denominational schools and, following amendments to the Indian Act in 1951, entering into joint agreements with provinces and local school boards. In 1961, 56 residential schools remained in operation compared with 377 day schools (Dominion Bureau of Statistics, 1963:79). The proportion of native children in elementary and secondary schools under federal control declined from two-thirds in 1961 to one-third in 1971 (Frideres, 1988:178).

The trend to integration of natives into the general school system had two major consequences. First, the move constituted a cost-saving measure for the federal government, allowing it to divert resources to other branches both in and outside of Indian affairs. Fields and Stanbury (1973: 25), for example, estimate with reference to British Columbia data from 1966 that the provincial government subsidized Indian public school education by about $223 per pupil per year, calculated according to shortfalls in the federal grant ($250 per year per Indian pupil compared with a provincial average net annual cost per pupil of $280), along with other expenditures on education borne by the province. Second, and more importantly, native youth were brought in direct contact with a broad range of non-native officials under conditions defined by the general ideology of open competition for jobs and other resources. No one but the individual could be blamed for success or failure.

Predictably, however, the native child encountered several barriers including language and cultural differences, teachers who were insensitive to or lacked training related to aboriginal concerns, and Eurocentric curricula and materials (Burnaby, 1982:20). These factors, in conjunction with social problems such as broken family ties (a common legacy of residential schooling) as well as overt racism left the native child at a pronounced disadvantage. Failure at school, failure to gain meaningful employment, and wider social failure became a familiar pattern for Canadian natives. By the late 1960s, in contact with a wider population base than previously, native peoples' problems as a visible minority began to capture public attention.

One of the most immediate responses to the problems came in the form of early childhood intervention by the state, given that between 40 and 50 percent of Canada's registered Indian population was less than 15 years of age throughout the 1950s and 1960s (Statistics Canada, 1977:287). The residential schools which had been so crucial in altering social relations among native communities gradually gave way to a less tightly bounded but equally punitive system of control conducted by armies of social workers, health-care workers, education specialists, and civil servants. Native peoples, authorities contended, required the proper institutional resources in order to allow them to gain the individual initiative that was the main ingredient for social advancement. State intervention would rectify home and community inadequacies by substituting a stable environment in which the individual could reclaim a sense of pride and worth. However well intended were those workers who marched onto reserves to remedy the plight of natives, their efforts contributed to the further destruction of the fabric of social life on reserves and native communities across the country (Johnston, 1983) while, in the process, creating a large new client base for the delivery of social services.

Under these conditions, it was questionable how successful even the most well-equipped public schools could be in integrating native children and providing them with the motivation and skill development that would allow them to succeed in life. However, the placement of native children in schools in contact and competition with the general population did hold out the tantalyzing possibility of success. Indian children began in the 1960s to remain in school longer and gain higher levels of education than in the previous period. By the early 1970s, nearly all Indians in the 10 to 13-year age group were attending school, and of all registered Indians who attended educational institutions, the proportion that was enrolled in courses above the Grade 8 level doubled in just over a decade to about 30 percent by the early 1970s (Statistics Canada, 1977: 289-290).

Nonetheless, native failure rates and low attainment were remarkably pronounced when compared with non-natives. Calls for action to rectify these educational shortcomings came from a variety of sources. In the early 1970s, the Federation of Saskatchewan Indians (1973:vii), in a task force on Indian education, criticized the state of education for Indians in Canada as a matter of "tragic proportion" and argued that, "generation after generation of Indian youth was being destroyed, consigned to a life of uselessness, despair, frustration, and indignity." An Ontario task force came up with similar findings, identifying the educational needs of native peoples in the province as a high priority area requiring "swift government response" (Task Force on the Educational Needs of Native Peoples of Ontario, 1976:8). These and other reports indicted the lack of services and support for native peoples in virtually every area of the education system, including administration, community relations, finance, curricula, personnel, and counselling. Evidence of the system's failure was presented in several forms, notably high dropout rates and age-grade retardation among aboriginal students, discrimination, and lack of recognition of native cultural backgrounds. A review of learning resources used in Alberta Social Studies courses, for example, revealed both that while many materials made no reference to native issues, nearly two-thirds (63 percent) of those that did "were found to be either seriously problematic or completely unacceptable" because of factual errors, stereotyping, and ideological distortions in the presentation of the issues (Decore, Carney, and Urion, 1982).

These conditions both reflected and exacerbated the "Indian problem," and fuelled contending visions of what was best for natives. The prevalent meritocratic ideology presenting skill development and individual initiative as the basis for economic success served to trap the Indian into a system in which neither the socioeconomic rewards nor the prerequisites for those rewards were within reach (Frideres, 1987). Research findings like those of Kelly (1973:139), whose analysis of the relationship between schooling attainment and income revealed "virtually no contribution by additional years of schooling to the ability of Indians to earn an income," pointed to the conclusion that "unlike the studies of white population,... additional schooling does not raise Indians' income-earning potential." Agencies and officials which had a vested interest in native problems tended to define the situation in terms of wasted human potential. Native leaders emerged with a wider audience to demonstrate, in the stark words of Harold Cardinal (1969:2), that "Canada shows more interest in preserving its rare whooping cranes than its Indians." As educational credentials became an increasingly important screening mechanism for entry into labour markets, the revamping of native policy in Canada had to pay heed to education and training priorities.

Steps Towards the Devolution of First Nations Education

The emergence of strong native groups such as the National Indian Brotherhood (NIB) coincided with federal and provincial reassessment and consolidation of state services in the 1970s to provide an impetus for greater native input into the organization of services for natives. Federal government initiatives such as the 1973 policy acknowledging aboriginal rights, amendments to the Indian Act in 1985, and negotiations on a number of fronts to arrange provisions for aboriginal self-government began to recognize the principle of Indian self-determination and "special status" (Department of Indian and Northern Affairs, 1986; Weaver, 1981). Gradually, the government began to transfer resources and services to bands or native organizations.

In principle, the recent policy directions have conformed to the interests outlined by aboriginal organizations. These were expressed most strongly and coherently in the National Indian Brotherhood's 1972 paper on "Indian Control of Indian Education," which asserted Indians' fundamental right to "parental responsibility" and "local control" as the foundation for building a viable and equitable education system for aboriginal peoples. While the federal government was quick to agree to these principles, the next year signing an agreement with the National Indian Brotherhood to adopt a policy of Indian control of Indian education, the mechanics of such control remain unclear and contested. Paquette (1986:32), reviewing self-government initiatives in the area of education up to the mid-1980s, observes that, "If there is one certainty about aboriginal education policy in Canada, it is the generally uncertain nature of the policy process across that arena." Several problems, including lack of legal clarity regarding the terms of self-government, inadequate fiscal arrangements, and conflicting or uncertain jurisdictional boundaries among federal, provincial, territorial, and First Nations governments, have created a diverse array of administrative and institutional forms of aboriginal-controlled education (see Paquette, 1986, for details).

The first exercise of band-controlled schooling in Canada occurred at the Blue Quills Native Education Centre in central Alberta in 1970 and in Rae-Edzo, Northwest Territories, in 1971. In the decade between 1975-76 and 1985-86, the number of schools operated directly by bands increased more than fourfold, from 53 to 229 (Department of Indian and Northern Affairs, 1990:41). By the end of the 1989-90 school year, 300 of the 379 Indian schools nationwide were band controlled, with an additional 21 scheduled to come under band control by the fall (Indian and Northern Affairs Canada, 1990b:19). Table 5.1 illustrates the increase in enrollment in band-controlled schools relative to Indian children enrolled in schools under federal and provincial jurisdictions. The data indicate that by 1990-91, nearly one-half (44.0 percent) of on-reserve Indian children enrolled in elementary and secondary schools were attending band-controlled schools, compared with less than one-quarter (23 percent) just five years earlier and only 4 percent in 1975-76.

Table 5.1

Enrollment Of On-Reserve Population By School Type
Expressed As Percentage Of Total Enrollment, 1975-76 to 1990-91

Year	Federal	Provincial	Band-Operated	Private	Total Number of Students
1975-76	41.2	53.0	4.0	1.8	71 817
1976-77	41.8	51.4	4.7	2.1	71 717
1977-78	37.7	53.0	7.2	2.2	78 088
1978-79	35.2	55.8	7.1	1.9	81 359
1979-80	34.1	56.3	7.8	1.8	81 237
1980-81	32.1	56.6	9.5	1.8	82 801
1981-82	28.0	54.2	16.3	1.4	80 466
1982-83	28.2	49.7	20.6	1.5	77 412
1983-84	28.0	50.6	21.4	n/a	78 082
1984-85	27.0	50.0	22.9	n/a	80 121
1985-86	24.7	49.3	26.0	n/a	80 623
1986-87	22.9	48.7	28.5	n/a	82 271
1987-88	20.6	48.1	31.4	n/a	84 271
1988-89	16.1	47.9	36.0	n/a	85 582
1989-90	13.3	47.3	39.3	n/a	88 158
1990-91	8.8	47.2	44.0	n/a	92 018

Source: Calculated from Indian and Northern Affairs Canada, *Basic Departmental Data 1991*. Ottawa: Minister of Supply and Services Canada, p. 43.

The shift towards First Nations control over education has had, both directly and indirectly, several positive consequences for aboriginal students and their communities. More native students are remaining in school longer and achieving higher levels of education. As the data in Table 5.2 reveal, among Indian children living on reserves, the enrollment rate (the proportion of the 4-18-year-old population who are enrolled in kindergarten, elementary and secondary schools) increased from just under three-quarters in 1960-61 to over 91 percent in 1990-91.

This trend, it must be noted, does not in itself constitute evidence of success for local control, since the enrollment rate peaked at over 93 per-

Table 5.2

Enrollment in Kindergarten, Elementary and Secondary Schools,
On Reserve, and Rate of On-Reserve[3] Students Remaining
Until Grade 12 or 13 for Consecutive Years of Schooling,
Canada, 1960/61 to 1990-91

Year	Enrollment [1]	Population 4-18 Years	Enrollment Rate (Percent)	Retention Rate (Percent)
1960/61[2]	41 671	57 550	72.4	3.4
1965/66[2]	54 670	73 632	74.2	6.0
1970/71	68 449	81 531	84.0	14.6
1975/76	71 817	88 660	81.0	15.8
1980/81	82 801	88 581	93.5	19.6
1985/86	80 623	92 080	87.6	33.9
1986/87	82 271	94 169	87.4	42.2
1987/88	84 271	95 336	88.4	40.2
1988/89	85 582	96 606	88.6	41.4
1989/90	88 158	97 751	90.2	41.6 [4]
1990/91	92 018	100 717	91.4	47.0 [4]

Notes:
1. Total enrollment include registered, non-registered Indians and Inuit in Grades K4 to 13.
2. A breakdown of on/off-reserve Indian population was not available in 1960/61 and 1965/66. Based on 1975 Indian Register data, off reserve was estimated to be 26 percent of the total population. Data were also not available for the 4-18 population for 1960/61 and was estimated to 42 percent of the total Indian population.
3. On reserve includes Crown lands and settlements.
4. Preliminary estimate.

Source: Indian and Northern Affairs Canada, *Basic Departmental Data 1991.* Ottawa: Minister of Supply and Services Canada, Cat. No. r-12-7/1991E, pp. 35, 37.

cent in 1980-81, followed by a marked decline and levelling off in subsequent years, despite an increase in the number of band-operated schools. Nonetheless, over this period there has been evidence of increased educational attainment by the native population as a whole. As Table 5.2 shows, the proportion of students who have attended school continuously from Grade 1 to the end of high school rose markedly from 3.4 percent in 1960-61 to 47 percent in the early 1990s. This has also increased the pool of native students who are eligible to attend post-secondary institutions. The advantages of band control have been experienced in additional ways by natives and their communities. Local community members have been able to gain, often for the first time, input into and expertise in educational decision-making processes. Provisions for local control has facilitated the development and introduction of curricula and language experiences that reflect rather than deny aboriginal heritage, as opposed to the alienating legacy of past practices.

Despite these indicators of success, however, the movement towards First Nations control of education has not been problem-free. A combination of chronic underfunding and resource-related issues, like a shortage of adequately trained teachers, have meant that there is often a gap between the services and outcomes associated with band-operated schools relative to the public school system; moreover, because of the special nature of aboriginal schools, it is difficult to assess the extent to which parity can and should exist between the two systems (Paquette, 1986:52-54). The politics of education contribute to additional dilemmas, through disagreement over the meaning and nature of aboriginal control. Issues such as the extent to which First Nations education systems should priorize local and cultural issues relative to the provision of training for broader labour-market integration have significance both for the direction taken by educational programs and for the establishment of guidelines through which resources are allocated. Moreover, because many legal issues remain to be resolved, some bands limit their efforts in educational control to curricular matters out of fear that the transfer of complete administrative control will not be accompanied by adequate funding to operate a comprehensive and successful education system (Mabindisa, 1989). All of these matters, in turn, are constrained by funding arrangements and policies established by federal, provincial, and local levels of government.

A further limitation to the success of First Nations educational developments lies in the reality that band control does not affect large numbers of native peoples who lack Indian status and those who live off reserve, particularly in larger urban centres. Despite their sizable concentrations in many public schools, aboriginal students often face chronic problems such as discrimination and lack of appropriate services. High dropout rates remain prevalent. An analysis of the Grade 7-12 population in a sample of Saskatoon and Regina schools, for example, reveals that in 1980-81, native students had a dropout rate of 43.2 percent compared with 15.0 percent for non-natives; projected over the six-year period, this would mean that out of every 100 students who enrolled in Grade 7, 90 natives and 40 non-natives would not complete Grade 12 (Saskatchewan Education, 1985b:20-21). Native students, particularly females and status Indians, also tended to drop out of school earlier than other school leavers, with over half of all native dropouts (except for Métis and non-status Indian males where the figure was just under half) leaving school prior to the completion of Grade 9 (Saskatchewan Education, 1985b:28).

Increasingly, public school districts have taken steps to resolve some of these problems, with mixed results. The experience of Saskatchewan, in which students of aboriginal ancestry constituted 12.5 percent of the provincial school population in 1989, with projections that that figure will reach nearly one-quarter (22.8 percent) by 2006 (Kuster, 1990:17), is indicative of these dilemmas. In the early 1980s, the provincial government began to consolidate its efforts to address native concerns in education. Although the province had developed several initiatives in this area in the previous decade, such as the hiring of a provincial Native Educational Program Consultant in 1971, the establishment a year later of the Saskatchewan Indian Cultural College, the creation of an Indian Teacher Education Program at the University of Saskatchewan in 1973 and subsequent programs for northern and urban native teacher education, and the introduction of a Native Survival School (now operating as Joe Duquette High School) within the Saskatoon Separate School Board, it was not until 1982 that the provincial education department appointed a Native Curriculum Review Committee to initiate and coordinate curricular and program activities pertaining to the special needs of native students (Native Curriculum Review Committee, 1984:1, 8-10). In 1984, the committee specified three priorities — the integration of native curricular materials into the province's core curriculum, the production of supplemental materials, and the development of courses in native studies and languages — as part of its "five year action plan" for native curriculum development in the province (Native Curriculum Review Committee, 1984:2). In a related measure, following consultation with selected educational participants across the province, the education department produced a document that outlined a coordinated approach to Indian and Métis education which favoured a strategy of improvements in the existing education system over the possible creation of an alternative system (Saskatchewan Education, 1985b:46). The province then adopted in 1985 the four principles set out in the report to guide Indian and Métis educational policy:

1. Indian and Métis peoples must be given the opportunity to participate fully in the education system at all levels.
2. The education system must recognize Indian and Métis students are the children of peoples whose cultures are, in many ways, very different from those of the people who established the school system. These differences which may include learning styles, language and world-view, must be accounted for in curriculum, programs, teaching methods and climate in the schools attended by Indian and Métis children.
3. There must be co-operation and consultation among all federal, provincial, local and Indian and Métis authorities to ensure co-ordination of efforts to meet the needs of Indian and Métis students.
4. Efforts to improve the success of Indian and Métis students in school are most effective at the school-community level (Saskatchewan Education, 1985a:1; Saskatchewan Education, 1989:5).

Consistent with these principles, a series of curricular and resource developments has been implemented to realize the objectives outlined in the five-year action plan under the auspices of a provincial Indian and Métis Curriculum Advisory Committee. Initiatives have included the development of curricula and materials with native content in the areas of Language Arts, Social Studies, Health, and the Creative Arts; steps to develop curricula in Native Studies, Cree, and other native languages; the production of audio-visual resources emphasizing aboriginal heritage and culture; and in-service training aimed at increasing cross-cultural awareness and reducing racial bias among education system participants (Saskatchewan Education, 1988).

In addition, beginning in 1986, several school districts began to establish programs and guidelines for education equity under terms of reference established by the Saskatchewan Human Rights Commission, directed to the goal of reducing the number of aboriginal school dropouts. Nineteen school boards, encompassing about 36 percent of the province's elementary and secondary school population, have designed education equity plans, based on five components of "ensuring school policies and procedures are not biased, cross-cultural training, participation of aboriginal parents, hiring of aboriginal teachers, and ensuring curriculum is relevant to aboriginal students" (Saskatchewan Human Rights Commission, 1990:18).

As with the education department's recent initiatives, the education equity programs have produced several tangible results, like in-service training, community involvement in the schools, learning resources developments, and cultural events that have been targeted, with some effectiveness, to ensure that aboriginal students are provided equal participation in the school system. The scope and success of such activities can be illustrated by the following sample of initiatives which constitute part of the "Circle of Life: Education Equity Program" offered by the Saskatoon Catholic Board of Education (1991): recruitment, orientation, and career counselling priorities for native teachers; the delivery and monitoring of cross-cultural workshops and conferences in areas such as teaching styles, family violence, and native art, as well as cultural awareness sessions with participation by native elders and community members; the organization of meals, community liaisons, family support services, and volunteer programs to involve parents and community members in the schools; and the introduction of curricular programs and resources relevant to aboriginal concerns in areas such as native studies, hoop dancing, and career work education.

It is clear that many of these initiatives, long overdue, are important steps towards the recognition of native peoples and their unique circumstances in the education system. While the changes are having some beneficial impact, they are also subject to severe limitations. Many proposed curriculum and program developments are proceeding, if at all, at a much slower pace than projected. Departmental and school board reports are full of glowing descriptions of promised initiatives, but there is no certainty that they will be delivered as outlined because of problems such as resource shortfalls, conflicting priorities, and lack of clear commitment to their development among school system personnel. In some cases, concern to attract and retain aboriginal students is motivated by financial considerations. Stated simply, school boards provide services to, and often stand to gain from having on their rolls, registered Indian students because of capital and tuition funding agreements between the Department of Indian Affairs and provincial governments. In 1988-89, $199.9 million was provided under these arrangements to the provinces for tuition of an estimated 40 925 Indian students attending provincial schools, for an average of $4884.54 per student, which constitutes a substantial proportion of the gross national cost per student of $5175.00 at the elementary and secondary school levels (calculated from Indian and Northern Affairs Canada, 1989b:3; Statistics Canada, 1989:22, 28).

School districts, under these circumstances, often make efforts to give the impression that progress is being made, even in the absence of any substantial results. A case in point is the hiring of teachers of aboriginal origin. As Table 5.3 reveals, education equity programs so far have

Table 5.3

Representation Of Students and Teachers of Aboriginal
Ancestry in Seventeen Saskatchewan School
Divisions, 1987-88 and 1990-91

	1987-88					
	Teachers			Students		
School Division	Aboriginal Ancestry (a.a.)	Total	a.a. as % of Total	Aboriginal Ancestry (a.a)	Total	a.a. as % of Total
Biggar	1.0	71.5	1.4	107	961	11.1
Broadview	0.0	90.5	0.0	216	1446	14.9
Cupar	0.0	94.7	0.0	205	1579	13.0
Indian Head	1.0	97.7	1.0	246	1642	15.0
Kamsack	4.0	75.0	5.3	250	862	29.0
Meadow Lake	5.0	147.4	3.4	631	2525	25.0
North Battleford						
Catholic	5.0	92.2	5.4	323	1579	20.5
Northern Lakes	0.0	100.0	0.0	327	1600	20.4
Northern Lights	64.0	268.5	23.8	3861	4516	85.5
Prince Albert						
Catholic	2.0	155.0	1.3	606	2471	24.5
Comprehensive	2.0	80.0	2.5	108	1551	7.0
Public	7.0	211.0	3.3	795	3764	21.1

Table 5.3 Continued

	a.a.	Total	a.a. as % of Total	a.a.	Total	a.a. as % of Total
Regina Catholic	1.0	509.0	0.2	800	9758	8.2
Saskatoon						
Catholic	10.5	660.0	1.6	1112	12 449	8.9
Public	38.0	1120.0	3.4	1511	21 898	6.9
Wadena	0.0	116.8	0.0	94	2134	4.4
Wilkie	1.0	87.0	1.1	89	1370	6.5
TOTAL	141.5	3976.3	3.6	11 281	72 155	15.6

1990-91

	Teachers			Students		
School Division	Aboriginal Ancestry (a.a.)	Total	a.a. as % of Total	Aboriginal Ancestry (a.a)	Total	a.a. as % of Total
Biggar	1.0	65.3	1.5	116	936	12.4
Broadview	1.0	89.5	1.1	264	1433	18.4
Cupar	0.0	88.1	0.0	194	1488	13.0
Indian Head	1.0	103.5	1.0	449	1776	25.3
Kamsack	2.8	61.0	4.6	176	970	18.1
Meadow Lake	11.0	154.0	7.1	600	2555	23.5
North Battleford						
Catholic	7.0	93.0	7.5	287	1614	17.8
Northern Lakes	1.0	104.0	1.0	276	1556	17.7
Northern Lights	72.0	284.0	25.4	n/a	4445	n/a
Prince Albert						
Catholic	5.0	144.7	3.5	737	2602	28.3
Comprehensive	3.0	84.0	3.6	295	1640	18.0
Public	8.5	223.5	3.8	n/a	4055	n/a
Regina Catholic	3.0	489.0	0.8	n/a	9642	n/a
Saskatoon						
Catholic	12.5	715.5	1.7	1185	12 880	9.2
Public	35.0	1212.0	2.9	1931	21 943	8.8
Wadena	0.0	113.8	0.0	203	1990	10.2
Wilkie	2.0	79.5	2.5	85	1272	6.7
TOTAL	165.8	4104.4	4.0	6798*	54 655*	12.4*

Note: * Total numbers of students do not include figures from school divisions with incomplete data, and are likely to underestimate the overall proportion of aboriginal students.

Source: Figures from Saskatchewan Human Rights Commission, Education Equity Reports submitted by school divisions, and from Saskatchewan Education statistical reports.

resulted only in slight improvements in the number and proportion of aboriginal teachers in most school districts, while some divisions including larger ones like Saskatoon Public Schools have even experienced a decline. Moreover, the objective of parity in the proportions of aboriginal students and teachers within the school system is continually subject to revision. While there has been an increase in the number and proportion of teachers of aboriginal origin in school districts with education equity programs, the evidence (after taking into account divisions with missing data for 1990-91) indicates that the number and proportion of aboriginal students are increasing at even higher rates. The major reasons cited by school boards for an inability to meet Education Equity hiring targets are restricted hiring opportunities or even cutbacks in teaching personnel combined with a lack of qualified applicants for the positions which do become available.

However, regardless of positive efforts taken by school boards to meet native students' needs and to attract and retain teachers of aboriginal origin, there remain within the structure and practices of the provincial school system serious inadequacies for aboriginal peoples. School divisions commonly experience high rates of attrition among teachers of aboriginal origin. Between 1987 and 1990, for example, the Saskatoon Catholic Board of Education (1991:2) hired fifteen teachers of native ancestry but lost 9.5 native teachers over the same period. Typically, aboriginal teachers encounter problems over the issue of complete integration into school systems. Regardless of their backgrounds and levels of qualification and competence, their identity as teachers of aboriginal origin places them at risk of being singled out as different from the general teaching force. This dilemma is often compounded by their placement in schools with high concentrations of native students which, of course, makes sense in the context of recognized special needs of aboriginal students. However, this also carries with it the strong possibility that these schools and school system personnel are, or are perceived to be, ghettoized within (and by implication inferior to) the school system as a whole. On the other hand, teacher placement practices which do not take into account students' and teachers' backgrounds create a different set of potential difficulties in which services do not fulfill the needs of the targeted groups. These problems are evident also with school system personnel other than teachers. Persons of aboriginal origin who are employed by school divisions are more likely to be in subordinate or teaching assistant roles, and are rarely found in administrative positions. In the Kamsack School Division (1991:2), for example, while there were equal numbers of native teachers and teaching assistants/native liaison counsellors in 1990, the former represented only 4.5 percent of the teaching staff, while the latter constituted over one-third (38.6 percent) of the total teaching assistant/native liaison counselling staff (by comparison, native students constituted 18 percent of the total student population). At the other extreme, native persons are grossly underrepresented in administrative positions. This can be illustrated with reference to the Northern Lights School Division, which encompasses the northern half of the province and has the province's highest concentration of teachers of aboriginal origin (25.4 percent of the total teaching staff). In 1990-91, the division employed only three native principals and two native vice-principals out of a total complement of thirty principals and twelve vice-principals in the division's schools (Northern Lights School Division, 1990:2). Finally, the education equity programs have not yet provided any significant indication of improvements in the attendance and attainment patterns among aboriginal students, particularly of status Indians. Efforts to track native students through schools within the Regina Catholic Board of Education, for instance, reveal that students of aboriginal origin have a higher than average risk in primary grades of developing problems in academic progress, face problems in transition from elementary to secondary school, have lower than average attendance rates in high school, and experience high rates of transiency and early school leaving (Kuster, 1990).

RECENT TRENDS IN POST-SECONDARY EDUCATION AND VOCATIONAL TRAINING

Consistent with patterns in elementary and secondary education, only partial improvements have been made in the rates of participation and attainment by aboriginal students in post-secondary education and vocational training programs. As the figures in Table 5.4 indicate, there have been substantial increases in both enrollment by and expenditures on natives in post-secondary institutions (colleges and universities). These trends, showing an increase of nearly four times in the number of Indians enrolled in post-secondary programs and an increase of about ten times in post-secondary funding in the decade between 1980-81 and 1990-91, indicate that, for various reasons, education systems have made great progress in their ability to extend the educational careers of many aboriginal peoples. Post-secondary institutions throughout Canada, particularly in the western provinces, have over the past five to ten years taken steps to become more receptive to native concerns, especially as they have faced competition for students and resources from institutions like the Saskatchewan Indian Federated College, which offers its own courses in Arts and Sciences and professional programs. Recent initiatives have included the provision of program offerings such as native studies, pre-professional training in areas such as nursing, teaching, law, and social work, and various counselling and student services in order to attract and retain native students (see McGivern, 1990, for details). Affirmative action and employment equity programs have also contributed to increased educational attainment among aboriginal peoples.

These trends, nonetheless, must be interpreted with some caution. As with programs in elementary and secondary schools, post-secondary institutions have sometimes been reticent to embrace initiatives to promote educational progress among natives, particularly if they are perceived to provide competition for resources in universities and colleges threatened with program and staffing cutbacks and rationalization of services. There are also several factors which restrict the number of aboriginal students who are able to attend and complete post-secondary studies, in addition to general problems such as discrimination and lack of success at previous levels of schooling discussed earlier. The matter of financial assistance has a strong bearing on individuals' chances of attending and completing higher educational studies (Wotherspoon, 1991). As a social group who occupy a generally disadvantaged socioeconomic position, native peoples face several impediments to educational success. Poverty, in addition to its association with health and nutritional problems that may impede learning, often makes it difficult to compete in a system that places great emphasis on an individual's access to material resources. Competing priorities like child care and the need to manage a family on a limited budget cut into the time and energy that an individual has to devote to educational studies.

One controversial issue in this regard is the question of federal financial assistance to Indian post-secondary students. In the mid-1970s, after

Table 5.4

National Indian Post-secondary Enrollment and
Expenditures, 1969-70 to 1990-91

Year	Post-secondary enrollment	Post-secondary expenditures ($ millions)
1969-70	808	0.4
1974-75	2500	3.0
1980-81	4999	17.0
1981-82	5467	25.1
1982-83	6810	33.1
1983-84	8062	42.0
1984-85	8617	52.9
1985-86	11 170	58.9
1986-87	13 196	92.7
1987-88	14 242	110.0
1988-89	15 104	123.3
1989-90	18 535	147.1
1990-91	21 300	170.0

Note: Figures for 1990-91 are preliminary estimates by Indian and Northern Affairs Canada.

Source: Data from Indian Affairs Annual Reports, Indian and Northern Affairs Canada Information Sheet No. 5 (April, 1989), and Indian and Northern Affairs Canada 1991-92 Expenditure Plan.

more than a decade of providing assistance for continuing education to Indian and Inuit students, the federal government consolidated the funding arrangements through a series of documents known as the E-12 guidelines. The guidelines, formally approved by the Treasury Board in 1977, provided for federal assistance to cover the costs of tuition, books and supplies, travel, and living allowances for Indian and Inuit students enrolled in university, college, and pre-entrance preparatory programs. In 1989, citing pressures caused by increasing costs and growing numbers of eligible students, the federal government replaced the program with a new one, the Postsecondary Student Assistance Program, which tightened eligibility and funding restrictions for Indian and Inuit post-secondary students (Indian and Northern Affairs Canada, 1989b:6-8; Lanceley, 1991). By arguing that under the E-12 guidelines, "People were going *to* school, but not enough were going *through* school," the Minister of Indian Affairs justified the implementation of performance standards and an annual ceiling on program expenditures that were part of the new guidelines (Cadieux, 1989). The announcement of the program changes provoked an outcry of protest from native groups, who claimed that the new terms of reference were even more inadequate than the previous guidelines. Protest centred on the specific concerns that large numbers of aboriginal students would not receive funding for post-secondary studies while other students would face cutbacks in the length and amount of funding for which they would be eligible. In the academic year beginning in 1991, the Assembly of First Nations and other native groups claimed that over 4000 native students would not be funded under the program, while even the Minister for Indian Affairs estimated that between 1000 and 1500 eligible students would not be covered under the program (Saskatoon *Star-Phoenix*, 1991:bB5).

Besides the question of severe inadequacies in the program, though, a more fundamental issue has been native peoples' concern that the federal government unilaterally altered the program guidelines without proper consultation with First Nations groups, combined with the perpetuation of the government's position that post-secondary education is not a treaty right (Lanceley, 1991). When the program changes were first announced, the student protest, which included the occupation of Indian and Northern Affairs offices in different regions of the country, a hunger strike by several students in Ontario and Saskatchewan, and the formation of a National Student Network, prompted the federal government to loosen some of the restrictions over the length and amount of assistance provided under the program (Cadieux, 1989:30-32; Lanceley, 1991:244-245).

One key consequence of the protest movement was its significance as an unprecedented step towards the politicization and unification of aboriginal students both within particular educational institutions and across the country. Formal education has long had contradictory implications for native peoples, serving to suppress the general aboriginal population but at the same time fostering the emergence of an articulate, knowledgeable corps of native leaders whose impact upon native organizations, in turn, has varied from reactionary to moderate to radical. In the past, the prominence attached to the relatively few native persons with post-secondary education made them susceptible to being perceived as token examples of Indian success or as role models who could lead the advancement of native issues and concerns. The recent expansion in the number of native students who enroll in and complete post-secondary studies has given aboriginal peoples access to a much broader range of occupational and political positions. Moreover, educational and professional contact among these students and graduates has provided the basis for collective action, using the student protest network as an important catalyst.

Nonetheless, this factor, which may serve to facilitate the rise of aboriginal power and influence, is also related to a significant limitation. In order to understand this constraint, it is necessary to refer to the general distribution of native peoples in the educational and occupational structure. As noted earlier, native peoples' overall educational attainment and occupational levels are well below those of the general Canadian population. Despite improvements and efforts to close these gaps, the majority of native peoples continue to have relatively low levels of formal education and are destined for entry into the lower reaches of the labour market. Those who do achieve entry into, and complete, higher education are part of a select group. In an analysis of 1986 census data pertaining to participation and success rates among eligible persons (those who have earned at least a high school diploma), Armstrong, Kennedy, and Oberle (1990:9) found that eligible non-Indians were 1.5 times more likely than eligible Indians to attend university and 3.6 times more likely to complete a degree program. In 1988-89, between one-quarter and one-third (29.4 percent) of Canadians in the 18-24-year age group were enrolled in full-time post-secondary studies, while the *total* number of registered Indians enrolled in full-time post-secondary programs constituted about 20 percent of the number of registered Indians in the 18-24-year age cohort (Indian and Northern Affairs Canada, 1989b:7; Loh, 1990:54-55; Statistics Canada, 1991:117). Moreover, about half of those Indians enrolled in post-secondary studies are at least 25 years of age, compared with a national median post-secondary age of between 20 and 21 (Indian and Northern Affairs Canada, 1991:2-66). While the trend for older Indian students to enter post-secondary institutions after interruptions in their educational career is encouraging, it also points to further aspects of selectivity that are attached to the educational process, which in turn reinforce the class structure that we discussed in Chapter 3.

These tendencies can be understood with reference to the kinds of educational and vocational studies engaged in by native peoples. It is particularly noteworthy that, while aboriginal students enroll in and complete a wide range of programs, they tend to be highly concentrated in only a few areas. At the university level, native students are concentrated in teacher education, nursing, and social work programs as well as in areas such as Native Studies, Cree, and native law which have native concerns as their specific focus. Community college and trades training programs also tend to emphasize native participation in para-professional work in the education, health, and social services sectors as well as in administrative services and vocations that correspond with broader federal aims in aboriginal economic development. Federally-sponsored initiatives like the Indian Community Human Resource Strategies program, the Indian Business Development program, and various on-the-job and work-experience programs provide funding and training for individuals to fill targeted positions in specific industries and enterprises. While increasing the diversity of credentials and employment situations to which native peoples have had access, these strategies have contributed to the formation of a hierarchical model of development which widens the opportunity gap among natives.

What is noteworthy about this process is that it appears to be shifting social relations among native peoples towards a replication of wider class and occupational structures. As we stressed in Chapter 3, Canadian labour markets in the late 20th century have been characterized by a "declining middle," in which new job creation has emphasized the proliferation of positions which tend to be concentrated at either high or low extremes in terms of the relative distribution of skills, wages, and working conditions (see, e.g., Economic Council of Canada, 1990; Myles, Picot, and Wannell, 1988). There is evidence of these same tendencies within the aboriginal population, in which class fractionalization is concentrating around two poles — a limited but relatively privileged sector of bourgeois entrepreneurs and new petite bourgeois professionals or highly-skilled workers, and a massive pool of wage labourers who are subject to exploitation by both native and non-native employers.

The first group has benefitted the most from state-sponsored educational and economic opportunities. Federal government activities, justified in part by the observation in the Hawthorn Report that there existed "a relatively high Indian motivation towards self-employment or individual proprietorship, and a consequent aversion to traditional employer/employee relationships" (Department of Indian Affairs and Northern Development, 1980:46), have contributed to the cultivation of an entrepreneurial and professional elite within the aboriginal population. As we observed in Chapter 3, 16.1 percent of single origin Indian men and 29.0 percent of Indian women, compared with 25.7 percent of men and 28.7 percent of women in the general Canadian population, were employed in managerial and professional occupations. While these data are potentially misleading in that many jobs included in these categories, especially those performed by women in government services, paraprofessional work, and low-level management positions, involve little real control and discretion for the employee, they do indicate that for natives, as with the general population, a small but substantial proportion of workers is fairly well-situated occupationally relative to most people.

Governments have directed many of their recent efforts and resources at programs which have fostered subclasses of native managers, state agents, and "safe" political leaders. Federal economic development initiatives, such as the Indian/Inuit Management Development program, produce native managers who ensure that band resources and enterprises are utilized productively and efficiently in terms defined by capital and the state. In 1985-86, for example, an Indian Management Assistance program produced twenty-nine student advisors to offer managerial services to band and tribal councils, and the Department of Indian and Northern Affairs allocated $1.5 million for a Native Business Summit and Trade Show (Department of Indian and Northern Affairs, 1986:18, 22). Similarly, those persons of aboriginal origin who have completed university degrees have opportunities open to them that are beyond the reach of the general native population, and in some instances even the non-native population. When work experience is controlled for among young people in the 15-24-years of age cohort, registered Indians with university degrees have a labour force participation rate of 90.6 percent compared with a rate of 88.0 percent among non-Indians, and a median income of $8158 compared with a median income of $7713 among non-Indians (Armstrong, Kennedy, and Oberle, 1990:42).

The growth of native enterprises combined with a belated embracing of the need for employment equity programs by many public- and private-sector employers has created new opportunities for employment and occupational advancement among aboriginal peoples, particularly those with educational credentials and other skills. Paradoxically, these practices have sometimes placed limits on the educational advancement of native peoples because large numbers of promising young aboriginal scholars have interrupted their studies, particularly at the post-graduate level, as they have been induced by the immediate prospects of careers that appear to be relatively attractive and well-paying. In addition, band economic development strategies and self-government initiatives have meant that native peoples themselves increasingly are called upon to manage not only aboriginal-specific enterprises, but also the economic and social problems that accompany them. The transfer to band control of federal funding for post-secondary education, for instance, has downloaded to aboriginal communities the difficult question of how to distribute resources that are often inadequate to meet local needs. Funds directed to specific purposes such as education are often diverted to more pressing community requirements for local administration and infrastructural services, often with the tacit consent of the Indian Affairs department which seeks little or no financial information or monitoring of programs delivered at the band level, as a 1991 inquiry into financial arrangements by Saskatchewan's Meadow Lake Tribal Council has revealed (Greenshields, 1991). Moreover, as federal policy initiatives in the 1980s and 1990s have shifted many of the risks of economic and educational development to native bands and individuals, there has been no assurance of a clear commitment to support for future stability.

At the same time, higher education and entrepreneurial capabilities are not in themselves tickets to a rosy future. As more aboriginal persons attain educational credentials, the persistent danger of underemployment increases. Structural barriers that limit the number of "good jobs" within labour markets are reinforced by other factors such as racial discrimination. Speaking at a forum on native employment in 1988, the chairperson of the Interprovincial Association on Native Employment observed that:

> There are thousands of young Indian people who have been told for years, "If you get an education you will get a job." They are getting educated ... but they are not getting jobs. Some employers still haven't changed their negative attitudes towards Indians (Munroe, 1988).

Moreover, there is considerable interaction between dimensions of gender and recent educational and labour force changes. Although comprehensive data are not available, trends we have pointed out in previous chapters indicate that women and men are likely to benefit or be restricted in different ways by these transformations. Because females constitute a higher proportion than males of Indians living off reserves, and because most Bill C-31 Indians are female, Indian women have potentially greater access to expanded educational services and support. As we saw in Chapter 3, the proportions of aboriginal women employed in professional occupations involving advanced education were greater than those of aboriginal men. Moreover, some of the strongest advocates of aboriginal rights, particularly as illustrated in student protests over changes in the Postsecondary Student Assistance Program guidelines and critiques over inadequate aboriginal representation in recent debates over national constitutional negotiations, have come from women attending or recently graduated from post-secondary institutions. Educational opportunities have provided for many aboriginal women new avenues of input into decision-making both on and off reserves. At the same time, though, native women often stand to benefit less than men from entrepreneurial support programs and other educational services. Domestic responsibilities and economic and political impediments, notably in the form of the structure of employment itself, continue to relegate most aboriginal women to subordinate positions both in and out of work.

For the majority of native peoples, along with growing proportions of the general population, the prospects for relatively stable, meaningful, and well-paying careers are highly limited. Formal schooling, vocational training, and other employment programs tend to be oriented to the production of low-cost labour power. The massive proportions of the native population who have low levels of educational attainment are in large part a reflection of the reality that credentials, in themselves, do not go very far in the absence of a fundamental restructuring of labour markets. Most of the vocational programs for natives are of short duration and highly specific in nature, providing limited skill development for jobs which may be in short supply or unavailable in particular geographical regions. Noting that the federal government in 1984-85 spent an estimated $163.8 million on sixteen training and short-term job creation programs, the federal Task Force on Program Review (1985:113) commented that "Training for training's sake, with no expectation or opportunity to use these skills in a job, appears to have become the norm rather than the exception." Consequently, the trainee becomes locked into a perpetual cycle of training, retraining, and upgrading. Those natives with limited schooling or job training are forced to seek work in whatever situations they can find it, often requiring considerable movement from one region to another. They become in the process dependent upon work opportunities that are highly elusive. Furthermore, the availability of a substantial pool of low-cost labour power is crucial to the success of many aboriginal enterprises and on-reserve economic development projects. Whether managed and employed by natives or non-natives, the social and economic circumstances are such that a massive underclass of aboriginal peoples will remain a long-standing reality within the Canadian social landscape.

Conclusion

This chapter has presented the development of education for aboriginal peoples in Canada as a contradictory endeavour. Changing education policies and practices, understood as elements of broader structural transformations, have served to shape the lives and opportunities (usually in a restrictive sense) open to aboriginal peoples. It is important here to reiterate the point made in the previous chapter that people do not simply "step in" to ready-made class, gender, and "race" positions and identities; instead, these social characteristics emerge out of people's lived realities. Education has been a powerful tool in structuring these realities. By shaping personalities as well as contributing to a person's utility and competitiveness as defined by prevailing social and economic circumstances, educational practices constitute a strategic part of the political agenda for any group which seeks to control its own destiny or that of other groups.

We have discussed in this chapter the ways in which formal systems of education for aboriginal peoples have been introduced and modified through state responsiveness to capitalist development. However, our analysis has shown that these educational transformations have not been accomplished either as simple consequences of narrow economic determinants or as one-sided, fully successful instances of capitalist domination over a homogeneous group of people. Schooling's relevance lies not so much in its ability to prepare people for entry into labour markets as in its broader capacities to manage populations. For aboriginal peoples, this has meant that formal education has been implicated as a powerful tool in the transition from subsistence-based modes of production through different stages of capitalist development. In the process, segments of the native population have made some gains, in terms of personal benefit, opportunities for resistance, and input into decision-making processes within and beyond the education system. However, these benefits have tended to be limited in scope and not equally distributed among aboriginal peoples, as education has contributed to and reinforced distinct gender, class, and racialized positions both in and out of the labour force.

Our observations reveal that recent trends in the direction of devolution of educational services to aboriginal communities and responsiveness to native concerns within the general education system will perpetuate the contradictory tendencies that are central to formal education. Clearly, increased direct involvement by native peoples in education planning and program delivery have enabled many aboriginal peoples to gain new credentials, a sense of respect, and access to positions that were previously denied them. Nonetheless, there remain significant structural limitations to educational success so long as educational programs operate within societies characterized by class, "race," and gender segmentation.

NOTE

1. Portions of this chapter have appeared in revised form in Terry Wotherspoon, "Indian Control or Controlling Indians? Barriers to the Occupational and Educational Advancement of Canada's Indigenous Population," in Terry Wotherspoon, ed., *Hitting the Books: The Politics of Educational Retrenchment*, Toronto and Saskatoon: Garamond Press and Social Research Unit, 1991, pp. 249-273.

CHAPTER 6

HEALTH STATUS AND HEALTH CARE

INTRODUCTION

The health status of a population reveals many things about its social and economic circumstances. Degrees of healthiness or ill health, chances and causes of death, and life expectancy reflect important characteristics about the nature and quality of people's living conditions. This chapter explores several dimensions of health conditions which among native peoples in general are significantly worse than those for the overall Canadian population. The list of problems is extensive, as indicated by such factors as life expectancy, chronic physical and mental health disorders, alcohol and drug-related problems, suicide, and injuries and deaths from violence (see, e.g., Health and Welfare Canada, 1988). We present these indicators of health status, as well as the organization and delivery of health care services, as products of shifting social, economic, and political relations, especially as experienced through the introduction and development of the capitalist mode of production. We argue that the dominant structure of medicine and health care institutions under capitalism, though offering some crucial advancements in aboriginal peoples' health status, interacts with existing social inequalities by subordinating the needs of minority populations. The capitalist "medicine chest," even with medicare and other state-supported services, serves to erode both traditional aboriginal medicinal practices and the health conditions of large proportions of Canada's aboriginal peoples.

BIOLOGICAL AND CULTURAL MODELS OF HEALTH STATUS

There are various ways in which differences in health status among populations are explained. Among the most common are biological and cultural explanations. Biological explanations locate the source of health problems in the physiological or genetic constitution of the individual, while cultural accounts, in common with pluralist and Chicago School models of assimilation discussed in Chapter 1, emphasize differences between two or more cultural standards and ways of life. Research supporting both approaches has gained increasing currency and sophistication in recent years. However, we argue after a brief assessment of each that both types of analysis are limited through their failure to account for the realities of unequal policies, social structures, and economic practices.

Biological explanations of health status focus on the intrinsic characteristics of particular individuals or groups of people. Common expressions such as those that point to a person's low tolerance for alcohol or sickly demeanour focus on supposed biological determinants of health problems. As Bolaria (1988:538-539) observes, this approach assumes that people's health is a product of their natural endowments, in terms of either their physical characteristics, their organic capacity to adapt to new diseases or conditions, or their mental capabilities to follow correct preventative procedures. There is a strong body of scientific research as well as common sensory evidence to validate these claims. It has been widely demonstrated, for instance, that health risks ranging from cancer and heart disease to visual and mental disorders are often hereditary, while ongoing research efforts attempt to uncover connections between such problems as alcoholism and genetic characteristics.

In the face of such knowledge, there is no denying that biological factors contribute to people's health status in very decisive ways. Nonetheless, the implications of attributing biological and individual characteristics as primary causes of health problems must be examined carefully. The danger of these explanations of health is that problems are reduced to the level of individual qualities and behaviours and, on the basis of attributes observed over a range of individuals, generalized to wider populations. Thus, the health status of particular subgroups such as the aboriginal population is often viewed as the manifestation of inherent qualities possessed by those people. However, any population, including native peoples, emerges historically as a composite of diverse social, political, and economic categories of persons. With respect to aboriginal people, the validity of claims that they inherently possess "Indian" characteristics is highly suspect. The argument that health is largely a consequence of inborn qualities ignores the variable impact that social environments have upon both health risks and the diagnosis of health problems. While biological factors set limits on a person's life chances, it is vital to recognize that exposure to health hazards and access to such necessities as clean air and water, adequate housing, proper sanitary facilities, nutritious food, and medical supplies are crucial determinants of health status. Persons who share similar living conditions are likely to experience similar health problems over the course of time.

A predisposition towards biological and individual characteristics of illness has been promoted by the dominance of medical models which emphasize the treatment of pathologies rather than the socioeconomic foundations and prevention of health problems (Bolaria, 1988). The isolation of various dimensions of health care into narrow components, justified by scientific foundations, enables the intervention by medical practitioners who possess particular forms of expertise. In the process, the social foundations of health problems, including unhealthy living and working conditions, are either ignored or transformed into matters of individual choice.

The implication of this dominant model of health care is that individuals or collectivities are blamed for their health conditions. Viewed in these terms, the recurrent health problems experienced by native peoples are deemed to signify the unfitness or inferiority of aboriginal peoples relative to the general population. However, such a focus is concerned especially with the identification of health problems after they occur, regardless of the social context within which they were produced. Consequently, given a treatment orientation that is concerned more with the symptoms than the causes of the problems, it is not surprising that the overall health status of Indian people remains inadequate.

Cultural explanations of health and illness have attempted to address deficiencies in the biological and individual approach. According to cultural analysis, differences in the health status of particular social groups are more a product of the everyday practices of those groups and of the standards employed in the health diagnosis and delivery process than of individual pathologies. Models derived from the dominant Eurocentric world view stand in contrast to the experiences of Indians through their traditional orientations to the world and the isolation experienced in reserve living (Nagler, 1975). Under these circumstances, health problems are examined not merely in terms of disorders and illnesses themselves, which are seen to be derived from living in a "culture of poverty," but also in relation to treatment processes. Medical professionals who have displaced traditional aboriginal healing and medicinal practices, and who are uneducated about native culture, may help to perpetuate rather than eradicate health problems (Shah and Farkas, 1985).

The cultural model points out many important aspects of the mainstream health care system which contribute to Indians' health care problems. Frideres (1988:144-145) emphasizes that native peoples, through their experiences with poverty, within which illness is common, and their holistic approach to life, which integrates health into a unified view of the social and natural environments, have been failed by the dominant medical system in several ways: non-native health care practitioners are often unaware of or insensitive to native perspectives on health and illness; Indians are undermined for living under conditions that are conducive to disease but from which they cannot escape; health-care service delivery is situated in urban environments or oriented to community circumstances foreign to the experiences of most native peoples; Indian input into the organization of health care services is minimal; and health problems are often magnified as a result of jurisdictional disputes and inefficient bureaucratic procedures. In short, the organization and delivery of health care services oriented to the demands and interests of white, middle-class administrators, professionals, and clients tend to conspire against the real health care needs of aboriginal peoples.

While these observations are important in showing that health care problems are not merely the consequences of individual or group characteristics, it is necessary to probe further in order to understand the social, economic, and political conditions within which these problems originate. In particular, we must be sensitive to the problems associated with adopting an uncritical notion of "culture" which is presented in such a way that it appears as a primordial feature of a particular group of people. As we have observed earlier with respect to education and social conditions, culture is not something that can be isolated from other aspects of life, since it refers to a total way of life, including both the experiences and the modes of understanding that people collectively employ to make sense of their shared existence (McLaren, 1989:171). Expressed in these terms, culture is not something that merely "belongs" to or reflects a particular social group but, rather, it expresses the total landscape that shapes and is shaped by ongoing social activity.

At the same time, some caution has to be employed in the interpretation of health indicators, because concepts of health are both relative and socially constructed (Doyal and Pennell, 1979; Waitzkin, 1983). Notions of longevity and quality of life, for example, are likely to have different meanings in pre-industrial societies where average life expectancy is 20 years in contrast to contemporary Canadian society where people may expect to live on average over 75 years. Similarly, modern industrial notions of health are driven by models of medical rationality which provide technical or science-based assumptions for the diagnosis and treatment of various health concerns.

A MATERIALIST ALTERNATIVE TO THE EXPLANATION OF NATIVE PEOPLES' HEALTH STATUS

The preceding comments have indicated that health conditions reflect much more than individual characteristics and the way in which they have come to be interpreted and treated within particular cultural contexts. They must, instead, be viewed as part of a group's struggle for stability and survival in terms of relations among members of that group as well as with other social groups. In other words, the story of the health status of Canada's indigenous population must be told in terms of the historical circumstances which have encompassed aboriginal life at particular times and places, recognizing as well the heterogeneous nature of aboriginal peoples' social circumstances, both under different modes of production and within capitalism.

All societies require at least minimal standards of health care in order to ensure that necessary social tasks are fulfilled and the population is able to maintain itself. The degree to which these conditions are adequate will vary in accordance with a society's resources and needs. As Marx (1970, 72) observed, so long as living standards and skill requirements are low, "A quick succession of unhealthy and short-lived generations will keep the labour market as well supplied as a series of vigorous and long-lived generations." Under real historical conditions, however, it is necessary to maintain a supply of workers with particular types of needs, skills, know-how, and physical attributes. The severe health care problems that have characterized Canada's aboriginal population for over a century are telling indicators of native peoples' marginalized position at least since confederation. But it is important, also, to recognize variations in policy and practice over this time period.

The remainder of this chapter documents the changing health status and health care services for Canada's native peoples in relation to shifting social, economic, and political factors. Unfortunately, our analysis of different subgroups of the population must of necessity be at a very general level in places, given limited sources of comprehensive data. Health care statistics, where they permit any basis of comparison at all, tend to refer to broad divisions such as native/non-native without further breakdown into gender and class categories.

We argue that European contact and colonization, while not solely responsible for deteriorating health conditions, advanced the destruction of Indian self-sufficiency through the process of primitive accumulation and eventual transitions towards advanced industrial capitalism. Initial capitalist development contributed to the desecration of the population's health and living standards to such a point that, by the middle of the 20th century, ethnologist Diamond Jenness (1977), in scattered references to several different Indian tribes and lineages, predicted the eventual demise of the aboriginal population. Although health care conditions remain severely inadequate for many contemporary aboriginal peoples, Jenness' prognosis has not been validated by recent experience. We argue that a combination of changing labour force requirements and First Nations peoples' struggles for change have contributed to several new but contradictory federal, provincial, and band initiatives to enter into agreements to improve health care conditions and services for indigenous people.

The Pre-Contact Period

It would be a gross oversimplification to present a stark contrast between robustly healthy Indians in the period prior to contact with Europeans and a debilitated and demoralized aboriginal population in the wake of colonization. Like other pre-industrial societies, the fate of North American Indian tribes was for several thousand years linked to various forms of hunting, gathering, cultivating, culture, trade, and commerce (see, e.g., McMillan, 1988; Miller, 1989; Patterson, 1972; and Trigger, 1985, for details). Periodic barriers to subsistence activities through extreme weather variations, warfare, and epidemics made the population vulnerable from time to time. This was particularly true for dependent members of the society including infants and the elderly whose inability to engage in intense physical activity or contribute to economic tasks made them expendable during times of hardship or migration. Infanticide, abandonment of ill tribal members, and deliberate killing of the elderly were practiced by some tribes, particularly in the eastern and northern regions of Canada (Jenness, 1977:163).

For aboriginal peoples in the pre-contact period, life and death matters, like other spheres of activity, were integrated into a total way of life. The health of tribal members, treatment of the ill, burial of the dead, and beliefs about the afterlife were all organized around the available resources and essential tasks necessary for the tribe's survival. Healing, and the role of the healer, was therefore crucial for ensuring or restoring wholeness for the individual in relation to the community and environment as a totality (see, e.g., Young, 1989). Although the lifestyle undoubtedly was often harsh, given the rugged demands of hunting, climate, and warfare, recent anthropological evidence suggests that when sustenance requirements were readily fulfilled, many early societies had ample time for leisure and cultural activities (Harris, 1977). Sophisticated healing practices, that would later be undermined by practitioners of European-based models of science and medicine, drew upon extensive knowledge of indigenous herbs and plants as well as of rituals and practices, such as the sweat lodge ceremony, that were founded in notions that adequate health required a proper balance between the individual and the social and natural environments. O'Neil (1988:30) observes that traditional Indian medicine "is a broad constellation of values that underpins the respectful relationships that Indian people insist characterize their relationships with each other, the physical environment and the spiritual world." Except under extraordinary circumstances, an abundance of meat, fish, edible vegetation, and medicinal plants and substances, combined with an active lifestyle, is likely to have contributed to the general well-being of the population. Given these conditions, aboriginal populations were probably relatively healthy, free of major infectious diseases and other disorders (Young 1988, 32-33), although periodic difficulties or crises certainly existed under particular circumstances.

Colonization

Primitive accumulation involves two major aspects of colonization — control over aboriginal labour power, and control over aboriginal lands —

within which several subtle but important variations have occurred over time. From the point of view of the colonizing power or dominant group, the health status of the indigenous population is more important under the former than under the latter. Whereas the deterioration or depletion of an indigenous population may foster the colonization of land, it is necessary to maintain at least some standards of health and fitness when labour is to be exploited. In the case of early European explorers and traders in North America, the aboriginal population provided both useful commodities for trade and knowledge about the land and its resources which were invaluable for long-term survival. As long as Indians, whether engaged through commercial, military, or other relations, were indispensable to the Europeans, it was important that traditional patterns of health and ways of life be maintained as much as possible. When labour needs were supplanted or transformed, such as with the development and subsequent demise of the fur trade, there was less reliance on traditional practices.

At the same time, the very fact of contact between Indians and Europeans altered life patterns. In some instances this was achieved indirectly, as when one isolated tribe encountered another that had some dealings with fur traders, missionaries, or explorers. Exposure to new foods, products, cultural traits, and diseases modified both social and material relations. These arrangements were not simply imposed and were reciprocal in the sense that through contact, both Europeans and Indians had to make adaptations in pre-existing living patterns. Nonetheless, the consequence was a steady deterioration in the conditions of aboriginal social existence as native peoples became increasingly separated from their means of subsistence and networks of sociocultural support. By the late 19th century, with the consolidation of land colonization in Canada, these processes of cultural genocide were not as extensive as they might have been as long as native labour power was required for mercantile capital.

Some of the earliest recorded Indian health problems were the consequences of unforeseen circumstances while others were direct outcomes of deliberate policies or practices. Examples of the former include parasites and infections transferred through herds and land cultivation and epidemics such as smallpox and measles, while instances of the latter include the introduction of alcohol, widespread starvation as a result of overfishing or herd devastation, and the withholding of food, supplies, and medicine by government or fur-trade officials. The patterns were not always clearcut, revealing the interplay among complex sets of factors involving regional differences, intergroup conflict and cooperation, and distinct positions within class, gender, and other social relations.

Many explorers and fur traders wrote with admiration of the health of the Indians they encountered, although as Young (1988:34) observes, such comment has to be qualified by recognition both of stereotypical assumptions about the "noble savage" and of the condition of the Europeans themselves, many of whom displayed various disorders and impediments which belied their lower-class origins. These early descriptions, nonetheless, stand in stark contrast to portrayals of starvation and devastation which highlighted later 18th- and 19th-century journals. The following account written to Hudson's Bay Company officials by John Fullartine at Albany Fort on James Bay in 1703, illustrates in dramatic fashion not only the serious nature of the problem but also the way in which Indians' behaviours were represented by non-native officials:

> It was a very hard winter (for provision) all over the country, for abundance of the poor Indians perished and were so hard put to it that whole families of them were killed and eaten by one another: the young men killed and eat their parents and the women were so put to it for hunger that they spared not the poor sucking infants at their breasts but devoured them. The reason of this famine amongst them was the little snow that fell so that they could not hunt beasts (Hudson's Bay Record Society, 1965:9).

Although aspects of these grisly events (at least as described) are consequences of natural conditions, it must be recognized that the fur trade began to incorporate aboriginal labour and family support in such a way as to foster dependency on schedules and quotas created in accordance with the company's needs. Constant demands for furs often stretched people's abilities to survive to the limits, sometimes forcing them to take risks or remain on traplines longer than they normally would. The traders' accounts of death and suffering due to starvation and disease tend to reveal a mixture of empathy and loyalty to company demands for useful labour power. Writing in 1738, company officials in Fort Prince of Wales observe that:

> And as to starved Indians, when any are here we observe they was always employed in hunting and making snow-shoes etc. at proper seasons for the use of the factory, which useful necessaries we cannot do without, likewise the great assistance we have had from them in bringing us meat and fowls, in particular this last winter they have brought in abundance of meat, some of which have come upwards of three hundred miles with provisions for us. In the time of trade here is great care taken that no persons has any commerce with the natives, Mr. Norton [the chief trader] excepted, or such as he at any time does appoint (Hudson's Bay Record Society, 1965:247-248).

This statement reveals several facets of the relations between Indians and the Hudson's Bay Company. The company's willingness to feed starving Indians was predicated by its desire to extract from the Indians particular use values through tasks such as producing implements, food, or furs. Trading patterns were determined by company needs and timetables so that Indians would be both available to and dependent upon the company. Insofar as Indians were indispensable to the economic survival of the fort, their health and fitness had to be maintained. While the company had no direct interest in those aboriginal peoples who were less central to the fur trade, tribal communities were important since the trappers' well-being often depended upon the preservation of links with Indian social networks and kinship ties. The creation of various levels of interdependencies that went beyond strict commerce often posed difficulties in maintaining social, economic, and political relations. Friendships and alliances were frequently instrumental in nature as a consequence of the expediency of survival in the North, as well as elements in the struggle for trade advantages. Nonetheless, children produced through both temporary and long-term liaisons between white traders and Indian women, and successive generations of Métis families, were part of a deeply interwoven fabric of social relations which commonly blurred strict delineations between cultures (Brown, 1982).

These social relations had mixed implications for health care. The introduction of European products, diseases, and medical models sometimes had devastating consequences for the aboriginal population. In remote areas, medical services were limited or absent. This lacuna proved tragic in a number of instances where epidemics of smallpox, diptheria, whooping cough, measles, influenza, bubonic plague, cholera, scarlet fever, syphilis, and tuberculosis spread rapidly throughout indigenous communities, which were not equipped to deal with the previously unknown diseases. Dobyns (1983, 16) observes that several factors, including high susceptibility to new strains of viruses, the spread of disease through trading patterns and informal social contact, and the absence or breakdown of social-support mechanisms during times of illness, contributed to high mortality. Some tribes were decimated directly by the diseases while survivors in other areas subsequently died from starvation, dehydration, or other infections after they became too weak to obtain food and maintain regular sanitary procedures. At the same time, the Indians' inability to cope with the epidemics made them increasingly dependent upon white people's services and provisions. However, aboriginal spiritualism, healing, and medicinal knowledge remained vital parts of the culture in many settings. Traditional healing practices had contradictory implications in these regards. While healers, by virtue of their knowledge and centrality to the community, possessed a power base that was often threatening to, and therefore to be undermined by, non-aboriginal missionaries and colonial authorities, they also had networks of support and knowledge of remedies that were indispensible to non-aboriginal officials (Young, 1989:11). In some instances, these practices were even adopted by whites as awareness of medicinal plants and other treatments indigenous to North America became incorporated into mainstream medical knowledge.

Through the interplay of cultures and various health factors, there was no denying the severe consequences for the aboriginal population. By the middle of the 19th century, the native population had declined drastically, while large proportions of the survivors were wracked by disease, alcoholism, weakness, and starvation. With the demise of the fur trade and a general lack of employment opportunities for native peoples, recognition of Indians' dismal health status was more a matter of pity or general comment to authorities than a basis for any plan of action.

State Building

As we have observed previously, preconditions for industrial capitalism and the development of the new nation of Canada in the latter half of the 19th century involved massive consolidation of land holdings and settlement of vast tracts, particularly in the West. For the state, this process involved gaining clear title to the land however possible by way of treaty signing, the creation of Indian reserves, and, where deemed necessary, police and military intervention and the forcible expulsion of aboriginal peoples to remote areas. With few remaining outlets for their labour power and often cut off from traditional patterns of subsistence, large segments of the native population were marginal or viewed as an obstruction to the nation-building project. Officially, there was much concern about Indians' health and social status as part of the formal policy of assimilation. Under the BNA Act of 1867, and as later spelled out in the 1876 Indian Act, the federal government assumed responsibility for jurisdiction over Indians in several areas, including health care and education, which were otherwise provincial matters. In addition, Indians covered under Treaty 6 were promised a medicine chest and assistance in the event of famine or pestilence, at the discretion of the Indian Agent.

Undoubtedly, these formal declarations of federal concern for Indian health were reinforced by the good intentions of many officials in the state bureaucracy as well as in various medical establishments. In practice, however, Indian health conditions frequently were neglected except under duress. As the following excerpt from the Manitoba Indian Commissioner's report in 1876 reveals, an outbreak of measles on St. Peter's reserve was left untreated until its epidemic proportions posed a threat to nearby white communities, at which time the commissioner

> sent a medical man to St. Peters to examine into the affair, and he pronounced the epidemic to be of a very malignant type, and in danger of reproducing itself amongst the surrounding White population, if not mitigated. Whereupon I authorized him to take such steps as he might think proper to give relief, and to make all possible efforts to prevent the spread of the mischief (Canada Sessional Papers, 1876:37).

The settlement and isolation of Indians on reserve lands which had little economic viability contributed to the development of malnutrition,

afflictions resulting from poor sanitary conditions, and the spread of con-
tagious diseases. In cases where agriculture was promoted, the cultivation
of land and maintenance of herds also proved to be breeding grounds for
illness. Moreover, displacement from traditional tribal lands and migration
patterns disrupted family and social life so as to further demoralize much
of the native population and undermine communal solidarity. The substi-
tution of cash economies for traditional subsistence patterns resulted in a
notable decline in Indian health status. The authors of a medical survey of
nutrition among Indians in northern Manitoba observed in 1946 that:

> It can be stated that without exception in those areas where the dietary
> habits of the Indian have changed from the consumption of foods from
> the country itself to "store food", which is largely white flour, lard and
> sugar, the physical condition of the Indian has markedly deteriorated in
> recent years (Moore et al., 1946:228).

As their social and health status worsened, many bands were characterized by extreme apathy and social disorganization. For large segments
of the population, social life lacked any clear unifying purpose. Epidemics,
alcoholism, and violence were rampant. People's lives were destroyed,
both inwardly and outwardly, in concert with idleness from lack of economic opportunity and the absence from any meaningful place in mainstream society. Isolation on reserves or remote areas of the country meant
that the health and living conditions of native peoples were problems hidden from most Canadians. At the same time, concentrations of aboriginal
peoples in small communities, combined with the establishment of segre-
gated residential schools, produced conditions which generated epidemics
of tuberculosis and other infectious diseases.

Although these circumstances might seem to pose a problem to state
authorities responsible for Indian affairs, the fact that Indians could be
easily contained or managed under conditions of isolation and disorder
provided officials little inclination to redress matters. The federal government, through its departments of Indian Affairs and Health, was reluctant
to act on any but the most severe health care crises, and in many cases
lacked the personnel, resources, or will to follow through even on these.
In 1918, for example, the Department of Indian Affairs refused to meet
an urgent request for medical personnel and supplies from the Indian
Agent at Bella Coola in northern British Columbia because of the severity
of an influenza epidemic which occurred nationally at the end of World
War I amidst a shortage of physicians. The Chief Inspector of Indian
Agencies emphasized his regrets "that it is absolutely impossible to get
either a physician or any nurses, owing to the prevalence of the epidemic
around the large centres of population every physician and nurse, professional or otherwise being taxed to their utmost" (Ditchburn, 1918).
Overall, despite repeated claims that it was willing and able to deliver on
demand adequate health care services for native peoples, the federal

government continually revealed through both its actions and claims of responsibility that it was adopting a most restrictive interpretation of its commitment to provide a "medicine chest" to Indians (Young, 1984:258-259). As in other routine aspects of life on reserves, approval of the Indian agent was required before an Indian could be admitted to hospital. Also, the provision of other medical services to Indians was not preventative in nature but emerged as a response to problems that already existed, filtered through the various discretionary channels of the federal bureaucracy. Regardless of intent, and in spite of high demands for medical services induced by tuberculosis and other health care problems experienced by native peoples, expenditures on health care for Indians remained far below those for the general Canadian population. In 1933-34, for example, the total cost of Indian health services paid out of public and band trust funds was slightly below $10 per capita, at least one-third below what the Director of Medical Services considered to be a level sufficient to provide highly effective service delivery to Indians, compared with health care expenditures of at least $30 per capita for the national population (Department of Indian Affairs, 1934).

Jurisdictional Transfers and Disputes

The political and economic crises which surrounded the depression in the 1930s provided an impetus to reexamine funding and service delivery arrangements that prevailed among different levels of government in Canada. The gradual expansion of the welfare state was accomplished by bringing together a diverse array of services already in existence and establishing new public services in areas like health care, education, and social security. The various social programs were established as a consequence of both political struggle and the desire on the part of large employers and state officials to maintain on an ongoing basis a healthy, stable, and accessible work force .

As we observe elsewhere, aboriginal peoples tended in various locales and periods in the first half of the 20th century to be pushed out of and reintegrated into wage labour, while they were denied systematic involvement in wider class and political struggles. Not surprisingly, then, with respect to health and welfare service delivery, the position of Indians, who were officially under the care and protection of the federal government until such time as assimilation could be accomplished, was often ambiguous, as federal and provincial governments began to enter into joint or transferred jurisdictional and funding arrangements. The lack of integration of aboriginal peoples into mainstream labour markets and social life suggested that there was no pressing need for governments to attend to Indian affairs, as evident in declining health standards observed in the early part of the century. However, the development of resource-based industries in northern and western Canada and the potential proletarianization of increasing numbers of aboriginal peoples made more pressing the issue of concern for native peoples' health and welfare.

One of the first measures to recognize these changing relationships was the transfer in 1945 of Indian health care services from the Indian Affairs Branch within the Department of Mines and Resources to the newly constituted Department of National Health and Welfare. The move offered several advantages in terms of providing the basis for a relatively unified administrative response to aboriginal health problems, resulting in the expansion of public health services, hospitals, and other medical resources. The identification of tuberculosis as a major health problem among Indian people, for example, stimulated the expansion of treatment centres and testing and innoculation programs which contributed to declines in the official rate of death among Indians from the disease from levels of 579 per 100 000 in 1946 to 48 per 100 000 in 1955 (Graham-Cumming, 1967:141-142). However, general health care services for aboriginal peoples often continued to be severely inadequate. The removal of health care from the Indian Affairs Branch caused some interdepartmental bitterness, with the consequence that concern for administrative procedures often took priority over actual service delivery (Graham-Cumming, 1967:128). Such problems were compounded by the isolated state of Indian bands which necessitated costly transfers, usually by air transport, of medical personnel into native communities and reserves, and of native peoples who required hospitalization out to larger centres.

Despite whatever efforts and services were provided for improving aboriginal health care, the major problems that needed to be addressed were related to underlying social and economic conditions. While federal authorities and health care workers were frequently aware of these concerns and presented them to appropriate officials, they commonly attributed the problems to matters of cultural difference. C.R. Maundrell, a former employee of the Indian Affairs Branch, quoted by Graham-Cumming (1967:152-153), observed in 1940 that

> Just at the time when better sanitation was required to combat the new European diseases, [the Indians] settled on reserves, built permanent habitations for winter use at least, and permitted their yards to become as dirty as pig stys.
>
> The Department was aware of the danger, keenly aware of it, when the tuberculosis epidemics on the Plains became acute, and did its best to ameliorate conditions.... Personal habits were investigated and the natives were urged to keep their clothes and themselves clean. The danger of chills from getting overheated and the ill effects of getting wet were pointed out. This educational policy was carried on in the schools as well as on the reserves, and the Indian children were told in a language of imagery, dear to all children but especially to the Indians, of the insidious character of disease....

> The situation elsewhere is far from satisfactory. The natives still slip
> into slovenly habits; they still misunderstand the need for personal clean-
> liness and they seem indifferent to diseases which are the result of these
> conditions.

These statements reveal the paternalistic, Eurocentric notions of disease, lifestyle, and culture through which non-native agents portrayed
Indians and their society as monolithic, backwards, and inferior. While
many accounts, such as the one just cited, identified the destruction of
aboriginal self-sufficiency by the encroachment of Europeans as the source
of Indians' loss of health status, they blame or pity the Indians for their
failure to adjust to the new conditions. The perpetuation of Indian health
problems is thus depicted as the product of either a primitive, unsophisticated culture or of a population unwilling to yield to the logic of reason.

At the same time, though, such an ideology also conveys a more subtle purpose of contrasting the apparently primitive ways of Indians living
on reserves with the more positive aspects of engaging in industrial wage
labour and adopting the ways of modern urban society. However, the
ability to gain meaningful employment and participation in mainstream
society was heavily restricted for most aboriginal peoples, especially as
northern development tended to have the consequence of continuing the
destruction of aboriginal subsistence and community patterns. Living in
an environment with few physical resources and often limited cultural support, aboriginal peoples all too frequently lived in settings akin to those
vividly described by Fanon (1968:39) as the condition of the colonized
people:

> They are born there, it matters little where or how; they die there, it
> matters not where, nor how. It is a world without spaciousness; [people]
> live there on top of each other, and their huts are built one on top of the
> other. The native town is a hungry town, starved of bread, of meat, of
> shoes, of coal, of light. The native town is a crouching village, a town on
> its knees, a town wallowing in the mire.

Under such conditions, the reorganization and improvement of
health-care service delivery could accomplish little more than to provide
temporary, localized relief from misery. Moreover, uncertainty over health
care provision for Indians living off reserves gave no assurance that migration and participation in wage labour would guarantee an escape from
these conditions.

The major immediate advantage of reorganization of Indian health
care services was to provide, to a greater extent than had been the case, a
vehicle through which aboriginal health and living conditions could be
identified officially as problems that demanded serious attention. The
systematic collection of data, the monitoring of particular disease trends,
and the employment of personnel committed to finding solutions to abo-

riginal problems offered definite improvements over earlier efforts to deal with native health care. Nonetheless, there were few significant coordinated plans in place to recognize and counter Indian health care concerns. The lack of attention to aboriginal health has been illustrated by the failure of several major reviews of Canada's health care system, notably the Royal Commission on Health Services, which reported in 1964, and the 1970 Task Force on the Cost of Health Services, to acknowledge or investigate fully the needs and problems associated with Indian health care (Badgley, 1973:158; Young, 1984:262).

As Canada and the provinces moved towards a national health insurance program in the late 1960s, characterized by federal standards and cost-sharing for health programs delivered by the provinces, the status of health care services for aboriginal peoples became even more indefinite and confusing. While Indians, like other Canadians, received coverage under the national health insurance program, there were no clearcut guidelines for the actual entitlement and delivery of Indian health care services. As Badgley (1973:153) observed:

> Under the terms of existing legislation the Indian is often placed in a confusing and cruel dilemma. Indians, like other Canadians, are entitled to health benefits as a right, depending on conditions for universality in the various provinces. However, if a Treaty Indian remains in his community he is provided primarily with preventive and midwifery health services. If he chooses to seek alternate care outside the reservation, he must get permission for transportation costs if these are required. The uncertainty of these regulations, how they are established and enforced pose equal difficulties for health workers and precludes a uniform policy where provincial regulations vary. Such doctors and nurses must frequently play the role of a collection agent at the point of treatment by determining whether an Indian is a band member, an indigent or entitled to a full range of services.

Indian organizations recognized and began to press the government to address three main areas of concern in relation to the delivery of health services to aboriginal peoples. First, levels of service and financial arrangements for health care on and near reserves were inconsistent and usually inadequate. Indians expressed their dissatisfaction with several aspects of the health care system, including variations in the range of services covered under medical insurance and treaty rights, irregular billing patterns, delays in federal reimbursement to medical practitioners for services rendered, and lack of monitoring to ensure that funds earmarked by the federal government for Indian health services were actually spent for that purpose by provincial governments. Severe inequities in health care delivery existed between northern and southern regions of the country. Second, increasing patterns of migration from reserves to urban areas meant that many Indians lost their health care entitlements either formally through loss of status or, more importantly, through the process of becoming uprooted from a community environment in which informal support networks could provide direct care or service referrals. The National Indian Brotherhood (1976:2), for instance, pointed to the existence of about one hundred registered Indians whom they termed "medical foster children" in medical care away from home while no visitation rights or information concerning their condition and discharge dates were extended to their parents. Third, Indian organizations became increasingly sensitive to the connection between socioeconomic conditions and health status, recognizing that political and administrative ambiguity over Indian affairs was prolonging what was clearly an intolerable situation. In 1976, the National Indian Brotherhood (1976:7), drawing upon position papers from its member organizations, recommended "a policy of free and complete medical care to Indian people" that included a comprehensive health plan and free dental care, eye care, and prescription drugs, funded completely by the federal government. In a submission to the federal government's special commissioner on national health services in 1979, the Federation of Saskatchewan Indians expressed the prevailing view of First Nations peoples that, for Indian people, demographic, health, and socioeconomic indicators all "clearly portray a situation that is getting worse rather than better" (Health and Welfare Canada, 1980:89).

By the 1980s, Indian organizations and federal and provincial government representatives agreed that some recognition should be given to aboriginal self-determination over many areas of life, including health care. Beginning in 1981, the federal government began to transfer control over local health services to native bands. These services supplement a growing array of programs offered through private and community agencies in response to specific areas of health concern, which we discuss briefly at the end of this chapter.

Growing formal attentiveness to the organization of health care services for, and the health status of, aboriginal peoples is a consequence of both political and economic factors. Native leaders and organizations, building upon the anger produced by the immediate experience of widespread ill health and suffering, have made health issues a major focus within their demands for official recognition of aboriginal rights and self-government. At the same time, significantly, growing reliance upon aboriginal labour power on and off reserves by both native and non-native employers has made it imperative that increasingly greater proportions of the aboriginal population be relatively healthy and ready to work. Moreover, there is a high degree of affinity between, on the one hand, the emergent prominence on national agendas of the apparent contribution of rising health care costs to government deficits and public debt and, on the other hand, the political attractiveness of community health services and traditional healing practices that potentially can be provided in an environmentally sensitive way at relatively low cost.

Recent Trends in Aboriginal Health Status

Health status is produced by the interaction of demographic and socio-economic considerations within particular material circumstances. In this section of the chapter, we present data which indicate that serious problems in health status and health care have not been eradicated for much of Canada's aboriginal population, even though improvements have been made with respect to several health indicators.

Figure 6.1 reveals that Canada's aboriginal population is characterized by its youth, relative to the national population, and the preponderance of females in every age category. Among First Nations people, persons aged 25 or less constituted 57 percent of the population in 1986 as compared with 39 percent among the general population (Assembly of First Nations, 1987:6). These facts indicate that continued population growth is likely. As the data in Figure 6.2 show, recent and projected population growth is also subject to regional variation, with the largest on-reserve population increases in Atlantic Canada and Quebec between 1966 and 1988, and the largest projected increases on-reserve as well as the highest overall increases in the off-reserve population in the prairie provinces.

These population distribution patterns have important implications for health care, affecting both the organization and dissemination of health care services and the kinds of health problems which are common to specific population groups such as children, the elderly, and men and women. Beyond the health care system, their significance lies in the recognition that for the next few decades, at least, there will be several large cohorts of aboriginal peoples who are likely to be seeking entry into labour markets. Regional, gender, and status variations in the population distributions are likely to have the consequence of perpetuating unevenness and inequality in opportunities, economic outcomes, and political demands.

Unfortunately, data concerning most health indicators, including birth and death rates, are available systematically only at the most general level. The trends depicted in Table 6.1 show that while there is a gradual convergence in crude rates of birth and mortality, or death, between Indians and the general population, substantial and persistent gaps characterize the comparison between the two groups.

The tabulated rates for Canada's Indians are broadly comparable to similar indicators for the less developed nations of the world, which in 1988 had an overall crude birth rate of 31 per 1000, a crude death rate of 10 per 1000, and an average life expectancy at birth of 60 years (Population Reference Bureau, 1988). Moreover, as Brady (1983) emphasizes, the disadvantaged position of native peoples becomes even

Figures 6.1a, 6.1b

Aboriginal (single origin) and Canadian Populations, Distribution by Age and Sex, 1986

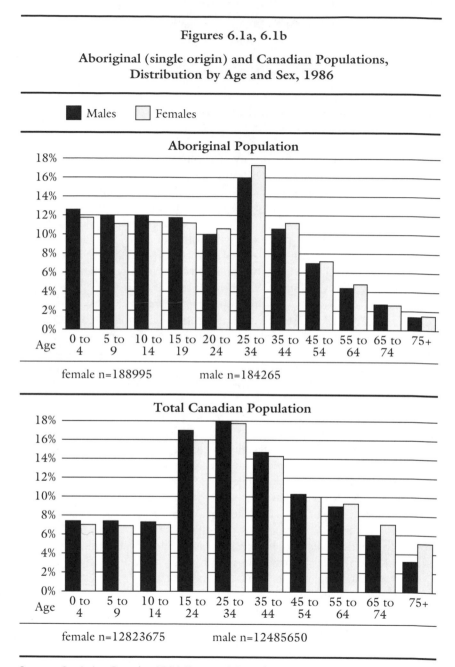

Source: Statistics Canada, *1986 Census of Canada*, Cat. Nos. 93-101 (1-1) and 93-154 (1-58).

Figure 6.2a

Registered Indian Population On Reserve and Off Reserve, By Region, 1966

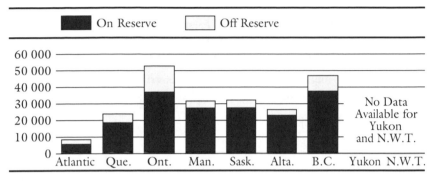

Figure 6.2b

By Region, 1989

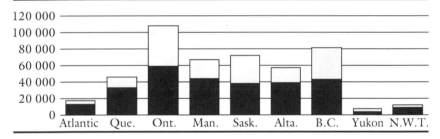

Figure 6.2c

By Region, 2001 (projected)

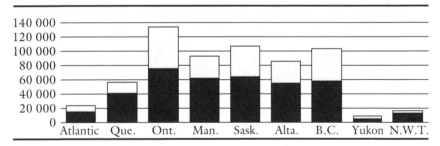

Source: Indian and Northern Affairs Canada, *Basic Departmental Data.*
Ottawa: Minister of Supply and Services Canada,
Cat. No. R-12-7/1990E, pp. 11, 13.

Table 6.1

Crude Death Rates, Infant Mortality Rates, And Birth Rates,
Selected Years, 1960-1988, Registered Indian And
Canadian Populations

	Death Rate (deaths per 1000 pop.)		Infant Mortality Rate (deaths of children 1 year or under per 1000 pop.)		Birth Rate (live births per 1000 pop.)	
Year	Canada	Registered Indians	Canada	Registered Indians	Canada	Registered Indians
1960	7.8	8.8	27.3	82.0	26.8	46.7
1967	7.4	8.4	20.8[1]	48.6[1]	18.2	39.9
1976	7.3	7.3	13.5	32.1	15.7	29.0
1978	7.2	7.4	12.0	26.5	15.3	n/a
1980	7.2	6.7	10.4	24.4	15.5	24.0
1981	7.0	6.3	9.6	21.8	15.3	25.2
1982	7.1	6.2	9.1	17.0	15.1	28.4
1983	7.0	5.7	8.5	18.2	15.0	26.8
1984	7.0	5.7	8.1	19.0	15.0	26.2
1985	7.2	6.0	8.0	17.9	14.8	29.8
1986	7.3	5.6	7.9	17.5	14.7	29.1[3]
1987	7.2	5.6[2]	7.3	11.7[2]	14.4	32.7[3]
1988	7.3	5.3[2]	7.2	12.7[2]	14.5	33.3[2]

Notes: 1. Figures are for 1968.
  2. Rates for 1987 and 1988 no longer include Northwest Territories
     Indians because of the transfer of health services to the
     government of the Northwest Territories.
  3. Data are for Saskatchewan only, and are provided only as an
     indication of general trends.
Sources: Indian and Northern Affairs Canada, *Basic Departmental Data 1990.*
     Ottawa: Minister of Supply and Services Canada, pp. 25, 27; Statistics
     Canada, *Vital Statistics.* Ottawa: Minister of Supply and Services
     Canada, Cat. 89-204 Annual Series to 1986; Statistics Canada, *Health
     Reports, Deaths.* Ottawa: Minister of Supply and Services Canada, Cat.
     82-003S15, Annual Series, 1987-88; and Health and Welfare Canada,
     Health Status of Canadian Indians and Inuit, Update 1987. Ottawa:
     Health and Welfare Canada, pp. 2, 6-7.

more visible when these rates are standardized according to the age structure of the population, demonstrating that Indian and Inuit people have
much higher than average mortality rates within every age cohort (see also
Health and Welfare Canada, 1988:20).

The average life expectancy at birth for aboriginal peoples increased
from 62.6 years in the 1978-80 period to 65.9 from 1984-1986. For
male registered Indians, average life expectancy at birth increased from
59.8 years in 1976 to 63.8 years in 1986, with a projected life expectancy
of 69.8 years by the year 2001, while for female registered Indians, the

respective figures are 66.3 years in 1976, 71.0 in 1986, and a projection of 77.0 by 2001 (Assembly of First Nations, 1987:9; Indian and Northern Affairs Canada, 1990:23). Nonetheless, Indians can expect to live on average about eight to nine years less than Canadians in general (Health and Welfare Canada, 1988:20).

A further indicator of health status is provided by patterns in infant mortality, also shown in Table 6.1. While the infant mortality rate, calculated as the number of deaths of children of 1 year of age and under expressed as a proportion of every 1000 live births in a given year, declined among registered Indians from 82.0 in 1960 to 12.7 in 1988, these rates remained about double those for the general Canadian population. While the highest rates of mortality existed at the perinatal stage (from 28 weeks after conception to 7 days after birth), mortality rates for aboriginal infants between 4 weeks and 1 year were nearly four times those for infants of the same age range in the general population. Additional evidence that pregnancy and early childhood problems exist among portions of the aboriginal population is provided by trends that reveal increases in fetal death rates between 1982 and 1985 (Assembly of First Nations, 1987:10). Among Indian infants, leading causes of death are respiratory ailments, infectious and parasitic diseases, and accidents, all of which are indicators of inadequate housing, sanitary conditions, and access to medical facilities (Health and Welfare Canada, 1988:21; Department of Indian Affairs and Northern Development, 1980:16).

These factors are also evident in patterns of causes of death among the overall aboriginal and non-aboriginal populations. Death rates from diseases of the circulatory system and neoplasms (cancer) are lower for native peoples than for non-natives, but natives have much higher than average rates of death from injury and poisoning, at about four times the national average (Assembly of First Nations, 1987:12; Indian and Northern Affairs Canada, 1990:29). Native peoples have experienced declining death rates from diseases of the respiratory and circulatory systems, but such rates remain between two and three times the national average. Death rates from infectious and parasitic diseases, which for aboriginal peoples remain consistently above national levels, began to increase in the mid-1980s after several years of steady decline. As in the case of infant mortality, these trends are indicative of pronounced differences in lifestyle and living conditions among large segments of the two population groups, although they conceal important differences within each group.

Certain diseases are more prevalent among aboriginal peoples than among the general population. As with death rates, Indians have high rates of hospitalization associated with injuries and accidents, pregnancy and childbirth, diseases of the digestive and circulatory systems, and infectious and parasitic diseases. In addition, Indians have high rates of diseases like tuberculosis and diabetes which are directly attributable to lifestyle and nutrition patterns (Assembly of First Nations, 1987:19). These trends are amplified when factors of age and geographic distribution are taken into consideration. In Saskatchewan, for example, rates of diabetes and essential hypertension (linked to increased risk of heart disease) are higher for registered Indians living on reserves in the southern regions than in the North, indicating differences in diet, lifestyle, and level of health care and monitoring services (Health and Welfare Canada, 1988:31-32, 50). A survey conducted in the early 1970s by the federal government on the nutrition status of Canadians revealed that Indian and Inuit populations, amplified by factors such as age, regional distribution, and gender, had serious deficiencies in terms of calcium, iron, and vitamins A and D intake, indicating improper diet, often as a consequence of inadequate provision of fresh fruit, produce, and dairy supplies in isolated and northern regions (Nutrition Canada, 1975). Moreover, Indian populations had considerable variations in body weight and caloric input, with frequently inadequate levels of caloric intake among pregnant women and widespread excessive caloric intake among children and adults to such a level that the survey concluded "that overweight, obesity and elevated cholesterol levels are health hazards of major proportions" (Nutrition Canada, 1975:37). In terms of comparisons among age cohorts within the aboriginal and non-aboriginal populations, aboriginal children and youth face much greater and more varied diseases, disabilities, and health risks while among the elderly, given the general pattern in which health problems tend to increase with age, the health indicators in the two populations are relatively similar.

As noted, one of the most striking aspects of Indian health status is the high rate of death from accidents, injuries, and poisoning. Among Canada's registered Indian population, injury and poisoning constituted the leading cause of death for all age cohorts below 45, accounting for 88 percent of all deaths among those aged 15 to 24, and just under two-thirds of deaths among persons under 15 and among those between 25 and 44 (Health and Welfare Canada, 1988:21). In Saskatchewan, deaths from accidents, suicides, homicides, and poisoning accounted for six of the top ten causes of death in 1987 (Health and Welfare Canada, 1989:23). Motor vehicle accidents constituted the leading cause of death among Saskatchewan's registered Indians for all age groups between 5 and 44 years, while the potential years of life lost due to injuries and poisoning were calculated as 5901, or 60 percent of the total potential years of life lost from all causes of death (Health and Welfare Canada, 1989:25-27). On a national basis, the rate of deaths among aboriginal peoples by motor vehicle accident was about three times the Canadian average, the rate of deaths by drowning was double the national average, and the rate of deaths by firearms was about nine times the Canadian average for the period from 1980 to 1983 (Assembly of First Nations, 1987:13). High rates of death by injury and poisoning are also common, especially among

Indians between the ages of 10 and 20. Siggner and Locatelli (1981:23) report that in British Columbia, based on data from the mid-1970s, "deaths due to accidents, poisonings and violence account for over 38 per cent of all Indian deaths in comparison with less than 11 per cent of all such deaths in the provincial population." Data from the early 1980s reveal that injury and poisoning constituted the leading cause of death among registered Indians in the North and all provinces from Ontario west, and the second leading cause of death in Quebec and the Atlantic region (Health and Welfare Canada, 1988:15). In 1986, injury and poisoning were the leading cause of death among Canada's on-reserve registered Indian population, constituting 31 percent of all deaths, or 508 cases out of a total of 1641 deaths (calculated from Indian and Northern Affairs Canada, 1989b:29). When population age distributions are taken into account, the average death rate from injury and poisoning for the years 1980 to 1984 was 3.9 times the national rate among registered Indians, and 3.6 times greater among the Inuit population (Health and Welfare Canada, 1988:19).

Table 6.2, showing data on Saskatchewan's registered Indian population in 1988, indicates rates of death from injury and poisoning of 151.4 per 100 000 population for males and 69.4 per 100 000 for females. As the figures reveal, suicide constitutes the largest single cause of injury and poisoning-related deaths, while motor vehicle and fire-related accidents are also prominent causes of mortality.

Nationally, the suicide rate among native peoples has been estimated as at least twice the rate for the total Canadian population. Data from 1982, for instance, reveal that suicides accounted for 36.1 percent of violent deaths among status Indians compared with a rate of 14.3 percent among the general population; most of these suicides occurred among males in the 15 to 24-year age group (Health and Welfare Canada, 1987:33).

Intertwined with the severe risks and alarming health statistics characteristic of aboriginal populations are above average incidences of alcohol and drug abuse. Though comprehensive data are not available, virtually all reports on aboriginal health status and social conditions emphasize the serious nature of alcohol and drug-related problems. For instance, a federal government survey in 1980 indicated that "Officials working in health services for Indians estimate that between 50 and 60 percent of Indian illnesses and deaths are alcohol-related" (Department of Indian Affairs and Northern Development, 1980:21). The federal Department of Health and Welfare estimates that 75 percent of deaths by accident, poisoning, and violence, and 90 percent of deaths by fire, are linked to alcohol abuse (Health and Welfare Canada, 1985:5). In Saskatchewan in 1987, about one-third, or 42 out of a total of 130 deaths were attributed to alcohol and drugs (Health and Welfare Canada, 1989:29). Jarvis and Boldt

Table 6.2

Injury And Poisoning Deaths by External Cause and Sex
On and Off Reserve
Saskatchewan Region, 1988

Cause of Death	Male		Female		Total		Age Group			
	No.	Rate	No.	Rate	No.	Rate	<15	15-24	25-44	45+
Motor Vehicle Accidents	10	29.7	9	26.0	19	27.8	1	3	10	5
Other Road Accidents	1	3.0	0	-	1	1.5	0	0	0	1
Accidental Poisoning	1	3.0	4	11.6	5	7.3	0	2	2	1
Accidental Falls	3	8.9	0	-	3	4.4	1	1	0	1
Accidents Caused by Fire & Flames	8	23.8	2	5.8	10	14.7	4	1	3	2
Accidents Due to Natural & Environmental Factors	2	5.9	1	2.9	3	4.4	0	1	1	1
Accidents Caused by Submersion, Suffocation & Foreign Objects	4	11.9	2	5.8	6	8.8	1	1	2	2
Other Accidents	1	3.0	0	-	1	1.5	0	0	0	1
Suicide and Self-Inflicted Injury	17	50.5	5	14.5	22	32.2	3	6	8	5
Homicide and Intentional Injury	4	11.9	1	2.9	5	7.3	0	0	2	3
Total	51	151.4	24	69.4	75	109.9	10	15	28	22

Rates per 100 000 population

Source: Health and Welfare Canada, *1988 Vital Statistics for the Registered Indian Population of Saskatchewan.* Ottawa: Health and Welfare Canada, 1990, p. 51.

(1982), by utilizing data derived from key informants in Indian communities throughout Alberta, suggest that heavy use of alcohol contributes to more deaths and related health problems than are officially reported. Moreover, alcohol and drug abuse are associated with other chronic conditions such as cirrhosis, heart disease, and birth defects. The combination of drug abuse, alcoholism, and inadequate or overcrowded living conditions is further linked to the rapid spread of sexually-transmitted diseases, notably AIDS, among aboriginal communities. Fritz and Darcy (1983) report also that Indians have much higher rates of institutionalization and treatment for psychiatric disorders related to alcoholism and drug addiction than do non-Indians.

Consistent with these observed patterns of illness, death, and other health disorders, aboriginal peoples have high rates of utilization of health services although, again, an overall picture is difficult to provide because of an absence of comprehensive data. Rates of hospitalization for aboriginal peoples are often more than double comparable rates for the general population, while the average length of stay for aboriginal peoples tends to be shorter. British Columbia recorded a hospital separation rate (calculated according to the numbers of persons per 1000 population released from institutional care through death or discharge) of 209.8 among registered Indians, compared with a rate of 148.6 among non-Indians, while the number of patient-days in hospitals was 1352.9 per 1000 for registered Indians and 1161.9 for non-Indians (Health and Welfare Canada, 1988:22).

In Manitoba in 1988-89, status Indians recorded a rate of 307 separations per 1000 population, compared with a rate of 146 for the total provincial population, while the gap between the two populations was narrower for rates of separated days, with 1703 per 1000 status Indians and an overall provincial rate of 1550 (Manitoba Health Services Commission, 1989:19). In Saskatchewan in 1987-88, the provincial population as a whole recorded a rate of separations of 195 per 1000, compared with a rate of 430 for the population on Indian reservations, with average durations of stay of 7.4 days for the general population and 5.9 for Indian reserve populations (Saskatchewan Health, 1988:13).

Rates of hospitalization also vary according to types of disorder and illness. Utilizing data from the 1970s, Fritz and Darcy (1983:73-76) observe that the Saskatchewan Indian population had a separation rate for psychiatric care 62 percent higher than the non-Indian population for treatment in public-sector institutions and 11 percent higher in private-sector institutions, although the trend was reversed for outpatient psychiatric treatment, with the Indian rate at over 20 percent lower than the rate of outpatient treatment for non-Indians. These patterns also reveal distinctions in the reasons for hospitalization, as illustrated in Table 6.3, which provides data from British Columbia in 1983-84 concerning

Table 6.3

Hospital Separations and Patient-Days, Registered Indians and Non-Indians, British Columbia, April 1, 1983 to March 31, 1984

Disease Category (I.C.D. Chapters)		Separation Rate*		Patient-Days*	
		Indians	Other	Indians	Other
I.	Infectious and parasitic diseases	7.2	2.4	55.0	16.3
II.	Neoplasms	4.0	10.3	40.5	117.6
III.	Endocrine, nutritional, metabolic diseases and immunity disorders	4.0	2.6	40.1	28.0
V.	Mental disorders	11.1	6.5	66.4	102.0
VI.	Diseases of the nervous system and sense ogans	12.9	7.2	69.0	43.4
VII.	Diseases of the circulatory system	8.7	16.5	89.5	183.7
VIII.	Diseases of the respiratory system	30.5	12.7	189.3	75.5
IX.	Diseases of the digestive system	23.8	15.9	152.3	113.3
X.	Diseases of the genitourinary system	10.2	12.3	63.0	71.7
XI.	Complications of pregnancy, child-birth and puerperium	31.3	20.6	135.7	89.7
XII.	Diseases of the skin and s.c. tissue	5.0	2.0	54.3	16.0
XIII.	Diseases of the musculoskeletal system and connective tissue	8.6	9.1	81.2	70.3
XVII.	Injury and poisoning	30.5	15.6	188.3	121.1
	All other categories	21.9	14.9	128.2	114.0
	Total	209.8	148.6	1352.9	1161.9

Calculated from data given by Hospital Programs, B.C., Ministry of Health.

* Per 1000 population

Source: Health and Welfare Canada, *Health Status of Canadian Indians and Inuit, Update 1987*. Ottawa: Health and Welfare Canada, 1988, p. 25.

hospital indicators for the registered Indian and non-Indian populations. Consistent with points noted earlier, registered Indians experienced much higher than average rates in several disease categories, notably injury and poisoning, pregnancy and childbirth-related complications, diseases of the respiratory, digestive, and nervous systems, as well as diseases related to the skin, nutrition, immunity and infectious and parasitic disorders, and mental disorders; by contrast, non-Indians were strongly overrepresented in rates of cancer (neoplasms) and diseases of the circulatory system.

The scenario that emerges from the data presented in this chapter portrays two realities in which native peoples and non-natives have distinctly different patterns of living and dying. In terms of disease and illness, injury, causes of death, and forms of treatment, Canadian aboriginal peoples in general experience conditions which, though improving, continue to be unsatisfactory in the context of an industrially and medically advanced society. This does not mean that natives as a whole are more prone to illness or injury, but reflects instead the highly disadvantaged position occupied by large segments of the native population.

The trends suggest the perpetuation of the aboriginal population as a distinct underclass. However, we have also seen a trend towards convergence between the two populations on many indicators, notably on such general measures as birth and death rates and life expectancy as well as on incidences of particular disorders. We have also observed several differences in people's health status according to gender, class, age, and area of residence. By recognizing health as a product of people's lived experiences, these trends can be understood to be indicative of diverse socioeconomic circumstances combined with particular inequalities in the arrangement and delivery of health care services. As we have seen, several organizations and studies, especially since the 1970s, have drawn attention to the urgency of the most serious of these problems. Nonetheless, any progress to redress matters has been slow. Attempted solutions have tended to be framed in terms of cultural differences and aboriginal rights to self-determination. These issues are the focus of the remainder of this chapter.

TRADITIONAL HEALING, STRUGGLES FOR SELF-GOVERNMENT, AND THE TRANSFORMATION OF FIRST NATIONS SOCIETIES

One of the prevalent themes of this book concerns the conflict between state policies and capitalist structures — which have subjugated many native peoples — and First Nations' attempts to reassert some degree of self-determination. This is commonly portrayed as a struggle in which a misguided and sometimes hostile white society has exerted its domination over a powerless, often voiceless minority. A stark description of these conflicting value systems is provided in a 1978 National Indian

Brotherhood statement of principle on Indian health which argues that, as Indian peoples:

> Our whole culture, our knowledge of thousands of years, has been devoted to developing ourselves as wise children, to changing ourselves rather than changing our environment, to humbling ourselves before the forces of nature, the forces and will of the Creator, to prevent our own egos from destroying us or our environment, to seeking balance and harmony within ourselves and to extend that balance and harmony to all our daily acts, to our very way of life (National Indian Brotherhood, 1978:1).

This harmonious and integrated approach to life, however, is presented as having been eradicated by the destructive forces of a dominant society:

> So today we are living with our fellow man who is in conflict with himself, whose attitude, values and culture are adverse to nature and the creation, a people who develop and inflate their egos and force all things in their sphere of influence to humble themselves to the will of those few whose way of life is that of adversity, conflict and imbalance. A people who freely manipulate the environment and yes, even the lives of their fellow men. A society whose culture and every act is one of manipulation, control and adversity to every living organism, even their very own (National Indian Brotherhood, 1978:2).

The vivid representation of these two world views presents a compelling case for First Nations control over health care and other aspects of aboriginal life. From the perspective of many aboriginal peoples who are seeking to regain control over their lives, the loss of traditional healing practices under the onslaught of a manipulative dominant medical model has drastic consequences that extend beyond health care. Referring to attempts to revive sacred rituals, for example, Alberta healer Russell Willier "says that many people have gotten careless about the rituals or have forgotten how to do them properly.... Thus, a kind of double bind exists: it is dangerous to take part in ceremonies conducted by incompetent people, but it is even more dangerous not to do the ceremonies at all" (Young, 1989:34).

It is important, in understanding these problems, to take into account the particular economic and political realities which affect health status and within which health care systems operate. While some cultural factors and other dimensions are unique to the health care concerns of native peoples as a whole, natives also enter into the health care system through their wider social relations compounded by distinctions of class, gender, age, and other characteristics. The high concentrations of aboriginal peoples who are in the younger age cohorts, for example, mean that natives as a whole are more likely to demonstrate susceptability to afflictions like childhood diseases and accidental deaths and injuries. Similarly, native women living in poverty are exposed to higher than average risks of problems such as malnutrition and pregnancy-related disorders. In short, aboriginal health care conditions reflect the socioeconomic circumstances experienced by native peoples and the way in which these are managed politically. (Details of the interrelationships among health care, socioeconomic conditions, and political decision-making are illustrated graphically in Culhane Speck's 1987 case study of health care delivery in a northern British Columbia community.)

An emphasis on First Nations control and delivery of aboriginal health care services is a preliminary step in the direction of recognizing that environmental factors rather than individual and cultural pathologies are the basis of health problems. This is a progressive step insofar as it represents a rejection of dominant models of medicine and health care which reinforce social inequalities under capitalism by emphasizing the medicalization of health problems, corporate and profit-driven services and decision-making structures, and responsiveness to system rather than consumer and community needs (Doyal and Pennell, 1979; Waitzkin, 1983).

Recent developments in band control of health services and recognition of traditional healing methods place health care in a context that takes into account peoples' life experiences. These can be illustrated with reference to initiatives such as the Four Worlds Developments Project, which started in southern Alberta in 1982. The project, funded by the federal government's National Native Alcohol and Drug Abuse Program, adopts a holistic approach which integrates support resources and training not only in response to serious drug and alcohol problems which the project addressed initially, but also to facilitate community development, educational, and research components (Four Worlds Development Project, 1985:59-60). Several other native communities have developed similar projects, spurred by the prominent example of British Columbia's Alkali Lake Band which in 1972 began a program of abstention from alcohol, personal development workshops, community cultural activities, and employment initiatives in order to counter serious alcohol-related problems.

General policy orientations which favour a shift towards aboriginal self-government have made health care a central component in band development. The landmark agreements made in 1975 and subsequent years among the federal and provincial governments and the Cree, Naskapi, and Inuit peoples of the James Bay and northern and northeastern Quebec regions provide a framework to enable the establishment both of special federal and provincial health programs to meet local needs and of administrative and fiscal transfers to facilitate the involvement by district and band councils in health care assessment and delivery processes (Peters, 1989:196-198). However, because of the wide diversity of interests, historical considerations, and local needs that enter into the health care field, there is no single path along which self-government initiatives in that area are likely to be established. At most, all that can be concluded, as emphasized in the analysis of self-government alternatives documented by Boisvert (1985:57), is that, "A judicious sharing of responsibilities among governments — including aboriginal governments — seems the only approach to use in the social policy field" in general. The precise nature of those relationships is uncertain, though, since ongoing jurisdictional disputes over the organization, financing, and delivery of aboriginal health care services are further complicated by an overall political atmosphere dominated by arguments for reducing health care expenditures and rationalizing services. Under such conditions, the availability of sufficient resources to provide native communities adequate health care remains in continual jeopardy.

Aboriginal health care concerns must also take into account the recognition that effective changes in health status require major transformations in the organization of social life that go beyond what native peoples can achieve on their own. This is accomplished in part by the increasing acknowledgment that health is a product of our social circumstances. The politicization of environmental concerns, for example, provides an opportunity to link aboriginal health care issues with broader reform strategies. But there are also deeper political and economic realities that must be confronted before any substantial progress can be made in the area of aboriginal health.

In particular, health prospects for native peoples tend to be disadvantaged at two levels. First, as persons who occupy primarily subordinate class positions, native peoples continue to face higher than average health risks. There is a systematic association between poverty and illness, with persons of lower socioeconomic status much more likely than those of higher socioeconomic status to experience physical, medical, and mental health problems (see, e.g., Health and Welfare Canada, 1981; Grant, 1988). As we have observed with reference to several historical examples, many of Canada's aboriginal peoples experience living conditions that are characterized by serious deficiencies. Inadequacies in areas such as housing, sewage, and nutrition contribute directly to increased health risks, and are related indirectly, as indicators of social disorganization and marginalization, to violence, mental illness, and other social problems. Second, native peoples' health tends to be further jeopardized by strategies for economic development, particularly in the North. Exposure to environmental hazards and displacement through massive mining, energy, and hydroelectric development projects both alter traditional patterns of life and create new health and safety risks. Table 6.4 provides a summary description of the widespread nature of these problems and their impact on native communities. A stark illustration of these concerns lies in a highly-publicized case from the mid-1970s in which mercury that flowed

Table 6.4

The Impact of Selected Contaminants on
First Nations Health Conditions

Effect or Impact	Source and Contaminant	Areas of Major Concern (Number of Projects or Developments)
Destruction of wildlife; restrictions on hunting and fishing rights	Flooding of First Nations lands through dams and hydro-electric developments	Atlantic (8) Northern Quebec (11) Ontario (17) Manitoba (4) Saskatchewan (2) B.C. (9)
	Acid rain from smelters, coal-fired electricity, transportation, and industrial processes	Quebec and Ontario (43% of lakes contaminated) Ontario (Serpent River, Wawa-Sudbury, 65% of headwaters in Muskoka-Haliburton area) Northwest Territories (lakes contaminated) Canada (40% of forest affected, a dozen rivers no longer support salmon or trout)
	Higher water temperature from large-scale forest harvesting	British Columbia (Meares Island, Lyell Island, Moresby Islands, Stein watershed)
	Aquaculture and fish farming in marine water	Bays traditionally harvested by First Nations in maritime areas
	Oil and gas exploration, drilling, pipelines, and refineries, and potential for spills	West coast offshore High and eastern Arctic (Beaufort Sea, MacKenzie Delta)
	Noise from military	Northern Canada

Table 6.4 continued

Water contamination and destruction of fisheries	Mercury and other heavy metals from mining, smelters and acid rain	Northwest Territories (lakes and rivers) Ontario (English-Wabigoon river system, St. Clair River, Sarnia)
	Toxic chemicals including PCBs, DDT, dioxin, and endosulfan	Great Lakes (1,000 chemicals) Ontario (Niagara River) Quebec (St. Lawrence River system)
Social and economic disruption	Dislocation of whole communities, disruption of industries, depletion of resources	All regions noted above

Source: Data from Assembly of First Nations, *Current Indian Health Conditions: A Statistical Perspective*. Ottawa: Assembly of First Nations, 1987, p. 23.

into rivers and lakes from Ontario's Reed Paper Company had poisoned drinking water and food supplies of some native communities. While levels of mercury found in the blood of residents of two Indian reserves in the province were reported to be from 40 to 150 times the Canadian average, the situation was not unique as medical observers noted that at least fourteen other areas across the country also had serious contamination problems (Bolaria, 1988:542).

Although media coverage and general environmental awareness in recent years have sensitized us to these kinds of problems, the likelihood that further health risks will be created through industrial activity remains strong. The process of northern development, whether constituted through massive public projects, corporate ventures, band initiatives, or some combination of these, tends to emphasize immediate economic priorities over social and cultural concerns. As Waldram (1988), for example, carefully documents with reference to the impact of hydroelectric developments on three native communities in Saskatchewan and Manitoba, promises and agreements which emerged from detailed negotiation procedures have tended to be negated by drives for the immediate removal of native peoples from their lands and communities. While projects guided by First Nations peoples may alleviate the most serious injustices in the development process, conflicting agendas mean that human justice and social services concerns are often subordinated to priorities for immediate economic gain or for projects whose benefits will not be equitably distributed throughout native communities.

Conclusion

The health status of native peoples has been characterized by significant shifts at different times and places. We have argued that the introduction and transformation of capitalist relations of production have had considerable impact upon both the health status of, and the provision of health care services for, Canada's aboriginal peoples. While it is difficult to document these changes fully because of incomplete historical records and inadequacies in contemporary health-reporting practices, there is a close relationship between the social and economic marginalization of aboriginal peoples and the deterioration of their health conditions. Health has become a public issue particularly under circumstances in which native peoples are valued as a source of real or potential labour power. Viewed in this way, recent state action and self-government initiatives directed at improving health care status and service delivery can be understood in terms of the increasing integration of aboriginal peoples into capitalist labour markets within both native and non-native sectors. Stated simply, under capitalism people gain adequate health care when their health is crucial to prevailing economic and political priorities. Moreover, as long as aboriginal peoples live in class-, "race-," and gender-divided societies, they are likely to experience ongoing inequalities in health status and the health services which they are provided.

CHAPTER 7

LAW, CRIME, AND THE CRIMINAL JUSTICE SYSTEM

INTRODUCTION

We had a situation a few months ago where two young offenders were picked up in a community. They first arrived in Souix [sic] Lookout, but were flown out by the Ontario Provincial Police after being held overnight in an adult cell, which is contrary to the Young Offenders Act. They were then taken to a close observation detention facility in Kenora, two hundred miles away and held there for two weeks. They were then returned to Souix [sic] Lookout which is the northern-most court. The Crown was requesting that both matters be put over for trial in their home community for the next circuit court, and requested that one of the youths be released and the other held in detention.

There was a long argument. The kids were a $500 airplane charter from their home community which had no scheduled air service. The parents had indicated their intention to come to Souix [sic] Lookout and had chartered a plane but were turned back because of bad weather. The next circuit court date in their home community, Cat Lake, was three months away. If they had been remanded until that time, they would have spent Christmas in detention. Neither youth spoke English and were each 14 years old.... We had a non-English speaking 14 year old who had never been out of the bush suddenly released in town and nobody is responsible for him and nobody is responsible for getting him home and he has no place to go. Child Services said he was not their problem; juvenile probation said he was not their problem and the police said "We just bring them out. We don't have any authority to take them back." The town said they didn't know anything about him. The judge

180

said, "I don't have any authority to order any expenditure in this case."

We were faced with a situation where we have a very undesirable result if the child was remanded in custody — a lengthy detention, a long separation from the community and the family; not speaking the language on the one hand and, on the other hand, we have a situation where the child, if released onto the street, had no place to go and nobody to take care of him there (Beamish, 1987:129-130).

Experiences like those depicted in the account above are lived daily, with slight variations, in communities across the country. Each of the phases in the criminal justice process, including the originating act or offence, the arrest and charge, detention, the judicial process, and the potential sentencing and incarceration, carries with it only part of the individual frustrations, technical difficulties, and cultural barriers which many aboriginal peoples regularly encounter. Viewed separately, each aspect of the process appears as a bewildering and perhaps unfortunate setback under unique circumstances. Depicted as a whole, these circumstances signify a structure of deep-rooted inequality and oppression which translates everyday lives into biographies characterized by failure, subjugation, and misery.

Since the late 1980s, media and political attention has been directed towards aboriginal peoples' problems with the criminal justice system through high-profile events like the Nova Scotia public inquiry in 1987-88 into the wrongful imprisonment of Donald Marshall on a murder conviction, tensions between natives and non-natives in The Pas, Manitoba, revealed in the 1987 trial of two men for the murder of Helen Betty Osborne in 1971, the 1988 police shooting of native leader J.J. Harper in Winnipeg, the explosive tensions between the Quebec provincial police and Mohawks at Oka in 1990, and the release of reports from aboriginal justice inquiries in the three prairie provinces in the early 1990s. As shocking as these incidents often appear, their sensationalism overshadows the more mundane but equally powerful realities that affect the daily lives of large portions of Canada's aboriginal population.

The objective indicators of natives' involvement with the criminal justice system provide a stark overview of the problem. Most analyses of natives and the law begin with accounts of the overrepresentation of native peoples throughout the criminal justice system. These trends hold for nearly all categories of offenders, all types of institutions, and all regions of the country. Native peoples constitute less than 3 percent of the total Canadian population but, according to 1991 figures, about 11 percent of the inmate population in federal correctional institutions — housing offenders sentenced to terms of two years or more — and 15 percent of provincial prison populations — constituting offenders sentenced to less than two years (Department of Justice Canada, 1991:7). These rates range from less than 1 percent in Quebec to 32.7 percent in the prairies region (which includes the far north). In 1987-88, 11 percent of new sentenced admissions into federal institutions were natives, while figures were even higher for inmate admissions into provincial institutions, ranging from 9 percent in Ontario to 55 percent in Manitoba, 66 percent in Saskatchewan, 60 percent in the Yukon, and 88 percent in the Northwest Territories (Solicitor General Canada, 1988:5; Griffiths and Verdun-Jones, 1989:564). Hylton (1982:122-123) observes that, based on data for admissions into provincial correctional institutions in Saskatchewan for 1976-77, "a male Treaty Indian turning 16 in 1976 had a 70% chance of at least one incarceration in a provincial correctional centre by the age of 25. The corresponding figure for a male non-status Indian or Métis was 34%, while for a non-Native male, the figure was 8%." These probabilities are substantiated by figures reported by the recent Task Force on the Criminal Justice System and its Impact on the Indian and Métis People of Alberta (Province of Alberta, 1991a:4-30) which indicate that 78 percent of Indian men surveyed by the Indian Association of Alberta reported having been arrested at some point in their lives.

Incarceration rates are often even more pronounced for female inmates. In 1990, aboriginal women constituted 15 percent of female inmates in federal prisons (Department of Justice Canada, 1991:62), though these proportions have been even higher. Native women constituted nearly one-third (31 percent) of the population in the federal prison for women in Kingston in 1983 and between 13 to 80 percent of inmates in provincial institutions in the prairie region and the northern territories (LaPrairie, 1987:103). Hylton (1982:122) reports that in 1976-77, 85.1 percent of all female admissions compared with 63.7 percent of all male admissions to provincial correctional centres in Saskatchewan were persons of aboriginal ancestry. Aboriginal women constituted 68 percent of all admissions to Manitoba's Portage Women's Jail in 1987, of which proportion 71 percent were status Indian, 19 percent were Métis, and 10 percent were non-status Indians (Barkwell et al., 1989:140).

Aboriginal peoples are also overrepresented among young offenders. In Ontario, for example, Jolly (1983) reports that status Indian youth under the age of 20 constituted less than 1 percent of the general population in that age cohort but their likelihood of being placed in an observation and detention facility and of being placed on probation was three times that of the general population in each instance, according to data for 1982. Mason (1988:61) reports that in Alberta, where native young persons constituted less than 5 percent of the total youth population, aboriginal young offenders as a proportion of all young persons in custody regularly ranged in the 1980s between 35 and 40 percent, while aboriginal youth represented about 20 percent of youth in community corrections programs (including probation, community service, and fine option).

More recent data indicate that these patterns are not reversing but, if anything, are becoming more pronounced. Throughout the 1980s, the annual rate of growth in the number of aboriginal inmates has regularly exceeded the growth rate for non-natives. In 1982-83, for example, the growth rate for the population of native inmates was 15.2 percent compared with 9.4 percent for non-natives, while by 1986-87, the non-native inmate population exhibited a growth rate of 1.3 percent compared with 3.5 percent for aboriginals (Solicitor General Canada, 1988:24). In 1991, the federal government admitted that, "There is every indication that the aboriginal inmate problem is worsening, given that the federal aboriginal inmate population is increasing at more than twice the national rate" (Department of Justice Canada, 1991:7).

Although these data are not complete, a consistent pattern emerges in which native peoples are far more likely than non-natives to be processed through the criminal justice system and far less likely to be involved as officials and employees in the system itself. Increasingly over the past two-and-a-half decades, these circumstances have been condemned as intolerable by aboriginal spokespersons. Gradually, politicians and representatives of the criminal justice system have come to acknowledge that questions about systematic inequality and discrimination within the system can no longer be ignored. From late 1964, when an inquiry by the Canadian Corrections Association (1967:9) declared its finding that "a situation of serious magnitude existed" with respect to Canadian Indian people and the legal system, several surveys and inquiries have attempted to identify the scope and nature of native peoples' involvement with the criminal justice system in an effort to rectify the major problems uncovered. A national conference on Native Peoples and the Criminal Justice System in 1975, attended by representatives from aboriginal groups as well as federal and provincial officials, reiterated the seriousness of these problems. The conference produced a series of guidelines for action which adopted the philosophy that native persons and communities must be more fully involved in the planning, staffing, and delivery of criminal justice services for native persons, that non-natives in the system needed to be sensitized to the particular needs and goals of aboriginal peoples, and that prevention and alternatives to institutionalization should be emphasized in planning and implementing programs for aboriginal peoples (Solicitor General Canada, 1975:38). In announcing the formation of a Canadian Advisory Council on Native Peoples and the Criminal Justice System, Solicitor General Warren Allmand indicated that the council's aim was "to make sure that what was started here and started the preparation for this conference is not forgotten and is not shoved under the rug, and that those things we agreed to do here today are, in fact, done" (Solicitor General Canada, 1975:59). However, four years later, Jolly, Peters, and Spiegel (1979) reported that many of the recommendations had not been followed by subsequent action and, moreover, several top-level bureaucrats had not even read the conference report or else were unfamiliar with its recommendations. A decade later, the federal Standing Committee on Justice and Solicitor General, chaired by David Daubney, included a section on native offenders in its report on national sentencing review and corrections issues. However, the report merely echoed many of the principles which had been established at the 1975 conference with little acknowledgment that those guidelines had been put into place by federal and provincial ministers (Canada House of Commons, 1988).

The Daubney report signifies the dual and often contradictory role increasingly established by government, especially at the federal level, with respect to natives and the criminal justice system. On the one hand, the serious nature of existing problems and their grounding in socioeconomic conditions are acknowledged. The Daubney report, emphasizing that, "The serious disruption of the Native culture and economy that has taken place in this century has had a devastating effect on the personal and family life of Native inmates," declares that "too many [Natives] are being unnecessarily sentenced to terms of imprisonment" (Canada House of Commons, 1988:211-212). Similarly, the report of the Task Force on Aboriginal Peoples in Federal Corrections, also released in 1988, stresses that, "It is evident that the greater socio-economic disadvantage of Aboriginal offenders points to the need for special remedial treatment" (Solicitor General Canada, 1988:12). At the same time as these special circumstances are recognized, however, the federal reports, consistent with the stated direction of both Indian affairs and corrections policies in general, place the burden of improving conditions upon offenders, communities, and aboriginal peoples themselves, as revealed in the title of the Daubney report, "Taking Responsibility."

In the 1990s, several important initiatives towards greater native participation in the criminal justice system have been introduced as officials have been forced to contend with the potentially explosive nature of problems in aboriginal justice. Nonetheless, these programs have contradictory aims and results. As Verdun-Jones and Muirhead (1982:278) observe:

> There is, of course, a certain irony in the attempt of the Federal and Provincial governments to deal with problems created by their predecessors in a manner which effectively requires natives to provide their own "solutions" through cooptation into the formal agencies of the criminal justice system. Furthermore, it is not clear whether these recent political developments reflect a genuine commitment to radical change or merely an overall governmental strategy of reducing costs by turning over part of its responsibility to volunteers and self-help groups of various kinds.

This chapter examines these contradictory policies in the context of the legal, economic, and political status of Canada's aboriginal peoples. We argue that consideration of these matters must begin with an assessment of the ways in which law has contributed to the marginal and subordinate place occupied by particular groups of aboriginal peoples as subjects within the Canadian nation-state. We then explore the implications of these legal frameworks for natives as peoples who occupy distinct positions within changing class and gender structures.

ABORIGINAL PEOPLES AND THE LAW

Legally, as we have shown in previous chapters, aboriginal peoples have been divided into distinct groups and defined in ways that separate many of them from the general Canadian population. Politically, state policy has until recently recognized a special status for Indians which has failed to acknowledge crucial forms of aboriginal rights. Economically, native peoples have been marginalized from the means of obtaining an adequate subsistence. Yet, commonly, Indians' problems with the law have been viewed in terms of individual responsibility rather than as reflections of these legal, political, and economic frameworks. This individualistic view of crime is not surprising, given a general tendency in criminological literature and criminal justice system policies to present criminal activities and legal problems as consequences of individual pathologies within a legal-political framework which is taken to be relatively unproblematic (Ratner and McMullan, 1987). Few people would wish to absolve individuals from responsibility for their actions. However, an approach that presents law violation and criminality primarily as symptoms of individual inadequacies or cultural failings draws attention away from legal and social structures derived from fundamentally unequal social relations.

Aboriginal peoples have been subjected to ongoing, systematic policies, legislation, and institutional practices which have singled them out for discriminatory treatment as either "Indians" or other racialized categories of peoples, sometimes in conjunction with other racial groups, notably the Chinese and Japanese. Moss (1987) outlines a continuous history of colonial, federal, and provincial laws which have discriminated against Canada's aboriginal peoples, beginning with slavery which ended formally in the Canadas in the 1790s, and continuing on through restrictions on Indians' civil and political rights and special provisions in criminal law oriented to the prosecution of aboriginal peoples.

Under these circumstances, the involvement of aboriginal peoples with the criminal justice system must be seen not simply in terms of individual law violators, but as the consequence of a political, legal, and socioeconomic framework which has contributed directly and indirectly to the criminalization of natives both as natives and as persons who occupy subordinate socioeconomic positions. That is, efforts to suppress native peoples, their traditions, and their socioeconomic independence have often involved placing Indians in situations where their everyday life activities are defined and acted upon as criminal in nature (such as legislation to ban cultural ceremonies such as the potlatch and sun dance and to restrict Indians from purchasing alcohol or to ban Indians from pool-rooms), or their responses to lived circumstances place them in conflict with the law (such as alcohol-related violations or imprisonment resulting from inability to pay fines).

The special status of Indians is a contradictory position which derives from deeper contradictions in government policy towards aboriginal peoples. The federal government's paternalistic obligation to care for and protect Indians historically has been managed through alternating policies of isolation, which in practice has meant minimal delivery of services, and assimilation, which has been oriented to the ending of Indians' special status. The peculiar problems which these policies have posed for native peoples, in turn, are reflections of a fundamental contradiction in Canadian confederation, in which the federal system of government has attempted to coordinate the aim to establish a distinct and unified nation with the will to preserve diverse cultural nationalities (Opekokew, 1987:1).

With reference to the sociological language that we employed in Chapter 4, these issues are commonly framed in terms of what kinds of individuals must be produced in order to maintain the cohesion of the collectivity. The "problem of social order" focuses upon the need to have social subjects who will acquiesce or conform to the demands for social order produced by a particular social system. In a complex society, this requires a balance between having individuals who possess a diverse range of social and cultural characteristics but who, nonetheless, are somehow unified in fundamental ways so that there are limits placed upon what are considered to be normal or acceptable citizens and citizenship actions. The minimal basis for this social organization in capitalist societies is the legal and political recognition of individuals and individual rights as the fundamental units in society.

Ideological conceptions of citizenship grounded in possessive individualism have two major implications for aboriginal peoples in Canada. First, citizenship is grounded in the notions of individual responsibility and acceptability within the limits of what is regarded as "normal" for society. People who are identified by formal authorities as deviating from these standards of appropriate behaviour, either through lack of readiness for full social participation or violation of laws and cultural practices, are subjected to some limitations of their citizenship rights. Historically, the denial of Indians' right to vote and legislation restricting Indians' right to own private property have served as examples of paternalistic policies based on ideologies that present aboriginal peoples as not yet ready for full citizenship. Second, the ideology of individualism is promoted to serve an assumed "common good" or public interest rather than loyalty to any particular group or collectivity. Enforcement of this ideology has the impact of destroying cultural traditions and bonds that do not conform with the dominant white, anglo framework.

It is important to recognize that while notions of "rights" and "citizenship" have been defined in accordance with general principles established within western capitalist nations, they have taken on distinct meanings whose implications have varied in accordance with changing state policies and practices regarding aboriginal peoples.

Under early British colonial rule, Indians were recognized (giving rise to the contemporary conception of "First Nations") to possess a degree of sovereignty which enabled them to regulate their own peoples and enter freely into alliances with other groups or authorities (Smith, 1975:xv). Significantly, this interpretation of sovereignty may have played an important role in legitimating the political alliances and subsequent treaties that were engaged in between Indians and colonial and state powers. In other words, under British law, the transfer of lands from First Nations to colonial and state authorities was regarded as legally and morally proper if it could be shown that due process was involved in the transaction between politically sovereign parties.

In addition, formally until at least 1826 and in practice after that time, British rule enabled First Nations peoples to police and prosecute offences by natives against other natives within their territorial lands. Traditional aboriginal justice, in contrast with the formally individualistic, bureaucratic, and adversarial models of contemporary criminal justice systems, emphasized collective decision-making and concern for community interests, usually guided by elders and other tribal leaders (Coyle, 1986:615). However, after 1826, following the unprecedented case of a warrant for execution of an Indian who had murdered another Indian, Indians were treated more directly as subjects under British and Canadian civil and criminal law (Smith, 1975:xv-xvi).

The clash between unequal conceptions of law and justice posed distinct difficulties in the context of expansion of non-native settlement and economic development. The case of Te-cha-malt, a Cowichan Indian chief who in 1869 was threatened with arrest for trespassing on reserve land which was improperly surveyed and subsequently sold to a non-Indian, illustrates some of these issues. In a letter to the Chief Commissioner of Land and Works, one official recommended that the government take no action either to acknowledge the error or to rectify it by returning the land to the Indians:

> In the case of dispute between Mr. Rogers and the Indians, I summoned Te-cha-malt on a charge of trespass, but as I found it was a case of dispute as to the ownership of the land, and on the Indians promising not to interfere until I received further instructions from the Government, Mr. Rogers also agreeing to let the matter stand over, I have taken no further action; since that time all has been quiet.
>
> I still firmly believe the Indian knew the land was open for pre-emption.... I believe it would be advisable not to restore it to the Indians; it

will only encourage them to make further demands. I have another case of a similar description in hand. A party of Indians have fenced a good portion of Mr. Munroe's land in, which he paid $5 per acre for.

I really believe the Indian Missions here do a deal to make the Indians dissatisfied. The Catholics appear to have a great influence over them.

Te-cha-malt made use of very improper language, and was very insolent. He said he was the Chief and that the land was his. He also said that Governor Seymour could not take the land from him, that if the Governor sent his gunboat he would fetch his friends from all parts and hold the land against him. He also said the Governor was a liar and had not fulfilled his promise to pay for the land he had taken. And then he told me he did not care for me, or the prison either, that I had no power over the Indians, and a good deal to the same effect (Morley, 1869).

Several points of note can be determined from the incidents described. Most importantly, regardless of the merits of the individual case, the events signify the emergent domination of non-native institutional practices over aboriginal lands and society. The dispute emphasizes the contending notions of legitimate authority as held by Indians and state officials. The immediate application, upon the transfer of land, of the "rule of law" ensured the extinguishment of whatever traditional land uses may once have been in effect. This process is reinforced by the threat of arrest, the imposition of jails and other aspects of the criminal justice system, and, if necessary, the use of force through "gunboat diplomacy." At the same time, the possible admission that the Indians could be in the right is overridden by the fact that the land had been paid for and by the fear that to give in to the Indians' demands, however legitimate they might be, would lead to continued problems by "[encouraging] them to make further demands." In addition, the situation is complicated by the allegations of intervention by missionaries, signifying the importance of struggles at various levels, including between denominations, between religious orders and the state, and between different groups of Indians.

Of central concern in all of these events is the ambivalent way in which Indians are treated as both political subjects and objects of the law. Under the general terms of civil and criminal law in a "free" society, Indians are held accountable for their individual actions. In addition, however, within the terms set out by laws and policies pertaining specifically to aboriginal peoples, Indians are subject to extensive paternalistic regulation by the state in accordance with recognition of their special status. The official justification for such a policy is assimilation, which entails both the loss of such status, accomplished primarily through the enfranchisement process, and the termination of federal obligations to the individual as an Indian. This legal position is outlined clearly in a statement on Canadian Indian policy by Duncan Campbell Scott, the Deputy Superintendent General of Indian Affairs in the 1930s:

The Indians are minors in the eye of the law; they are protected by the Indian Act which exempts real and personal property on Indian reserves from seizure for debt, prohibits the sale or gift of intoxicants to Indians, the consumption or possession of intoxicants by Indians or on an Indian reserve, restricts trading with Indians, and otherwise provides for the safe guarding of their interests. In respect to those matters, which are not specifically covered by the Indian Act, the Indians are subject to the criminal and civil laws of the country. The duties of the Department are to administer and protect the estate of the Indians and to carry out the policy of the Government for their advancement towards civilization (Scott, 1931:5).

Concerns about the legal definition and designation of who is an Indian, which we discussed in Chapter 2, add further dimensions of ambiguity and inequality to these conditions. The Indian Act employs racial discrimination by classifying individuals who are defined as Indians, and until the Bill C-31 amendment in 1985, by authorizing the Minister for Indian Affairs to enfranchise Indians by removing Indian status of an Indian deemed "capable of assuming the duties and responsibilities of citizenship" and "capable of supporting himself and his dependants" and of a band which could be deemed "capable of managing its own affairs as a municipality or part of a municipality" (R.S., c. I-6, sec. 109[1] and 112[1]). Moreover, the legislation in its original formulation was also sexist since it discriminated against persons on the basis of gender and marital status as we observed in Chapter 2, citing Jamieson's (1978:1) summary of the dire consequences of the provisions to remove Indian status from Indian women who married men not legally defined as Indian.

As we have stressed earlier, the state's selective exertion of regulations over the lives of aboriginal peoples has served to amplify control over differentiated segments of the population. Such distinctions have come to assume even greater importance as the question of aboriginal title is considered in the context of current negotiations over self-government and economic development. Opekokew (1987:5) observes in this regard that

> The recognition which Canadian and English law and policy gave to the historic fact of who had original possession of the North American continent, is the basis of the present legal and political inequalities among the aboriginal peoples. This diversity created by legislative limitations translates only to a certain group of aboriginal peoples having the right to exercise fully their aboriginal rights whether as communities or individuals. The government of Canada has generally chosen not to provide for programs and services to Non-Status Indians and have [sic] claimed that they have no constitutional responsibility for the Métis. Except for Alberta, the provinces have also denied any responsibility over the Métis people.

Statutory and policy distinctions among aboriginal peoples are not simply abstractions, for they outline differential access to rights and obligations which translate into differences in opportunities and barriers experienced in the lives of aboriginal peoples. In the process of legally defining who is an Indian, the federal government has contributed to the division of families and communities and undermined aboriginal peoples' ability to become equal participants (however such participation is defined) in Canadian society. This is not simply an unfortunate by-product, but is rather a central structural feature of class and socially-divided capitalist societies. It is within this context that we can now explore native involvement with the criminal justice system.

ABORIGINAL PEOPLES IN CONFLICT WITH THE LAW

Our knowledge of the extent and nature of criminal activity is limited by the problems involved in compiling reliable and valid data. Most comprehensive crime data come from police records which are based on officially reported incidents of crime. However, as self-reporting studies such as the Canadian Urban Victimization Survey reveal, over half of all crimes are not reported to police, with even higher non-reporting rates for categories of offences like assault, vandalism, and personal theft, and in particular geographical regions (Solicitor General Canada, 1982). These problems are particularly significant with respect to visible minorities, especially native peoples in the Canadian context. As observed earlier in this chapter, the overrepresentation of native peoples in correctional institutions helps to produce an image that aboriginal peoples are involved in proportionately more criminal activity than are members of the general population. Common characteristics emerge among those persons who are actually convicted and sentenced: they are typically young, male, aboriginal, poorly educated, and of low socioeconomic status. The incarcerated population, though, includes only a small proportion of all persons who have committed a criminal offence. Evans and Himelfarb (1987:44), for example, estimate that one person is sentenced to prison or penitentiary for every 43 break-and-enter offences that occur in Canada. Because of selectivity and possible bias in reporting and processing cases at various points within the criminal justice system, the inmate population is not a representative group of those who have committed crimes. Consequently, indicators of native criminality which are based upon the incarcerated population tend to tell us more about class, "race," and gender inequalities within the criminal justice system and the socioeconomic and political system within which it operates than about the actual nature of criminal activity.

Unfortunately, as in many other areas, sufficiently detailed data are not widely available that can offer us much more than a broad comparison between native and non-native offenders in federal custody and provincial custody. Data from 1989 show that 10.8 percent of inmates in federal custody were native, as determined by the proportion of inmates who identified themselves as either status or non-status Indian, Métis, or Inuit (Correctional Service of Canada, 1989; Canadian Centre for Justice Statistics, 1990). With respect to admissions to provincial and territorial custody, there are wide discrepancies across provinces. Jolly (1983:3) reports that the rate of incarceration in Ontario jails in 1981-82 was 1849 per 100 000 population for natives compared with 518 per 100 000 for non-natives. More comprehensive data from 1982 and 1983 indicate that the ratio of native to non-native rates of admission to custody (as determined by expressing the number of custodial admissions as a proportion of the total population aged 15 and over for each group) ranges between 7.1 in the Yukon to 31.8 in Saskatchewan (see Table 7.1). These variations, however, must be interpreted in the context of discrepancies among jurisdictions which reveal that some provinces — notably Manitoba and British Columbia — have relatively low rates of admission for both natives and non-natives, while others, including Ontario and the Yukon, have relatively high overall rates (see Moyer et al., 1985:2.24-2.25).

Closer examination of these data reveals that native offenders, relative to the general population, tend to be incarcerated for more serious crimes in federal institutions and less serious offences under provincial custody. Table 7.2 presents data which show that, as of early 1989, federally-incarcerated native offenders were more likely than non-native offenders to be admitted for crimes of violence, with the greatest differences between the two offender groups under the categories of manslaughter, assault, and sex-related offences. Native offenders in federal institutions were also likely to be serving longer sentences than non-native offenders, with nearly two out of five (39.7 percent) native inmates serving aggregated sentences of five years or more compared with just under one-quarter (23.2 percent) of the total inmate population.

However, native offenders, like the general federally-incarcerated population, tend to be young, male, and single — 75.6 percent of federal native inmates in 1989 were under age 35, over 98 percent of on-register federal native inmates in 1989 were male, and 52 percent of that population were single, 41 percent were married or cohabiting, and 7 percent were widowed, divorced, or separated (Correctional Service Canada, 1989:A5). These parallels indicate that native and non-native offenders share some common experiences based on class and gender characteristics, reflective in particular of a segment of the population for which only marginal and intermittent employment is likely.

Native inmates, reflecting a more highly marginalized legal and social status, are even more disadvantaged in other respects. McCaskill (1985), in a study of federal inmates in the prairie region, indicates that aboriginal offenders were born predominantly in rural or isolated areas (only 20.4 percent were born in communities of over 10 000 people) but lived in

Table 7.1

Rates of Custodial Admissions of Natives and Non-Natives

Jurisdiction	Year	Native Admissions as a Percentage of Native Population	Rank	Non-native Admissions as a Percentage of Non-native Population	Rank	Ratio of Native to Non-native Rates of Admission
Yukon	1983	9.24	3	1.30	1	7.1
British Columbia	1982-3	4.15	6	0.54	4	7.7
Alberta	1982	7.87	4	0.56	3	14.1
Saskatchewan	1982-3	13.36	1	0.42	5	31.8
Manitoba	1982	4.45	5	0.27	6	16.5
Ontario	1982-3	11.44	2	0.93	2	12.3

Source: Sharon Moyer, Paigie Kopeiman, Carol LaPrairie, and Brenda Billingsley, *Native and Non-Native Admissions to Federal, Provincial and Territorial Correctional Institutions.* Ottawa: Research Division, Ministry of the Solicitor General of Canada No. 1985-34; p. 2.23.

Table 7.2

Major Offence Types and Aggregated Sentence Lengths,
Native and Total On-Register Population in Federal
Correctional Institutions, March 31, 1989

Major Offence Type	Native (Percent)	Total Federal Offender Population (Percent)
Violent		
Murder and Attempted Murder	13.5	15.0
Manslaughter	11.1	5.0
Sex Offences/Rape/Sexual Assault	17.0	11.0
Kidnap & Abduct/Wounding	1.3	1.0
Assault	12.2	4.0
Robbery	18.1	23.0
Offensive Weapons	1.7	1.0
Violent Total	74.9	60.0
Property		
Break and Enter	14.0	15.0
Theft/Fraud/Possession of Stolen Goods	3.1	5.0
Criminal Negligence	0.9	1.0
Arson & Attempted Arson	1.0	n/a
Property Total	19.0	21.0
Other	5.8	16.0
Total	99.7	97.0
Aggregated Sentences (Years)		
<3	33.1	41.2
3<4	15.8	24.4
4<5	10.4	12.0
5<6	7.5	6.6
6<7	4.5	3.8
7<8	3.9	2.6
8<10	5.1	2.5
10<15	4.4	2.2
>15	1.1	1.0
Indefinite	0.5	1.0
Life	12.7	3.5
Total	99.0	100.8
Total Number of Offenders	1407	13 066

Note: Figures do not total 100 because of rounding.

Sources: For native offenders, Correctional Service of Canada, *Native Population Profile Profile Report, Population on Register 03/31/89*. Ottawa: CSC Management Services. For total population, Canadian Centre for Justice Statistics, *Adult Correctional Services in Canada 1989-90*. Ottawa: Statistics Canada Cat. No. 85-211.

larger urban communities at the time of admission (67.2 percent lived in centres of over 10 000) (also reported in Solicitor General Canada, 1988:25). Another recent report based on a comparison of aboriginal and non-aboriginal inmates who became eligible for release in 1983-84 reveals that fewer than 20 percent of aboriginal inmates, compared with 30 percent of non-aboriginal inmates, had Grade 10 education or lower and that less than one-quarter of aboriginal inmates had any vocational training; furthermore, fewer than 17 percent of aboriginal inmates, compared with nearly 30 percent of non-aboriginal inmates, were employed at the time of their offence, while about two-thirds of aboriginal inmates did not have any previous skilled employment (Solicitor General Canada, 1988:26).

Data for aboriginal offenders in provincial and territorial custody further confirm the impact of class through social and economic disadvantage on the likelihood of incarceration, especially when it is acknowledged that high proportions of such admissions are related to default of fine payment and alcohol use. According to 1982-83 data for selected jurisdictions, the proportion of natives relative to total admissions to provincial or territorial custody was 59.7 percent in Saskatchewan, 56.4 percent in the Yukon, 46.3 percent in Manitoba, 26.6 percent in Alberta, 16.1 percent in British Columbia, and 11.6 percent in Ontario (Moyer et al., 1985:2.4). Between about one-fifth (22.7 percent in Manitoba) and just under one-half (47.9 percent in Alberta) of these natives in all jurisdictions except British Columbia (where the proportion was 16.6 percent) were admitted into custody on the basis of fine default (calculated from Moyer et al., 1985:2.4). The federal Department of Justice, citing Saskatchewan data, observed in 1991 that

> while the sentences given aboriginal offenders have become shorter on average, they have become more frequent and increasingly involve offenses against the justice system itself in the form of failure to appear for court and default in paying fines (Department of Justice Canada, 1991:7).

The proportion of native persons admitted for liquor offences as a percentage of total native sentence admissions appears to be relatively small in most jurisdictions (ranging from 0 percent in Manitoba to 4.0 percent in the Northwest Territories); the notable exception is Ontario, where the comparable rate is 42.0 percent as a result of legislative differences, lack of adequate short-term detoxification facilities, and greater "visibility" of native drinking in public places (Moyer et al., 1985:4.3-4.5). However, alcohol is a prominent factor in admissions to custody for other reasons. Schmeiser (1974:81), in a report prepared for the Law Reform Commission of Canada in 1974, concludes that

> Much, if not most, Native crime is associated with the use of alcohol. The association may be direct, such as in the offences of impaired driv-

ing, public drunkenness, and causing a disturbance; or it may be indirect, such as assault following drinking, or theft or breaking and entering to obtain alcohol.

McCaskill (1985:35), in a longitudinal analysis of native offenders in Manitoba, reports that three-quarters of crimes committed by native offenders in 1984 involved alcohol either directly or indirectly, although this figure is less than the rate of 90 percent recorded in 1970. Similarly, Hagan (1977:203), analysing data on Alberta offenders incarcerated in early 1973, estimates that while 64 percent of native, compared with 34 percent of non-native, offenders were incarcerated in default of fine payments, the gap between the two groups decreases when those who are incarcerated for default of fine payment involving liquor offences are removed, in which case the comparable figures are 46 percent for natives and 32 percent for non-natives.

In summary, native offenders are overrepresented in the institutionalized population, most particularly for those incarcerated for the most serious offence categories, as well as for relatively minor offences including offences against the justice system. Alcohol is a prominent factor in much native crime, and high proportions of native peoples are incarcerated in default of fine payments. However, we must be wary of overgeneralizing on the basis of these trends in order to avoid making simplistic or misleading conclusions about the nature of native peoples' involvement in the criminal justice system. For example, we cannot conclude from the evidence that native crime is a product of a particular pathology associated with alcohol abuse among native peoples, since in many cases comparable proportions of non-natives are incarcerated for alcohol-related offences. Hylton (1982:124) reports that nearly half of all admissions to provincial correctional institutions in Saskatchewan in 1975-76 were related to drinking or driving, and 60 percent of admissions were relatively minor, involving a sentence of ninety days or less. Bonta (1989), in a study of inmates who were serving terms of between ninety days and two years in three provincial jails in northern Ontario, found few significant differences between natives and non-natives in terms of sentencing, offence categories, unemployment rates at the time of incarceration, and institutional behaviour. Regional variations in incarceration patterns also suggest that it is not so much the inmate characteristics that must be taken into account when comparing groups within the criminal justice system, but differences in laws, policing, sentencing, and facilities. The findings of recent provincial aboriginal justice inquiries have given official recognition to the importance of these factors (see, e.g., Province of Manitoba, 1991:103ff.; Saskatchewan Indian Justice Review Committee, 1992:6-9; Saskatchewan Métis Justice Review Committee, 1992:6-9).

The picture that emerges is one whereby "race" and socioeconomic circumstances have an interactive effect which varies the chances and nature of involvement in the justice system for different groups of people. By focusing only on the most visible aspects of that system in terms of who is processed through it, we ignore the complex mechanisms which operate to produce the observed outcomes. As Hylton (1982:125) stresses:

> All too often the involvement of native people in social service and social control programs is seen as "the problem". We often hear that Natives are "drunks" and "criminals"; that they are "mentally unstable" and "morally degenerate". These pronouncements fail to take account of underlying causes and concentrate instead on symptoms of problems.

At the point of incarceration, we tend to see only the individuals who have been processed all the way through the system. We do not see the experiences that led up to and generated the arrest or that accompanied the journey through the system. We see neither the comparable cases that were not processed nor the discretionary decisions that led to the observed statistics. And we do not call into question the legitimacy of the whole criminal justice system and the legal-political framework which it represents. However, as the following overview of the positions of aboriginal female offenders and young offenders reveals, those structures contain serious inadequacies and inequalities.

Aboriginal Women and Crime

Most of the trends described in the previous section appear to hold true for both male and female aboriginal offenders, although data on women and the law, and aboriginal women in particular, are maintained only sporadically. As noted earlier, aboriginal women constitute 15 percent of federal female inmates (Department of Justice Canada, 1991:62). In the early 1980s, native women constituted between 13 to 80 percent of the provincial female inmate populations in the provinces west of Quebec and in the Northwest Territories, and all or nearly all of the female inmate populations in some institutions such as the Newfoundland Correctional Centre for Women, the Kenora District Jail, and the Whitehorse Correctional Centre (Jolly, 1983:7; LaPrairie, 1984:162; LaPrairie, 1987:103). Although there is some indication that the rates are declining (the proportion of federal female inmates who were of native ancestry was 21.7 percent in 1982 and 31 percent in 1983), it remains evident that native women tend to be even more highly overrepresented in prison than are native men (LaPrairie, 1984:162; LaPrairie, 1987:103). Data from Saskatchewan, for instance, reveal that 85 percent of females, compared with 65 percent of males, admitted by sentence to provincial correctional centres in 1990-91 were aboriginal (Saskatchewan Indian Justice Review Committee, 1992:11).

Native women under federal custody tend to be incarcerated for relatively serious offences. The rates of those in custody for violent crime exceed comparable rates for women offenders in general as well as for native men (Canada House of Commons, 1988:220-221; LaPrairie, 1984:164). In 1989, seventeen of the nineteen (89 percent) aboriginal women in Kingston's Prison for Women (P4W) were admitted for violent offences, including murder, manslaughter, assault, robbery, and wounding (Correctional Service of Canada, 1989:B112). Data presented by LaPrairie (1984:164) indicate that about 28 percent of native female inmates, compared with 7.3 percent of non-native female inmates, are incarcerated for violent crimes in provincial institutions. However, as with males, the majority of female offenders are in custody for relatively minor offences. Jolly (1983:10) observes that, in 1981-82, 73 percent of native females who were admitted to Ontario jails on sentences were serving terms of thirty days or less, compared with 63 percent of their native male counterparts, with the consequence that "there continued to be five times as many Native male admissions and almost 15 times as many Native female admissions serving short sentences of less than one month than their proportion of the population would seem to warrant." Data from Saskatchewan's Pine Grove Correctional Centre for women, in which 83.4 percent of inmates were of native ancestry in June, 1986, indicate that 60 percent of inmates were serving sentences of less than thirty days and an additional 14 percent were serving sentences of between thirty and sixty days. Nearly two-thirds of Pine Grove inmates were serving sentences for either drinking and driving (21 percent) or non-payment of fines (45 percent) (Canada House of Commons, 1988:221).

These trends are symptomatic of the particular problems encountered by aboriginal women as a segment of the population which is doubly disadvantaged or worse, facing discrimination on gender, class, and racial grounds. Profiles of female inmates who had been incarcerated in or recently discharged from Pine Grove Correctional Centre between April 1, 1985, and April 30, 1987, appear to be indicative of the characteristics of aboriginal women offenders in general:

> 58.5 percent had at least one dependent child; 78 percent had more than two children (includes non-dependent children); 72 percent had a Grade 9 education or less; 89.4 percent were unemployed prior to incarceration;.... 55.2 percent had been victims of sexual abuse; and 79.3 percent admitted to serious addictions problems (Canada House of Commons, 1988:222).

These data include non-aboriginal women (who constituted about 17 percent of the inmates), thereby suggesting some commonalities among the social positions of female offenders in general. Lack of education and meaningful employment, poverty, motherhood at an early age, and domestic violence all interact for some women in such a way as to further block opportunities for social advancement, creating in turn ongoing frustrations and tensions which may manifest themselves in drug depen-dencies, crime, and other personal problems.

These characteristics are indicative of the reality whereby native women, on the whole, constitute one of the most oppressed groups in Canadian society (LaPrairie, 1984; LaPrairie, 1987; Task Force on Federally Sentenced Women, 1990:15). They are compounded by the evidence that prison is a form of containment rather than a means to address the problems seriously. Sugar and Fox (1989-90:468-469), stress-ing that, "Aboriginal women who end up in prison grow up in prison," cite on the basis of interviews with incarcerated aboriginal women several factors that impede the promotion of "healing instead of rage." These include severely inadequate prison facilities and programs, cultural- and gender-biased assessment standards, failure to acknowledge and treat the realities of aboriginal women's abusive life histories, and unsympathetic prison regimes. Among aboriginal inmates in particular, suicide, attempted suicide, and slashings are a recurrent feature of prison experi-ence at P4W and other institutions (Sugar and Fox, 1989-90:473). However, the victimization of aboriginal women commonly begins well before their own conflict with the law and is reinforced in prison where aboriginal women encounter humiliation and, frequently, painful separa-tion from their children and supportive family members (Barkwell et al., 1989:141). As a recent Task Force on Federally Sentenced Women (1990:15-23) stresses, the lack of meaningful participation and choice available to incarcerated aboriginal women is symptomatic of the posi-tions of nearly all aboriginal women.

Aboriginal Youth in Conflict with the Law

The common problem of an absence of systematic data is particularly acute with respect to native young offenders. However, consistent with the general experience of native peoples within the criminal justice system, there is substantial evidence to demonstrate that native youth are highly overrepresented throughout the juvenile justice system, especially within custodial institutions. Alberta data reveal that over one-third (34.9 per-cent) of admissions to young offender correctional facilities in the province in 1989 were native persons, while native offenders constituted 18.8 percent of new cases added to community corrections caseloads involving young offenders (Province of Alberta, 1991b:1-57-1-58). These trends are consistent with the findings of previous surveys in Alberta which reveal that while native youth represent less than 5 percent of the province's total youth population, native young offenders constitute between 35 and 40 percent of the province's youth custody populations and about one-fifth of community corrections caseloads, involving proba-tion, community service, and fine options programs (Mason, 1988:61). Data from Saskatchewan for 1989 indicate that the rate of youths charged for violent crimes is 1.6 per 100 persons aged 12 to 17 on reserves compared with an off-reserve rate of 0.6, while the rates for property offences are 8.8 per 100 youth on reserves (primarily for break-and-enter charges) and 5.0 off reserve (Canadian Centre for Justice Statistics, 1991:19-21). The Ontario Native Council on Justice (1981:17) reports that of youth under 16 years admitted to adult correctional institutions in Ontario in 1979-80, 25 percent of the 56 male admissions and 76 percent of the 17 female admissions were native.

Problems experienced by young offenders are particularly significant because they tend to be strongly associated with personal histories of repeat offences, frequent conflict with the law, and restricted opportunities for future social success. Native young offenders tend to be relatively more disadvantaged than non-native young offenders with respect to factors such as income, education, and family arrangements, though the two groups are likely to be in custody for similar types of offences (LaPrairie and Griffiths, 1982). The Alberta Task Force on the Criminal Justice System and its Impact on the Indian and Metis People reports that native young offenders have consistently higher rates of drug and alcohol abuse than both the non native young offender population and the adult offender population, while native young offenders have on average 8.5 years of completed formal education, about half a year less than levels attained by non-native young offenders (Province of Alberta, 1991b:1-150, 1-156). These problems are commonly revealed in patterns of repeat offences and frequent incarceration. Among native offenders surveyed in Ontario correctional institutions, for example, 37 percent of repeat offenders indicated that they had first been convicted as juveniles (Ontario Native Council on Justice, 1981:17).

There is substantial documentation on the special nature of the problems that face young offenders in general, and aboriginal young offenders in particular. The federal government implemented the Young Offenders Act in 1984 in an attempt to manage the peculiar needs of young offenders in such a way as to maintain individual accountability, responsibility, and protection of the public while providing for alternatives to custody. Several commentators have argued that the legislation has not had the desired effect, with the most severe consequences experienced by native youth in isolated rural and northern communities (Griffiths and Verdun-Jones, 1989:569). Among the major problems are:

> access to legal counsel for youth, the lack of understanding of the justice process among northern youth, the involvement of parents and the community, the development of alternative measures, and the separation of adult and youth cases in northern circuit courts (Dube, 1987:92).

These concerns are illustrated by the incident described at the beginning of this chapter. The inadequacies of the juvenile and wider criminal justice systems, when combined with the socioeconomic disadvantages faced by many native youth, contribute to ongoing histories of victimization and failure. Community intervention and child welfare practices often serve to reduce the likelihood that the individual will have a supportive, stable environment, thereby adding to the tensions and experiences which produce ongoing conflict with the law (see, e.g., Ontario Native Council on Justice, 1981).

THE QUESTION OF RACIAL DISCRIMINATION IN THE CRIMINAL JUSTICE SYSTEM

To what extent is the serious overrepresentation of aboriginal peoples in custodial institutions and community correctional programs the consequence of differential treatment and discrimination in the Canadian criminal justice system? This question has a seductive simplicity that is lost when we make a distinction between competing conceptions of fairness and justice.

The operation of a system of "justice" implies that all individuals within its scope are subject to equitable, fair, and just treatment. Liberal notions of due process and equality of treatment are of central importance to the rule of law in democratic capitalist nations, since the absence of these phenomena potentially undermines the system's legitimacy and therefore its ability to operate effectively. There are, however, different meanings to conceptions of equality before the law. Most importantly, legal systems under capitalism are based on principles of *formal* rather than substantive equality; they are, in other words, premised upon notions of justice based upon procedures that enable people to be treated in a fair and equitable manner regardless of the real circumstances and implications which surround those procedures. As Fine (1984:112), paraphrasing Marx, stresses, "equal treatment of unequal individuals — and individuals would not be individuals if they were not unequal — leads to inequality."

The judicial system's primary concern is with *law* as opposed to *justice*. This distinction can be illustrated with reference to the case of two Saskatchewan native women who were part of a group of persons charged with unlawfully occupying Saskatoon's Indian Affairs branch office in protest against the federal government changes to funding post-secondary education for treaty Indians. In his delivery of a suspended sentence to the defendants, the provincial court judge argued in part that the defendants were permitted "to outline the entire issue, as they saw it, in relation to their long-term struggle for the protection and recognition of aboriginal rights," but that "while I indicated that my sympathy rested with the students, I held that the issue of post-secondary education rights was not within the jurisdiction of this court, and therefore one which this court would not be at liberty to rule upon in these proceedings" (Provincial Court of Saskatchewan, 1990:6). Questions of justice, in other words, take us beyond the bounds of procedures within the operation of the criminal justice system.

Having already observed the unequal outcomes of the legal process, we now turn to an examination of the workings of that system. The literature that concerns the question of discrimination in the Canadian criminal justice system yields mixed findings. Nonetheless, it becomes clear that groups which are disadvantaged in terms of class, "race," and gender stand a much higher than average probability of being processed through the criminal justice system by persons who occupy more favourable positions in social, political, economic, and legal hierarchies. These data and conclusions are discussed below in relation to the areas of policing, sentencing, correctional programs and facilities, and community services.

Native-police relations have a long, often controversial history in Canada. Violence and tensions have been explosive on occasions ranging from the paramilitary roles played by the Northwest Mounted Police in the Northwest Rebellion in 1885 to more recent barricade skirmishes over land use and title disputes, most notably in the antagonism between the Quebec Provincial Police and Mohawk warriors at Oka during the summer of 1990. Similarly, police forces frequently have been subject to widespread accusations of racism, lack of tolerance, and harassment of aboriginal peoples, especially in communities where police have come to symbolize the victimization of natives by white society. At the same time, the publicity which has surrounded the most visible of these incidents has made it difficult to assess on a day-to-day basis the degree to which problems are either real or perceived.

Griffiths and Verdun-Jones (1989:551-552) cite research that demonstrates disparities in policing whereby native peoples are more vulnerable than is the general population to surveillance, frequent arrest, and strict interpretation of legal and criminal authority, at the same time as police and law enforcement services are inadequate for responding to requests for assistance by natives. Alberta's Task Force on the Criminal Justice System and its Impact on the Indian and Métis People, for example, reports that residents on reserves, Indian communities, and Métis settlements view day-to-day policing activities as inadequate, while police are prone to overreact to relatively minor offences committed by natives in public places, exercising differential policing and sometimes abusing the native offender (Province of Alberta, 1991a:2-6, 2-48). These patterns cannot necessarily always be attributed to racism on the part of police officers, since larger than average proportions of the native population are in the "high risk" categories of both offenders and victims (predominantly persons who are male, young, non-white, and with low family incomes), particularly for violent crimes (Koenig, 1987). Moreover, the nature and availability of policing practices has an impact on the amount of crime that is reported and how it is responded to. A recent report by the Canadian Centre for Justice Statistics (1991:12) observes that it is "important to note that geographic isolation, community culture, and police-community relations may have an impact on whether or not a criminal incident is reported to the police, and if reported, how it is dealt with.

Further, police presence on a reserve has a direct impact on the amount of activity reported." Nonetheless, as Griffiths and Verdun-Jones (1989:553) summarize, "The relations between the police and native Indians in many urban and rural areas are characterized by mutual hostility and distrust, increasing the likelihood of conflict and high arrest rates" in conditions where natives and police have little sympathy for or knowledge of each other's circumstances. The degree to which this mistrust exists is evident in a national survey of native offenders in which three-quarters of respondents (81 percent of male inmates and 55 percent of female inmates in the sample) indicated that they felt that police employed differential treatment towards natives and non-natives, expressing the view "that a deep rift exists in their mind between the police and Native people" (Morse and Lock, 1988:33). These perceptions were given further substance in the conclusions of the Royal Commission which investigated the prosecution of Donald Marshall, Jr. that pointed towards racism and bias both directly on the part of police investigators as well as indirectly in the nature and organization of policing in general (Province of Nova Scotia, 1989:250).

The federal government and other agencies have been slow to act on these problems, even though as far back as 1973 a federal Task Force on Policing on Reserves concluded that policing practices on reserves were inadequate and more oriented to deal with complaints and petty crime than with preventive practices (Indian and Northern Affairs Canada, 1973:1, 27). In many urban areas, despite increasing concentrations of aboriginal peoples and persistent accusations by minorities of police bias, there continues to be little demonstrable progress in the direction of addressing such matters as the recruitment of aboriginal police officers. The Saskatchewan Indian Justice Review Committee (1992:20), for example, reports that despite a stated intent of commitment on the part of chiefs of police to increase the complement of aboriginal staff on three urban police forces in the province, in September 1991, only 5 percent of police officers in Prince Albert, 2 percent in Regina, and less than 1 percent in Saskatoon were of aboriginal origin. Nonetheless, federal authorities maintain an inclination to define problems in relations between police and aboriginal peoples as matters of perception rather than as real inadequacies. In its summary of aboriginal justice issues in the 1990s, the Department of Justice (1991:33) states that:

> Recognizing that the relationships between some police forces and some aboriginal communities are quite good, it appears nevertheless that aboriginal people, and particularly aboriginal offenders, perceive that they are treated more harshly by the police, that the police discriminate against aboriginal people and that this is one of the reasons for the persistent over-representation of aboriginal people in correctional institutions.

Regardless of public statements concerning perceptions about the matter, though, the real problems are sufficiently acute to mobilize police forces and government officials to develop strategies such as "A National Action Plan for Police-Minority Relations in Canada," which proposes to integrate race relations sensitivity into police recruitment, training, and operating practices (International Briefing Associates, 1990). These attempts to manage the crisis are consistent with the general concern of the criminal justice system with formal law and procedures as opposed to justice.

A somewhat stronger preoccupation with justice issues exists with respect to sentencing. The Daubney committee's review of sentencing and related correctional issues concludes bluntly that "too many [Native inmates] are being unnecessarily sentenced to terms of imprisonment" (Canada House of Commons, 1988:211-212). Some data appear to contradict this assessment. Schmeiser (1974:45), for example, observes that in 1970-71, 38.6 percent of native admissions compared with 59.8 percent of all non-native admissions to provincial correctional centres in Saskatchewan were for initial jail sentences. Clark (1989a:74), in accordance with more general findings across Canada, does not observe any significant variation in sentences received by natives and non-natives in two Nova Scotia districts, although both crown prosecutors and defence counsel identified consistent disparities (which were alternatively advantageous and disadvantageous to native offenders) in the criteria employed by different judges in their sentencing decisions. Hathaway (1986:231) observes that, while there is evidence to show that natives are not convicted or sentenced to incarceration at rates that are disproportionate to the general population, natives are more likely than non-natives to be charged and convicted for relatively minor offences. These findings lend credence to the argument that class and socioeconomic circumstances both contribute to, and interact with, aboriginal status as significant contributors to the overrepresentation of natives in the criminal justice system.

The lack of services such as probation officers in many native communities restricts viable alternatives to incarceration, while problems of poverty result in high proportions of natives being incarcerated for default of fine payment. Moreover, there are other subtle and blatant forms of discrimination that enter into the sentencing process. Ross (1989:2), observing that "Sentencing is nothing more than an institutional response to an act or a word," argues that cultural differences between white officials and native accused often produce inappropriate interpretations of particular actions and statements in courtroom settings. Clark (1989b:47-48) relates testimony from the Donald Marshall inquiry which illustrates the dilemmas produced by language differences, noting:

> that many Micmacs translated the judge's question, "How do you plead: guilty or not guilty?" as "Are you being blamed?" Heard in this way, the

natural response is to answer in the affirmative, which can then be interpreted by the Court to mean "guilty."

Stevens (1991:229) stresses that even where equal treatment is afforded natives and non-natives, natives are at a disadvantage because the legal system and adversarial process, as well as specific terms such as "guilt," "innocent," and "lawyer" are absent from aboriginal people's traditional vocabularies and systems of justice.

These problems have resulted in the wrongful conviction and sentencing of uncounted numbers of aboriginal peoples. This can be illustrated historically by a case in the 1870s of a Cowichan Indian man who was sentenced to fifteen years in prison for the murder of an Indian woman. Petitioning for a pardon for the man, the Cowichan chiefs contended that the man was not guilty but was imprisoned only because he did not disclose the name of the real murderer. In their submission to the Governor General, the chiefs added that:

> We also beg to remind your Excellency of the disadvantages at which we are placed in trials of this kind by our not understanding the English Language and being unacquainted with the customs of the courts we are often, (as in the present case) unprovided with important witnesses for the defence (Chiefs of the Cowichan Indians, 1877).

The striking parallels between this case and that of Donald Marshall, Jr. makes it clear that persistent problems of bias and inequity which operate within the criminal justice system are not merely historical remnants.

It is not surprising, under these conditions, that the existence of bias is evident in people's perceptions of the justice system. Morse and Lock (1988:48) report in their survey of native offenders that 54 percent of respondents felt that natives received higher sentences than non-natives, 16 percent felt that treatment was the same, and only 2 percent felt that natives received more lenient treatment than non-natives. The same survey also reveals a widespread sentiment that judges were either too harsh or inconsistent in their sentencing (Morse and Lock, 1988:48).

However, the problem of unequal outcomes in the sentencing process is not simply a matter of perception. Alberta's Cawsey inquiry reached the "disturbing conclusion" that "while the police are charging fewer people, more people are going to jail" and that, "While Aboriginal offenders are generally given lower sentences by the courts than non-Aboriginals, they spend more time in prison" (Province of Alberta, 1991a:4-33). As with other areas of the criminal justice system, the judicial and sentencing process places native peoples in a highly disadvantaged position.

In addition to sentencing and policing problems, there are further disparities with respect to programs and services offered to convicted offenders. These are a product both of the inadequacies of existing programs and of the reality whereby native offenders who might not otherwise be subject to institutionalization are processed through the system and, upon conviction, are likely to be sentenced to prison rather than to an alternative program. The federal Daubney report on sentencing and corrections, noting that "Incarceration has a destructive impact on [Native] offenders and their relationship with the community," cites low rates of native participation in rehabilitative programs in federal custody and natives' lack of familiarity with and utilization of release-eligibility programs as evidence of the correctional system's failure to meet the particular needs of native offenders (Canada House of Commons, 1988:212). The Correctional Law Review (1988:5) notes that the lack of meaningful native participation in rehabilitative programs remains even with the introduction of a greater variety of programs and services into the correctional context, although participation rates are higher in spiritual, cultural, and educational programs delivered by native organizations themselves. However, the Manitoba Attorney General (1989:26-27) reports, to the contrary, that according to "informal feedback" from provincial institutions, natives and non-natives have equitable rates of participation in programs such as life skills, education, and substance abuse and anger management.

Regardless of the levels of participation in custodial programs, there are clear indications that correctional institutions have limited success in fulfilling their mandate to provide meaningful opportunities for the reform and rehabilitation of offenders. The observed overrepresentation of native peoples in custody is partly a consequence of the fact that native offenders tend to serve longer sentences because of delays in their release relative to the general inmate population. Data from Alberta for 1989, for example, reveal that while natives on average had a lower aggregate sentence (122 days) than non-natives (149 days), the average length of time actually served in provincial custody by adult offenders was nearly equal (43.2 days for natives compared with 44.5 days for non-natives). A substantial degree of disparity also exists between male and female offenders in this regard — the average length of time in custody as a proportion of the average aggregate sentence was 35.1 percent for native males, 44.3 percent for native females, 29.1 percent for non-native males, and 45.5 percent for non-native females (Province of Alberta, 1991b:1-104) — indicating the complex nature of problems related to inequalities in the criminal justice system. Similarly, Jolly (1983:16-17), referring to Ontario data for 1981-82, indicates that 45 percent of native male admissions compared with 28 percent of non-native male admissions, and 50 percent of native female admissions compared with 30 percent of non-native female admissions, served their complete sentences prior to release, while native admissions were only half as likely as non-native admissions to be released on bail.

Many of these trends are related to difficulties experienced by minority populations in the granting of parole. In 1987, nationally, only 18.3 percent of the native inmate population in federal custody, compared with

42.1 percent of the general inmate population, was released on full parole (Canada House of Commons, 1988:211). There are some indications of a possible reversal of these trends. The difference in full parole rates granted to non-natives relative to natives declined from a factor of 3:1 in 1983 to the 1987 ratio of just under 2.5:1, while in Saskatchewan, evidence from the early 1980s suggests that native federal offenders may be more likely than non-natives to be granted parole (Correctional Law Review, 1988:7; Solicitor General Canada, 1988:27). Nonetheless, the proportion of parole decisions in which full parole was granted to aboriginal offenders declined from 25.6 percent of cases in 1984-85 to 20.5 percent in 1986-87 (Solicitor General Canada, 1988:30). Several factors indicate the problems that native inmates have in gaining favourable parole decisions. Aboriginal offenders, relative to non-aboriginal offenders, are more likely to have served a greater proportion of their sentence prior to the granting of parole. Aboriginal offenders are also more likely than non-aboriginal offenders to have special conditions imposed upon the terms of their release programs. Finally, upon release, aboriginals are more likely than non-aboriginals to be readmitted to prison, particularly for technical violations rather than for new offences (Correctional Law Review, 1988:7; National Parole Board, 1990:4; Solicitor General Canada, 1988:28-31).

Several reasons are cited for native offenders' relative inability to secure early release. There are widespread perceptions among offenders and other observers of racial bias and lack of understanding of natives' concerns in the parole assessment and decision-making process. Morse and Lock (1988:64-69) report that over half of native inmates they surveyed believed the parole system was unfair, with just under one-third of the respondents indicating that there were disparities in treatment of natives and non-natives in the parole process in general, as well as by parole and probation staff in particular. As a consequence of these perceptions, many native offenders do not apply for parole because they feel their applications will not be successful. In addition, the absence of factors such as familiarity with parole procedures, employment opportunities, supervisory facilities, and community support that are crucial determinants in the parole assessment process makes it unlikely for many native offenders to gain a favourable parole decision (Correctional Law Review, 1988:6-7; Hathaway, 1984:232). Moreover, the imposition of release conditions such as dissociation (which prohibits the offender from having contact with persons with a criminal record) poses special difficulties for native offenders to become reintegrated into community life, particularly, given the overrepresentation of natives in the criminal justice system, because there is a strong likelihood that the offender's friends and family members may at some point in time have been convicted of an offence (Canada House of Commons, 1988:215-216).

These difficulties are not confined to native inmates. A recurring series of reports and studies has pointed to persistent inadequacies in the services and programs in the correctional system which have placed tremendous doubt on the whole question of the system's ability to rehabilitate and reform the offender (Mohr, 1990). The criminal justice system has commonly been employed as a method for the containment and control of problem populations such as transients, the chronically unemployed, the dispossessed, and alcoholics, drug addicts, and prostitutes (Samuelson, 1991). Consistent with problems related to lack of meaningful employment and educational opportunities, large proportions of the native population have been continually suppressed both outside of and within the criminal justice system as well as through the pathological images that are created and reinforced through their involvement in crime and corrections.

THE QUEST FOR ABORIGINAL JUSTICE

The disadvantaged position of many native peoples within the criminal justice system, their special needs, and the interrelationships between involvement in the criminal justice system and wider socioeconomic problems have, especially since the late 1960s, been recognized by state officials as matters which must be addressed as part of formal government policy and institutional practice (see, e.g., Canadian Corrections Association, 1967; Law Reform Commission of Canada, 1974; Solicitor General Canada, 1975; Canada House of Commons, 1988; Solicitor General Canada, 1988; Province of Alberta 1991a, 1991b; Province of Manitoba, 1991; Province of Nova Scotia, 1989; Saskatchewan Indian Justice Review Commission, 1992; Saskatchewan Métis Justice Review Committee, 1992). In this section, we review briefly some of the practices which have developed as responses to these concerns, discussing their implications for a possible shift towards the de-marginalization of First Nations and their peoples.

The widespread refrain that the criminal justice system is failing native peoples has been substantiated through several common themes. The Alberta native justice inquiry provides a list of the "top ten" recommendations as summarized in its review of twenty-two major reports on aboriginal peoples and the justice system published between 1967 and 1990:

— Have cross-cultural training for non-Native staff.
— Employ more Native staff.
— Have more community-based programs in corrections.
— Have more community-based alternatives in sentencing.
— Have more special assistance to native offenders.
— Have more Native community involvement in planning, decision-making and service delivery.

— Have more Native advisory groups at all levels.
— Have more recognition of Native culture and law in Criminal Justice System service delivery.
— Emphasize crime prevention programs.
— Self-determination must be considered in planning and operation of the Criminal Justice System (Province of Alberta, 1991b: 4-7).

These recommendations point in particular to the recognized need to involve natives more directly in consultative and participatory roles throughout the criminal justice system. It must be stressed that the frequent recurrence of these themes in various reports is indicative of the fact that, often, little substantive action has been taken to redress the problems. Table 7.3, with reference to Alberta, illustrates the striking contrast between the proportions of aboriginal persons who are employed in different positions within the criminal justice system and those who are sentenced within that system. Most notable are the observations that there are no judges, and negligible proportions of other court officials and municipal police, of aboriginal ancestry. Persons of aboriginal origin are underrepresented in every category but two — about one-third of all young offender admissions to provincial correctional centres, and nearly 30 percent of all adult admissions are aboriginal. These trends, significantly, appear nearly a quarter century after the Canadian Corrections Association (1967:58) recommended to the Minister of Indian Affairs

Table 7.3

Representation of Aboriginal People as Employees and as Inmates in the Alberta Criminal Justice System, 1989-90

Criminal Justice System Component	Total Number of Employees	Number of Aboriginal Employees	Aboriginal Employees as a (%) of Total Employees
Police			
R.C.M.P.	2052	50-55	2.4-2.7
Municipal Police	2583	27	1.0
All Police	4635	77-82	1.7-1.8
Alberta Solicitor General[a]			
Corrections	2000	54[b]	2.7
Correctional Service of Canada			
Prairie Region	2071[c]	93	4.5
Alberta	894	31	3.5
National Parole Board	n/a	6	n/a

Table 7.3 Continued

Alberta Attorney General			
Crown Prosecutors	125	Not Known	n/a
Justices of the Peace	398	4	1.0
Provincial Court Judges	111[d]	0	0
Court of Queen's Bench Judges	64	0	0
Appeal Judges	8[e]	0	0
Legal Aid Lawyers Roster	2647[f]	28[g]	0.9

Admissions to Provincial Correctional Centres

	Total Number of Offenders	Number of Aboriginal Offenders	Aboriginal Offenders as a Percentage of Total Offenders
Adult Admissions	31 316	8972	28.6
Young Offender Admissions	4160	1451	34.9
Total Admissions	35 476	10 423	29.4

Notes: a. Includes salaried staff in Corrections and Law Enforcement.
b. Does not include thirty-seven non-salaried Aboriginal staff wage positions, for example, in the Summer Temporary Employment Program.
c. Number of employees.
d. Excludes two supernumerary and one vacant position.
e. Excludes one vacant position.
f. From an alphabetical listing of lawyers willing to accept Legal Aid cases, provided by Legal Aid Society. Ethnic status was not defined.
g. The number of members of the Indigenous Bar Association has been used as an indicator of the potential number of Aboriginal lawyers. However, not all members of the Indigenous Bar Association provide Legal Aid services. Therefore, the percentage of Legal Aid lawyers of Aboriginal ancestry is very likely to be lower than 0.9.

Source: Province of Alberta, *Report of the Task Force on the Criminal Justice System and its Impact on the Indian and Métis People of Alberta.* Edmonton: Province of Alberta, 1991, Volume I, p. 8-42 and Vol. III, p. 1-57.

that, "Indians and Eskimos should be hired much more frequently than is now the case to work with Indians and Eskimo offenders in all aspects of law enforcement, judicial and correctional services."

Nonetheless, several initiatives have been implemented recently to facilitate greater aboriginal involvement in the organization and operations of the criminal justice system. Efforts to redress the previous lack of native participation have been oriented to two general paths to reform: (1) programs such as employment equity guidelines and cross-cultural training which operate within the existing institutional structure of the criminal justice system; and (2) the development of a system of indigenous justice composed of either autonomous local community programs or a more extensively coordinated framework organized under a broader First Nations mandate (Clark, 1989a:58; Correctional Law Review, 1988:26; Griffiths and Verdun-Jones, 1989:551). Table 7.4 provides a sample of the diverse array of programs that has been established within each of these categories.

Table 7.4

A Cross-section of Aboriginal Justice Programs

A: Initiatives Within the Criminal Justice System

Program	Program Description
(i): Services for the Special Needs of Aboriginal Offenders	
Native Courtworker Program	Counselling and referrel services for Natives accused of offences. In all provinces and territories except Sask., N.S., N.B. & P.E.I.
Native Spirituality Program	Spiritual and cultural guidance to inmates provided by Native elders in institutions throughout Canada.
Court Interpreters Program	Native language interpreter services for accused persons in 50 Alberta communities.
Programs for Aboriginal Inmates	Cultural, spiritual, lifeskills, literacy and counselling programs for Aboriginal male and female inmates in Saskatchewan.
Wilderness Camps	Culturally responsive residential services provided to Native young offenders in 2 camps in Ontario.
Native Elders Visitation Program For Young Offenders	Spiritual and cultural guidance provided by Native elders to Native young offenders in Alberta.
Native Inmate Liaison Worker Program	Counselling and discharge planning provided by Aboriginal workers to Native offenders in Ontario.

Table 7.4 continued

Dene Tha Native Youth Service Centre	Youth attendance centres providing a sentencing option on remote reserves in Alberta.
Native Programming at Whitehorse Correctional Center	Native cultural and spiritual programing.
Native Brotherhood/Sisterhood Program	Native awareness activities and cultural events organized for adult offenders in 8 Alberta correctional centres.
Conditional Release Services	Access to Aboriginal halfway houses provided in Vancouver, Edmonton, Winnipeg, Sudbury and Halifax.
Native Probation Supervision Program	Supervision and counselling of Native persons on probation by Native workers in Alberta.
(ii): Programs to Increase Native Representation in the Criminal Justice System	
RCMP Special Constable Program	Policing by Indian people under the supervision and training of the RCMP. In all provinces and territories except Quebec, Ontario & New Brunswick.
Legal Studies For Aboriginal People	Financial assistance offered through the Dept. of Justice to Native people attempting to enter the legal profession.
Native Justice of the Peace Appointments	The services of Native Justices of the Peace are sought to increase Native involvement in Alberta provincial courts.
First Nations Policing Arrangements Program	Indian policing service for the residents of 67 First Nations in Ontario, currently administered through OPP.
Native Criminal Justice Studies Training Program	A certificate program preparing Native students in Vancouver for employment in the criminal justice system.
Native Special Constable Training Program	A three week training program for Native Special Constables in Alberta.
Native Human Justice Program	A two year course developed in conjunction with Correctional Service of Canada to train Native students in Sask. for employment in corrections.

Table 7.4 continued

Ontario Indian Special Constable Program	OPP sponsored training and supervision of Indian constables on reserves.
Native Policing Program	Native Special Constables are actively recruited by the RCMP in NWT, to become regular members of the force.
Policing of Reserves Adjacent to Municipalities Program	Provides for Indian policing on reserves within/adjacent to municipal boundaries, with support from municipal police in B.C., Ont., N.B., & N.S.
Grierson Community Correctional Centre	A correctional centre in Edmonton staffed and operated by Native personnel.
Auxiliary Constable Program Yukon	Offers 8 weeks employment to Native students in their home community to provide career exposure to police work.

(iii) Cross-Cultural Training Programs

RCMP Cross-Cultural Training Program	Cross-cultural training of officers at a recruit level and on an in-service basis. In all provinces and territories except Ontario & Quebec.
Western Judicial Education Centre	Education and discussions of the social context of judicial decisions as they relate to Native people and the law. For justice professionals in B.C., Alta., Sask., Man., NWT & Yukon.
Cross-Cultural Awareness Program	Two-day awareness courses offered to justice professionals in Alberta.
Northern Justice Education Forums	Maintenance of a resource center and organization of an annual conference to provide a forum for Northern and Native justice issues.
Native Courtworker Program	In addition to direct service to Native offenders, this program seeks to enhance the awareness of Native culture and socio-legal conditions among justice administrators.
Ontario Native Council on Justice	Aids the development of justice policy, programs and research pertaining to Aboriginal people.

Table 7.4 continued

Cross-cultural Awareness Training Program	Two-day sessions offered to correction workers in Sask. to provide awareness of diverse cultural backgrounds.

B: Initiatives Implemented By Aboriginal Communities

Dakota Ojibway Tribal Council Police Program	Indian policing service for 8 Manitoba reserves.
Special Band Constable Program	Band controlled policing of civil matters to supplement RCMP on reserves. In all provinces and territories except B.C., Ont., and NWT.
Community Service Work Supervision	Band-supervised Community Service Orders in Northern B.C.
Amerindian Police Program	Indian-delivered policing service for 23 Quebec reserves.
Crime Prevention Coordinators (Blood Tribe and Yellowhead Tribal Council, Alberta)	Crime prevention coordinators selected by the band and council.
Dakota Ojibway Probation Services Program	Tribal council-supervised probation orders and community correctional programs on various Manitoba reserves.
Quebec Aboriginal Police Program	Transfer of policing authority to 23 Aboriginal communities pursuant to the James Bay and Northern Quebec Agreement.
Counselling/Supervision/Substance Abuse Education Program	Education, supervision and counselling services provided to Native offenders by band councils throughout Ontario.
St. Therese Point Indian Government Youth Court System	Indian court system established for young offenders on the St. Therese Point reserve in Manitoba.
Community Holistic Circle Healing	A Native healing program for sexual abuse offenders prior to court appearances. In 4 Manitoba Native communities.
Hobbema Four Nations Police Service	Indian policing service for 4 Alberta reserves.
Blood Tribal Police Force Program	Native peace officer services for the Blood Reserve in Alta.

Source: Compiled from Department of Justice Canada, *National Inventory of Aboriginal Justice Programs, Projects and Research*. Ottawa: Minister of Supply and Services, 1990.

Programs introduced within mainstream criminal justice system operations are intended to provide services which recognize the special needs of native offenders, to increase sensitivity among system employees to native offenders and cultural traditions, to increase native representation in the system, or to meet some combination of these objectives. It is often difficult to assess the relative success of each initiative, partly because many of the programs have been introduced only recently and partly because of the particular circumstances associated with the implementation of the programs. Moreover, as a consequence of the latter concern, the programs tend to be offered in a somewhat haphazard way with little or no systematic interconnection on a regional or national basis.

Overall, while many of the special native program initiatives do offer certain advantages over general criminal justice procedures that do not take into account the special problems faced by the aboriginal offender, there remain several major limitations. (See the review of these programs by Griffiths and Verdun-Jones, 1989, for details). It might be expected, given the strong likelihood of sentencing and high rates of incarceration for relatively minor offences committed by native offenders, that even minor modifications to existing practices would have a positive effect on reducing native overrepresentation in the criminal justice system. In fact, the major benefits provided by such programs appear to be in the areas of increasing knowledge and confidence on the part of the natives who become part of the criminal justice system, whether as offender, liaison, or official, and of heightening the sensitivity of non-native officials to native concerns (Hathaway, 1986:220). However, the success of initiatives like the RCMP Indian Special Constable program, which beginning in 1973 provided for the recruitment, training, and placement of native police officers to improve policing practices and relations with native communities, has been uncertain. The special constables — who have the same powers as regular force members, but are trained for a shorter period of time, are paid lower wages, and have a different status — tend to have a marginalized position both within the police force and in relation to the native communities, which view them with some skepticism (Griffiths and Verdun-Jones, 1989:556). Other officials such as native courtworkers experience similar dilemmas related to conflicting expectations and sometimes suspicion and hostility among clients and justice system officials, disparities in caseload sizes, and restricted or uncertain terms of reference in job descriptions (Hathaway, 1986).

One of the major limitations to these types of programs is that, by virtue of their delivery within the existing framework of the criminal justice system, they do not adequately address problems which lie within the system itself. Griffiths and Yerbury (1984:156-157), in an assessment of native policing programs, observe astutely that, "It is of questionable utility to merely staff white criminal justice structures, such as policing, with natives," given the predominance of "a 'white' crime control oriented model of policing." To this could be added the significance of class and patriarchal forms of domination that reinforce the observed inequalities. Insofar as the roots of native overrepresentation in the criminal justice system originate in the political and socioeconomic structures of Canadian society, of which that system is a major component, any program modifications or reforms which are carried out within the system are likely to be oriented toward symptoms rather than core problems.

It is in response to these issues that many proponents have argued for the development of a parallel system of indigenous justice. Probably to a greater extent than with other program initiatives, local and community-controlled justice services have arisen on an ad hoc basis as conditioned by specific circumstances. A growing number of tribal councils, particularly since the mid-1980s, has acted to deliver justice services tailored to local needs in response to community frustration over the justice system's inadequate treatment of both offenders and victims, as well as its insensitivity to the conditions which surround the criminalization of life activities.

Most common are programs such as community policing, counselling, mediation, and diversion services which complement or replicate services offered by the general criminal justice system, substituting local or band control and native officials for a non-native administration. Some native organizations and bands have sought more radical proposals for autonomous tribal courts and local justice authorities. This type of alternative has also received endorsement from several influential non-native authorites and inquiries (see, e.g., Clark, 1989a:70-76; Correctional Law Review, 1988:40; Morse and Lock, 1988:92; Province of Manitoba, 1991:733). Examples of initiatives in this direction include the Saddle Lake (Alberta) Tribal Justice Centre, which since 1985 has drawn upon community mediators and a council of elders to replace adversarial structures with conciliatory measures of conflict resolution; the Swampy Cree (Manitoba) Tribal Justice Proposal, introduced in 1987 to foster community justice committees and provide long-term planning towards a comprehensive tribal justice system; and the Sandy Lake (Ontario) Band proposal to involve elders in the determination of sentencing as well as to provide a local detention centre and youth diversion programs. As Coyle (1986:628) observes, one of the major advantages of a shift towards community control is that many of the principles embodied in traditional conceptions of aboriginal justice increasingly have become incorporated into the Canadian criminal justice system. These include the use of coercive punishment only as a last resort; lay and community involvement in place of exclusively expert decision-making regarding offenders; decentralized administration of justice system programs; mediation, reconciliation, and compensation by offenders to victims; and informal or diversionary alternatives to incarceration.

Tribal justice programs have an added significance because of their implications for wider questions concerning aboriginal self-government.

As with the issue of self-government, the matter of tribal justice has many definitions and conceptions that, in turn, are confounded by practical difficulties concerning their implementation. Because jurisdiction over criminal justice is divided in different instances between provincial and federal governments, negotiations over the creation of aboriginal justice programs are often protracted and uncertain. While most bands such as the ones we have described have introduced alternative programs in conjunction with official government agencies, in some instances, such as the Quebec reserve communities of Akwesasne and Kahnawake, bands have sought greater recognition for tribal court systems which operate in an unofficial capacity (Morse and Lock, 1988:92).

Government officials and agency representatives either tend often to fail to seek solutions to criminal justice problems outside the national justice system (see, e.g., Canada House of Commons, 1988) or are hesitant to transfer full control over justice programs to band councils (see, e.g., Province of Alberta, 1991a:1-7), for a variety of reasons. In many instances, the state's failure to recognize aboriginal justice needs echoes a common theme in the reluctance of colonial states to relinquish control over a colonized people. Such a position is sometimes justified by claims that aboriginal justice systems won't work because of divisiveness in community sentiment and in band governance.

However, there are also some valid questions that must be raised over the implications of various models of aboriginal justice. One emergent issue concerns the matter of how conflicts between two systems of justice may ultimately be arbitrated. There is the further problem that some programs, such as Alberta's High Level Diversion Project, that were introduced to facilitate community participation in order to alleviate the problems experienced by natives in the criminal justice system, have become little more than additional mechanisms of control within the existing justice bureaucracy (Native Counselling Services of Alberta, 1982). Similarly, as with other aboriginal self-government initiatives, there are concerns about the extent to which a real commitment to justice is undercut by state concerns to download a problem area to aboriginal communities without adequate long-term arrangements for financial and political stability. For First Nations, as for other groups of people, the development of any real or substantive system of justice must be grounded in a clear assessment of the socioeconomic and legal implications of a people's life chances and conditions.

The Politics of Indigenous Justice

It is important to consider why, after decades of relative inaction, governments have moved recently to recognize problems and alternative solutions to natives' involvement with the criminal justice system. An adequate response to this question must take into account several factors.

First, government management of the criminal justice system, as well as of Indian affairs and of social services in general, has been characterized especially since the early 1980s by the rhetoric of fiscal responsibility and rationalization under the neoconservative guise of debt reduction (Neilsen, 1985; Myles, 1988). In the criminal justice field, the state has emphasized crime prevention and community alternatives such as victim-offender mediation and diversion as low-cost solutions to traditional patterns of sentencing and incarceration. These reforms have neither substantially altered the criminal justice system nor reduced the cost of program delivery; instead, they have served simultaneously to focus attention on crime as a social problem and to increase the network of social control that regulates persons designated as offenders and potential offenders (Mandel, 1991). Moreover, as a result of socioeconomic changes as well as differential responses by the criminal justice system, native criminality has come to be recognized as a complex and changing phenomenon which requires an understanding of social structures more than of individuals (McCaskill, 1985:39-40). As in the areas of health and education, discussed in previous chapters, the viability of existing criminal justice practices is being challenged as aboriginal peoples are regarded as an exploitable source of labour power and integrated in new ways into changing labour markets. Finally, native issues have been politicized as a consequence of frustration over the lack of progress on outstanding aboriginal concerns combined with the emergence of a sophisticated native leadership able and willing to take action of various sorts, including working through formal political and legal channels as well as direct militancy. Growing recognition of the problems encountered by natives in their treatment by and dealings with the criminal justice system has made justice officials and native offenders more sensitive to new dilemmas and alternatives. As Nielsen (1991) observes, the native population has come to constitute a form of "social dynamite" to which traditional control strategies are limited because "the very existence of a problem population such as Native inmates calls into question the fundamental economic, political and social relationships within Canadian society."

Underlying all of these factors is the recognition by the Canadian state that the persistent realities of inadequate socioeconomic conditions for the majority of Canada's aboriginal peoples can no longer be ignored in the context of land claims and self-government issues which threaten to reshape the nature of the Canadian state. These issues, in turn, have become significant because of the changing material circumstances which native peoples experience as part of the broader transformation of Canadian socioeconomic reality under advanced capitalism. As we have shown in previous chapters, these changes hold out differential opportunities which are limited for the majority of the population. Consequently, while the terms and conditions may vary, large proportions of aboriginal peoples appear to have little chance of fully overcoming their disadvantaged position of involvement with criminal justice systems.

Conclusion

This chapter has emphasized how Canada's criminal justice system has operated as a vehicle for the containment and control of large segments of Canada's aboriginal population. We have presented considerable evidence of aboriginal peoples' disproportionate involvement as clients of the criminal justice system and their long-standing exclusion from most of the system's central decision-making and operating processes. These phenomena, we argue, are consequences of dominant social, economic, and legal-political structures which employ ideologies of formal justice as means to legitimize fundamental social inequalities.

Various forms of discriminatory policies and practices have distinguished aboriginal peoples as a "racialized" minority or as distinct "racial" subgroupings within Canada's legal and criminal justice systems, while the system has reflected the simultaneous impact of systematic inequalities in class and gender structures. Recent reforms in criminal justice system operations have begun to take into account the relatively disadvantaged socioeconomic status of aboriginal peoples in conflict with the law, but they have tended to ignore the structural mechanisms which have produced those inequalities within the framework of capitalist social relations. The next chapter addresses the broader question of the extent to which aboriginal peoples' quest for political representation and citizenship rights is able to provide an effective solution to the problems we have outlined in this chapter and the preceding ones.

CHAPTER 8

ABORIGINAL ORGANIZATIONS:
Struggles Over Citizenship

For a time it seemed that they would be doomed. But the government determined that the race should be saved (MacInnes, 1943:154).

The concept of citizenship refers to the norms that define the nature of membership of a society (Mishra, 1977:27). In the 1950s, British sociologist T.H. Marshall (1963) argued that there are three forms of citizenship rights under capitalism: civil, political, and social. Civil rights refer to guarantees of individual liberty and equality before the law, access to a fair trial, and trial by *habeus corpus*; political rights refer to rights associated with political enfranchisement, particularly the right to vote and to seek political office; social rights refer to a broader and more loosely defined set of rights linked to the ability to maintain a minimum standard of living, social welfare, and economic security.

While concerned specifically with the case of Britain, Marshall implied that a general tendency in all Western capitalist societies was towards a progessive expansion in citizenship rights: under capitalism, more rights have been extended to more people. In Britain, the 18th century witnessed the expansion and spread of civil rights, the 19th century the expansion and spread of political rights, and the 20th century the progressive expansion of social rights. There has been a widening of the scope of each of these rights so that entire populations within western nation-states now possess common citizenship rights.

Bryan Turner (1986) elaborates on this theme in his recent book *Citizenship and Capitalism*. He suggests that in the course of capitalist development, there has been a move away from particular to universal

219

standards of citizenship rights. Social groups have engaged in struggles to eliminate differential bases for according citizenship rights. In their efforts to establish universal citizenship rights, groups have questioned the legitimacy of according citizenship rights on the basis of ascribed criteria like sex, age, and ethnicity. In Turner's view,

> the development and modernization of any society can be seen as a struggle to establish citizenship rights of egalitarian membership within a common community. Where these struggles are effective they have the consequences of destroying or weakening particularistic criteria of social value ... (Turner, 1986:65).

There are four aims of this chapter. First, we argue that while aboriginal peoples historically have been denied various citizenship rights, they were not the only social group denied such rights. Class, "race," gender, and immigration status have all affected the character of citizenship rights accorded to groups in Canada. Second, citizenship rights are the objects of social struggles. We suggest that the emergence, development, and activities of aboriginal organizations are rooted in the problem of citizenship: their struggles have been over access to, and the definition of, citizenship rights. Third, aboriginal peoples' struggles over citizenship rights have had a twofold character: they have struggled to eliminate certain particular restrictions on their citizenship rights, but at the same time have struggled to retain other particular citizenship rights which recognize their status as First Nations. Finally, we argue that some of the disillusionment associated with the current activities of national aboriginal organizations stems from their primary focus on the definition of civil and political rights at the expense of the realization of social rights.

HISTORICAL DIMENSIONS OF INDIAN CITIZENSHIP

The "special status" of Indian people within Canada has had, and continues to have, profound and contradictory implications for the character of their citizenship rights. Historically, Indians have been denied certain citizenship rights that some other Canadians have taken for granted. But at the same time they possess, and wish to retain, certain particular citizenship rights associated with their status as First Nations. In the course of the development of industrial capitalism in Canada from the middle of the 19th century to the middle of the 20th century, Indian people were denied a range of political, civil, and social rights. The Indian Act and subsequent amendments to the act provide a litany of examples of the denial of citizenship rights.

At various times, Indians were denied political rights of voting in provincial and federal elections. During the late 19th century all provinces, with the exception of Nova Scotia, passed legislation which specifically barred status Indian people living on reserves from voting in provincial elections. The acquisition of the provincial franchise began after World War II, but in an uneven fashion from province to province. The first provinces to grant Indians who lived on reserves the franchise were British Columbia and Newfoundland in 1949. However, it took two more decades for all other provinces to agree to the Indian franchise. Indian people were accorded the franchise in Manitoba in 1952; Ontario in 1954; the Yukon and Saskatchewan in 1960; New Brunswick and Prince Edward Island in 1963; Alberta in 1965; and in Quebec in 1969. Indian people were not denied the right to vote in Nova Scotia and the Northwest Territories (Hawthorn, 1966:262).

Between the periods 1867-1885 and 1898-1920, provincial voters' lists were used for federal elections. Therefore, those excluded from voting by provincial statutes were also thereby excluded from voting in federal elections. The first federal legislation to establish criteria for federal elections was the Electoral Franchise Act of 1885. It was the first instance of specifically federal legislation that restricted Indian franchise. The act excluded Indians living in Manitoba, British Columbia, Keewatin, and the Northwest Territories from the federal vote. As well, it denied the right to vote to any Indian living on a reserve in eastern Canada who was not in possession and occupation of a separate and distinct tract of land and whose improvements on that land were less than $150 (Statutes of Canada, 1885). This meant that Indians in eastern Canada who held property in a fashion akin to European forms of private property were allowed to vote in federal elections. In this case, class location seemed to override "racial" considerations to the extent that Indians with private property were regarded by Sir John A. Macdonald and the Conservative Party (the authors of the legislation) as potential Conservative supporters.

Since the enfranchisement of Indian people who owned private property was defined by the Liberals under Laurier as a measure undertaken by Macdonald to win Indian votes in eastern Canada, when the Liberals assumed federal office in 1898 they proceeded to disenfranchise Indian people with private property by forcing a return to the use of provincial voters' lists (Titley, 1986:113). Federally defined electoral criteria were reintroduced in 1921, but this time Indians remained disenfranchised. With the exception of Indian war veterans who were given the vote in 1917, Indian people were not granted the unconditional extension of the federal franchise until 1960.

Indians were also denied civil rights associated with equal treatment before the law. As noted previously, whereas non-Indians faced a multiplicity of government departments and agencies, Indians faced a single government department: the Indian Affairs Branch. Within this context, the Indian agent was the chief administrator of justice on reserves, and Indian people had few channels to seek redress over the quality of justice and administration the agent provided. According to Kellough

(1980:348) "the dependence of Indians upon the agent for their very being made it very unlikely they would do or say anything to anger him."

The denial of other civil rights involved laws restricting cultural and religious practices such as the potlatch in British Columbia and the sun dance on the Prairies. The potlatch was formally outlawed in 1884, and while it proved to be difficult to enforce, the law remained on the statutes until the revision of the Indian Act in 1951 (LaViolette, 1961:43). As noted in previous chapters, Indian women were denied their Indian status if they married non-Indian men.

In relation to social rights, Indians could not take up homesteads in the late 19th and early 20th centuries and remain an Indian under the government's definition of the term. Indian people's formal right to move about freely in the country was curtailed by the pass system introduced following the Riel Rebellion in 1885, although this regulation also appears to have been difficult to enforce (Barron, 1988). Indians did not have the right to freely market produce or livestock which was raised on reserve land, and they were not allowed to mortgage reserve-based property to acquire a loan to improve their land or establish a business.

A close examination of the Indian Act and the various amendments over the years provides many more examples of the nature and extent to which Indian people were denied full citizenship rights and readers are directed to that source for more details. At this point, however, we want to make three observations about the citizenship status of Indian people.

First, much of the rationale for the denial of citizenship rights was racist in nature to the extent that aboriginal peoples were regarded as culturally, if not genetically, inferior to groups of European origin. However, it is also the case that aboriginal culture was defined as a "problem" because it interfered with the provision of labour power and with agricultural activities. According to T.L.R. MacInnes, the Secretary for the Indian Affairs Branch in the 1940s:

> The Indian Act prohibits the appearance of Indians in native costume without consent at pageants, and also dances or ceremonies involving mutilation of the body. It may seem arbitrary on our part to interfere with native culture. The position of the Department, however, may be understood, when it is pointed out that Indians will spend a fortnight preparing for a Sun-Dance, another fortnight engaging in it, and another fortnight to get over it. Obviously this plays havoc with summer ploughing (MacInnes, 1943:162-63).

Second, Indians were not the only Canadians to be denied basic citizenship rights. The first prime minister of Canada, Sir John A. Macdonald, was a noted opponent of universal suffrage. Less than enamoured with more advanced forms of democracy, he argued that universal suffrage was the "greatest scourge that could be inflicted on a land." In a rather innovative interpretation of the need to maintain minority rights in the country, Macdonald argued that "the rights of the minority must be protected, and the rich are always fewer in number than the poor" (Verney, 1986:130). George-Etienne Cartier, another father of confederation, told the Legislative Assembly that "there must be power of resistance to oppose the democratic element" (Verney, 1986:130).

As such, Canadian confederation was initially constructed on the premise that only certain kinds of men, namely "white" men with property, should have the right to vote and stand for office. As noted above, between 1867 and 1885, provincial voters' lists were used for federal elections. The first federal election in 1867 was held with an electorate which varied among the initial four provinces (Ward, 1950: 211). In addition to the exclusion of Indian people, the two other common denominators to the right to vote in that election were gender and the possession of property. According to Norman Ward (1950:211), only 15 percent of the population of the four provinces were allowed to vote: the remainder were excluded from the vote because of age, gender, the lack of property, and Indian status.

After 1867, the provinces slowly began to eliminate property qualifications for suffrage. By the early 1880s, the Conservatives were sufficiently concerned about the possible extension of suffrage to the male working class and poor farmers via provincial legislation that they decided to formulate federal legislation. According to Dawson (1970:321), the rationale for the formulation of federal elections legislation was that "Macdonald and the Conservative party generally had little sympathy with such advanced ideas of democracy and wished to retain a property qualification." The Electoral Franchise Act of 1885 established universal criteria for the federal franchise but at the same time aimed to maintain unequal access to the franchise. While it allowed, as noted, some Indian men in eastern Canada the right to vote, it denied Indian women this right too and also excluded non-Indian women, poor non-Indian men, and Chinese people. This act remained in effect until 1898, when there was a return to the use of provincial voters' lists. By that time the provinces had established more or less universal suffrage for white males, but universally excluded Indian men and women.

Provincially, women were accorded the franchise in Manitoba, Saskatchewan, and Alberta in 1916; British Columbia and Ontario in 1917; Nova Scotia in 1918; New Brunswick in 1919; Prince Edward Island in 1922; Newfoundland in 1925; and in Quebec in 1940. Women were given the right to vote in federal elections in 1918 (Cleverdon, 1950:2).

Political, civil, and social rights were also denied to various other minority groups, including the Chinese, Japanese, East Indians, and blacks (Bolaria and Li, 1988; Li, 1988: 28-30). Chinese people did not have the right to vote in provincial elections in British Columbia and Saskatchewan, or in federal elections, until 1947. In British Columbia, the Chinese could not be nominated for municipal offices and the provincial legislature, or be school trustees or serve as jury members. They were denied the right to form families, they could not take up the positions of law or pharmacy, and they could not hold liquor or hand logger's licences in British Columbia (Li, 1988).

Historically, migrant workers who have come to Canada to fill particular occupational categories have also been denied basic citizenship rights. While female domestics from the Philippines and the Caribbean and male farm workers from the Caribbean and Mexico have become relatively permanent parts of the Canadian labour force, they have been denied rights to family formation, access to state-funded social services, and rights of political participation (Satzewich, 1991; Arat-Koc, 1992).

The practices which restricted the citizenship rights of these collectivities have been justified by racist and sexist claims that these groups possessed particular social deficiencies which made them unable to assume the responsibilities and obligations of citizenship. However, the denial of citizenship rights also reflected a process in which groups in power wished to maintain their privileged positions by excluding subordinate groups from decision-making processes. Thus, bourgeois democratic forms of political participation were denied to various groups (including Indians), in part because of the belief that granting such rights would undermine the power of "white" men with property. Thus, the denial of citizenship rights to Indian people was rooted in a much larger class project which aimed to maintain hegemony over a number of subordinate groups.

The third general observation about the citizenship status of Indian people is that while they were denied many citizenship rights that other Canadians have taken for granted, the entire category of aboriginal peoples also possess, and have struggled to retain and further define, certain "extra" citizenship rights that non-aboriginal people do not possess. As noted previously, these rights consist of aboriginal and treaty rights. The aboriginal rights of Indian, Métis, and non-status Indian people are currently being negotiated. The treaty rights of Indian people are more clearly defined and stem from agreements signed between governments and various bands throughout much of what is now western Canada. Treaties accord the Indian people, among other things, the right to hunt, fish, and trap on reserve and on unoccupied crown land. The Income Tax Act accords Indians exemption from taxation for income earned on reserve, and the Indian Act exempts from taxation the interest of an Indian or a band in reserve lands or surrendered lands and the personal property of an Indian or a band situated on a reserve. In some provinces Indian people are exempt from provincial sales tax regardless of whether they live on or off reserve, and Indians who purchase goods from businesses on reserves are not required to pay the federal Goods and Services Tax if the goods are taken to a home on the reserve.

In addition to the desire by legislators to maintain control over Indian people by denying them the right to vote, for Indian people, the existence of some special social rights coupled with other restricted social, civil, and political rights also revolved around the issue of taxation. In its consideration of Indian voting rights, the Canadian federal government inverted the American Revolution axiom of "no taxation without representation" to "no representation without taxation." According full civil, political, and social rights to Indian people was seen as inconsistent with extant special social rights stemming from treaties and the Indian Act. Consistent with the wider government policy of enfranchisement, the state's position was that if Indians wished to retain the state's special social rights, then granting them full civil and political rights would put them in an advantageous position in relation to non-aboriginal people. According to Hawthorn (1966: 257), "until all restrictions [on voting] were finally removed in 1960 the government consistently coupled the retention of certain priviledges [particularly taxation] founded either on treaty or the Indian act, with exclusion from the franchise." In fact, in 1950, the government introduced legislation which allowed voting rights to Indians if they signed a waiver of exemption from taxation (Hawthorn, 1966:258). In explaining the government's position on this matter to the Special Committee Appointed to Consider Bill 79, An Act Respecting Indians, Walter Harris, the Minister of Citizenship and Immigration, explained in 1951:

> We provided that it was entirely a matter of their own choice, if they felt they were losing certain rights they had, which were more valuable than exercising the vote in the federal elections, they should have the right to make that choice; and we have provided that the Indian does not have to vote if he does not want to do so, and, therefore, we are continuing the advantage of this tax exemption in the Indian Act.... Alternatively if he wishes to vote he may do so on precisely equal terms with non-Indians; that is, without enjoying the tax exemptions.... [An Indian] can make his own choice as to the advantages of voting (Hawthorn, 1966:258).

In other words, for many years enfranchisement (the loss of Indian status) and paying taxes were defined by government officials as the price that Indians would have to pay for the privilege to vote (Gibbins, 1986:370). Since the 1970s, the federal government has accepted the view that the possession of special rights need not preclude the possession of the full range of extant civil, political, and social rights.

Indian Struggles Over Citizenship Rights Prior to 1970

Until various revisions and amendments to the Indian Act occurred in the 1950s and 1960s, the ability of Indians to pressure the state to fulfill its citizenship obligations was directly restricted by the state. Without the franchise, Indian people could not utilize the lines of political influence that extended through the parliamentary system. While some members of parliament did occasionally take up issues on behalf of Indian people (LaViolette, 1961), Indian people had neither direct nor consistent influence over MPs through the franchise. Furthermore, after a bid to have the issue of land claims in British Columbia settled in 1927, the government made it illegal for Indians to raise money or use band funds to bring land claims disputes to court (Patterson, 1978:50). Also in 1927, an amendment to the Indian Act prohibited national political organizing of Indian people (Ponting and Gibbins, 1980:196).

However, while there were clear power differentials between aboriginal peoples and state officials, and while Indian Affairs officials, and even some provincial governments, took efforts to obstruct Indians in their attempts to attend meetings and form organizations where they could collectively pursue their interests, Indians did not simply cave in to the demands and whims of state policies and state agents (Ponting and Gibbins, 1980:197; Miller, 1989). Despite various obstacles placed in their way to use the political and legal systems in their struggles over citizenship rights, prior to the 1960s Indians did engage in struggles, both organized and not, to force the Canadian state to recognize the existence of their treaty and aboriginal rights and to eliminate restrictions on their civil and political rights (LaViolette, 1961; Cuthand, 1978; Dempsey, 1978; Patterson, 1978; Miller, 1989). Thus, what is particularly interesting about the struggles of aboriginal organizations is that they have been both universal and particular in nature. In some cases, they have resisted pressures to become "full" citizens, they have pressed to retain their special citizenship status, and have pressed to eliminate many of the special restrictions placed on their rights.

The particular nature of these struggles was shaped by a variety of ecological, cultural, economic, and political forces which surrounded the nature of the state's and private capital's interests in Indian land, labour, and culture. That is, prior to the 1960s, aboriginal peoples' struggles were primarily local in nature.

In British Columbia, Indian people first became politically organized around the outlaw of the potlatch. The potlatch, outlawed in 1884, was a cultural practice which involved, in part, the redistribution of wealth and the repayment of debts. In addition to passive resistance, Indians pressured politicians for the repeal of the law. For example, in 1896 the Nass River tribes sent a petition to a British Columbia member of parliament. The petition claimed, not unreasonably, that there were a number of European customs such as Christmas in which "money is spent in squandrous profusion with no benefits to the poor of your race" and that it was therefore contradictory for the state to outlaw the potlatch and not outlaw similar European cultural practices (LaViolette, 1961:70).

European encroachment on their land and the provincial government's unwillingness to participate in land claims and treaty negotiations provided a second basis upon which the politicization of British Columbia Indians occurred. In 1906, they sent a deputation of three chiefs to London to petition King Edward VII to protest against the Canadian state's dealings with respect to their land. Commenting on the position of the Indians in the Nass Valley, a representative of an organization calling itself the Friends of the Indians of British Columbia (1912:5) advised British officials that "although what [the Indians] regard as their country is being sold over their heads, they have borne all this with remarkable patience. They have recently been writing and imploring us to secure that some decisive action shall be taken during the present year." And while it did not appear to have accomplished much, British Columbia Indians did manage to get the government to appoint a Joint Royal Commission on Indian Affairs in British Columbia, which sat from 1912 to 1916, to examine the land issue (LaViolette, 1961: 126-28).

In western Canada, aboriginal peoples engaged in struggles to assert their status as self-governing people, over restrictions on their citizenship rights and the fulfillment of special citizenship rights stemming from treaties. The best known struggle, the Riel Rebellion in 1885, involved both Métis and Indians (with some sympathy from white merchants and farmers) in a complex struggle over the control of land, poor economic conditions, and representative government (Bourgeault, 1988a; Adams, 1990). In seeking to assert control over territory they defined as rightfully theirs, Métis people were attempting to establish their own state and hence define for themselves their citizenship rights.

Other struggles focused more specifically on unfulfilled treaty promises and government policies. At the turn of the century Indians protested the lack of assistance given to agriculture — a treaty obligation of the government (Carter, 1990). Also in relation to agricultural policy, Indians of the Piapot reserve, the Pasquah and Muscowpetung bands in southern Saskatchewan, and from the Oak River reserve in southern Manitoba resisted efforts to subdivide their reserves and allot land to individual Indians. In addition to locally-based passive resistance (which involved a lack of cooperation with Indian agents), Indians sent delegations, petitions, and letters outlining their grievances to the Indian Affairs Branch in Ottawa (Carter, 1990:224-229).

Unfilled promises for land stemming from treaties have been a source of conflict between Indian people and the government for nearly a century, and remain of paramount importance today. The widely-publicized struggle in 1988 by Lubicon Indians of northern Alberta has long historical roots. While the government agreed in principle to set aside reserve land for the Lubicon Indians in 1940, it has yet to fulfill this obligation. In the past fifteen years, the Saskatchewan government has appointed two treaty commissions in order to settle issues associated with unfilled land entitlements in that province. Little came of the first commission's report of 1977, in part because of a change of government and in part because of protests by farmers and ranchers over the growth of reserve land and the loss of crown land for pastures. The second commissioner, appointed in September 1989, issued his report in May of 1990. The report provided a formula for the resolution of these historical claims. This formula provided for the transfer of 841 419 acres of land and cash compensation of $74.3 million to 27 Saskatchewan bands.

Indians in Ontario were the first to attempt to organize a nationally-based Indian organization. The League of Indians of Canada was formed at the end of World War I. Founded by F.O. Loft of the Six Nations Reserve near Brantford, the aims of the league were to win the vote for the Indian people, protect hunting rights, gain more freedom from government bureaucracy, and establish a new system of secular schools (York, 1989:246). While the organization acquired a considerable degree of support across the country in the 1920s, it eventually folded, in part because of government suppression (Titley, 1986:102-109). The western branch of the league lived on and provided the foundation for the formation of provincial associations in Alberta and Saskatchewan (Titley, 1986:109).

National Indian Organizations and Struggles for Citizenship Rights

While various Indian organizations have been in existence since the turn of the century, it is clear from Table 8.1 that the 1970s marked a turning point in the history of the politicization of Indians in Canada. This politicization is interpreted by some as an intended (Burke, 1976), and by others as an unintended, consequence of the Liberal government's White Paper of 1969 (Frideres, 1988).

The federal government's White Paper of 1969 declared succinctly the state's position on the nature of Indian people's citizenship rights before the 1970s. It also outlined the Liberal government's intentions in the area of Indian policy for the future. Prior to the 1970s, successive Canadian governments did not recognize the existence of aboriginal rights; while treaty rights were recognized, these were interpreted in a narrow, literal fashion, and, as noted above, as incompatible with full civil and political rights.

In relation to treaty rights, the White Paper stated that "a plain reading of the words used in the treaties reveals the limited and minimal promises which were included in them." It went on to suggest that while the government was prepared to live up to unfilled treaty promises for reserve land, the importance of the treaties in serving the contemporary needs of Indian people were minimal, and it was their intention that "the anomaly of the treaties between groups within society and the government of that society will require that these treaties be reviewed to see how they can be equitably ended."

In relation to aboriginal claims for land, the White Paper stated that

Table 8.1

Major Native Political Voluntary Associations in Canada, by Date of Formation

	Prior to 1799	1800-49	1850-99	1900-09	1910-19	1920-29	1930-39	1940-49	1950-59	1960-69	1970-73	1974-80
National	2				1		2	1	1	4	6	2
Regional		1	1		1	4	1	1		1	1	4
National-regional total	2	1	1		2	4	3	2	1	5	7	6
Newfoundland-Labrador										1	2	1
Prince Edward Island												1
New Brunswick								1		1	3	2
Nova Scota								1		2	2	2
Quebec			1		1	2		2	1	3	5	1
Ontario			1		1	2		1	1	6	7	3
Manitoba						1	1	5	1	2	6	2
Saskatchewan						1	2	1	2	1	4	3
Alberta		1				1	3	1	1	4	3	3
British Columbia			1	1	2				4	8	3	4
Northwest Territories							1			3	3	4
Yukon										2	3	1
Provincial total		1	3	1	4	7	7	12	9	33	41	27
Grand total	2	2	4	1	6	11	10	14	10	38	48	33

Source: Frideres, 1988:268.

"these are so general and undefined that it is not realistic to think of them as specific claims capable of remedy except through a policy and program that will end injustice to Indians as members of the Canadian community." In other words, the existence of legitimate aboriginal rights was dismissed.

The White Paper, in addition to suggesting that the unique citizenship rights of Indian people was the source of their "problems," outlined the government's intentions with respect to their future citizenship rights. In order to solve the "problem," it was argued that the special citizenship rights had to be terminated: "special treatment has made of the Indians a community disadvantaged and apart." In an effort to establish universal criteria of citizenship, the government intended to transform Indians into persons with the same citizenship rights and obligations as non-Indians.

In this light, the government was prepared to: 1) repeal the Indian Act and pass legislation necessary for Indians to control Indian lands and to acquire title to them; 2) propose to the provinces that they consider Indians to be provincial citizens so that they would receive the same services through the same channels as other provincial citizens; 3) make available "substantial funds" for Indian economic development; 4) phase out the Indian Affairs Branch of the Department of Indian and Northern Affairs; 5) appoint a commissioner for the adjudication of land claims.

In sum, the underlying theme of the White Paper was the devolution of legislative responsibility for Indians to the provinces. The federal government, in wishing to terminate the special citizenship rights for Indian people, sought to accord Indian people the same citizenship rights as non-Indians and nothing more.

The White Paper proposals sparked an unprecedented backlash within Indian communities. The government was forced to back down from its proposals, and in 1970 the White Paper was formally withdrawn. However, many argue, including an ex-Assistant Deputy Minister of Indian Affairs (Nicholson, 1984:60), that the aim of government policy has remained consistent with the White Paper proposals: it remains committed to the termination of its special relationship with Indian people and to the devolution of legislative and fiscal responsibility for Indians to the provinces (Cassidy and Bish, 1989:9-10).

Given the White Paper's emphasis on the termination of the special rights of Indian people, Indian organizations became increasingly politicized around the issues of citizenship rights. The Indian Association of Alberta, under the leadership of Harold Cardinal, put forward an alternative conception of the nature of Indian citizenship rights in their "Red Paper" of 1970. Their position was that Indians should not be treated in the same manner as other Canadians because they were the first occupants of the land, and because they had signed treaties with the government which were to run in perpetuity. In their view, they should be accorded full citizenship rights consistent with those rights held by non-

Indians, but they should also continue to be accorded special status. Drawing on the terminology of the Hawthorn Report of 1966, the Alberta Indian Chiefs argued that Indians should be regarded as "Citizens Plus." In addition to the customary rights and duties of citizenship, Indians should possess certain extra rights as "charter members of the Canadian community." In direct contrast to the White Paper, the recognition of some special rights was regarded as not inconsistent with the possession of the full range of other rights which Canadians deserved.

Since the publication of the Red Paper, national and provincial aboriginal organizations have been concerned with the definition of their citizenship rights, and to establish the "authority, resources and structures necessary to implement and enjoy those rights" (Ponting and Gibbins, 1980:195).

The National Indian Brotherhood (NIB) was formed in 1968 out of a split within the National Indian Council (NIC). The NIC, itself formed in 1961, aimed to provide a political voice for treaty and non-treaty Indians as well as non-status Indians and Métis people. With the split of the NIC, status Indians formed their own organization (the NIB) and Métis and non status Indians formed the Canadian Métis Society.

When the NIB was first formed, its efforts were focused on organizational matters: formulating a constitution, establishing relationships with provincial and territorial organizations, and raising funds. By the mid-1970s, however, the NIB began to focus its resources on constitutional issues and the articulation of problems pertaining to Indian citizenship (Ponting and Gibbins, 1980:213). Indian sovereignty, self-government, and the entrenchment of Indian rights in the constitution have also been the primary concerns of the Assembly of First Nations (AFN), which was formed out of the dissolution of the National Indian Brotherhood in 1980. According to Georges Erasmus, the national leader of the AFN between 1982 and 1991,

> I think [the constitutional entrenchment of rights] is the centrepiece action, one that would propel native people out of a situation where so many of our agenda items are outstanding, unfulfilled, and virtually impossible to be implemented. We could deal in the Constitution with the fundamental relationship between First Nations, their governments, their land, and other governments in Canada. And on an equal footing. Any other way of dealing with these issues — whether through legislation or anything else — skirts the issue and does not deal with the primary relationship that can be dealt with through the Constitution (quoted in Krotz, 1990:208-209).

The election in 1991 of Ovide Mercredi as leader of the AFN signalled no significant departure from this focus, although at times it is acknowledged that more needs to be done about social rights associated with the maintenance of a minimum standard of living.

Recently, the focus on self-government by the AFN has come under sharp criticism from the Native Women's Association of Canada (NWAC), which claims to represent about 120 000 native women from across the country. The criticisms of this strategy came to a head during the course of the Constitutional Conference on Aboriginal Self-Government held in Ottawa in March 1992. The leader of the NWAC, Gail Stacey-Moore, was unwilling to accept the argument put forward by the AFN that the Canadian Charter of Rights should be set aside within the proposed structure of aboriginal self-government. The NWAC recognizes that aboriginal organizations, which historically have been dominated by men, have not always acted to protect the interests of aboriginal women. In fact, it appears that much of the opposition to the AFN's proposal stems from a recognition that the most stringent opponents to Bill C-31, which as noted in Chapter 2 provided for the reinstatement of status to Indian women who married non-Indian men, came from male-dominated organizations. Thus, Stacey-Moore was unwilling to support the proposal for self-government unless women's rights were protected. The NWAC's position was that "we will not accept a regime of self-government without guarantees of basic human rights" (Delacourt, 1992:A4). Shortly after the conference ended, the NWAC asked the federal court to curtail federal funding of the main aboriginal organizations, including the AFN, until such time as the NWAC is given financial support and a voice at self-government negotiations.

The Canadian Métis Society, formed in 1968, was recast as the Native Council of Canada in 1970 and represented Métis and non-status Indians (Sealey and Lussier, 1975:167). In the early 1980s, some Métis members of the Native Council of Canada felt that the organization did not reflect specifically Métis aspirations for land and self-government. The Métis National Council was therefore formed out of this split in 1983.

In the mid-1970s, Sealey and Lussier (1975:169) argued that "Indians claim to be people with special rights and privileges. Most Métis claim only to be people with special problems." While this statement is true to the extent that Métis people consider themselves to be a distinct "people" and do not wish to become "Indians," Métis struggles historically, and at present, have been over the recognition of their special rights as a people. Since the entrenchment of their "existing aboriginal rights" in the constitution in 1982, Métis organizations, like their Indian counterparts, have attempted to specify the nature of these rights (Purich, 1986:180-181).

The Federal Government and Citizenship Rights: After the White Paper

Since the early 1970s, federal court decisions on land claims cases have forced successive federal governments to change, at least their public positions, on the nature and meaning of aboriginal and treaty rights. The case which appeared to have forced the hand of the federal government was Calder v. the Attorney General of British Columbia in 1973. In the early 1970s, Nishga Indians took the British Columbia provincial government to court to force it to recognize that they had never given up their aboriginal title to land. While the Nishgas lost the case, six of seven judges of the Supreme Court of Canada recognized the existence of Indian title to the land in general, and three ruled more specifically that the Nishgas had yet to relinquish this title (Purich, 1986:54).

Following that decision, Prime Minister Trudeau rather sardonically admitted that "perhaps you have more legal rights than we thought you had when we did the white paper." That same year, while in Opposition, the Progessive Conservative Party gave "wholehearted recognition to the concept of aboriginal rights" (Task Force to Review Comprehensive Claims Policy, 1985:12).

Since then, and after extensive struggles which involved court action and lobbying in Canada and Britain, aboriginal organizations were able to force the federal government to entrench both aboriginal and treaty rights in the Constitution Act of 1982. The act states that "the existing aboriginal and treaty rights of the aboriginal peoples [Indian, Inuit and Métis] of Canada are hereby recognized and affirmed" (quoted in Purich, 1986:34). The entrenchment of aboriginal and treaty rights into the constitution means that the parliament of Canada can no longer unilaterally extinguish or modify aboriginal rights, and that "changes in existing aboriginal rights require the consent of the aboriginal groups concerned or a constitutional amendment" (Task Force to Review Comprehensive Claims Policy, 1985:14).

In the decade since the entrenchment of aboriginal and treaty rights in the 1982 Constitution Act, the main area of struggle between aboriginal organizations and various levels of the state has been over the definition of these rights. Four constitutional conferences (1983, 1984, 1985, and 1987) have been held between aboriginal leaders and federal and provincial authorities to provide substance to this broad recognition. While initially intended to establish and define the nature of "existing aboriginal and treaty rights," eventually the conferences focused on the specific entrenchment of the right to self-government in the constitution and the definiton and meaning of self-government (Cassidy and Bish, 1989:16).

As these constitutional talks progressed, two federally-appointed committees, the Special Committee on Indian Self Government (Government of Canada, 1983) and the Task Force to Review Comprehensive Claims Policy (1985), supported the principle that the right to aboriginal self-government should be entrenched in the constitution. More specifically, the Special Committee on Indian Self Government in 1983 recommended that band-based Indian governments should constitute a third order of government within Canada (Gibbins, 1986:369).

While both committee reports have been supportive of the concept of aboriginal self-government, federal and provincial governments appear to be less than enamoured with it, although in 1991, the provincial NDP government in Ontario declared its support for self-government. At the last constitutional conference, held in 1987, a proposal was put forward which provided for the entrenchment in principle of aboriginal peoples' right to self-government, with the specific content of this right and the associated jurisdictional arrangements to be defined by negotiations with all governments participating (Long and Boldt, 1988:16). The proposal also suggested that the courts would be able to decide on the form and content of these rights in the absence of a political agreement. This conference ended in failure, in part because four provinces — Saskatchewan, British Columbia, Alberta, and Newfoundland — found unacceptable the argument that self-government could only be defined in practice and not *a priori*. Furthermore, these provinces were unwilling to accord the courts final authority over what they defined as a political process (see Long and Boldt, 1988, for more details of the provincial governments' positions).

During the debate about the Meech Lake Accord, aboriginal peoples have not failed to point out the double standard associated with the treatment of aboriginal and French-Canadian constitutional issues. Some provincial premiers were willing to allow Quebec the opportunity to define what it meant by a distinct society after an agreement was reached, but only a few years earlier were unwilling to allow Indian people the same opportunity in the context of self-government. Indeed, it was this double standard, along with the accord's conception of Canada as consisting of "two nations" (neither of which was aboriginal) that led to the rejection of the accord by Elijah Harper and the Indian people. One year after the accord's demise, Chief Ted Moses, the ambassador of the James Bay Cree Nation, told a hearing of the United Nations Working Group on Indigenous Populations in Geneva that "Canada's steadfast refusal to discuss indigenous self-determination, while it openly entertains Quebec's claims to self-determination, reflects a double standard based on racial prejudice" (Picard, 1991).

While constitutional discussions over the entrenchment of the right to aboriginal self-government failed in the late 1980s, the federal government has nevertheless allowed Indian nations some limited forms of self-government on a band basis that would integrate Indian government into the existing provincial-municipal framework of services and legislation (Long and Boldt, 1988:17). These limited forms of self-government involve the right to develop band membership codes stemming from the passage of Bill C-31, Alternative Funding Agreements (AFAs), and granting municipal-style powers to bands.

Bill C-31, passed in 1985, amended the Indian Act, in part to resolve the long-standing issue of the loss of status to Indian women who married non-Indian men. The bill eliminated many of the gender-based discriminatory provisions of the act and provided for the reinstatement of Indian status to people who had lost their status over the years. The bill also provided bands with the opportunity to create their own membership codes. These must be approved by a majority of existing band members and DIAND must be notified. Therefore, bands now have the right to create their own citizens (Cassidy and Bish, 1990: 58-64). As of 1989, 39 percent, or 231 of 596 bands in Canada, have formulated their own membership codes (Department of Indian and Northern Affairs, 1990).

Alternative Funding Agreements were established in 1986 by DIAND in part as a response to recommendations of the Special Committee on Indian Self-Government (Government of Canada, 1983). The stated aim of AFAs is to allow Indian bands and band councils more flexibility in their administration and control of certain programs. AFAs involve block grants to bands on a five-year basis. With some restrictions, AFAs provide the opportunity for bands or band councils to move funds from one budget line to another (Cassidy and Bish, 1990). Excluded from the scope of AFAs are decisions relating to child welfare, business development, resource development projects, and larger capital projects: these areas remain subject to DIAND or other governmental control. To qualify for an AFA, a band or tribal council must have participatory and governing procedures that are satisfactory to DIAND, and the band and tribal council must also agree to submit to a yearly audit of its financial affairs. Table 8.2 provides information on the number of AFAs by the stage of agreement. It shows that by 1990, there were 36 signed agreements covering 79 bands; 27 proposals representing 45 bands were deemed eligible for an AFA and were at the draft stage of an agreement; and 49 applications for an AFA, representing 95 bands, were being assessed.

To date, the federal government has committed itself to what it defines as "self-government" in two cases: the Cree-Naskapi (of Quebec) Act (1984) and the Sechelt Indian Band Self-Government Act (1986), the latter of which will be discussed here. While the form of self-government provided in this legislation is different from the constitutional entrenchment of the right to self-government and the establishment of a third order of government that aboriginal organizations are seeking, they have nevertheless been defined by the federal government as appropriate models of self-government for other bands to follow. The Sechelt agreement of 1986 involves the provision of enhanced municipal powers of government for the Sechelt band. This resulted in the passage of the federal Sechelt Indian Band Self-Government Act in 1986 and the provincial Sechelt Indian Government District Enabling Act in 1987. These acts delegate various municipal-style powers to the band. The band is able to make laws in twenty-one areas of concern including lands, taxation, and social and welfare services (Cassidy and Bish, 1990).

Table 8.2

Alternative Funding Arrangements —
Canada, 1988-1990

Status[1]	Number of Proposals			Bands Involved		
	1988	1989	1990	1988	1989	1990
Signed Agreements	9	16	36	21	38	79
Entry Confirmed	16	19	27	29	27	45
Applications	33	36	49	54	45	95

Note: 1. Alternative Funding Arrangements (AFA):
AFA agreements were established by DIAND with Indian bands to
allow new and more flexible financial and administrative arrangements
in which the primary accountability of the band council is to the band
members. The following steps are required to reach an agreement:
    Agreements: The draft agreement is signed by DIAND and Indian
representatives.
    Entry Confirmed: The applicant has been confirmed eligible for AFA
and the draft agreement is being developed.
    Applications: Formal application has been made for AFA and the
entry assessment is proceeding.

Source: Indian and Northern Affairs Canada, *Basic Departmental Data*. Ottawa,
Minister of Supply and Services, 1990, pp. 69, 78.

Table 8.3 provides information on the status of various types of self-government negotiations. It shows that in addition to the two existing agreements, seven proposals representing 29 bands were in the final stages prior to legislation by parliament, 16 proposals representing 31 bands were at the stage of developing a framework for negotiations; 40 proposals representing 160 bands were received by DIAND for research and community consultation, and 30 workshops were held. Fifty-three proposals were inactive.

While the government's hidden agendas in areas of membership codes, AFAs, and municipal-style governments are complex, these intiatives are generally seen with skepticism by national Indian organizations. They are not providing self-government but rather new forms of control.

BUREAUCRATIZATION OF INDIAN ORGANIZATIONS

For some aboriginal peoples, particularly those living in urban areas (Reeves, 1986), their organizations' struggles with the state over the definition and implementation of particular citizenship rights associated with aboriginal rights may seem rather abstract and distant from the problems of finding work, finding decent accommodations, and ensuring that children receive adequate health care and education. In this section, we suggest that the focus by national and provincial aboriginal organizations on citizenship issues, particularly those relating to political and civil rights, has led to some resentment directed toward those organizations and their leadership. We argue that this resentment is rooted, in part, in a process of bureaucratization of aboriginal organizations (Valentine, 1980). Two recent examples are instructive. During the summer and fall of 1990, the leadership of the Federation of Saskatchewan Indian Nations (FSIN) came under criticism from some aboriginal peoples of Saskatchewan for its stance on the events at Oka, Quebec. During the course of the crisis, the federation avoided overt political support for the Mohawk cause. Indeed, while he stated that he was sympathetic to their cause, Roland Crowe, the First Chief of the FSIN, tended to be implicitly critical of their tactics. He stated, for example, that "we've been counselled by our elders and maintain violence and militancy is not the answer.... We agreed not to pick up arms in our treaties and we would be breaking what we feel is sacred to do it or support it" (Struthers, 1990b).

The lack of support for, and indirect criticisms of, the struggle by Mohawks at Kahnawake and Kahnesetake by the leadership of the FSIN during the course of the summer led to criticisms from some aboriginal peoples. During a rally in Saskatoon in support of the Mohawks, one aboriginal spokesperson stated "I'm very disappointed in the leaders of some of the status quo organizations. They are nowhere to be seen when the fight is there, but they're there to pick up the paychecks" (Struthers, 1990a).

While difficult to gauge the degree of support they had, some aboriginal people in Regina called for the resignation of the leadership of the FSIN because of their position during the crisis.

The second example stems from the controversy over the Conservative government's effort to revise the guidelines for funding Indian post-secondary education. Consistent with its view that post-secondary education is not a treaty right, Bill McKnight, the federal Minister of Indian Affairs, announced in June 1987, that the government would place a cap of $130 million on federal funding of Indian post-secondary education, as well as reduce the number of months for which Indian students would be eligible for funding.

The announcement of this new policy sparked protest, particularly amongst Indian students. To press the government to either withdraw or revise the new policy as noted in Chapter 5, Indian students engaged in hunger strikes, sit-ins, and marches in a number of cities. The students argued that education was a treaty right and that a cap on the funding of education was therefore in violation of treaties. Even though the students were able to win some changes to the newly-announced guidelines, the cap on funding remained in place.

Table 8.3

Self-Government Negotiations —
Canada, June 1990

Status[1]	Number of Proposals	Number of Bands
Substansive Negotiations	7	29
Framework Negotiations	16	31
Developmental	40	160
Inactive Proposals	53	n/a
Workshops	30	n/a
Total Proposals Received to Date	146	

Note: 1. Self-government Negotiations:
Process in which government authority is transferred to Indian and Inuit people. The following steps are required:
Substansive negotiations: Negotiations leading directly to new arrangements which will be effected through legislation.
Framework negotiations: Terms of reference for negotiations: a community's itemization of the authorities desired beyond the Indian Act, the proposed modifications to its governing structures and the new legislative arrangements sought to enable these changes. Work plan and budget for substansive negotiations and the ratification process for any agreements.
Developmental: Research and community consultation.
Workshops: Meetings held by a community or communities to explore and discuss self-government issues and exchange information and experiences among communities.

Source: Indian and Northern Affairs Canada, *Basic Departmental Data—1990.* Ottawa: Minister of Supply and Services, 1990, pp. 67, 100-101.

In addition to criticizing the federal government for its lack of consultation in the development of the new guidelines and heavy-handed tactics used to control student dissent, student leaders also criticized Indian organizations for their muted protests over the new guidelines. According to Lanceley (1991:247), one of the outcomes of the student protests over cutbacks to educational funding was that in addition to questioning "the often reactionary leadership of their own Indian nations," they "awoke the Indian nations to the fact that the new generation of Indian students is unwilling to be submissive to either government or Indian leadership when it ignores their interests." Since then mainstream organizations such as the FSIN have become more sensitive to the needs and demands of Indian students with respect to education rights.

However, both cases highlight a common theme where extant organizations have been reluctant to support particular issues that may jeopardize the larger, long-term goals of the organization. What is of interest here is that disagreements between the leadership and the "grassroots" reflect a structural process in which aboriginal organizations are undergoing a process of bureaucratization. In a society in which various class- and non-class-based forces are in constant contact with state officials to press for funding, legislation, and programs, there is a complex process by which relationships between particular state agencies and their respective client groups are established and maintained. Thus, while it appears that state and aboriginal organization representatives are in perpetual conflict, there is in reality a degree of mutual interdependence between the two parties (Valentine, 1980:99).

One of the key problems for state officials, particularly cabinet ministers, whether dealing with aboriginal or non-aboriginal issues, is to seek out individuals in their target client groups with whom they can work. While the position of Minister of Indian Affairs is not an attractive one for prospective cabinet ministers (Ponting and Gibbins, 1980), the position nevertheless requires a minimal degree of recognition and support from aboriginal leaders in order to maintain its legitimacy. In the Mulroney cabinet shuffle of April 1991, in which most ministers were reassigned cabinet positions, one of the only ministers who did not change portfolios was Tom Siddon, the Minister of Indian Affairs. While there was a difference of opinion amongst Indian leaders over the minister's effectiveness, some leaders engaged in extensive lobbying of the Prime Minister's Office because Siddon was "sincere in his efforts.... [and was] prepared to make a commitment to Native People and get the prime minister to commit" (Santoro, 1991).

Similarly, while provincial Indian leaders and the leader of the Assembly of First Nations are elected by band chiefs, they need to "get results" from the state and appear to be effective in order to maintain their positions of leadership (Valentine, 1980:100). As such, there are times when both parties need to cooperate in order to accomplish their respective aims and to maintain legitimacy. This mutual dependence of state and organization officials, then, creates the conditions for conflict with grass roots elements in communities.

The Federation of Saskatchewan Indian Nations appears to have developed a workable relationship with both federal and provincial Indian Affairs officials. Prior to the Oka crisis, the FSIN was engaged in negotiations with both federal and provincial government officials over land claims settlements, and funding special projects in Saskatchewan. With many of these deals close to fruition, it is likely that the leadership was unwilling to make precipitous comments that might have jeopardized the success of these negotiations and years of hard work. In return, it appears that the federal government rewarded the FSIN for its restraint during the crisis with the announcement of a commitment to resolve outstanding lands claims; a $230 000 program to ensure all people in the 27 bands covered by the Treaty Commissioner of Saskatchewan's Report were informed of its contents; $25 000 to inform Indian people about treaty land entitlements; a $2.3 million child-care program for the Meadow Lake Tribal Council; and the funding of a new office complex for the FSIN in Regina (Zaretsky, 1990; Struthers, 1990c). It appears that these announcements were timed, in part, to shore up the leadership when its legitimacy was being challenged by some people in the rank and file.

Thus, while some of the hostility directed towards current Indian leadership may be personal in nature, and may entail personal attacks on the integrity of the leadership, we suggest that some of the conflicts between the leadership and the rank and file of aboriginal organizations represents a bureaucratization of these organizations (see also Dosman, 1972).

LOCAL INDIAN ORGANIZATIONS

Beginning in the 1950s and 1960s, the federal government became committed to accelerating the movement of Indian people off reserve and to partially funding programs to integrate them into urban social relations. The coupling of the promotion of out-migration with programs for integration into urban areas was an explicit strategy of "assimilation" in the 1960s. According to the Director of the Indian Affairs Branch in 1962, "a successful and accelerated movement of Indians to non-Indian communities is a goal of many of our programs" (Department of Citizenship and Immigration, 1962b). In this context, a variety of "relocation projects" were undertaken to remove Indian and Inuit people from their reserves or other rural areas and place them in urban centres or small towns (Stevenson, 1968; Weaver, 1981:31). Since then the process of urbanization of aboriginal peoples has occurred apace (see Chapter 4) and a whole range of urban-based service organizations have emerged in its wake.

Among the first organizations to emerge to facilitate the incorporation of aboriginal peoples into urban social relations were the Friendship Centres. First formed in Winnipeg in 1958 with funding from federal, provincial, and charitable organization sources, Friendship Centres were established in a number of cities during the course of the 1960s. Now, most major cities in Canada have at least one Friendship Centre.

Friendship Centres do not make a formal distinction between the categories of status and non-status Indians and Métis; their functions are aimed at aboriginal peoples as a whole. Their objective is to ease the transition from rural or reserve-based communities to urban life by providing a place for Indian and Métis to drop in, and counselling services which direct them to extant federal and provincial service agencies to resolve particular problems related to housing, health care, social services, and employment. Other service organizations are more limited in their activities in that they are concerned with access to specific services for specific categories of aboriginal peoples. Some of these are directly funded by the federal and provincial governments, others have resisted state funding, and yet others have been refused state funding (Ryan, 1978).

In other words, the activities of organizations like Friendship Centres are oriented to informing Indian people of their social citizenship rights and ensuring that Indian people take advantage of those social rights through their utilization of services and programs. That is, they are primarily aimed at ensuring that aboriginal peoples receive their citizenship rights to a full social minimum in practice.

The full history of Indian and Métis Friendship Centres has yet to be written. However, some of the historical background to their formation and the federal government's interest in providing funding for them provides insights into what the government hoped to accomplish. The apparent success of the Winnipeg "pilot project" first given federal funding of $4000 in 1959, and the establishment of other Friendship Centres in other cities in the early 1960s, meant that by 1962 the federal government was faced with a number of requests for the funding of similar centres. In order to develop a more systematic policy on funding such organizations, the Department of Citizenship and Immigration (the home of the Indian Affairs Branch between 1950 and 1966) undertook a review of the activities of these centres in order to recommend an appropriate course of action.

In its review to determine whether more systematic funding should be provided, the problem which the Department of Citizenship and Immigration faced was framed in these terms:

> the question basic to social policy should be stated as follows:— How may we continue to do justice to the Indians on the reserve, leaving aside the questions of enfranchisement and the reserve system, without making their lives so secure that a steady movement off the reserve will be impeded? On the other hand, given the barriers that now exist socially and occupationally in urban and industrial centres, how can programmes be developed that will ensure the good adjustment of Indians in urban centres without using paternalistic methods? (Department of Citizenship and Immigration, 1962a:11).

Clearly, the federal government defined its role as one in which it had, at least minimally, to live up to its statutory obligations to Indian people, but to do this in such a way as to make Indian people's lives on reserves just difficult enough to encourage them to leave. It was also clearly concerned about maintaining *de facto* control of an urban integration organization without appearing to do so.

Generally, the federal government was, and continues to be, opposed to funding programs for urban Indians on the grounds that once urban Indians leave the reserve, they cease to be the government's responsibility. However, the federal government's rationale for financially supporting Friendship Centres for urban Indians was framed in the following terms:

It would seem that to refrain from being involved is not a practical course of action, even though such a policy would make crystal clear the federal government's resolve not to give Indians off reserves the same help and services it provides for those on reserves. There is too much at stake in the integration of Indians into urban life to stand idly by. Moreover, the eventuality of some crisis, for example, race riot or a crime wave involving Indians as principal characters, might force the federal government, by political necessity, to take action that in the long run would delay the realization of the goals that are now agreed on (Department of Citizenship and Immigration, 1962a:17).

Thus, funding for the establishment of Friendship Centres was part of the state's attempt to facilitate a policy of urbanization of Indians that would save the government money and reduce its obligations to Indian people, and to ensure that "social problems" resulting from this urbanization would be contained. Friendship Centres were formed not in opposition to state policies and controls, but rather in order to accommodate Indians into urban social relations and support systems. The principle of refusing to financially support programs for urban Indians was to be sacrificed because of the expected political fallout associated with the urbanization of Indian people.

However, this support was managed in such a way that it was still possible to retain control over the activities of the organization. Since that time the federal government has entered into cost-sharing agreements with a number of provinces for the funding of Friendship Centres, although these agreements still only commit the government to funding on a yearly basis. While Indian Affairs officials contemplated a requirement that a member of the branch sit on the board of each Friendship Centre, it rejected this option on the grounds that it would create hostility and the impression that the department wanted direct control over the activities of such centres. It is likely that state funding of these organizations has been provided on a yearly basis in part as a mechanism of social control and to ensure that they do not become "political" organizations that will criticize government policy (Frideres, 1988:276).

Conclusion

Restrictions on the citizenship rights of Indian people were part of a larger context in which gender, "race," class, and immigration status all affected the character of citizenship rights accorded to people in Canada. Indian people were not the only ones to be denied basic citizenship rights. What is unique, though, about Indian people is that more of their rights were denied for longer periods of time. What is also unique about the character of their citizenship rights is that they possess certain extra citizenship rights, stemming from treaties and the Indian Act, which other Canadians do not have.

The struggles by Indian organizations over citizenship rights are fundamental to the future well-being of Indian people in Canada. However, as numerous commentators on the concept of citizenship have noted, the granting of full citizenship rights to groups of people does not constitute a fundamental challenge to the economic inequalities that exist within capitalist societies. Indeed, what is interesting about the possession of full citizenship rights is that they are perfectly compatible with the existence of economic inequalities. Indeed, as T.H. Marshall noted, "citizenship creates an equality of conditions in certain respects in order that a stucture of social inequality may be built all the more securely" (Mishra, 1977:29). In other words, one consequence of the struggles by aboriginal organizations to gain full citizenship rights and to retain other particular citizenship rights is that they may make the existence of other social and economic inequalities become more acceptable.

Thus, the struggles over citizenship rights do not occur in opposition to the existence of capitalist relations of production, based as they are on complex systems of class, "racial," and gender inequities. While the nature of social participation is the essence of struggles over citizenship, these struggles appear to leave intact the larger inequalities associated with Canadian capitalism.

The next chapter examines how the struggles over citizenship rights have been accommodated within the wider structure of Canadian capitalism via the process of economic development. "Red capitalism," while an indication of the larger political and civil equality between Indians and non-Indians, still retains the unequal aspects of Canadian society.

CHAPTER 9

CONFLICT, COMPETITION, AND THE
CONTRADICTIONS OF ECONOMIC DEVELOPMENT

... our officials are not out there slowing the pace of progress because they like to. They are doing so because they are required by an act of Parliament to do it (Harry Swain, Deputy Minister of Indian Affairs and Northern Development, November, 1990, quoted in Aubrey, 1990:6).

As noted in the previous chapter, despite its intention to terminate the historically unique relationship with Indian people, the Liberal government's White Paper of 1969 nevertheless made a commitment to establish a five-year $50-million fund earmarked for the economic development of Indian people. While the White Paper was publicly withdrawn as a statement of intended policy in 1970, economic development remains one of the stated priorities of the federal and some provincial governments. Indeed, the economic development of aboriginal peoples is a motherhood issue for various levels of the state: everyone agrees that it is necessary, and that it is a general good that will resolve the range of problems that aboriginal peoples experience. In addition to alleviating immediate problems of poverty and welfare dependence, economic development is defined as central to the establishment and reproduction of self-government. Without an economic base separate from federal and provincial government funding, aboriginal self-government would be vacuous; indeed, it would be a contradiction in terms. As many aboriginal leaders have clearly recognized over the years, the old adage of "who pays the piper calls the tunes" is true to the extent that along with state funding come the controls of state funding (Ng, 1988). Despite the apparently universal support amongst politicians, government officials, and the wider public for the principle of the economic development of aboriginal peoples, and despite the critical importance it is accorded in the process of self-government, there is little consensus as to the overall impact of two decades of economic development expenditures by the state. There are four aims of this chapter. First, it provides an estimate of the scale of economic development expenditures undertaken by various branches of the federal government in the past two decades. Second, it critically assesses some of the explanations for the failure of economic development initiatives. Third, it outlines an alternative explanation rooted in the concepts of conflict and competition. And fourth, it examines some of the new directions in government policy pertaining to aboriginal peoples, and some of the possible consequences.

ECONOMIC DEVELOPMENT EXPENDITURES

As noted in previous chapters, Indian people have had many obstacles placed in the way of acquiring capital through private lending institutions. Given the nature of restrictions in the Indian Act, it is extremely difficult for Indian people to acquire loans or other private-sector financing to establish new, or expand existing, businesses. This has resulted in a situation where Indians have been forced, out of necessity, into seeking financial assistance and support from within the state for economic development initiatives.

An indication of the degree to which Indian businesses are dependent upon government support is provided in Figure 9.1. It shows that in 1984-85, only 12 percent of capital funds and 12.5 percent of operating funds for existing Indian businesses came from private-sector lending institutions. Figure 9.1 also shows that Indian and Northern Affairs Canada and other government programs accounted for nearly 70 percent of capital funds and 68.5 percent of operating funds of Indian businesses. Band-owned sources made up only 18.1 percent and 27.7 percent, respectively, of capital and operating funds, while less than 1.5 percent of funds came from provincial contributions (Department of Indian and Northern Affairs, 1986 b:17). The dependence of Indian businesses on the government is even greater when considering that most of the private-sector loans to Indian people have also been guaranteed by DIAND.

Since the White Paper on Indian policy was announced in 1969, the federal government has spent nearly $2.5 billion on the economic development of aboriginal peoples (Comeau and Santin, 1990:67). Funds for these expenditures have come from three main government sources: the Department of Industry, Science and Technology (previously, the Department of Regional Industrial Expansion and the Department of Regional Economic Expansion), the Department of Indian Affairs and Northern Development, and the Canada Employment and Immigration

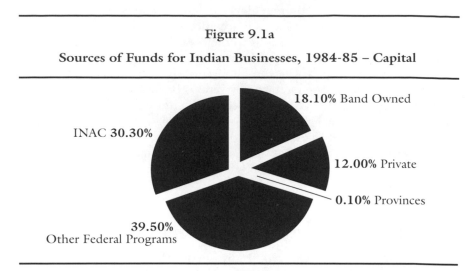

Figure 9.1a

Sources of Funds for Indian Businesses, 1984-85 – Capital

Source: Indian and Northern Affairs Canada, *Task Force on Indian Economic Development*. Ottawa: Minister of Supply and Services, 1986.

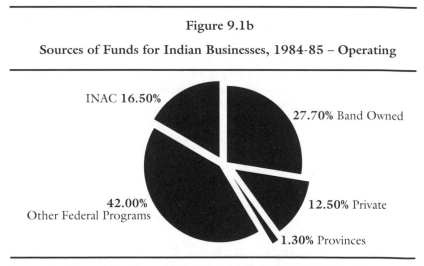

Figure 9.1b

Sources of Funds for Indian Businesses, 1984-85 – Operating

Source: Indian and Northern Affairs Canada, *Task Force on Indian Economic Development*. Ottawa: Minister of Supply and Services, 1986, p. 17.

Commission. Table 9.1 shows the scale and type of expenditures that government departments have provided between 1973 and 1988.

Table 9.1 indicates that within each department, there has been a number of general categories of economic development expenditures. Within each of these expenditure areas, there has been a plethora of specific programs and initiatives aimed at the promotion of aboriginal economic development. The mandate of the Department of Industry, Science and Technology (and its predecessor DRIE) has been to support regional development and small businesses. Until 1989, the department administered three programs: the Native Economic Development Program (NEDP), the Special Agricultural and Rural Development Agreements (Special ARDA), and the Northern Development Agreements (NDAs). Within the Department of Indian Affairs and Northern Development, business financing programs have been undertaken in the context of the Indian Economic Development Fund which provided contributions, direct loans, and loan guarantees to prospective businesses. The department also administered the Indian Community Human Resources Strategy which involved job training for unemployed reserve-based residents. The mandate of the Canada Employment and Immigration Commission has been primarily to provide "human resource development" involving urban-based job-training programs like the Canadian Jobs Strategy.

Over the years, then, economic development expenditures have been rather loosely defined to include expenditures on everything from loans, loan guarantees, business support services, business counselling, job training, skills acquisition, management consulting, and community development. As we shall show in more detail in the final section of this chapter, a clearer division of labour has emerged within the government in the area of aboriginal economic development with the introduction of the Canadian Aboriginal Economic Development Strategy (CAED) in 1989.

Explanation of Failures of Economic Development

Despite the impressive array of programs, initiatives and resources channelled through economic development for the last twenty years, there is no consensus as to the impact of this on aboriginal peoples. Perhaps not surprisingly, government officials acknowledge that while some money may have been misspent over the years, economic development has generally achieved positive results. In the fall of 1990, Harry Swain, the Deputy Minister of DIAND, claimed that "the government is getting value for its money" (Aubrey, 1990). In its summary of the history of economic development initiatives in 1989, the Canadian Aboriginal Economic Development Strategy suggested that "the results from economic development efforts to date, taken as a whole, have been most encouraging" (Government of Canada, 1989:19).

An even more positive picture is painted in the annual reports of the

Table 9.1

Federal Economic Development Expenditures, 1973-1988 ($ millions)

		1973-1974	1978-1979	1983-1984	1984-1985	1985-1986	1986-1987	1987-1988	TOTAL
Economic Development	INAC	21.9	44.9	39.5	34.5	30.4	30.4	30.4	232.0
	DRIE	1.1	8.3	18.0	39.4	144.5	169.8	90.8	471.9
Natural Resource Agreements	INAC	0.0	0.0	1.1	1.8	1.8	2.0	0.3	7
	F&O	*	*	2.7	2.7	2.7	2.7	2.7	13.5
Regional Development Agreements	INAC	85.0	255.7	462.0	495.6	578.0	615.0	666.0	3175.3
	DRIE	0.0	24.7	32.2	37.3	32.2	31.6	4.4	164.4
Training and Mobility	INAC	5.1	8.4	26.1	20.7	20.1	20.1	20.1	120.6
	EIC	19.2	27.0	118.1	137.5	114.8	101.3	101.3	619.2
	JUST	*	*	0.2	0.2	0.3	0.4	0.4	1.5
		*	*	2.6	5.6	6.8	6.8	6.8	28.6
TOTAL		132.3	369.0	702.5	775.3	931.6	980.1	923.2	4814.0

* Figures not available in this format.

Source: Compiled from H. Bherer, S. Gagnon, J. Roberge, *Wampum and Letters Patent*. Halifax: Institute for Research on Public Policy, 1990, pp. 22-23.

Department of Indian Affairs and Northern Development. Each year the Economic Development Sector outlines its "significant achievements," and in the 1988/89 *Annual Report*, the sector supported, among other things:

> funding for 380 advisors in 200 bands and 55 tribal and sectoral development corporations to assist hundreds of Indian businesses, and thousands of self-employed farmers, fishermen, trappers, outfitters and arts and crafts producers; provision of work experience for 1,500 Indians in community enterprises, and another 2,700 on housing construction and maintenance projects ...; the drilling of 44 wells on 12 reserves; 39 of these were completed: eight were for heavy oil, three for conventional oil and 28 for gas (Department of Indian and Northern Affairs, 1989).

Aboriginal peoples, and independent "outsiders" have, however, come to considerably different conclusions about the effectiveness of economic development expenditures over the years. Lester Lafond, of the DC Financial Corporation, suggested in 1986 that "While Indian economic development has received much attention over the years, it has been given the status of low man on the totem pole amongst the Department's (DIAND's) array of programs to assist Indian people" (Department of Indian and Northern Affairs, 1986 b:3).

In addition, unpublished reports prepared for the government provide a biting condemnation of past economic development initiatives. Comeau and Santin (1990) show that unpublished consultants' evaluations of the Northern Development Agreements signed between 1974 and 1989 by the federal Department of Regional Industrial Expansion and provincial governments in Manitoba, Saskatchewan, and Alberta demonstrate that economic development initiatives have been uncategorical failures. These evaluations show that

> the programs failed to improve conditions. Millions of dollars were spent on capital improvements, including housing, recreation centres, telephone systems and roads, but there was no attempt to establish a local economy which would in turn lead the residents to some level of economic independence (Comeau and Santin, 1990:69).

They go on to demonstrate that in the case of expenditures of $200 million in Manitoba between 1982 and 1989, the only thing that changed was that "more native residents were collecting welfare" (Comeau and Santin, 1990:72).

Others have also cast a much more critical eye on the successes and failures of economic development initiatives. Driben and Trudeau (1983), in their detailed case study of economic development initiatives undertaken by and for the Fort Hope Band in northern Ontario during the early 1980s, suggest that

... when we looked at the new businesses, we found that none had succeeded. Nor did it seem likely that any of them would, and this was dis-
heartening to everyone concerned, not just because DIAND had spent
well over 1.5 million dollars to establish the businesses but also things
actually looked quite promising from the start (Driben and Trudeau,
1983:51).

There are divergent views as to why state expenditures have failed to
accomplish "economic development." Generally, three types of explanations have been offered as to the obstacles faced by aboriginal peoples in
the area of economic development and why economic development initiatives have generally not been successful: human capital and cultural obstacles, political-legal obstacles to the acquisition of equity, and internal
colonial obstacles.

The first explanation, which is a supply-side explanation in that it
defines the source of the problem as aboriginal peoples themselves, suggests that aboriginal peoples lack the human and cultural capital necessary
to compete economically in an industrial society like Canada. The lack of
education and managerial skills are identified as two of the main human
capital obstacles to economic development. This appears to be the main
premise of the Canada Employment and Immigration Commission's programs.

Others, as noted earlier, stress the absence of certain forms of cultural
capital which make it difficult for Indian people to succeed in a competitive capitalist economy. Hawthorn (1966:119-134) suggested that in
addition to a number of other variables, Indian culture is incompatible
with European culture and that this incompatibility is one source of the
underdeveloped state of aboriginal communities.

Second, some argue that legal factors placed in the way of aboriginal
entrepreneurs have been the chief obstacles to economic development. As
already noted, Indians face a unique set of difficulties in their efforts to
establish businesses to the extent that their access to capital markets is
restricted by the Indian Act and the Income Tax Act (Department of
Indian and Northern Affairs, 1986).

The third, and more radical explanation of the failure of aboriginal
economic development is rooted, in part, in the internal colonial model.
Within the internal colonial model the blame for the failure of economic
development is placed squarely on the shoulders of the state and state
officials. According to Frideres (1988:413), "the biggest impediment" to
self-determination and economic development "has always been the policies of the federal and provincial governments." Officials within DIAND
have been defined as the primary malefactors.

There are several strands to this argument. While not necessarily
accepting all of the implications of the internal colonial model, the Special
Committee on Indian Self-Government, for example, argued in 1983 that

past economic development initiatives have been unsuccessful largely because of the hesitance of government officials to spend government funds on "risky" projects for which they would have been accountable; their lack of personal business experience; and their lack of confidence in the personal abilities of aboriginal peoples (Government of Canada, 1983:73).

Driben and Trudeau (1983) argue more pointedly that because of paternalism, Indian Affairs and other government officials have simply mismanaged the process of economic development. Economic development initiatives have failed due to bad planning and poor management on the part of government officials, the lack of clearly defined goals of government programs, and the reluctance of government officials to relinquish power and control to aboriginal peoples.

Associated with this, Driben and Trudeau (1983) also argue that the definition of "success" by government agencies in the area of economic development differs from that of aboriginal peoples and that of the marketplace. For government officials, success is defined in terms of the number of people who are processed through a particular program or initiative. Profitability is the main criterion of success for the market, while for aboriginal communities, the main criterion of success is the establishment of an economic base of long-term employability and viablity. Thus, the emphasis of government programs has been on short-term job creation projects that have little long-term employment potential or economic viability. Officials who administer these projects can, however, claim to have realized their own bureaucratically-defined goals if there is a high output of participants from a particular program, or if a large number of individuals are provided funding.

Yet others, including Frideres (1988) and Ponting and Gibbins (1980), argue for a related but more subtle process of subterfuge within the bureaucracy. They suggest that instead of being the result of bad planning on the part of government officials, failures of economic development programs may actually reflect the rather "good planning" of middle ranks of DIAND and other government departments. They argue that there are both manifest and latent functions associated with government policies and programs. Manifest functions consist of the publicly-stated aims of policies and programs, while latent functions are the unstated and hidden aims of those policies and programs. They argue that in social and economic spheres, there is oftentimes a contradiction between the manifest and latent functions of government programs, policies, and initiatives. Ponting and Gibbins (1980) contend that one of the unstated aims of mid-level officials working within DIAND is to maintain the client status of Indian people as a dependent population. They argue that if economic development programs are successful (in the sense of Indian people becoming less dependent on government programs), then those officials will have essentially worked themselves out of their jobs. Thus, whether consciously or unconsciously, government officials stonewall and sabotage such intiatives in order to protect their own interests.

This explanation is shared by Georges Erasmus, the past leader of the Assembly of First Nations, as well as many other aboriginal peoples. In 1990, Erasmus argued that "You're talking about a bureaucracy — you don't have to know Indians there, all they know is how to be managers — and asking them to work themselves out of a job" (Aubrey, 1990). Thus, in order to maintain their positions, government officials must sabotage any real effort to improve the conditions of aboriginal peoples: without the poverty of aboriginal peoples there would be no need for Indian Affairs officials whose job it is to improve aboriginals' socioeconomic conditions.

Taken together, these explanations shed considerable light on the reasons for the failure of state-sponsored economic development initiatives. Clearly, the lack of human capital and the existence of legal obstacles to the acquisition of capital are realities faced on a daily basis by prospective entrepreneurs and entrants to the labour market who are attempting to carve out niches for themselves in the wider economic system. Moreover, many government officials continue to display a colonial mentality in their dealings with aboriginal peoples, and there is often a contradiction between the publicly-stated aims of government policy and the internal, hidden agendas of those policies (Satzewich, 1991).

However, these are incomplete explanations, and indeed, there is a number of analytical problems with them. The problems with supply-side human capital and cultural deficit arguments have been noted already and shall not be reviewed here. The second view, with its focus on particular pieces of legislation, is incomplete in that it fails to contextualize the meaning of such legislation. Thus, while it is clear that the Indian Act has been an obstacle to the economic development of Indian people, it is necessary to go a step further and ask why particular regulations were implemented in the Indian Act.

In relation to the internal colonial model, we agree that a focus on the state is crucial to understanding the dynamics of aboriginal economic development and underdevelopment. Where we disagree is in the explanation of the dynamics of the activities of state agents. To a certain degree, mid-range bureaucrats may be fighting defensive manoeuvres to protect their jobs. This is particularly the case since the federal Progressive Conservative government has been committed to downsizing DIAND for the past five years, and since there appears to be general agreement amongst both politicians and aboriginal leaders that the department should eventually be phased out. However, the nature of civil service employment is such that it is unlikely that Indian Affairs officials would work themselves out of a job because of successful economic development projects. For example, in the context of the downsizing of DIAND, it appears that most of the positions have been phased out through early assisted retirement, severance packages, hiring freezes, and voluntary transfers to other departments; over the past four years of downsizing, less than 2 percent of the workers within DIAND have been involuntarily laid off (Department of Indian and Northern Affairs, 1990:35). Thus, it appears that only a very small fraction of the total work force of DIAND would be faced with the immediate prospect of joblessness because of Indian economic success.

Such explanations also tend to overly personalize the failures of economic development initiatives, and to be overly conspiratorial in their interpretation of the activities of Indian Affairs officials. The failures of state policies are explained in terms of the personal inadequacies and insecurities of government bureaucrats. While some officials working within DIAND may be incompetent, these explanations abstract the activities of the state and state officials out of existing political-economic relations. It assumes that departmental officials act as independent agents, uninfluenced by other social forces.

Furthermore, while it is true that many of the economic development initiatives undertaken in the past two decades have failed to improve the conditions of aboriginal peoples generally, it is also the case that there are some "success" stories associated with Indian economic development. As noted in Chapter 3, there is an extant petite bourgeoisie within the aboriginal population and an embryonic capitalist class. Some economic development corporations and individual and band-based enterprises have been able to establish themselves in competitive positions in the marketplace by either selling goods or providing services. Thus, in the context of a mixture of failures and some successes of economic development initiatives, the manifest and latent function argument does not specify the conditions under which state officials sabotage economic development programs in order to protect their own interests and the conditions under which they allow those programs to succeed. Presumably, if Indian Affairs officials have consciously intervened in particular ways to sabotage economic development, then it must also be the case that when initiatives succeed, officials must have either failed to intervene to sabotage them, or they intervened to allow them to succeed. If one of the main latent interests of Indian Affairs officials is to keep themselves in work, then the model has some difficulty in explaining the success stories associated with economic development. In light of the existing explanations of the failures of economic development initiatives and our critical comments, we turn in the next section to an alternative conceptualization of the meaning of state involvement in aboriginal economic development activities.

THE STATE AS A SITE OF STRUGGLE: THE CONTRADICTIONS OF ECONOMIC DEVELOPMENT

In this section we would like to offer an adjunct to the three explanations already presented. We suggest that the meaning of economic development initiatives supported through the state should also be located in the context of the wider set of class forces within Canada. As noted in earlier chapters, within a capitalist society, the state is a site of struggle: it is an arena in which class and other struggles are played out (Stasiulis, 1988). Social and economic policies and programs are the outcomes of contradictory forms of struggle occurring within the state. The various branches of the Canadian state do not act in a fashion independent of larger class relations in Canada. State officials and government departments must manage a series of contradictions arising from its role in the representation and social control of a whole range of client groups, not all of whom have equal degrees of power. Social and economic policies that emerge, and the way they are implemented, are the outcomes of contradictions inherent in the nexus of representation and social control responsibilities of the state. As such, policies are ridden with contradictions (Offe, 1975). The success and failure of aboriginal economic development initiatives must therefore be rooted in a dialectical analysis which examines the pressures and counter-pressures placed on the state by other classes and social groups.

Historically, one of the ongoing interests of business and labour within capitalist societies has been the nature of competition they face (see Bonacich, 1979). While one of the apparent hallmarks, and indeed virtues, of capitalism is that it is based on the principle of competition, too much competition can have negative consequences for individual producers. In other words, under capitalism, too much competition is a vice which can put individual producers out of business or workers out of jobs. Thus, while espousing the virtues of competition in the abstract, business and labour are sometimes keen to limit the size and scope of the competition they face. The state (through policy and legislation) has been used as a means by which groups have attempted to limit this competition.

For example, in relation to the activities of labour, evidence suggests that the "white" working class in British Columbia was central to the establishment of a split labour market that limited the ability of Chinese people to gain certain positions (Li, 1988:34). In relation to business interests, the tariffs on the import of finished goods produced abroad introduced as part of the Conservative government's National Policy of 1879 appear, in part, to have been implemented to protect the interests of eastern Canadian manufacturers from American competition. The tariff involved the establishment of duties on cheap imported consumer and industrial commodities from the United States. Some have suggested that the tariffs were undertaken on behalf of Canadian manufacturers to limit the ability of American companies to compete for Canadian markets (Pentland, 1981:164-175).

A more contemporary example comes from recent debates about free trade with the United States (and now Mexico). While many sectors of Canadian business were in favour of the establishment of free trade with the United States, other sectors (like the Canadian Textiles Institute, the

Brewer's Association of Canada, the Wine Institute of Canada, and the Canadian Council of Furniture Manufacturers) were opposed because the elimination of tariffs on American imports would increase competition and hurt them economically (Warnock, 1988:114-118).

One of the central contradictions faced by the state, then, is to maintain the general conditions for the profitable accumulation of capital (Offe, 1975), but at the same time it is forced by political and economic pressure to limit the degree of competition faced by individual capitalists or labour groups.

The implication of this argument for the issue of aboriginal economic development is that, stucturally, it is difficult for federal and provincial government departments to help establish and support successful Indian owned and controlled businesses, particularly if that support helps put those businesses in a position of direct competition with non-aboriginal interests. One of the constraints successive federal governments have faced in the area of aboriginal economic development are charges of "unfair competition" from non-aboriginal business interests. While often willing to seek state support, subsidies, or loan guarantees for their own activities, businesses tend to be resentful of state support for projects which do not benefit them directly, and are hostile to forms of support which might harm them. Thus, the contradiction for the state is that successful economic development programs put aboriginal peoples in a position of potential conflict with non-aboriginal producers who are seeking the same markets.

Several historical and contemporary examples highlight our argument. The first example concerns the land-surrender process in the Prairies during the turn of the century. As noted in Chapter 3, the Indian Affairs Branch appears to have actively undermined the development of reserve agriculture. This took the form of, among other things, dispossessing Indian bands on the Prairies of their most valuable and productive farm land which they had chosen under the terms of the treaties. As noted by Carter (1990), during the turn of the century, residents in the Broadview area of southern Saskatchewan had for several years covetously eyed the lands reserved for the Crooked Lakes band. They sent letters and petitions, and met with government officials, to press for the annexation of Indian land. For example, a 1902 petition to Clifford Sifton, the Minister of the Interior, stated that "whereas the proximity of the Reservation seriously retards the development of these towns [Broadview and Whitewood] ... [and] whereas the Reservation which occupies an area of two hundred and eighty-five square-miles is much in excess of the requirements of the present Indian population ... that the Honorable Minister of the Interior use his best offices to provide the assent of the Indians to the sale of this land to actual settlers" (Department of the Interior, 1902). Of the approximately 200 signatures on the petition, the majority consisted of those of town merchants or surrounding area farmers. While federal

officials initially resisted this pressure, they eventually relented and transferred the most productive of the reserve lands to private settler control.

There are several points of interest in this episode for the issue of
Indian economic development. First, the dispossession of Indian lands was
not effected simply because of "bad planning," incompetence, or mali-
ciousness on the part of state officials. Second, it was not "white" people
in the abstract that pressed for the dispossession of Indians from their
land, but rather "white" people who occupied particular positions in the
relations of production: those who had particular class-based interests.
Third, the existence of land reserved for Indians was identified as a barrier
to the economic interests of farmers and small businesses. And fourth,
businessmen and farmers placed pressure on the state to engage in particular practices that were in their best interests, but that were clearly not in
the best interests of Indian people. Certain classes of "white" people were
able to use the political system to suppress the ability of Indians to establish an independent agricultural base. In sum, what appears to have been a
case where Indian Affairs officials simply did not have the Indians' best
interests at heart begs the question of whose interests did Indian Affairs'
officials take into account. It is clear that in this case they also had land
speculators and small business interests in mind when they undertook to
dispossess Indian people of their land.

The second, more contemporary, example of the contradictory nature
of the pressures faced by the state in the area of aboriginal economic
development is the debate about the implementation of the Goods and
Services Tax on reserves. For a short time after the Goods and Services
Tax was introduced in January of 1991, it appeared that businesses on
reserves would be exempt from charging the tax on the sale of all goods
and services. The implication of this was that in addition to the tax
exemption for status Indians living on reserves, the purchases of non-
Indians shopping at stores on reserves would also not be subject to the
GST. When the tax-exempt status of stores on reserves came to public
light, there was an outcry from white-owned businesses in rural areas of
western Canada, particularly from businesses in those communities
located near reserves which depended heavily on the expenditures of
Indian people. An owner of a small business in a northern Saskatchewan
town explained, with a slight note of panic, the implications of GST
exemptions in the following terms: "This town is on the map because of
the native trade. It was a fur trading centre before anybody set foot in
Saskatchewan and people are here because it was an Indian settlement.
But you're going to see a shadow business district develop on the reserves
and you'll see stores boarded up on Main Street" (Goulding, 1991).
Among others, the Saskatchewan Urban Municipalities Association was
adamant in its criticisms of this loophole. Shortly after this loophole
became a public issue, it was closed off by Revenue Canada.

It is unclear whether the initial loophole was simply an oversight on the part of Revenue Canada officials and whether the reaction from non-Indian business interests forced Revenue Canada to change this provision. What was interesting about the reaction to reserve-based stores' exemption from the GST, though, was that it brought into sharp focus the nature of the contradiction faced by the state in the area of Indian economic development. This special provision might have had a positive effect on the process of Indian economic development to the extent that non-aboriginal people might have been attracted by the prospect of cheaper prices to shop for goods and services at reserve-based enterprises. This would have helped resolve at least one problem that reserve-based businesses face, namely the existence of limited markets for their goods and services (Department of Indian and Northern Affairs, 1986:11). However, this was politically indefensible. White business owners were quick to protest what they defined as unfair competition which was created for them by virtue of Indian people's special tax-exempt status, and they were not reluctant to use their associations, along with the media, to expose the "unfairness" of this situation.

The third and final example which we use to illustrate our argument about the contradictory nature of state support for aboriginal economic development comes from provincial economic development programs. The Saskatchewan government's Indian Economic Development Program, instituted in 1983, provides financial assistance to bands and band-based development corporations, tribal council development corporations, and Indian institutions, and to status Indian individuals who have lived in the province for at least one year. The policy guidelines and procedures for the program provide a list of the types of business activities which are accorded high and low priority for funding under the program. High-priority businesses are those that require less than $10 000; demonstrate the greatest potential for long-term viability and employment over the long run; attract conventional financing; demonstrate a personal commitment and willingess to take risk; are integrated into the existing business environment; create spin-off business and employment activities; and make the greatest impact on the diversification of the provincial economy. Low-priority activities include those which seek assistance for training and make-work projects; funds for organizational and community infrastructure; feasibility studies; debt retirement or financial bailouts; conventional agricultural projects; and which duplicate or displace existing program mandates and budgets. In addition, businesses accorded low priority for funding are those which "obviously displace or create unfair competition for existing businesses and employees" (Indian and Native Affairs Secretariate of Saskatchewan, 1990-91:2-3).

The aim of the program, then, is to support businesses which are small in nature (which require less than $10 000), and which will not be in competition for markets with existing businesses in Saskatchewan. This means that the potentially most profitable industries which require higher degrees of capitalization, and which are already characterized by the presence of "white" business interests, are out of bounds for Indians if they wish to use this form of state assistance. The provincial government's economic development policy forces potential entrepreneurs into those sectors of the economy which have either been vacated by existing businesses because of unprofitability, or which have never been very profitable. Thus, in order to qualify for funding under this program, aboriginal business people must consent to regulations which limit their ability to compete with existing businesses. Clearly, then, the Saskatchewan provincial government has effectively institutionalized the relationships which have historically limited the economic options and activities of Indian people. In other words, this program has concretized, within a specific policy, the contradiction associated with aboriginal economic development.

In short, the task that aboriginal businesses will face in the future is finding profitable niches in markets that are not already filled, or dominated, by white-owned businesses. The difficulty, of course, is that given the nature of capitalism, which contains a tendency towards monopolization and centralization, it is extremely difficult to find new niches in the economy that are profitable, and which will remain profitable in the long run. Many of the niches available to potential aboriginal business people are likely to be ones which have not been filled by white-owned businesses, or which are currently being vacated, because of low profit margins. They are more likely to succeed here because they involve those activities in which they will face the least amount of resistance to the introduction of their competition. Conversely, economic development initiatives are less likely to succeed in those contexts where there are existing producers who are able to become mobilized and exercise their political and economic influence to oppose this competition.

THE CANADIAN ABORIGINAL ECONOMIC DEVELOPMENT STRATEGY

In 1989, the federal government committed itself to the Canadian Aboriginal Economic Development Program (CAED). The program provides for a reorganization of existing federal government initiatives, and the development of a number of new initiatives, in the area of aboriginal economic development. This new program appears to have been rooted, in part, in the recommendations of the 1985 Neilsen Task Force on Improved Program Delivery for Aboriginal People (Neilsen, 1985). In its review, the Task Force recommended that greater effort be placed on the coordination of program delivery and the elimination of program and administrative duplication. It also recommended that the Department of Industry, Science and Technology should assume primary control over aboriginal economic development programs, with the Department of

Indian Affairs and Northern Development and Canada Employment and Immigration assuming subsidiary responsibilities. The program is "status blind" to the extent that Métis, Inuit, and status and non-status Indians are eligible for funding.

The strategy has a budget of $873.7 million for an initial five-year period, and consists of seven program areas to be administered by one of the three departments and one program area to be administered jointly. The eight program areas, along with their stated mandates and the administrative department, are as follows:

1) Business Development (ISTC) — the aim is to continue in a more effective way the commercial enterprise components of various government programs, including the Special Agricultural and Rural Development Agreements (Special ARDA), the Native Economic Development Program (NEDP), and the Indian Business Development Program (IBDP), so that aboriginal individuals or communities can obtain the capital and support services to start or expand a business;

2) Joint Ventures (ISTC) — to help aboriginal businesses forge new and profitable links with other firms in the mainstream economy thereby providing opportunities for the transfer of management, technical, and other business skills to aboriginal peoples;

3) Capital Corporations (ISTC) — support and build the network of autonomous aboriginal financial institutions established across the country in recent years through the efforts of ISTC's NEDP and CEIC's Community Futures;

4) Community Economic Planning and Development — DIAND — to build on the current DIAND, CEIC, and ISTC initiatives, to assist aboriginal peoples living in rural, remote, and isolated communities to plan, program, organize, and direct their own businesses and employability development services;

5) Access to Resources (DIAND) — to assist aboriginal communities to develop their employment bases by gaining access to commercially relevant renewable and non-renewable resources;

6) Skills Development (CEIC) — to augment managerial, professional, and vocational skills among aboriginal individuals under programs such as the Canadian Jobs Strategy by greater involvement of aboriginal peoples in the planning and implementation of local strategies;

7) Urban Employment (CEIC) — in consultation with local provincial and municipal authorities, to assist aboriginal peoples who live in urban areas to find employment through training and work experience initiatives so that they can share fully in the growing prosperity of our cities; CEIC will be proactive in involving representatives of the aboriginal communities, the private sector, and governments in development of local planning strategies;

8) Research and Advocacy (ISTC, DIAND, CEIC) — to ensure the

effective management of the new strategy, to coordinate the programs, and to conduct research and policy analysis. The advocacy role will be played to build support for aboriginal businesses within the federal government and in all quarters of the Canadian economy.

It is too early to predict the outcome of this new program, but some preliminary observations may be in order. First, the federal government's decision to include Métis and non-status Indians in the terms of reference of the program, while laudible in itself, appears to have been intended to undermine status Indians' claim for special status; it does not appear to be an affirmation of Métis and non-status Indian rights. According to Weaver (1986:18), one of the assumptions of the Neilsen report, upon which the CAED strategy is based, is that "aboriginality did not exist and should not be given validity as a basis for the new Indian-government relationship." Thus, the lumping together of all aboriginal peoples into one program area may be seen, particularly by status Indians, as an attempt to negate their special citizenship status.

Second, the emphasis on the development of joint ventures with non-aboriginal businesses is likely to have contradictory outcomes. The stated aim of joint ventures is to help facilitate the transfer of management, technical, and business skills from non-aboriginal to aboriginal peoples. Care needs to be taken in these efforts because they may ultimately undermine self-government. Given that private corporations have one aim (profitability), and given that business decisions are made on the basis of the maximization of profit, control over these investments may ultimately lie with the non-aboriginal decision makers.

Third, the requirement that business proposals be evaluated on the basis of potential profitability and likelihood of long-term economic success may have the effect of sharpening class divisions within aboriginal communities. If the profit motive is to be paramount to funding decisions, aboriginal businesses, like their non-aboriginal counterparts, will be under pressure to keep the wages of its work force low and resist efforts to unionize aboriginal workers. What needs to be avoided is the use of anti-colonial terminology, and Indian nationalism (see Boldt, 1982), to suppress struggles by the aboriginal working class to improve wages and working conditions within "Indian owned" enterprises (Daniels, 1986).

Fourth, and on a more positive note, the establishment of Indian owned and controlled capital corporations may be beneficial to the extent that decisions for funding of economic development initiatives will become disentangled from the state. This is likely to have the positive effect of depoliticizing the decisions surrounding financial support for economic development initiatives, and taking those descisions out of an arena in which there is not, in the words of our free trade negotiators, a "level playing field."

Conclusion

The perspective advanced in this chapter should be seen as an adjunct to existing explanations of the dynamics of aboriginal economic development programs. Conceiving of economic development as contradictory in nature means that sense can be made of failures as well as successes. We have suggested that the nature of aboriginal economic competition has been, and continues to be, a highly contested and politicized process. Given that Indian people are forced to compete in the marketplace through a state which is not a neutral arbiter of the interests of competing groups, but rather a representative of class rule, the character of the struggles that occur within the state is an important determinant of the success and failure of economic development initiatives. Politically, governments simply cannot afford to have aboriginal peoples as successful competitors to the extent that their primary support, both electoral and financial, comes from classes within the non-aboriginal population. To support those economic activities which would put aboriginal peoples into a position where they could compete for markets and services with white-owned businesses, would, to say the least, be imprudent for any political party or government.

Given the analysis presented in this book, it is perhaps inevitable that we pose the question: will economic development that follows the form of the development of capitalist relations of production amongst aboriginal peoples solve the many problems they experience? Governments, and some aboriginal peoples, argue that the development of free enterprise within aboriginal communities will benefit all aboriginal people to the extent that fewer will be on welfare, more will have jobs, and more will be in business. We would not deny that some aboriginal peoples will benefit by the further spread of capitalist relations of production into their communities, as has been the case in other contexts. However, as noted previously, capitalism, has, at best, been a mixed blessing for those who have participated in its logic. During the recession of the late 1980s and early 1990s, food banks, welfare agencies, and unemployment lines in dozens of cities across the country were swamped with both aboriginal and non-aboriginal Canadians who lost their businesses or were put out of work by forces beyond their immediate control. As people in what used to be East Germany are now learning first-hand, the existence of the capitalist mode of production, while creating staggering wealth for some people, also creates equally staggering degrees of poverty for others. The contradiction for aboriginal peoples is, of course, that while the status quo is no longer acceptable, a future characterized by the further penetration of capitalism into their lives may also be unacceptable.

CONCLUSIONS

We began this book by asking the question of how we can justify another study of aboriginal/non-aboriginal relations in Canada given the abundance of studies already in existence. We have argued that, despite the valuable insights about aboriginal life and history produced by several of these studies, key dimensions of these relationships have tended to be ignored or undertheorized. Too often, descriptive and analytical accounts have focused upon attempts to define the "Indian problem" and crises that emerge from aboriginal peoples' relations with white society in ways that assume that aboriginal and non-aboriginal peoples constitute two distinct social groups. Without trying to undermine the significance of "race," our analysis has situated these relations within the oppression, struggle, and systematic inequalities that characterize capitalist societies.

Our political economy approach has emphasized capitalism as a contradictory and changing form of social organization in which particular social practices and problems give rise to, and are shaped by, requirements for distinct forms of land, labour, and capital at different historic junctures. Central to capitalist development are processes of domination and resistance insofar as capitalism is premised upon the accumulation of profit in private hands through the extraction of surplus labour. It is widely assumed that, because Canada's aboriginal peoples have tended for the most part to be exluded from, or at the margins of, wage labour, a political economy and class analysis does not apply to their experience. We have contended, to the contrary, that such analysis can serve as a valuable tool for understanding the complexities of relations between aboriginal and non-aboriginal peoples in three main ways. First, capitalism, as we have shown with respect to various spheres of native life, has produced far-reaching changes in the economic, political, and social conditions experienced by aboriginal peoples. Second, native peoples to varying extents, in different places and periods of time, alternatively have been integrated into, or excluded from, wage-labour markets, often in highly regulated and managed ways. Finally, capitalism has not simply "acted upon" aboriginal peoples but, rather, the particular form that capitalist development has taken in Canada has been shaped by interactive relations among aboriginal peoples, capital, labour, and the state.

This last point is highly significant to our analysis. The existence, in many varied socially-developed forms, of First Nations in Canadian territory prior to European contact and colonization has posed a series of recurrent dilemmas for state and capitalist interests in terms of access to land, labour power, and other resources. Throughout the book we have shown how aboriginal peoples have stood, in diverse ways, as both barriers to and facilitators of capitalist development. These issues are still being resolved, as evident in negotiations and debate over the meaning and consequences of "aboriginal title," "self-government," "special status," and other related phenomena. Because of the complex and far-reaching nature of many of these problems, the state has been heavily involved in regulating both aboriginal life and interaction between aboriginal peoples and other groups. Nonetheless, given the Canadian state's prominent historical role in creating conditions favourable to capitalist development and in its engagement in class and other social struggles, aboriginal peoples are not unique as a "race" or group of people controlled and constrained by state management.

The crux of our analysis has been that while state policy and capitalist development have often been directed towards and had many distinct consequences for aboriginal peoples as a collectivity or as "Indians" and other indigenous subgroupings, aboriginal peoples have also experienced and responded to capitalism through their class and gender relations. It is not just as natives, but as boys and girls, men and women, employers and employees, and as persons who bear other social characteristics, that aboriginal peoples engage in social interaction and have unequal access to social opportunities and rewards. Moreover, these identities and relations are not ready-made, but constructed through the course of people's life experiences. Consequently, we have maintained throughout the book an emphasis on social production and reproduction, conceptualized as the ways in which aboriginal peoples, as human subjects who possess distinct social attributes, both shape and are shaped by the social structures and practices that they encounter in their daily lives. These structures and practices, within capitalist societies, are based upon relations of domination and resistance.

Recognition of the interactive effects of class, "race," and gender within capitalist societies carries with it important policy as well as analytical implications. While we have acknowledged that periodically, and especially in the past decade, aboriginal peoples' struggles have enabled them to make many important gains in areas such as acknowledgment of aboriginal and citizenship rights, economic development, and access to quality health care, education, welfare, housing, and criminal justice services, we have been somewhat cautious in our assessment of these advances. This is not to deny either the significance of these initiatives or the pressing need that continues to exist to find effective, aboriginal-controlled means of addressing the tremendous disadvantages which many native peoples experience relative to other segments of Canadian society. Instead, we have contended that efforts to redress aboriginal subjugation and to explore opportunities for self-determination cannot adequately be pursued in isolation from class, gender, and wider "race" relations. Inequalities of class and gender, as well as of "race," remain fundamental to the constitution of aboriginal life within capitalist societies.

There is also another side to the dialectic of domination and subordination. Persons who are not of aboriginal origin can benefit substantially from an understanding of aboriginal peoples' social history and cultural contributions, their experiences of subordination, their periodic struggles to resist oppressive policies and practices, and their efforts to alleviate pressing social problems at the community level. At the same time, aboriginal organizations and unorganized fractions of the aboriginal population can gain useful knowledge, as many have already recognized, from an analysis of the victories and setbacks experienced by other racial minorities, the women's movement, the labour movement, and democratic community organizations. Again, it is important to remember that while aboriginal peoples face certain unique problems and challenges as aboriginals, they also experience life through collective interests structured by gender, class, and other important social relations.

Of course, the political agenda remains far from clear. We have pointed out that class, "race," and gender alignments are rarely entirely unified and cohesive, especially amidst changing economic and political circumstances. We cannot, therefore, predict with certainty the outcomes and consequences of First Nations struggles to gain self-determination or meaningful coexistence within the Canadian nation-state. National boundaries and policies themselves are shaped in conjunction with the reordering of capitalism on an international scale. These processes, in turn, have significant potential either to limit or augment the impact of the aboriginal voice, at least as it emerges from particular segments of the aboriginal population.

Our analysis and concluding comments point toward several general kinds of investigation that remain to be pursued in greater depth than has so far been the case by social scientists and other persons who are concerned to examine aboriginal social relations and alternative futures. In order to address our starting concern about observers who contend that "Native people have been studied to death," there is a need to produce studies that will not merely restate the obvious and those, more seriously, that are not motivated by agendas either to control or naively to "help" aboriginal peoples. We have pointed out several times the lack of data which enable us to observe in a systematic way the impact of class, gender, and other structured inequalities upon all aspects of aboriginal life. As long as major statistical summaries highlight general comparisons between aboriginal and non-aboriginal peoples, other important distinctions are hidden so that we cannot determine the opportunities and experiences that are distinctive for particular types of people within these population groups. It is also essential that future studies explore fully the interconnections between features of everyday social life and the social structures which shape and are shaped by these experiences. This task involves the crucial task of integrating the aboriginal voice into social analysis, both through increasing the direct participation of aboriginal peoples in social scientific endeavours and by means of greater sensitivity to the concerns and experiences of aboriginal peoples who occupy diverse social positions. Social science offers useful tools and analytical approaches that can clarify the significance of people's lived realities in ways that go beyond what individuals are attuned to in their daily activities. Those tools, however, can be effective in stimulating democratic change only when they are linked to possibilities for action that are guided by the people who live those circumstances.

REFERENCES

Abele, F. and D. Stasiulis
1989 "Canada as a White Settler Colony: What About Natives and Immigrants?" In W. Clement and G. Williams, eds., *The New Canadian Political Economy*. Kingston: McGill-Queen's University Press, pp. 240-277.

Aborigines' Protection Society
1846 *The Ninth Annual Report of the Aborigines' Protection Society*. London: Aborigines' Protection Society.

Adam, B.A.
1991 "Abuse in Schools Linked to Problems of Natives." Saskatoon *Star-Phoenix*, Sept. 27, p. A10.

Adams, H.
1990 *Prison of Grass*, 2nd ed. Saskatoon: Fifth House Publishers.

Advisory Commission on Indian and Inuit Health Consultation
1980 *Report of the Advisory Commission on Indian and Inuit Health Consultation*. Ottawa: Department of Indian Affairs and Northern Development.

Advisory Committee on Indian Affairs in British Columbia
1951 Minutes of the Meeting of the Advisory Committee on Indian Affairs in British Columbia, January 31. Provincial Archives of British Columbia, Government Records 1071, Box 1, file 2.

Ahenakew, D.
1985 "Aboriginal Title and Aboriginal Rights: The Impossible and Unnecessary Task of Identification and Definition." In M. Boldt, J.A. Long, and L. Little Bear, eds., *The Quest for Justice*. Toronto: The University of Toronto Press, pp. 24-30.

Alberta, Province of
1991a *Report of the Task Force on the Criminal Justice System and its Impact on the Indian and Métis People of Alberta, Volume I: Main Report* (The Cawsey Report). Edmonton: Province of Alberta.

1991b *Report of the Task Force on the Criminal Justice System and its Impact on the Indian and Métis People of Alberta, Volume III: Working Papers and Bibliography*. Edmonton: Province of Alberta.

Allan, D.J.
1943 "Indian Land Problems in Canada." In C.T. Loram and T.F. McIlwrath, eds., *The North American Indian Today*. Toronto: University of Toronto Press, pp. 184-198.

Anderson, C.
1974 *The Political Economy of Social Class*. Englewood Cliffs: Prentice Hall.

Anthias, F.
1990 "Race and Class Revisited — Conceptualizing Race and Racisms," *Sociological Review* 38, 1:19-42.

Arat-Koc. S.
1992 "Immigration Policies, Migrant Domestic Workers and the Definition of Citizenship in Canada." In V. Satzewich, ed., *Deconstructing A Nation: Immigration, Multiculturalism and Racism in 90s Canada.* Halifax: Fernwood Publishers.

Armstrong, P.
1984 *Labour Pains: Women's Work in Crisis.* Toronto: The Women's Press.

Armstrong, R., J. Kennedy, and P.R. Oberle
1990 *University Education and Economic Well-Being: Indian Achievement and Prospects.* Ottawa: Indian and Northern Affairs Canada.

Asch, M.
1985 "Native Peoples." In D. Drache and W. Clement, eds., *The New Practical Guide to Canadian Political Economy.* Toronto: James Lorimer & Company, pp. 152-161.

1989 "Capital and Economic Development: A Critical Reappraisal of the Recommendations of the Mackenzie Valley Pipeline Commission." In K. Coates and W. Morrison, eds., *Interpreting Canada's North.* Toronto: Copp Clark Pitman.

Assembly of First Nations
1987 "Current Indian Health Conditions: A Statistical Perspective." Assembly of First Nations research document. Ottawa: Assembly of First Nations.

Aubrey, J.
1990 "Battling the Bureaucrats," Saskatoon *Star-Phoenix,* November 17, Prism 6.

Auditor General of Canada
1990 *Report to the House of Commons.* Ottawa: Minister of Supply and Services.

Badgley, R.F.
1973 "Social Policy and Indian Health Services in Canada," *Anthropological Quarterly* 46, 3:150-159.

Ballis Lal, B.
1990 *The Romance of Culture in an Urban Civilization.* London: Routledge.

Baran, P.A.
1973 *The Political Economy of Growth.* Middlesex, England: Penguin Books.

Barkwell, L.J., D.N. Gray, D.N. Chartrand, L.N. Longclaws, and R.H. Richard
1989 "Devalued People: The Status of the Métis in the Justice System," *The Canadian Journal of Native Studies* 9, 1:121-150.

Barkwell, L.J., L.N. Longclaws, and D.N. Chartrand
1989 "Status of Metis Children Within the Child Welfare System," *The Canadian Journal of Native Studies* 9, 1:33-53.

Barman, J., Y. Hébert, and D. McCaskill
1986 "The Legacy of the Past: An Overview." In J. Barman, Y. Hébert, and D. McCaskill, eds., *Education in Canada. Volume I: The Legacy.* Vancouver: University of British Columbia Press, pp. 1-22.

Barron, F.L.
1988 "The Indian Pass System in the Canadian West, 1882-1935," *Prairie Forum* 13, 1 (Spring): 25-42.

Barsh, R. and J. Henderson
1982 "Aboriginal Rights, Treaty Rights and Human Rights: Indian Tribes and Constitutional Renewal," *Journal of Canadian Studies* 17, 2:55-81.

Bartlett, R.H.
1990 *Indian Reserves and Aboriginal Lands in Canada: A Homeland.* Saskatoon: University of Saskatchewan Native Law Centre.

B.C. Indian Arts and Welfare Society
1948 *Report of the Conference on Native Indian Affairs,* Vancouver, April 1-3. Provincial Archives of British Columbia, Government Records 1071, Box 1, file 2.

B.C. Socio-Economic Development Commission
1977 *Socio-Economic Study of the Indian Population of British Columbia.* North Vancouver, B.C.: Union of British Columbia Indian Chiefs.

Beamish, C.
1987 "The Circuit Court and Young Offenders." In C.T. Griffiths, ed., *Northern Youth in Crisis: A Challenge for Justice.* Burnaby, B.C.: Simon Fraser University for the Northern Conference, pp. 129-133.

Bell, S.
1991 "Urban Natives Desperately Need Day Care Centres, Council Says," Vancouver *Sun,* June 28, p. E2.

Berger, T.
1977 *Northern Frontier, Northern Homeland: The Report of the Mackenzie Valley Pipeline Inquiry,* Volume I. Ottawa: Minister of Supply and Services.

1980 *Report of the Advisory Commission on Indian and Inuit Health Consultation.* Ottawa: Department of Indian Affairs and Northern Development.

Bherer, H., S. Gagnon, and J. Roberge
1990 *Wampum and Letters Patent: Exploratory Study of Native Entrepreneurship.* Halifax: Institute for Research on Public Policy.

Bienvenue, R.
1985 "Colonial Status: The Case of Canada's Indians." In R. Bienvenue and J. Goldstein, eds., *Ethnicity and Ethnic Relations in Canada.* Toronto: Butterworths, pp. 199-214.

Bienvenue, R. and A.H. Latif
1974 "Arrests, Dispositions and Recidivism: Comparison of Indians and Whites," *Canadian Journal of Criminology and Corrections* 16, 1:105-116.

Blainey, G.
1983 *The Tyranny of Distance*. Melbourne: Sun Books.

Blauner, R.
1969 "Internal Colonialism and Ghetto Revolt," *Social Problems* 16 (Spring): 393-408.

Boisvert, D.A.
1985 *Forms of Aboriginal Self-Government*. Kingston, Ont.: Institute of Intergovernmental Relations Background Paper Number 2.

Bolaria, B.S.
1988 "Sociology, Medicine, Health, and Illness: An Overview." In B.S. Bolaria and H.D. Dickinson, eds., *Sociology of Health Care in Canada*. Toronto: Harcourt Brace Jovanovich, pp. 1-14.

Bolaria, B.S. and P.S. Li, eds.
1988 *Racial Oppression in Canada*, 2nd edition. Toronto: Garamond Press.

Boldt, E.D., L.E. Hursch, S.D. Johnson, and K.W. Taylor
1983 "Presentence Reports and the Incarceration of Natives," *Canadian Journal of Criminology* 25, 1:269-276.

Boldt, M.
1980 "Canadian Native Indian Leadership: Context and Composition," *Canadian Ethnic Studies Journal* 12, 1:15-33.

1981a "Social Correlates of Nationalism: A Study of Native Indian Leaders in a Canadian Internal Colony," *Comparative Political Studies* 14, 2:205-231.

1981b "Enlightenment Values, Romanticism and Attitudes Toward Political Status: A Study of Native Indian Leaders in Canada," *Canadian Review of Sociology and Anthropology* 18, 4:545-565.

1981c "Social Correlates of Romanticism in an Internal Colony: A Study of Native Indian Leaders in Canada," *Ethnic Groups: An International Journal of Ethnic Studies* 3, 4:307-322.

1982 "Intellectual Orientations and Nationalism Among Leaders in an Internal Colony: A Theoretical and Comparative Perspective," *British Journal of Sociology* 33, 4:484-510.

Boldt, M., J.A. Long, and L. Little Bear, eds.
1985 *The Quest for Justice*. Toronto: University of Toronto Press.

Bonacich, E.
1979 "The Past, Present and Future of Split Labor Market Theory." In C.B. Marret and C. Leggon, eds., *Research in Race and Ethnic Relations*, Vol. 1. Greenwich: JAI Press, pp. 17-64.

Bone, R.
1989 "Economic Development and Country Food." In P. Kariya, ed., *Native Socio-Economic Development in Canada: Adaptation, Accessibility and Opportunity*. Winnipeg: Institute of Urban Studies, pp. 19-32.

Bonta, J.
1989 "Native Inmates: Institutional Response, Risk, and Needs," *Canadian Journal of Criminology* 31, 1:49-62.

Boston, T.D.

1988 *Race, Class, and Conservatism.* Boston: Unwin Hyman.

Bourgeault, R.

1983 "The Indian, the Métis and the Fur Trade: Class, Sexism and Racism in the Transition from 'Communism' to Capitalism," *Studies in Political Economy* 12 (Fall):45-80.

1988a "Race and Class Under Mercantilism: Indigenous People in Nineteenth-century Canada." In B.S. Bolaria and P.S. Li, eds., *Racial Oppression in Canada.* Toronto: Garamond Press, pp. 41-70.

1988b "The South African Connection," *Canadian Dimension* 21, 8 (January):6-10.

Brady, P.D.

1983 "The Underdevelopment of the Health Status of Treaty Indians." In P.S. Li and B.S. Bolaria, eds., *Racial Minorities in Multicultural Canada.* Toronto: Garamond., pp. 39-55.

1984 "Contradictions and Consequences: The Social and Health Status of Canada's Registered Indian Population." In J. Fry, ed., *Contradictions in Canadian Society.* Toronto: John Wiley and Sons, pp. 140-155.

Braroe, N.

1975 *Indian and White: Self-image and Interaction in a Canadian Plains Community.* Stanford: Stanford University Press.

Brett, E.A.

1973 *Colonialism and Underdevelopment in East Africa.* New York: NOK Publishers, Ltd.

Brody, H.

1971 *Indians on Skid Row: The Role of Alcohol and Community in the Adaptive Process of Indian and Urban Migrants.* Ottawa: Northern Science Research Group, Department of Indian Affairs and Northern Development. Information Canada.

Brown, C., ed.

1969 *Minorities, Schools and Politics.* Toronto: University of Toronto Press.

Brown, J.S.H.

1977 "Ultimate Respectability: Fur Trade Children in the 'Civilized World'" (Part one of two parts), *The Beaver* (Winter): 4-10.

1978 "Ultimate Respectability: Fur Trade Children in the 'Civilized World'" (Part two of two parts) *The Beaver* (Spring): 48-55.

1980a "Linguistics, Solitudes, and Changing Social Categories." In C.M. Judd and A.J. Ray, eds., *Old Trails and New Directions: Papers of the Third North American Fur Trade Conference.* Toronto: University of Toronto Press, pp. 147-159.

1980b *Strangers in Blood.* Vancouver: University of British Columbia Press.

1982 "Children of the Early Fur Trades." In J. Parr, ed., *Childhood and Family in Canadian History.* Toronto: McClelland and Stewart, pp. 44-68.

Buckley, K. and T. Wheelwright

1988 *No Paradise for Workers*. Melbourne: Oxford University Press.

Burke, J.

1976 *Paper Tomahawks: From Red Tape to Red Power*. Winnipeg: Queenston House.

Burnaby, B.

1982 *Language in Education Among Canadian Native Peoples*. Toronto: OISE Press.

Cadieux, P.H.

1989 "Notes for Remarks by the Honourable Pierre H. Cadieux to the Standing Committee on Aboriginal Affairs," April 26. Ottawa: Indian and Northern Affairs Canada.

Campbell, C.S.

1912 Letter to Rev. A.E. Green, March 13. City of Vancouver Archives, A.E. Green papers, Additional Manuscripts 330, Volume 1, file 1.

Canada, Government of

1973 *Report of the Task Force: Policing on Reserves*. Edmonton: Department of Indian and Northern Affairs.

1974 *The Native Offender and the Law*. Ottawa: The Law Reform Commission of Canada.

1978a *A Recommended Plan for Evaluation in Indian Education*. Ottawa: IIAP, Department of Indian Affairs and Northern Development, Program Evaluation Branch.

1978b "Evaluation of the RCMP Indian Special Constable Program (Option 3B)." Ottawa: IIAP, Department of Indian Affairs and Northern Development, Program Evaluation Branch.

1979 *Social Assistance and Related Social Development Programs of the Department of Indian and Northern Affairs*. Ottawa: IIAP, Department of Indian Affairs and Northern Development.

1983 *The Report of the House of Commons Special Committee on Indian Self-government* (The Penner Report). Ottawa: Minister of Supply and Services.

1989 *The Canadian Aboriginal Economic Development Strategy*. Ottawa: Minister of Supply and Services.

1990 *Creating Choices: The Report of the Task Force on Federally Sentenced Women*. Ottawa: Correctional Service Canada.

Canada House of Commons

1988 *Taking Responsibility: Report of the Standing Committee on Justice and Solicitor General on its Review of Sentencing, Conditional Release and Related Aspects of Corrections*. Ottawa: Minister of Supply and Services.

Canada Sessional Papers

1876 *Annual Report of the Department of the Interior*. Ottawa: Sessional Papers 9, 7 (9), A.1876.

Canadian Centre for Justice Statistics

1990 *Adult Correctional Services in Canada 1989-90.* Ottawa: Statistics Canada.

1991 *Crime in Aboriginal Communities: Saskatchewan 1989.* Ottawa: Statistics Canada.

Canadian Civil Liberties Union

1947 "Brief Submitted to the Special Joint Committee on the Indian Act." Vancouver: Vancouver Branch, Canadian Civil Liberties Union.

Canadian Corrections Association

1967 *Indians and the Law.* Ottawa: The Canadian Corrections Association.

Canadian Indian Lawyers Association

1980 "Summary of Proceedings, Indian Child Welfare Workshop," Winnipeg, April 15-17.

Canadian Welfare Council and the Canadian Association of Social Workers

1947 *Joint Submission to the Special Joint Committee on the Indian Act.* Ottawa.

Cardinal, H.

1969 *The Unjust Society.* Edmonton: Hurtig Publishers.

1977 *The Rebirth of Canada's Indians.* Edmonton: Hurtig Publishers.

Carnoy, M.

1984 *The State and Political Theory.* Princeton: Princeton University Press.

Carter, S.

1990 *Lost Harvests.* Montreal: McGill-Queen's University Press.

Cassidy, F. and R. Bish

1989 *Indian Government: Its Meaning and Practice.* Halifax: Institute for Research on Public Policy.

Centre for Contemporary Cultural Studies

1982 *The Empire Strikes Back.* London: Hutchinson.

Chiefs of Cowichan Indians

1877 Letter to the Governor General of Canada, February 7. City of Vancouver Archives, William Henry Lomas Files, Additional Manuscripts 986.

Clark, S.

1989a *Sentencing Patterns and Sentencing Options Relating to Aboriginal Offenders.* Ottawa: Department of Justice Canada.

1989b *The Mi'kmaq and Criminal Justice in Nova Scotia.* Research study prepared for The Royal Commission on the Donald Marshall Jr., Prosecution. Halifax: Province of Nova Scotia.

Clatworthy, S.J.

1981 *Patterns of Native Employment in the Winnipeg Labour Market.* Winnipeg: University of Winnipeg, Institute of Urban Studies.

Clement, W.

1975 *The Canadian Corporate Elite.* Toronto: McClelland and Stewart.

1988 *The Challenge of Class Analysis.* Ottawa: Carleton University Press.

Clement, W. and G. Williams
1989 "Introduction." In W. Clement and G. Williams, eds., *The New Canadian Political Economy*. Kingston, Ont.: McGill-Queen's University Press, pp. 3-15.

Cleverdon, C.
1950 *The Woman Suffrage Movement in Canada*. Toronto: University of Toronto Press.

Coates, K. and J. Powell
1989 *The Modern North: People, Politics and the Rejection of Colonialism*. Toronto: James Lorimer.

Cohen, L.
1983 *Affirmative Action in Canada: Ten Years After*. Ottawa: Department of the Secretary of State.

Cohen, R.
1987 *The New Helots: Migrants in the International Division of Labour*. Aldershot: Gower.

Comeau, M. and J. Santin
1990 *The First Canadians*. Toronto: James Lorimer.

Commission on Equality in Employment
1984 *Report of the Commission on Equality in Employment*. Ottawa: Minister of Supply and Services Canada.

Coqualeetza Residential School
1928 "Coqualeetza Residential School Commencement Annual," Sardis, B.C., June. City of Vancouver Archives, Additional Manuscripts 336, Volume 28, file 32.

Correctional Law Review
1988 *Correctional Issues Affecting Native Peoples*, Correctional Law Review Working Paper No. 7. Ottawa: Solicitor General Canada.

Correctional Service of Canada
1989 *Native Population Profile Report, Population on Register 03/31/89*. Ottawa: CSC Management Services.

Corrigan, P. and D. Sayer
1985 *The Great Arch: English State Formation as Cultural Revolution*. Oxford: Basil Blackwell.

Corrigan, P., B. Curtis, and R. Lanning
1987 "The Political Space of Schooling." In T. Wotherspoon, ed., *The Political Economy of Canadian Schooling*. Toronto: Methuen, pp. 21-43.

Cox, B.A.
1987a "Introduction." In B.A. Cox, ed., *Native People, Native Lands: Canadian Indians, Inuit and Métis*. Ottawa: Carleton University Press.

1987b "Prospects for the Northern Canadian Native Economy." In B.A. Cox, ed., *Native People, Native Lands: Canadian Indians, Inuit and Métis*. Ottawa: Carleton University Press, pp. 256-265.

Coyle, M.

1986 "Traditional Indian Justice in Ontario: A Role for the Present?" *Osgoode Hall Law Journal* 24, 3:605-633.

Cree-Naskapi Commission

1988 *Report of the Cree-Naskapi Commission.* Ottawa: Indian and Northern Affairs.

Culhane Speck, D.

1987 *An Error in Judgement: The Politics of Medical Care in an Indian/White Community.* Vancouver: Talonbooks.

Cumming, P. and N. Mickenberg

1972 *Native Rights in Canada,* 2nd. ed. Toronto: Indian-Eskimo Association of Canada.

Curtis, B.

1983 "Preconditions of the Canadian State: Educational Reform and the Construction of a Public in Upper Canada, 1837-1846." *Studies in Political Economy* 10 (winter):99-121.

1988 *Building the Educational State: Canada West, 1836-1871.* London, Ont.: The Althouse Press, pp. 31-42.

Cuthand, S.

1978 "The Native People of the Prairie Provinces in the 1920's and 1930's." In I. Getty and D. Smith, eds., *One Century Later.* Vancouver: University of British Columbia Press, pp. 31-42.

Daniels, D.

1986 "The Coming Crisis in the Aboriginal Rights Movement: From Colonialism to Neo-colonialism to Renaissance." *Native Studies Review* 2, 2:97-115.

1987 "Canada." In J. Sigler, ed., *International Handbook on Race and Race Relations.* New York:Greenwood Press.

Davin, N.F.

1879 *Report on Industrial Schools for Indians and Half-breeds to the Right Honourable the Minister of the Interior.* Ottawa: Department of the Interior.

Dawson, M.

1970 *The Government of Canada.* Toronto: University of Toronto Press.

Decore, A., R. Carney, and C. Urion

1982 *Native People in the Curriculum,* Report Summary. Edmonton: Alberta Education.

Delacourt, S.

1992 "Natives Divided over Charter," The *Globe and Mail* (Toronto), March 14, p. A4.

Dempsey, H.

1978 "One Hundred Years of Treaty Seven." In I. Getty and D. Smith, eds., *One Century Later.* Vancouver: University of British Columbia Press.

Department of Citizenship and Immigration

1962a "A Study of Friendship Centres," Public Archives of Canada, R.G. 26, Vol. 69, File 2-38-6.

1962b "Memo from the Director of Indian Affairs to the Director of the Citizenship Branch," *Public Archives of Canada*, R.G. 26, Vol. 69, file 2-38-6.

Department of Indian Affairs

1901 *Annual Report of the Department of Indian Affairs 1900.* Ottawa: Queen's Printer.

1902 *Annual Report of the Department of Indian Affairs 1901.* Ottawa: King's Printer.

1910 *Annual Report of the Department of Indian Affairs 1909.* Ottawa: King's Printer.

1911 *Annual Report of the Department of Indian Affairs 1910.* Ottawa: King's Printer.

1921 *Annual Report of the Department of Indian Affairs 1920-1921.* Ottawa: King's Printer.

1929 *Annual Report of the Department of Indian Affairs 1928.* Ottawa: King's Printer.

1931 *Annual Report of the Department of Indian Affairs 1930-1931.* Ottawa: King's Printer.

1934 *Annual Report of the Department of Indian Affairs 1933-34.* Ottawa: King's Printer.

1941 *Annual Report of the Department of Indian Affairs 1940-41.* Ottawa: King's Printer.

Department of Indian Affairs and Northern Development

1980 *Indian Conditions: A Survey.* Ottawa: Minister of Supply and Services.

1988 *A Northern Political and Economic Framework.* Ottawa: Minister of Supply and Services.

Department of Indian and Northern Affairs

1973 *Report of Task Force: Policing on Reserves.* Ottawa: Minister of Supply and Services.

1986a *Annual Report, 1985-1986.* Ottawa: Minister of Supply and Services.

1986b *Task Force on Indian Economic Development.* Ottawa: Minister of Supply and Services.

1987 *Annual Report, 1986-1987.* Ottawa: Minister of Supply and Services.

1988a *Annual Report, 1987-1988.* Ottawa: Minister of Supply and Services.

1988b *Basic Departmental Data.* Ottawa: Minister of Supply and Services.

1989a *Annual Report, 1988-1989.* Ottawa: Minister of Supply and Services.

1989b *Basic Departmental Data .* Ottawa: Minister of Supply and Services.

1990 *Annual Report, 1989-90.* Ottawa: Minister of Supply and Services.

Department of the Interior

1875 *Report for the Year ending June 30, 1874.* Ottawa: Queen's Printer.

Department of Justice Canada

1990 *National Inventory of Aboriginal Justice Programs, Projects and Research.* Ottawa: Minister of Supply and Services Canada.

1991 *Aboriginal People and Justice Administration: A Discussion Paper*. Ottawa: Minister of Supply and Services Canada.

Department of Mines and Resources
1941 *Indian Affairs Branch, Annual Report 1940-1941*. Ottawa: King's Printer.

Deprez, P. and G. Sigurdson
1969 *Economic Status of the Canadian Indian: A Re-Examination*. Winnipeg: Centre for Settlement Studies, University of Manitoba.

Dickinson, H.D. and B.S. Bolaria
Forthcoming "Expansion and Survival: Canadian Sociology and the Development of the Canadian Nation." In R.P. Mohan and D. Martindale, eds., *Handbook of Contemporary Developments in World Society*, 2nd ed. New York: Greenwood Press.

Ditchburn, W.E.
1918 Letter to Ivor Fourgner, Indian Agent, Bella Coola, November 5. *Public Archives of Canada*, British Columbia Superintendency, Inspector of Indian Agencies, Letterbook, 1918. RG 10, Volume 1321.

Dobb, M.
1963 *Studies in the Development of Capitalism*. London: Routledge and Kegan Paul.

Dobyns, H.F.
1983 *Their Number Became Thinned: Native American Population Dynamics in Eastern North America*. Knoxville: The University of Tennessee Press.

Dolan, R.
1980 *Native Employment: Opportunities for the Future*. Ottawa: Minister of Indian Affairs and Northern Development.

Dominion Bureau of Statistics
1953 *Ninth Census of Canada. Volume I. Population*. Ottawa: King's Printer.

1963 *Survey of Elementary and Secondary Education 1960-1961*. Ottawa: Queen's Printer.

Dosman, E.
1972 *Indians: The Urban Dilemma*. Toronto: McClelland and Stewart.

Doyal, L. with I. Pennell
1979 *The Political Economy of Health*. London: Pluto Press.

Drache, D. and W. Clement
1985 "Introduction: The Coming of Age of Canadian Political Economy." In D. Drache and W. Clement, eds., *The New Practical Guide to Canadian Political Economy*. Toronto: James Lorimer & Company, pp. ix-xxiv.

Driben, P.
1983 "The Nature of Métis Claims," *The Canadian Journal of Native Studies* 3, 1:183-196.

Driben, P. and R. Trudeau

1983 *When Freedom is Lost: The Dark Side of the Relationship Between Government and the Fort Hope Indian Band.* Toronto: University of Toronto Press.

Dube, P. M.

1987 "The Young Offender's Act: One Year Later (1985)." In C.T. Griffiths, ed., *Northern Youth in Crisis: A Challenge for Justice.* Burnaby, B.C.: Simon Fraser University for the Northern Conference, pp. 91-98.

Dunning, R.

1959 "Ethnic Relations and the Marginal Man in Canada," *Human Organization* 18, 3:117-122.

Durst, D.

1990 "Unemployment and Aboriginal People: A New Understanding." In G. Riches and G. Ternowetsky, eds., *Unemployment and Welfare.* Toronto: Garamond Press.

Dyck, L.

1986 "Are North American Indians Biochemically More Susceptible to the Effects of Alcohol?" *Native Studies Review* 2:85-95.

Dyck, N.

1980 "Indian, Métis, Native: Some Implications of Special Status," *Canadian Ethnic Studies* 12, 1:34-36.

1981 "The Politics of Special Status: Indian Associations and the Administration of Indian Affairs." In J. Dahlie and T. Fernando, eds., *Ethnicity, Power and Politics in Canada.* Agincourt, Ont.: Methuen Publications, pp. 279-291.

1983 "Representation and Leadership of a Provincial Indian Association." In A. Tanner, ed., *The Politics of Indianness.* St. John's: Institute of Social and Economic Research.

Easterbrook, M.A. and H.G.J. Aitken

1956 *Canadian Economic History.* Toronto: Macmillan.

Economic Council of Canada

1990 *Good Jobs, Bad Jobs: Employment in the Service Economy.* Ottawa: Minister of Supply and Services.

Eichler, M.

1988 *Families in Canada Today,* 2nd ed. Toronto: McGraw-Hill Ryerson.

Ekstedt, J. and C. Griffiths

1988 *Corrections in Canada: Policy and Practice,* 2nd ed. Toronto: Butterworths.

Elias, P.

1975 *Metropolis and Hinterland in Northern Manitoba.* Winnipeg: Manitoba Museum of Man and Nature.

1988 *The Dakota of the Canadian Northwest: Lessons for Survival.* Winnipeg: University of Manitoba Press.

Employment and Immigration Canada
1989 *Success in the Works: A Profile of Canada's Emerging Workforce.* Ottawa: Employment and Immigration Canada.

1990 *Employment Equity Act 1990 Annual Report.* Ottawa: Minister of Supply and Services Canada.

Erasmus, G.
1986 "NSR Comment," *Native Studies Review 2,* 2:53-63.

Evans, J. and A. Himelfarb
1987 "Counting Crime." In R. Linden, ed., *Criminology: A Canadian Perspective.* Toronto: Holt, Rinehart and Winston, pp. 43-73.

Fanon, F.
1968 *The Wretched of the Earth.* New York: Grove Press.

Federation of Saskatchewan Indians
1973 *Indian Education in Saskatchewan, Volume I.* Regina: Federation of Saskatchewan Indians.

Ferrier, T.
1906 *Indian Education in the North West.* Toronto: Department of Missionary Literature, Methodist Church.

Fields, D. and W. Stanbury
1975 *The Economic Impact of the Public Sector Upon the Indians of British Columbia.* Vancouver: University of British Columbia Press.

Fine, B.
1984 *Democracy and the Rule of Law.* London: Pluto Press.

Fisher, R.
1977 *Contact and Conflict: Indian-European Relations in British Columbia, 1774-1890.* Vancouver: University of British Columbia Press.

Forcese, D.
1975 *The Canadian Class Structure.* Toronto: McGraw-Hill Ryerson.

Four Worlds Development Project
1985 *Developing Healthy Communities: Fundamental Strategies for Health Promotion.* Lethbridge: The Four Worlds Development Project.

Frank, A.G.
1967 *Capitalism and Underdevelopment in Latin America.* New York: Monthly Review Press.

Frideres, J.S.
1987 "Native People and Canadian Education." In T. Wotherspoon, ed., *The Political Economy of Canadian Schooling.* Toronto: Methuen, pp. 275-289.

1988 *Native Peoples in Canada: Contemporary Conflicts,* 3rd ed. Scarborough, Ont.: Prentice-Hall.

Friends of the Indians of British Columbia
1912 "Notes of Interview Had at Colonial Office, Downing Street, 13th June, 1912." City of Vancouver Archives.

Friesen, G.
1984 *The Canadian Prairies: A History.* Toronto: University of Toronto Press.

Fritz, W. and C. D'Arcy
1983 "Comparisons: Indian and Non-Indian Use of Psychiatric Services." In P.S. Li and B.S. Bolaria, eds., *Racial Minorities in Multicultural Canada.* Toronto: Garamond Press, pp. 68-85.

Gaffield, C.
1990 "The Social and Economic Origins of Contemporary Families." In M. Baker, ed., *Families: Changing Trends in Canada, 2nd ed.* Toronto: McGraw-Hill Ryerson, pp. 23-40.

Gans, H.
1974 *More Equality.* New York: Vintage Books.

Gerber, L.M.
1990 "Multiple Jeopardy: A Socio-economic Comparison of Men and Women Among the Indian, Metis and Inuit Peoples of Canada," *Canadian Ethnic Studies* 22, 3:69-84.

Geshwender, J.
1978 *Racial Stratification in America.* New York: Wm. Brown and Company.

Gibbins, R.
1986 "Citizenship, Political and Intergovernmental Problems with Indian Self-Government." In J.R. Ponting, ed., *Arduous Journey.* Toronto: McClelland and Stewart.

Gibbins, R. and J.R. Ponting
1977 "Contemporary Prairie Perceptions of Canada's Native Peoples," *Prairie Forum* 2, 1 (May):57-81.

Giddens, A.
1971 *Capitalism and Modern Social Theory.* Cambridge: Cambridge University Press.

1979 *Central Problems in Social Theory.* London: Macmillan.

1985 *The Constitution of Society.* Cambridge: Polity Press.

Gladstone, P. and S. Jamieson
1950 "Unionism and the Fishing Industry of British Columbia," *Canadian Journal of Economics and Political Science* 26, 1:146-71.

Gonzalez, E.
1981 *Changing Economic Roles for Micmac Men and Women.* Ottawa: National Museum of Canada.

Gordon, M.
1964 *Assimilation in American Life.* New York: Oxford University Press.

Gorham, H.
1987 "Families of Mixed Descent in the Western Great Lakes Region." In B.A. Cox, ed., *Native People, Native Lands: Canadian Indians, Inuit and Métis.* Ottawa: Carleton University Press, pp. 37-55.

Goulding, W.
1991 "Reserve Stores, GST Spark Controversy." Saskatoon *Star-Phoenix,* January 12, p. C1.

Graham-Cumming, G.
1967 "The Health of the Original Canadians 1867-1967," *Medical Services Journal Canada* 23 (February):115-166.

Grant, G.
1983 *The Concrete Reserve: Corporate Programs for Indians in the Urban Workforce.* Montreal: Institute for Research on Public Policy.

Grant, K.R.
1988 "The Inverse Care Law in Canada: Differential Access Under Universal Free Health Insurance." In B.S. Bolaria and H.D. Dickinson, eds., *Sociology of Health Care in Canada.* Toronto: Harcourt Brace Jovanovich, pp. 118-134.

Green, M.B. and D.A. Stewart
1986 *Community Profiles of Socio-economic Change, 1982 1985.* Ottawa: Report 9-85, prepared for the Department of Indian Affairs and Northern Development.

Greenshields, V.
1991 "Tribal Council Report," Saskatoon *Star-Phoenix,* November 8, p. A11.

Gresko, J.
1979 "White 'Rites' and Indian 'Rites': Indian Education and Native Responses in the West." In D.C. Jones, N.M. Sheehan, and R.M. Stamp, eds., *Shaping the Schools of the Canadian West.* Calgary: Detselig, pp. 84-106.

1986 "Creating Little Dominions within the Dominion: Early Catholic Indian Schools in Saskatchewan and British Columbia." In J. Barman, Y. Hébert, and D. McCaskill, eds., *Indian Education in Canada. Volume 1: The Legacy.* Vancouver: University of British Columbia Press, pp. 88-109.

Griffiths, C.T.
1987 *Northern Youth in Crisis: A Challenge for Justice.* Burnaby, B.C.: Simon Fraser University for the Northern Conference.

Griffiths, C.T. and S.N. Verdun-Jones
1989 *Canadian Criminal Justice.* Toronto: Butterworths.

Griffiths, C.T. and J.C. Yerbury
1984 "Natives and Criminal Justice Policy: The Case of Native Policing," *Canadian Journal of Criminology* 26, 2:147-160.

Guilleman, J.
1978 "The Politics of National Integration: A Comparison of United States and Canadian Indian Administrations," *Social Problems* 25, 3:317-332.

Gustafson, R.W.

1978 "The Education of Canada's Indian Peoples: An Experience in Colonialism." University of Manitoba, unpublished M.A. thesis.

Hagan, J.

1974 "Criminal Justice and Native People: A Study of Incarceration in a Canadian Province," *Canadian Review of Sociology and Anthropology,* Special Issue (Aug.): 220-236.

1977 *The Disreputable Pleasures.* Toronto: University of Toronto Press.

Hamilton, R. and M. Barrett, eds.

1986 *The Politics of Diversity.* London: Verso.

Harding, J.

1971 "Canada's Indians: A Powerless Minority." In J. Harp and J. Hofley, eds., *Poverty in Canada.* Scarborough, Ont.: Prentice-Hall, pp. 239-252.

Harris, M.

1977 *Cannibals and Kings: The Origins of Cultures.* New York: Random House.

Hartnagel, T.

1987 "Correlates of Criminal Behavior." In R. Linden, ed., *Criminology: A Canadian Perspective.* Toronto: Holt, Rinehart and Winston, pp. 74-101.

Hartwig, M.

1978 "Capitalism and Aborigines: The Theory of Internal Colonialism and its Rivals." In E.L.Wheelwright and K. Buckley, eds., *Political Economy of Australian Capitalism* vol. 3. Sydney: Australia and New Zealand Book Company, pp. 119-141.

Hathaway, J.C.

1986 "Native Canadians and the Criminal Justice System: A Critical Examination of the Native Courtworker Program." *Saskatchewan Law Review* 49, 2:201-237.

Haveman, P., K. Couse, L. Foster, and R. Matonvich

1985 *Law and Order for Canada's Indigenous People.* Regina: School of Human Justice, University of Regina.

Hawkes, D.

1985 *Aboriginal Self Government.* Kingston, Ont.: Institute of Intergovernmental Relations.

Hawthorn, H.B., ed.

1966 *A Survey of the Contemporary Indians of Canada,* 2 Volumes. Ottawa: Queen's Printer.

Health and Welfare Canada

1980 *Canada's National-Provincial Health Program for the 1980s: A Commitment for Renewal.* Ottawa: Minister of Supply and Services.

1981 *The Health of Canadians: Report of the Canada Health Survey.* Ottawa: Minister of Supply and Services.

1985 *National Native Alcohol and Drug Abuse Program: A Progress Report.* Ottawa: Minister of Supply and Services.

1987 *Suicide in Canada,* Report of the National Task Force on Suicide in Canada. Ottawa: Minister of National Health and Welfare.

1988 *Health Status of Canadian Indians and Inuit, Update 1987.* Ottawa: Health and Welfare Canada.

1989. *1988 Vital Statistics for the Registered Indian Population of Saskatchewan.* Ottawa: Health and Welfare Canada.

1990. *1989 Vital Statistics for the Registered Indian Population of Saskatchewan.* Ottawa: Health and Welfare Canada.

Hepworth, H.P.

1980 *Foster Care and Adoption in Canada.* Ottawa: Canadian Council on Social Development.

Holmes, J.

1987 *Bill C-31, Equality or Disparity? The Effects of the New Indian Act on Native Women.* Ottawa: Canadian Advisory Council on the Status of Women.

Hooks, B.

1982 *Ain't I A Woman: Black Women and Feminism.* London: Pluto Press.

House, J.D.

1989 "Towards Sustainable Native Communities: Lessons from Newfoundland Outports." In P. Kariya, ed., *Native Socio-Economic Development in Canada: Change, Promise and Innovation.* Winnipeg: Institute of Urban Studies, pp. 47-65.

Hudson, P.

1987 "Manitoba's Indian Child Welfare Services: In the Balance." In J.S. Ismael and R.J. Thomlison, eds., *Perspectives on Social Services and Social Issues.* Ottawa: Canadian Council on Social Development, pp. 251-265.

Hudson, P. and B. McKenzie

1981 "Child Welfare and Native People: The Extension of Colonialism," *Social Worker* 49, 2 (Summer).

Hudson's Bay Record Society, The

1965 *Letters from Hudson Bay 1703-40,* Volume XXV, edited by K.D. Davies. London: The Hudson's Bay Record Society.

Hull, J.

1982 *Natives in a Class Society.* Saskatoon: One Sky.

Hylton, J.H.

1982 "The Native Offender in Saskatchewan: Some Implications For Crime Prevention Programming." *Canadian Journal of Criminology* 24, 2 (April): 121-131.

Indian Affairs Branch

1873 *Annual Report on Indian Affairs: Year ending June 30, 1872.* Sessional papers #23, 6(5). Ottawa: Queen's Printer.

Indian and Native Affairs Secretariate

1991 *Indian Economic Development Program.* Regina: Province of Saskatchewan.

Indian and Northern Affairs Canada

1987 *Indian Child and Family Services in Canada,* Indian Child and Family Services Task Force Final Report. Ottawa: Minister of Indian Affairs and Northern Development.

1989a "Indian and Inuit Education," *Department of Indian Affairs and Northern Development Information Binder,* Information Sheet No. 5 (April).

1989b *Basic Departmental Data 1989.* Ottawa: Minister of Supply and Services Canada.

1990 *Basic Departmental Data 1990.* Ottawa: Minister of Supply and Services Canada.

Indian-Eskimo Association of Canada

1966 *Conference on Concerns of Indians in British Columbia,* Theme: "Equal Opportunity in Our Land." Vancouver, December 2-4.

Innis, H.A.

1956 *Essays in Canadian Economic History.* Toronto: University of Toronto Press.

1970 *The Fur Trade in Canada.* Toronto: University of Toronto Press.

International Briefing Associates, Inc.

1990 *A National Action Plan for Police-Minority Relations in Canada,* An Agreement. Hull, P.Q.: International Briefing Associates, Inc.

Jamieson, E.

1922 "Indian Education in Canada." McMaster University, unpublished M.A. thesis (Education).

Jamieson, K.

1978 *Indian Women and the Law in Canada: Citizens Minus.* Ottawa: Minister of Supply and Services.

1981 "Sisters Under the Skin: An Exploration of the Implications of Feminist-Materialist Perspective Research," *Canadian Ethnic Studies* 13, 1:130-143.

Jenness, D.

1977 *The Indians of Canada,* 7th ed. Toronto: University of Toronto Press.

Johnston, B.H.

1988 *Indian School Days.* Toronto: Key Porter Books.

Johnston, P.

1983 *Native Children and the Child Welfare System.* Toronto: James Lorimer and Company.

Jolly, S.

1983 *Warehousing Indians: Fact Sheet on the Disproportionate Imprisonment of Native People in Ontario, 1981-1982.* Toronto: Ontario Native Council on Justice.

Jolly, S., C. Peters, and S. Spiegel
1979 *Progress Report on Government Action Taken Since the 1975 Federal-Provincial Conference on Native Peoples and the Criminal Justice System.* Ottawa and Toronto: Solicitor General of Canada and the Ontario Native Council on Justice.

Kamsack School Division #35
1991 "Education Equity Monitoring Report." Kamsack, Sask., January 3.

Katz, M.
1975 *The People of Hamilton, Canada West.* Cambridge: Cambridge University Press.

Kellough, G.
1980 "From Colonialism to Economic Imperialism: The Experience of the Canadian Indian." In J. Harp and J.R. Hofley, eds., *Structured Inequality in Canada.* Scarborough, Ont.: Prentice-Hall, pp. 343-377.

Kelly, A.R.
1974 "The Effectiveness of Indian Education in Saskatchewan." In *Indian Education in Saskatchewan, Volume II.* Regina: Federation of Saskatchewan Indians, pp. 136-139.

Kirkness, V.J.
1974 "Education of Indian and Metis." In D.B. Sealy and V.J. Kirkness, eds., *Indians Without Tipis.* Agincourt, Ont.: The Book Society of Canada, pp. 137-173.

Kline, M.
1989 "Women's Oppression and Racism: A Critique of the 'Feminist Standpoint," in Society for Socialist Studies, eds., *Race, Class, Gender: Bonds and Barriers.* Toronto: Between the Lines Press.

Knight, R.
1978 *Indians at Work: An Informal History of Native Indian Labour in British Columbia, 1858-1930.* Vancouver: New Star Books.

Koenig, D.J.
1987 "Conventional Crime." In R. Linden, ed., *Criminology: A Canadian Perspective.* Toronto: Holt, Rinehart and Winston, pp. 242-269.

Krauter, J.F. and M. Davis
1978 *Minority Canadians: Ethnic Groups.* Toronto: Methuen.

Krotz, L.
1990 *Indian Country: Inside Another Country.* Toronto: McClelland and Stewart.

Kuster, J.
1990 "Issues to Initiatives in the Inner-City Schools of the Regina Roman Catholic Separate School Division No. 81," November. Regina: Regina Catholic Board of Education.

Lachapelle, C.
1982 "Beyond Barriers: Native Women and the Women's Movement." In M. Fitzgerald, C. Guberman, and M. Wolfe, eds., *Still Ain't Satisfied.*

Toronto: The Women's Press.

Lanceley, D.
1991 "The Post-Secondary Assistance Program for Indian Education: The Vehicle for Change and the Voice of Opposition." In T. Wotherspoon, ed., *Hitting the Books: The Politics of Educational Retrenchment.* Toronto: Garamond Press, pp. 235-248.

LaPrairie, C.
1983 "Native Juveniles in Court: Some Preliminary Observations." In T. Fleming and L. Visano, eds., *Deviant Designations.* Toronto: Butterworths, pp. 337-350.

1984 "Selected Criminal Justice and Socio-demographic Data on Native Women," *Canadian Journal of Criminology* 26, 2:161-169.

1987 "Native Women and Crime in Canada: A Theoretical Model." In E. Adelberg and C. Currie, eds., *Canadian Women in Conflict with the Law.* Vancouver: Press Gang Publishers, pp. 103-112.

1988 "The Young Offenders Act and Aboriginal Youth." In J. Hudson, J.P. Hornick, and B.A. Burrows, eds., *Justice and the Young Offender in Canada.* Toronto: Wall and Thompson, pp. 159-168.

LaPrairie, C.P. and C.T. Griffiths
1982 "Native Indian Delinquency and the Juvenile Court: A Review of Recent Findings," *Canadian Legal Aid Bulletin* 5:39-46.

Larocque, G.Y. and R.P. Gauvin
1989 *1986 Census Highlights on Registered Indians: Annotated Tables.* Ottawa: Minister of Supply and Services.

LaRusic, I.E., S. Bouchard, A. Penn, T. Brelsford, J.G. Deschenes, and R.F. Salisbury
1979 *Negotiating a Way of Life: Initial Cree Experience with the Administrative Structure Arising from the James Bay Agreement.* Ottawa: Department of Indian and Northern Affairs.

Lasch, C.
1977 *Haven in a Heartless World.* New York: Basic Books.

LaViolette, F.E.
1973 *The Struggle for Survival.* Toronto: University of Toronto Press.

Leadbetter, D.
1984 *Essays on the Political Economy of Alberta.* Toronto: New Hogtown Press.

Leslie, J. and R. Maguire
1978 *The Historical Development of the Indian Act.* Ottawa: Indian and Northern Affairs Canada.

Li, P.
1988 *Ethnic Inequality in a Class Society.* Toronto: Wall and Thompson.

Lithman, Y.G.
1984 *The Community Apart: A Case Study of a Canadian Indian Reserve Community.* Winnipeg: University of Manitoba Press.

Loh, S.
1990 *Population Projections of Registered Indians, 1986-2001.* Ottawa: Department of Indian Affairs and Northern Development.

Loney, M.
1987 "The Construction of Dependency: The Case of the Grand Rapids Hydro Project," *The Canadian Journal of Native Studies* 7, 1:57-78.

Long, J.A. and M. Boldt
1988 "Introduction." In J.A. Long and M. Boldt, eds., *Governments in Conflict? Provinces and Indian Nations in Canada.* Toronto: University of Toronto Press.

Long, J.A. M. Boldt, and L. Little Bear
1982 "Federal Indian Policy and Indian Self-government in Canada: An Analysis of a Current Proposal," *Canadian Public Policy* 8, 2:189-199.

Loxley, J.
1981 "The 'Great Northern' Plan." *Studies in Political Economy* 6 (Autumn): 151-182.

Lysyk, K.M.
1977 *Alaska Highway Pipeline Inquiry.* Ottawa: Minister of Supply and Services.

Mabindisa, I.K.
1989 "Indian Control of Indian Education in Alberta: The Picture in 1989." *Our Schools/Our Selves* 1, 3 (April): 107-114.

McCaskill, D.
1985 *Patterns of Criminality and Correction Among Native Offenders in Manitoba: A Longitudinal Analysis.* Saskatoon: Correctional Service of Canada, Department of the Solicitor General, Prairie Region.

MacDonald, J.A.
1987 "The Program of the Spallumcheen Indian Band in British Columbia as a Model of Indian Child Welfare." In J.S. Ismael and R.J. Thomlison eds., *Perspectives on Social Services and Social Issues.* Ottawa: Canadian Council on Social Development, pp. 237-249.

McGivern, R.N.
1990 *Communities of Learners: A Study of Models of Brokerage and Affiliation between Native Organizations and Public Post Secondary Institutes.* Vancouver: Joint Steering Committee of Secwepemc Cultural Education Society and Simon Fraser University.

Mackie, C.
1986 "Some Reflections on Indian Economic Development." In J. Ponting, ed., *Arduous Journey: Canadian Indians and Decolonization.* Toronto: McClelland and Stewart, pp. 211-227.

McLaren, P.
1989 *Life in Schools: An Introduction to Critical Pedagogy in the Foundations of Education.* New York: Longman.

McLean, L.A.
1912 Letter to Rev. A.E. Green, March 25. City of Vancouver Archives, A.E. Green Papers, Additional Manuscripts 330, Volume 1, file 1.

McLean, P.
1991 Interview on the Roy Norris Show, CFQC Radio (Saskatoon), April 15.

McMillan, A.D.
1988 *Native Peoples and Cultures of Canada: An Anthropological Overview.* Vancouver: Douglas & McIntyre.

Mahon, R.
1977 "Canadian Public Policy: The Unequal Structure of Representation." In L. Panitch, ed., *The Canadian State: Political Economy and Political Power.* Toronto: University of Toronto Press, pp. 165-198.

Mandel, M.
1991 "The Great Repression: Criminal Punishment in the Nineteen-Eighties." In L. Samuelson and B. Schissel, eds., *Criminal Justice: Sentencing Issues and Reform.* Toronto: Garamond Press, pp. 177-226.

Manitoba Attorney General
1989 *Submission to the Aboriginal Justice Inquiry.* Winnipeg: Manitoba Attorney General.

Manitoba Health Services Commission
1989 *Annual Statistics 1988-89.* Winnipeg: Province of Manitoba.

Manuel, G. and M. Poslums
1974 *The Fourth World: An Indian Reality.* Toronto: Collier-Macmillan Canada Ltd.

Marchak, P.
1985 "Canadian Political Economy." *The Canadian Review of Sociology and Anthropology* 22, 5 (December): 673-709.

Marshall, T.H.
1963 *Sociology at the Crossroads and Other Essays.* London: Heinemann.

Marx, K.
1967 *Capital.* Edited by F. Engels. New York: International Publishers Co.

1970 *Wages, Price and Profit.* Peking: Foreign Languages Press.

1973 *Grundrisse: Foundations of the Critique of Political Economy.* New York: Vantage Books.

Mason, B.
1988 "Implementing the Young Offenders Act: An Alberta Perspective." In J. Hudson, J.P. Hornick, and B.A. Burrows, eds., *Justice and the Young Offender in Canada.* Toronto: Wall and Thompson, pp. 51-63.

Mason, D.
1986 "Controversies and Continuities in Race and Ethnic Relations." In J. Rex and D. Mason, eds., *Theories of Race and Ethnic Relations.* Cambridge: Cambridge University Press, pp. 1-19.

Matthews, J.S.
1934 "Figures re: Award by Arbitrators for 8 Acres Taken for Burrard Bridge Footings." City of Vancouver Archives, J.S. Matthews Papers, Additional Manuscripts 54, Volume 13, file 17.

Medical Services Branch, Saskatchewan
1989 *1988 Vital Statistics for the Registered Indian Population of Saskatchewan.* Regina: Health Planning Unit, Medical Services Branch, Saskatchewan Region.

Miles, R.
1982 *Racism and Migrant Labour.* London: Routledge and Kegan Paul.

1987 *Capitalism and Unfree Labour.* London: Tavistock Publications.

1989 *Racism.* London: Routledge.

Miller, J.
1989 *Skyscrapers Hide the Heavens.* Toronto: University of Toronto Press.

Miller, L.
1991 "Family Problems and Problem Families." In B.S. Bolaria, ed., *Social Issues and Contradictions in Canadian Society.* Toronto: Harcourt Brace Jovanovich, pp. 57-85.

Mishra, R.
1977 *Society and Social Policy.* Toronto: Macmillan.

1986 *The Welfare State in Crisis.* Brighton: Wheat Sheaf.

Mitchell, M. and A. Franklin
1984 "When You Don't Know the Language, Listen to the Silence: An Historical Overview of Native Indian Women in B.C." In B. Latham and R. Pazdro, eds., *Not Just Pin Money.* Victoria: Camosun College.

Mohr, J.W.
1990 "Sentencing Revisited," *Canadian Journal of Criminology* 32, 3:531-535.

Moore, P.E., H.D. Kruse, F.F. Tisdall, and R.S.C. Corrigan
1946 "Medical Survey of Nutrition Among the Northern Manitoba Indians," *Canadian Medical Association Journal* 54 (March): 223-233.

Morinis, E.A.
1982 "Skid Row Indians and the Politics of Self." *Culture* 2, 3:93-105.

Morley, J.
1869 Letter to Joseph Trutch, Chief Commissioner of Land & Works, April 27. In *Papers Connected with the Indian Land Question, British Columbia.* Victoria: Government Printer, pp. 58-59.

Morris, A.
1880 *The Treaties of Canada with the Indians of Manitoba and the North-West Territories.* Toronto: Belfords, Clark & Co. [1971]

Morse, B. and L. Lock
1988 *Native Offenders' Perceptions of the Criminal Justice System.* Ottawa: Department of Justice Canada.

Moss, W.
1987 *History of Discriminatory Laws Affecting Aboriginal People.* Ottawa: Library of Parliament Research Branch.

Moyer, S. P. Kopeiman, C. LaPrairie, and B. Billingsley
1985 *Native and Non-Native Admissions to Federal, Provincial and Territorial Correctional Institutions.* Ottawa: Solicitor General of Canada, working paper no. 1985-34.

Munroe, V.
1988 "Educated Natives Have Difficulty Finding Work," Saskatoon *Star-Phoenix,* June 3.

Myers, G.
1972 *A History of Canadian Wealth.* Toronto: James Lewis and Samuel.

Myles, J., G. Picot, and T. Wannell
1988 "The Changing Wage Distribution of Jobs, 1981-1986." In *The Labour Force,* Statistics Canada, October: 85-129.

Nagler, M.
1972 "Minority Values and Economic Achievement: the Case of the North American Indian." In M. Nagler, ed., *Perspectives on the North American Indian.* Toronto: McClelland and Stewart, pp. 131-141.

1973 *Indians in the City.* Ottawa: Canadian Research Centre for Anthropology, St. Paul University.

1975 *Natives Without a Home.* Don Mills, Ont.: Longman.

National Council of Welfare
1979 *In the Best Interests of the Child.* Ottawa: National Council of Welfare.

1985 *Poverty Profile 1985.* Ottawa: Minister of Supply and Services Canada.

1990 *Women and Poverty Revisited.* Ottawa: Minister of Supply and Services Canada.

National Indian Brotherhood
1972 "Indian Control of Indian Education: A Position Paper." Ottawa: National Indian Brotherhood.

1976 "Policy on Indian Health Services: Working Draft." Ottawa: National Indian Brotherhood.

1978 "National Indian Brotherhood Commission Inquiry on Indian Health: Statement of Principle — Adopted November 9." Ottawa: National Indian Brotherhood.

National Parole-Board
1990 "Study of Suspensions on Conditional Release Programs for Aboriginal and Non-Aboriginal Offenders, 1987-88." Ottawa: National Parole Board.

Native Counselling Services of Alberta
1982 "Creating a Monster: Issues in Community Program Control," *Canadian Journal of Criminology* 24, 3 (July): 323-328.

Native Curriculum Review Committee
1984 *Developments in Indian and Metis Curriculum, Annual Report.* Regina: Saskatchewan Education.

Naylor, T.
1975 *The History of Canadian Business, 1867-1914, Vols. I and II.* Toronto: James Lorimer.

Neilsen, E.
1985 *Improved Program Delivery: Indians and Natives, A Study Team Report to the Task Force on Program Review.* Ottawa: Minister of Supply and Services.

Ng, R.
1988a "Racism, Sexism and Canadian Nationalism." In Society for Socialist Studies, eds., *Race, Class, Gender: Bonds and Barriers.* Toronto: Between the Lines Press.

1988b *The Politics of Community Services.* Toronto: Garamond Press.

Nicholson, D.
1984 "Indian Government in Federal Policy: An Insider's Views." In L. Little Bear, M. Boldt, and A. Long, eds., *Pathways to Self-Determination.* Toronto: University of Toronto Press.

Nielsen, M.O.
1990 "Canadian Correctional Policy and Native Inmates: The Control of Social Dynamite," *Canadian Ethnic Studies* 22, 3:110-121.

Nock, D.A.
1978 "The Social Effects of Missionary Education: A Victorian Case Study." In R.W. Nelsen and D.A. Nock, eds., *Reading, Writing and Riches: Education and Socio-Economic Order in North America.* Toronto: Between The Lines, pp. 233-250.

Northern Lights School Division #113
1990 "Education Equity Report," December.

Nova Scotia, Province of
1989 *Royal Commission on the Donald Marshall Jr. Prosecution, Volume I: Findings and Recommendations.* Halifax: Province of Nova Scotia.

Nutrition Canada
1975 *The Indian Survey Report.* Ottawa: Department of National Health and Welfare.

Offe, C.
1975 "The Theory of the Capitalist State and the Problem of Policy Formation." In L. Lindberg et al. eds., *Stress and Contradiction in Modern Capitalism.* Lexington: D.C. Heath.

Olson, D.
1980 *The State Elite.* Toronto: McClelland and Stewart.

O'Malley, M.
1980 "Without Reservation," *Canadian Business* 4 (April): 37-43.

O'Meara, Rev. A.E.

1910 "The British Columbia Indian Land Situation," Lecture, January 4. City of Vancouver Archives, Wade Family Papers, Additional Manuscripts 44, Volume 18, file 9.

Omi, M. and H. Winant

1986 *Racial Formation in the United States.* New York: Routledge & Kegan Paul.

O'Neil, J.D.

1988 "Referrals to Traditional Healers: The Role of Medical Interpreters." In D.E. Young, ed., *Health Care Issues in the Canadian North.* Edmonton: Boreal Institute for Northern Studies Occasional Publication Number 26, pp. 29-38.

Ontario Native Council on Justice

1981 *Justice-Related Children and Family Services for Native People in Ontario,* A Discussion Paper. Toronto: Ontario Native Council on Justice.

Opekokew, D.

1987 *The Political and Legal Inequalities Among Aboriginal Peoples in Canada.* Kingston, Ont.: Institute of Intergovernmental Relations Background Paper Number 14.

Osberg, L.

1988 *The Future of Work in Canada: Trends, Issues and Forces for Change.* Ottawa/Montreal: Canadian Council on Social Development.

Palmer, B.

1983 *Working Class Experience: The Rise and Reconstitution of Canadian Labour, 1800-1980.* Toronto: Butterworths.

Panitch, L., ed.

1977 *The Canadian State: Political Economy and Political Power.* Toronto: University of Toronto Press.

Paquette, J.

1986 *Aboriginal Self-Government and Education in Canada.* Kingston, Ont.: Institute of Intergovernmental Relations Background Paper Number 10.

Park, R.

1950 *Race and Culture.* Glencoe, Ill.: Free Press.

Patterson, E.P.

1972 *The Canadian Indians: A History Since 1500.* Toronto: Collier-Macmillan Canada Ltd.

1978 "Andrew Paull and the Early History of B.C. Indian Organizations." In I. Getty and D. Smith, eds. *One Century Later.* Vancouver: University of British Columbia Press.

Pentland, H.C.

1981 *Labour and Capital in Canada 1650-1860.* Toronto: James Lorimer and Company.

Perreault, J., L. Paquette, and M.V. George

1985 *Population Projections of Registered Indians, 1982 to 1996.* Ottawa: Indian and Northern Affairs Canada.

Peters, E.J.

1984 *Native Households in Winnipeg: Strategies of Co-Residence and Financial Support.* Winnipeg: Institute of Urban Studies.

1989 "Federal and Provincial Responsibilities for the Cree, Naskapi and Inuit Under the James Bay and Northern Quebec, and Northeastern Quebec Agreements." In D.C. Hawkes, ed., *Aboriginal Peoples and Government Responsibility.* Ottawa: Carleton University Press, pp. 173-242.

Phillips, C.E.

1957 *The Development of Education in Canada.* Toronto: W.J. Gage.

Phizacklea, A. and R. Miles

1980 *Labour and Racism.* London: Routledge & Kegan Paul.

Picard, A.

1991 "Crees Vow to Seize Land if Quebec Separates," The *Globe and Mail* (Toronto), July 31, p. A3.

Platiel, R.

1991 "Native Election Features Drama, Whisper Campaign," The *Globe and Mail* (Toronto), June 13, p. A7.

Ponting, J.R.

1986 "Relations Between the Bands and the Department of Indian Affairs: A Case of Internal Colonialism?" In J.R. Ponting, ed., *Arduous Journey: Canadian Indians and Decolonization.* Toronto: McClelland and Stewart.

1988a *Profiles of Public Opinion on Canadian Natives and Native Issues: Module 4 — Native People, Finances, & Services.* Calgary: Research Unit for Public Policy Studies Research Report #88-01.

1988b "Public Opinion on Aboriginal Peoples' Issues in Canada." *Canadian Social Trends* 11 (Winter): 9-17.

Ponting, J.R. and R. Gibbins

1980 *Out of Irrelevance: A Socio-political Introduction to Indian Affairs of Canada.* Toronto: Butterworths.

Population Reference Bureau

1988 *1988 World Population Data Sheet.* Washington: Population Reference Bureau, Inc.

Porter, J.

1965 *The Vertical Mosaic.* Toronto: University of Toronto Press.

Powless, R.C.

1985 "Native People and Employment: A National Tragedy." In R.S. Abella, ed., *Research Studies of the Commission on Equality in Employment.* Ottawa: Minister of Supply and Services, pp. 591-610.

Pratt, A.

1989 "Federalism in the Era of Aboriginal Self-Government." In D.C. Hawkes, ed., *Aboriginal Peoples and Government Responsibility.* Ottawa: Carleton University Press, pp. 19-57.

Province of Manitoba

1991 *Report of the Aboriginal Justice Inquiry of Manitoba, Volume 1: The Justice System and Aboriginal People.* Winnipeg: Queen's Printer.

Provincial Court of Saskatchewan

1990 (June) "Judgement between: Her Majesty the Queen, and Dolly Pratt and Winona Luanne Stevenson." J.B.J. Nutting, PCJ. Saskatoon: Provincial Court of Saskatchewan.

Purich, D.

1986 *Our Land: Native Rights in Canada.* Toronto: James Lorimer.

Ratner, R. and J. McMullan

1987 *State Control: Criminal Justice Politics in Canada.* Vancouver: University of British Columbia Press.

Ray, A.

1974 *Indians in the Fur Trade.* Toronto: University of Toronto Press.

1989 "Periodic Shortages, Native Welfare and the Hudson's Bay Company, 1670-1930." In K. Coates and W. Morrison, eds., *Interpreting Canada's North.* Toronto: Copp Clark Pitman.

1990 *The Canadian Fur Trade in the Industrial Age.* Toronto: University of Toronto Press.

Rea, K.

1968 *The Political Economy of the Canadian North.* Toronto: University of Toronto Press.

1976 *The Political Economy of Northern Development,* No. 36. Ottawa: Science Council of Canada Background Study, Information Canada.

Reeves, W.

1986 "Native Societies: The Professions as a Model for Self-determination for Urban Natives." In J.R. Ponting, ed., *Arduous Journey: Canadian Indians and Decolonization.* Toronto: McClelland and Stewart, pp. 342-358.

Review Committee on Indian and Metis Adoptions and Placements

1983 *Interim Report.* Winnipeg: Province of Manitoba.

Rex, J.

1970 *Race Relations in Sociological Theory.* London: Routledge.

Richardson, R.L.

1886 "The Indian Problem." In *Facts and Figures — The Highest Testimony,* compiled by R.L. Richardson. Ottawa, pp. 26-29.

Ross, R.

1989 "Leaving Our White Eyes Behind: The Sentencing of Native Accused," *Canadian Native Law Reporter* 3:1-15.

1990 *Cultural Blindness and the Justice System in Remote Native Communities.* Paper presented at the "Sharing Common Ground" conference on Aboriginal policing services. Edmonton.

Rowe and Associates
1989 *The Vancouver Urban Indian Needs Assessment Study*, final report. Vancouver: Rowe and Associates.

Rushforth, S.
1979 "Country Food." In M. Watkins, ed., *The Dene Nation: the Colony Within*. Toronto: University of Toronto Press.

Ryan, J.
1978 *Wall of Words: The Betrayal of the Urban Indian*. Toronto: Peter Martin Associates.

Ryerson, S.
1960 *The Founding of Canada*. Toronto: Progress Books.

Samuelson, L.
1991 "Social Reproduction and Social Control: A Political Economy of Sentencing Reform in Canada." In L. Samuelson and B. Schissel, eds., *Criminal Justice: Sentencing Issues and Reform*. Toronto: Garamond Press, pp. 59-80.

Santoro, A.
1991 "Wilson Decries Lobby to Keep Siddon," *Windspeaker* 9, 6:7.

Saskatchewan Education
1985a *Plan of Action in Response to "Reaching Out"*. Regina: Saskatchewan Education.

1985b *Reaching Out: The Report of the Indian and Métis Education Consultations*. Regina: Saskatchewan Education.

1988 *Report on Developments in Indian and Métis Curriculum*. Regina: The Indian & Métis Curriculum Advisory Committee, Saskatchewan Education.

1989 *Indian and Métis Education Policy from Kindergarten to Grade XII*. Regina: Saskatchewan Education.

Saskatchewan Health
1988 *Statistical Tables Supplementing the Annual Report 1987-88, Saskatchewan Hospital Services Plan*. Regina: Government of Saskatchewan.

Saskatchewan Human Rights Commission
1990 *Meeting the Challenge: Annual Report 1990*. Saskatoon: Saskatchewan Human Rights Commission.

Saskatchewan Indian Agriculture Program
1989 *Annual Report 1988-1989*. Regina: Saskatchewan Indian Agriculture Program.

Saskatchewan Indian Justice Review Committee
1992 *Report of the Saskatchewan Indian Justice Review Committee*. Regina: Government of Saskatchewan.

Saskatchewan Métis Justice Review Committee
1992 *Report of the Saskatchewan Métis Justice Review Committee*. Regina: Government of Saskatchewan.

Saskatoon Catholic Board of Education
1991 "Circle of Life: Education Equity Program Progress Report — Year Four." Saskatoon: Saskatoon Catholic Board of Education.

Saskatoon Star-Phoenix
1991a "Business Potential for Natives Tremendous: Spokesman," Saskatoon *Star-Phoenix*, May 24, p. A5.

1991b "Native Educational Funding Request Rejected by Siddon," Saskatoon *Star-Phoenix*, October 1, p. B5.

Sassen, S.
1988 *The Mobility of Labor and Capital.* Cambridge: Cambridge University Press.

Satzewich, V.
1989 "Racisms: The Reactions to the Chinese Migrants in Canada at the Turn of the Century," *International Sociology* 4, 3:311-327.

1991 *Racism and the Incorporation of Foreign Labour.* London: Routledge.

Schmeiser, D.
1974 *The Native Offender and the Law.* Ottawa: Information Canada.

Schultz, T.W.
1961 "Investment in Human Capital." *American Economic Review* 51 (March): 1-17.

Schwartz, B.
1985 *First Principles: Constitutional Reform with Respect to the Aboriginal Peoples of Canada, 1982-1984.* Kingston, Ont.: Institute of Intergovernmental Relations Background Paper Number 6.

Scott, D.C.
1931 *The Administration of Indian Affairs in Canada.* Ottawa: The Canadian Institute of International Affairs.

Sealey, D.B.
1974 "The Indians of Canada: An Historical Sketch." In D.B. Sealey and V.J. Kirkness, eds., *Indians Without Tipis.* Agincourt, Ont.: The Book Society of Canada, pp. 9-37.

Sealey, D.B. and A. Lussier
1975 *The Métis: Canada's Forgotten People.* Winnipeg: Pemmican Publications.

Shah, C.P. and C.P. Farkas
1985 "The Health of Indians in Canadian Cities: A Challenge to the Health Care System." *Canadian Medical Association Journal* 133: 859-863.

Shore, M.
1987 *The Science of Social Redemption.* Toronto: University of Toronto Press.

Shumiatcher, M.
1971 *Welfare: Hidden Backlash.* Toronto: McClelland and Stewart.

Siggner, A.

1980 "A Socio-demographic Profile of Indians in Canada." In J.R. Ponting and R. Gibbins, eds., *Out of Irrelevance: A Socio-political Introduction to Indian Affairs of Canada*. Toronto: Butterworths, pp. 31-65.

1986 "The Socio-demographic Conditions of Registered Indians" *Canadian Social Trends* (Winter): 2-9.

Siggner, A. and C. Locatelli

1980 *Regional Population Projections by Age, Sex and Residence for Canada's Registered Indian Population, 1976-1991*. Ottawa: Research Branch, Department of Indian Affairs and Northern Development.

1981 *An Overview of Demographic, Social and Economic Conditions Among British Columbia's Registered Indian Population*. Ottawa: Minister of Indian Affairs and Northern Development.

Silman, J.

1987 *Enough is Enough: Aboriginal Women Speak Out*. Toronto: Women's Press.

Slattery, B.

1987 "Understanding Aboriginal Rights," *The Canadian Bar Review* 66: 727-783.

Smith, D.G., ed.

1975 *Canadian Indians and the Law: Selected Documents, 1663-1972*. Toronto: McClelland and Stewart.

Smucker, J.

1980 *Industrialization in Canada*. Scarborough, Ont.: Prentice-Hall.

Solicitor General Canada

1975 *Native Peoples and Justice*. Reports on the National Conference and the Federal-Provincial Conference on Native Peoples and the Criminal Justice System, both held in Edmonton. Ottawa: Communication Division, Ministry of the Solicitor General.

1982 *Canadian Urban Victimization Survey*. Ottawa: Solicitor General Canada.

1988 *Final Report: Task Force on Aboriginal Peoples in Federal Corrections*. Ottawa: Minister of Supply and Services.

Solomos, J.

1989 *Black Youth, Racism and the State*. Cambridge: Cambridge University Press.

Stabler, J.C.

1989a "Dualism and Development in the Northwest Territories," *Economic Development and Cultural Change* 37, 4 (July):805-839.

1989b "Jobs, Leisure and Traditional Pursuits: Activities of Native Males in the Northwest Territories," *Polar Record* 25, 155:295-302.

1990 "Native Participation in Northern Development: The Impending Crisis in the NWT," *Canadian Public Policy* 16, 3:262-283.

Stamp, R.M.

1977 "Canadian Education and National Identity." In A. Chaiton and N. McDonald, eds., *Canadian Schools and Canadian Identity.* Toronto: Gage, pp. 29-37.

Stanbury, W. and J. Siegel

1975 *Success and Failure: Indians in Urban Society.* Vancouver: University of British Columbia Press.

Stasiulis, D.

1987 "Rainbow Feminism: Perspectives on Minority Women in Canada," *Resources for Feminist Research* 16, 1:5-9.

1988 "Capitalism, Democracy and the Canadian State." In D. Forcese and S. Richer, eds., *Social Issues: Sociological Views of Canada.* Scarborough: Prentice-Hall, pp. 223-261.

Statistics Canada

1974 *Perspective Canada.* Ottawa: Information Canada.

1977 *Perspective Canada II.* Ottawa: Minister of Supply and Services.

1978 *Historical Compendium of Education Statistics from Confederation to 1975.* Ottawa: Minister of Industry, Trade and Commerce.

1983 *Historical Statistics of Canada,* 2nd ed. Ottawa: Minister of Supply and Services.

1984 *Canada's Native People.* Ottawa: Minister of Supply and Services.

1986 *Mortality: Summary List of Cause, Vital Statistics Volume III.* Ottawa: Minister of Supply and Services.

1988 *Household Facilities and Equipment, 1988.* Ottawa: Minister of Supply and Services.

1989 *Data Book on Canada's Aboriginal Population from the 1986 Census of Canada.* Ottawa: Minister of Supply and Services.

1990 *Women in Canada: A Statistical Report,* 2nd ed. Ottawa: Minister of Supply and Services.

1991 *Education in Canada 1989-90.* Ottawa: Minister of Industry, Science and Technology.

Steinberg, S.

1981 *The Ethnic Myth.* Boston: Beacon Press.

Stevens, S.

1991 "Aboriginal People and the Canadian Justice System." In L. Samuelson and B. Schissel, eds., *Criminal Justice: Sentencing Issues and Reforms.* Toronto: Garamond Press, pp. 227-241.

Stevenson, D.

1968 *Problems of Eskimo Relocation for Industrial Employment.* Ottawa: Department of Indian Affairs and Northern Development.

Stevenson, W.L.
1991 "Prairie Indians and Higher Education: An Historical Overview, 1876-1977." In T. Wotherspoon, ed., *Hitting the Books: The Politics of Educational Retrenchment.* Toronto: Garamond Press, pp. 215-234.

Stewart, D.A.
1986 *Perceived Impacts of the Norman Wells Project on Social Conditions and Native Peoples.* Ottawa: Report 5-85, prepared for the Department of Indian Affairs and Northern Development.

Stirling, R. and D. Kouri
1979 "Unemployment Indexes: The Canadian Context." In J. Fry, ed., *Economy, Class and Social Reality.* Toronto: Butterworths.

Struthers, G.
1990a "Mohawk Supporters Rally in Saskatoon," Saskatoon *Star-Phoenix,* August 18, p. A3.

1990b "Saskatchewan Chiefs Maintain Stand Against Violence," Saskatoon *Star-Phoenix,* August 28, p. A10.

1990c "Saskatchewan Indian Leaders Opposed to Violence," Saskatoon *Star-Phoenix,* August 17, p. A7.

Stymeist, D.H.
1975 *Ethnics and Indians: Social Relations in a Northwestern Ontario Town.* Toronto: Peter Martin Associates.

Sugar, F. and L. Fox
1989-90 "Nistum Peyako Sht'wawin Iskwewak: Breaking Chains," *Canadian Journal of Women's Law* 3:465-482.

Sutherland, N.
1976 *Children in English Canadian Society, 1880-1920.* Toronto: University of Toronto Press.

Tabb, W.
1970 *The Political Economy of the Black Ghetto.* New York: W.W. Norton and Company.

Task Force on Federally Sentenced Women
1990 *Creating Choices: The Report of the Task Force on Federally Sentenced Women.* Ottawa: Correctional Services Canada.

Task Force on the Educational Needs of Native Peoples of Ontario
1976 *Summary Report of the Task Force on the Educational Needs of Native Peoples of Ontario.* Toronto, June 30.

Task Force to Review Comprehensive Claims Policy
1985 *Living Treaties: Lasting Agreements, Report of the Task Force to Review Comprehensive Claims Policy.* Ottawa: Department of Indian Affairs and Northern Development.

Titley, B.
1986 *A Narrow Vision.* Vancouver: University of British Columbia Press.

Tobias, J.

1976 "Protection, Civilization, Assimilation: An Outline of Canada's Indian Policy," *Western Canadian Journal of Anthropology* 6, 2:13-30.

1987 "Indian Reserves in Western Canada: Indian Homelands or Devices for Assimilation?" In B.A. Cox, ed., *Native People, Native Lands: Canadian Indians, Inuit and Métis.* Ottawa: Carleton University Press, pp. 148-157.

Trigger, B.

1985 *Natives and Newcomers: Canada's Heroic Age Reconsidered.* Montreal and Kingston: McGill-Queen's University Press.

Turner, B.

1986 *Citizenship and Capitalism.* London: Allen and Unwin.

Tyler, E.

1966 "The Farmer as a Social Class in the Prairie Region." In M. Tremblay and W. Anderson, eds., *Rural Canada in Transition.* Ottawa: Agricultural Economics Research Council of Canada.

Upton, L.F.S.

1973 "The Origins of Canadian Indian Policy," *Journal of Canadian Studies* 8, 4:51-61.

Urry, J.

1981 *The Anatomy of Capitalist Societies: The Economy, Civil Society and the State.* London: Macmillan.

Usher, P.J.

1976 "Evaluating Country Food in the Northern Native Economy," *Arctic* 29, 2:105-120.

Valentine, V.

1980 "Native Peoples and Canadian Society: A Profile of Issues and Trends." In R. Breton, J. Reitz, and V. Valentine, eds., *Cultural Boundaries and the Cohesion of Canada.* Montreal: Institute for Research in Public Policy, pp. 45-135.

Vallee, F.

1988 "Inequality and Identity in Multiethnic Societies." In D. Forcese and S. Richler, eds., *Social Issues: Sociological Views of Canada*, 2nd ed. Scarborough, Ont.: Prentice-Hall, pp. 129-150.

Van Kirk, S.

1980 *Many Tender Ties.* Winnipeg: Watson and Dwyer Publishing.

Veltmeyer, H.

1986 *Canadian Class Structure.* Toronto: Garamond Press.

Verdun-Jones, S.N. and G.K. Muirhead

1982 "The Native in the Criminal Justice System: Canadian Research." In C. L. Boydell and I. A. Connidis, eds., *The Canadian Criminal Justice System.* Toronto: Holt, Rinehart and Winston, pp. 266-281.

Verney, D.

1986 *Three Civilizations, Two Cultures, One State: Canada's Political Traditions.* Durham: Duke University Press.

Waitzkin, H.

1983 *The Second Sickness.* New York: Free Press.

Waldram, J.B.

1988 *As Long as the Rivers Run: Hydroelectric Development and Native Communities in Western Canada.* Winnipeg: University of Manitoba Press.

Ward, M.

1984 *The Adoption of Native Canadian Children.* Cobalt, Ont.: Highway Book Shop.

Ward, N.

1950 *The Canadian House of Commons: Representation.* Toronto: University of Toronto Press.

Wardhaugh, R.

1983 *Language and Nationhood.* Vancouver: New Star Books.

Warnock, J.

1988 *Free Trade and the New Right Agenda.* Vancouver: New Star Books.

Watkins, M.

1972 *The Dene Nation: A Colony Within.* Toronto: University of Toronto Press.

Weaver, S.

1981 *Making Canadian Indian Policy: The Hidden Agenda 1968-1970.* Toronto: University of Toronto Press.

1985 "Federal Policy-Making for Métis and Non-status Indians in the Context of Native Policy," *Canadian Ethnic Studies* 17, 2:80-102.

1986 "Indian Policy in the New Conservative Government, Part II: The Nielson Task Force in the Context of Recent Policy Initiatives," *Native Studies Review* 2, 2:1-45.

1990 "A New Paradigm in Canadian Indian Policy for the 1990s," *Canadian Ethnic Studies* 22, 3:8-18.

n.d. "Report on Archival Research" (Reasons for introduction of s.6 into s.c. 1869, c.6).

Welfare and Training Service of the Indian Affairs Branch

1947 *Brief to the Special Joint Committee on the Indian Act.* Ottawa.

Wharf, B.

1989 *Toward First Nation Control of Child Welfare: A Review of Emerging Developments in B.C.* Victoria: University of Victoria.

Wien, F.

1986 *Rebuilding the Economic Base of Indian Communities: the Mic Mac in Nova Scotia.* Montreal: Institute for Research on Public Policy.

Wilson, J.D.

1986 "'No Blanket to be Worn in School': The Education of Indians in Nineteenth-century Ontario." In J. Barman, Y. Hébert, and D. McCaskill, eds., *Indian Education in Canada. Volume I: The Legacy.* Vancouver: University of British Columbia Press, pp. 64-87.

Wilson, J.D.

1980 *The Declining Significance of Race.* Chicago: University of Chicago Press.

Wolf, E.

1982 *Europe and the People Without History.* Berkeley: University of California Press.

Wolfe, J. G. Cunningham, and L. Convey

1989 "Supporting Native Canadian Micro-Enterprises: A Southern Ontario Case Study." In P. Kariya, ed., *Native Socio-Economic Development in Canada: Change, Promise and Innovation.* Winnipeg: Institute of Urban Studies.

Wolpe, H.

1975 "The Theory of Internal Colonialism: The South African Case." In I. Oxaal, T. Barnett, and D. Booth, eds., *Beyond the Sociology of Development: Economy and Society in Latin America and Africa.* London: Routledge and Kegan Paul.

Wotherspoon, T.

1987 "Introduction: Conflict and Crisis in Canadian Education." In T. Wotherspoon, ed., *The Political Economy of Canadian Schooling.* Toronto: Methuen, pp. 1-15.

1991 "Educational Reorganization and Retrenchment." In T. Wotherspoon, ed., *Hitting the Books: The Politics of Educational Retrenchment.* Toronto: Garamond, pp. 15-34.

Yancey, W., E.P. Erikson, and R. Juliani

1976 "Emergent Ethnicity: A Review and Reformation," *American Sociological Review* 41, 3:391-403.

York, G.

1987 "Questions Surfacing on Native Child Welfare Groups." The *Globe and Mail* (Toronto), July 2, p. A4.

1989 *The Dispossessed.* Toronto: Lester & Orpen Dennys.

Young, D.E., ed.

1988 *Health Care Issues in the Canadian North.* Edmonton: Boreal Institute for Northern Studies, Occasional Publication Number 26.

Young, D.E., with G. Ingram and L. Swartz

1989 *Cry of the Eagle: Encounters with a Cree Healer.* Toronto: University of Toronto Press.

Young, T.K.

1984 "Indian Health Services in Canada: A Sociohistorical Perspective." *Social Science and Medicine* 18, 3:257-264.

1988 *Health Care and Cultural Change: The Indian Experience in the Central Subarctic.* Toronto: University of Toronto Press.

Zakreski, D.

1990 "Saskatchewan Indians' Approach Lauded," Saskatoon *Star-Phoenix*, August 3, p. A3.

Zentner, H.

1972 "Reservation Social Structure and Anomie; A Case Study." In M. Nagler, ed., *Perspectives on the North American Indian*. Toronto: McClelland and Stewart, pp. 214-226.

1973 *The Indian Identity Crisis*. Calgary: Strayner Publications.

COPYRIGHT ACKNOWLEDGMENTS

Province of Alberta, *Report of the Task Force on the Criminal Justice System and its Impact on the Indian and Metis People of Alberta* (Edmonton: Province of Alberta, 1991), Volume I, pp. 4-7, 8-42 and Volume III, pp. 1-57. Reprinted by permission of the Government of Alberta, Department of the Solicitor General.

Auditor General of Canada, *Report to the House of Commons* (Ottawa: Minister of Supply and Services, 1990), p. 473. Reprinted by permission.

R.F. Badgley, "Social Policy and Indian Health Services in Canada," *Anthropological Quarterly* 46, p. 153. Reprinted by permission of the Anthropological Quarterly/Catholic University of America Press.

P.A. Baran, *The Political Economy of Growth.* Copyright © 1957 by Monthly Review Inc. Reprinted by permission of Monthly Review Foundation.

C. Beamish, "The Circuit Court and Young Offenders." In C.T. Griffiths, ed., *Northern Youth in Crisis: A Challenge for Justice* (Burnaby, B.C.: Simon Fraser University for the Northern Conference, 1987), pp. 129-130. Reprinted by permission of Simon Fraser University, Northern Justice Society.

H. Bherer, S. Gagnon, and Jacinte Roberge, *Wampum and Letters Patent: Exploratory Study of Native Entrepreneurship* (Halifax: Institute for Research on Public Policy, 1990), pp. 22-23. Reprinted by permission.

G. Blainey, *The Tyranny of Distance* (Melbourne: Sun Books, 1983), pp. 3-4. Reprinted by permission of Pan Macmillan Publishers Australia.

Commission on Equality in Employment, *Report of the Commission on Equality in Employment* (Ottawa: Minister of Supply and Services, 1984), p. 38. Reprinted by permission.

Cree-Naskapi Commission, *Report of the Cree-Naskapi Commission* (Ottawa: Indian and Northern Affairs, 1988), p. 11. Reprinted by permission.

D. Daniels, "The Coming Crisis in the Aboriginal Rights Movement: From Colonialism to Neo Colonialism to Renaissance," *Native Studies Review* 2, 2:104, 111. Used with the permission of Native Studies Review.

D. Daniels, "Canada." Reprinted by permission of Greenwood Publishing Group, Inc., Westport, CT, from *International Handbook on Race and Race Relations,* edited by J. Sigler. Copyright by Greenwood Press, 1987.

Department of Citizenship and Immigration, "A Study of Friendship Centres," *Public Archives of Canada,* R.G. 26, Vol. 69, File 2-38-6, 1962, pp. 11, 17. Reprinted by permission.

Department of Indian and Northern Affairs, *Annual Report, 1988-1989* (Ottawa: Minister of Supply and Services, 1989). Reprinted by permission.

T.L.R. MacInnes, "The History and Policies of Indian Administration in Canada." In C.T. Loram and T.F. McIlwraith, eds., *The North American Indian Today* (Toronto: University of Toronto Press, 1943), pp. 162-163. Reprinted by permission of the University of Toronto Press.

Sharon Moyer, Paigie Kopeiman, Carol LaPrairie, and Brenda Billingsley, *Native and Non-Native Admissions to Federal, Provincial and Territorial Correctional Institutions* (Ottawa: Research Division, Ministry of the Solicitor General of Canada), working paper no. 1985-34, p. 2.23. Reprinted by permission.

National Council of Welfare, *In the Best Interests of the Child* (Ottawa: National Council of Welfare, 1979), p. 7. Reprinted by permission.

D. Opekokew, *The Political and Legal Inequalities Among Aboriginal Peoples in Canada* (Kingston, Ont.: Institute of Intergovernmental Relations, 1987), Background Paper Number 14, p. 5. Used with the permission of the Institute of Intergovernmental Relations.

Saskatchewan Education, *Plan of Action in Response to "Reaching Out"* (Regina: Saskatchewan Education, 1985), p. 1; *Indian and Métis Education Policy from Kindergarten to Grade XII* (Regina: Saskatchewan Education, 1989), p. 5. Used with permission of the Government of Saskatchewan—Queen's printer.

Duncan Campbell Scott, *The Administration of Indian Affairs in Canada* (Toronto: The Canadian Institute of International Affairs, 1931), pp. 5, 25-26. Reprinted with permission of The Canadian Institute of Intergovernmental Affairs.

Statistics Canada, *A Data Book on Canada's Aboriginal Population from the 1986 Census of Canada* (Ottawa: Minister of Supply and Services, 1989), pp. 15-16. Reprinted by permission.

E. Tyler, "The Farmer as a Social Class in the Prairie Region." In M. Tremblay and W. Anderson, eds., *Rural Canada in Transition* (Ottawa: Agricultural Economics Research Council of Canada, 1966), p. 287. Reprinted by permission.

H. Veltmeyer, *Canadian Class Structure* (Toronto: Garamond Press, 1986), p. 105. Reprinted by permission of Garamond Press.

S.N. Verdun-Jones and G.K. Muirhead, "The Native in the Criminal Justice System." In C.L. Boydell and I.A. Connidis, eds., *The Canadian Criminal Justice System* (Toronto: Holt Rinehart & Winston, 1982), pp. 266-281. Reprinted by permission of Holt Rinehart & Winston.

INDEX